SOCIAL JUSTICE IN HUMAN RELATIONS VOLUME 1
Societal and Psychological Origins of Justice

CRITICAL ISSUES IN SOCIAL JUSTICE

Published in association with the International Center for Social Justice Research, Faculty of Social Sciences, ISOR, University of Utrecht, The Netherlands.

Series Editors: **MELVIN J. LERNER** AND **RIËL VERMUNT**
University of Waterloo   *University of Leiden*
Waterloo, Ontario, Canada   *Leiden, The Netherlands*

A Continuation Order Plan is available for this series. A continuation order will bring delivery of each new volume immediately upon publication. Volumes are billed only upon actual shipment. For further information please contact the publisher.

SOCIAL JUSTICE IN HUMAN RELATIONS VOLUME 1
Societal and Psychological Origins of Justice

Edited by

Riël Vermunt
and
Herman Steensma

University of Leiden
Leiden, The Netherlands

PLENUM PRESS • NEW YORK AND LONDON

Library of Congress Cataloging-in-Publication Data

Social justice in human relations.
    p.   cm. -- (Critical issues in social justice)
    Includes bibliographical references and indexes.
    Contents: v. 1. Societal and psychological origins of justice /
edited by Riel Vermunt and Herman Steensma -- v. 2. Societal and
psychological consequences of justice and injustice / edited by
Herman Steensma and Riel Vermunt.
    ISBN 0-306-43625-6 (v. 1). -- ISBN 0-306-43626-4 (v. 2)
    1. Social justice.   I. Vermunt, Riel. II. Steensma, Herman.
III. Series.
HM216.S556 1991
303.3'72--dc20
                                                         90-25382
                                                             CIP

ISBN 0-306-43625-6

© 1991 Plenum Press, New York
A Division of Plenum Publishing Corporation
233 Spring Street, New York, N.Y. 10013

Printed in the United States of America

Contributors

Liesbeth Aleva, Department of Developmental Psychology, University of Leiden, 2333 AK Leiden, The Netherlands

Michael Billig, Department of Social Sciences, University of Loughborough, Leicestershire, LE11 3TU, England

Ronald L. Cohen, Social Science Division, Bennington College, Bennington, Vermont 05201

Morton Deutsch, Teachers College, Columbia University, New York, New York 10027

Nicholas Emler, Department of Psychology, University of Dundee, Dundee DD1 4HN Scotland

Janus L. Grzelak, Psychological Institute, University of Warsaw, 00-183 Warsaw, Poland

Dan. R. Jonsson, Department of Sociology, University of Göteberg, Göteberg, Sweden

Jan ter Laak, Department of Child Studies, University of Utrecht, 3508 TC Utrecht, The Netherlands

H. F. M. Lodewijkx, Institute of Social Psychology, University of Utrecht 3584 CS Utrecht, The Netherlands

Melvin J. Lerner, Department of Psychology, University of Waterloo, Waterloo, Ontario, Canada N21 361

Barry Markovsky, Department of Sociology, University of Iowa, Iowa City, Iowa 52242

Solveig M. Mühlhaøusen, Department of Sociology, University of Göteberg, Göteberg, Sweden

J. M. Rabbie, Institute of Social Psychology, University of Utrecht 3584 CS Utrecht, The Netherlands

Herman Steensma, Department of Social and Organizational Psychology, University of Leiden, 2333 AK Leiden, The Netherlands

J. E. M. M. Syroit, Department of Social and Organizational Psychology, University of Utrecht, 3384 CS Utrecht, The Netherlands

Kell J. Törnblom, Department of Sociology, University of Colorado at Denver, Denver, Colorado 80217-3364

Riël Vermunt, Department of Social and Organizational Psychology, University of Leiden, 2333 AK Leiden, The Netherlands

Ad. L. W. Vogelaar, Department of Social and Organizational Psychology, University of Leiden, 2333 AK Leiden, The Netherlands

Preface

Justice plays an important role in our culture. The topic of justice has attracted the attention of scholars all over the world. Beginning in 1985, a continuing series of international conferences on social justice started in the Netherlands. Scientists present and discuss papers, exchange information, and choose new roads to theory building.

In this volume, a selection of papers presented at the International Conference on Social Justice in Human Relations (Leiden, 1986) is published. There has been some refinement and improvement, thanks to the comments made by experts in the field. The chapters in this volume represent second (and in some cases, even third or fourth) versions of the papers.

As organizers of the conference and editors of this volume, we hope that the reader will be pleased by the content and the high quality of the contributions.

There is some diversity, but there also are some common themes. We organized the chapters in this volume with respect to what we think are two important themes: (1) justice and societal and developmental processes and (2) justice in intra- and intergroup relations. These categories are not mutually exclusive, for some chapters could have been placed in both categories. Still, we think the distinction between these themes has value.

The contributors to this volume are all well known for their commitment to the study of justice. This book demonstrates that such commitment can take many forms. We believe that all these forms are necessary for finding solutions to what we think is the most important problem in human beings: finding just procedures to allocate outcomes in a way that give rise to feelings of justice.

The present book could not have been published without the efforts of many persons, who deserve our sincere acknowledgment. We wish to thank the Royal Dutch Academy of Sciences and the Department of Social and Organizational Psychology of Leiden University for their financial support, which made the conference possible. Also, we wish to acknowledge the support of the ''Dienst Sociaal Wetenschappelijk Onderzoek'' of Leiden University for the valuable assistance in running the conference, and our secretary Maja Metselaar for her help in preparing this book.

Eliot Werner of Plenum Press, and Melvin J. Lerner, editor of the Critical Issues in Social Justice series, have been very kind, patient, and most of all very helpful in the process of preparing this volume. Also, we should mention the help of Faye Crosby, who reviewed the manuscript. And, of course, we wish to thank all of the contributors to the Social Justice in Human Relations conference. Without their contribution, neither the conference nor this book would have been possible.

RIËL VERMUNT
HERMAN STEENSMA

Contents

2. Prospects for a Cognitive–Structural Justice Theory 33

Barry Markovsky

3. The Allocation of Positive and Negative Outcomes: When Is the Equality Principle Fair for Both? 59

*Kjell Y. Törnblom, Solveig M. Mühlhausen,
and Dan R. Jonsson*

PART II JUSTICE IN INTRAGROUP
AND INTERGROUP RELATIONS

7. Consistency and Group Ideology: Toward a
Rhetorical Approach to the Study of Justice 169

Michael Billig

8. Egalitarianism in the Laboratory and at Work 195

Morton Deutsch

Introduction

Riël Vermunt and Herman Steensma

Recently scholars have attempted to improve the exchange of inter-disciplinary and cross-cultural views on justice. Psychologists, sociologists, economists, legal scholars, and philosophers have discussed several justice topics, and exciting ideas have been expressed.

With respect to the cross-cultural approach to justice, although most of the research on justice has been conducted in the countries of Europe and North America, which are said to be similar in many respects, differences in opinions from people of both groups of countries about several aspects of justice are considerable. It is not uncommon that research projects about the same topics in North America and in Europe produce different results. It is too early to conclude whether these differences are due to different cultural traditions or to the use of different research methods, although some scholars are convinced that the different empirical findings reflect genuine differences in theoretical views about justice. The present volume consists of the contributions of scientists from Europe and North America, so that the reader is given the opportunity to compare the several views and findings. The present volume, *Societal and Psychological Origins of Justice*, consists of two parts: Justice: Societal and Developmental Processes and Justice in Intra- and Intergroup Relations. As the titles of the parts of this volume reflect, we will pay attention to justice at diferent levels of analysis: the individual, the group, and the societal level. At the individual level we are interested in the way individuals acquire a sense of justice, how they cognitively grasp the complexity of

Riël Vermunt and Herman Steensma • Department of Social and Organizational Psychology, University of Leiden, 2333 AK Leiden, The Netherlands.

the justice phenomenon, and how they react to violations of what they conceive of as the justice norm. At the group and organizational level, we are interested in the distribution of resources in situations of cooperation and competition and in the relationship between cooperation and competition, on the one hand, and the development of rules of fairness, on the other hand. Social dilemma research tries to discover the factors influencing the conflict between individual and group gains, as exemplified in the tragedy of the commons. Another important research area concerns not only the influence of intergroup relations on the development of group norms of justice but also the interplay between individual and group reactions to injustice. At the societal level, we are interested in people's perception of the overall distribution of rewards in the social system, the distribution of income as well as the distribution of social security.

In the two parts of Volume I, the previously mentioned aspects will be presented in detail. In the next section of this introduction, we will present an overview of the content of the two parts, starting with studies reflecting certain general obeservations about justice. Next, we will summarize studies on issues of the multilevel explanation of justice behavior, and finally we give an overview of studies on the generality of justice data.

Some General Observations

In every situation where people live and work together, some form of social coordination (Lerner, 1975, 1981; Moore, 1978) of the actions of individuals is necessary. Problems of authority, division of labor, and distribution of resources have to be met in every human society, no matter how primitive or modern the society may be. The development of forms of social coordination is accompanied by the development of moral codes as what is a fair distribution of resources for what kinds of (groups of) individuals. Differences in the degree of authority individuals have or differences in the kind of work individuals perform create inequalities in society. Besides that, in every society, it is a common feature to set aside a high proportion of the goods and services produced as a reward for the managerial function. The ubiquity of these processes in societies and the development of moral codes may indicate the generality of the justice phenomenon. To this statement should be added, however, the idea that each society solves the problems of authority, division of labor and distribution of resources in its own way, dependent on the special social and physical circumstances. One can therefore distinguish general as well as special features of justice: genotypical as well as phenotypical aspects of justice.

But also within society, social and physical circumstances may be different for different kinds of people and systems, so that irregularities can be discerned even within a society. It is not surprising, therefore, that research data reveal regularities as well as irregularities in justice behavior and in judgments about justice phenomena. Törnblom, Muhlhausen, and Jonsson (Chapter 3) present data indicating the complexity of justice behavior. The authors assert that opinions about justice are influenced by several psychological and sociological factors. They studied the influence of positive and negative outcomes on the application of the equality rule. In a judgmental task, male subjects assumed the perspective of a recipient who was responsible or not responsible for the conduct resulting in an equal allocation of outcomes to four persons. Overall, the equal allocation was judged as fair, except for the anonymous/responsible subject who rated equality as unfair for a negative outcome. Vogelaar and Vermunt (Chapter 4) could show that individuals in allocating fictitious amounts of money for different amounts and types of inputs apply the equity rule. However, depending on the social status and political party preference of the individuals, interesting deviations from this pattern could be found.

More data could be presented to prove the complexities of justice in human relations. One of the main reasons for the complexities of justice behavior is that it is not only influenced by factors on the individual psychological level (the psychological factors mentioned by Lerner in Chapter 1) but also by factors on the group or category level (see Markovsky, Chapter 2; Cohen, Chapter 10; Syroit, Chapter 11; Rabbie & Lodewijkx, Chapter 12) and even on the societal level (Lerner, Chapter 1; Billig, Chapter 7).

The Multilevel Explanation of Justice Behavior

In a simplified way, society may be viewed as consisting of three levels: the societal, group, and individual levels. It seems obvious that the influence of all three levels should be taken into account in order to explain individuals' justice behavior. This is not an easy task because the influence of the three levels is often not consistent with each other. These inconsistencies are, in most cases, not dramatic, and the individual can easily deal with it in his or her daily routine activities. However, with respect to the issue of justice inconsistenties play a major role, because justice is a salient value in the lives of most people. It is therefore necessary to concentrate justice research on the multilevel causes of justice behavior and to multilevel explanations of justice behavior.

Until now, theories of justice confined themselves mostly to the one-level explanation of justice behavior. Grzelak's comments on research on social dilemmas (Chapter 9) point in that direction. Grzelak states that, in many real life dilemmas, in addition to two parties directly involved in the conflict, local authorities or local power groups are present as well. Groups or authorities on the higher level influence important aspects of the dilemma situation. They can change the amount and type of payoffs or the rules regulating the use of common resources. The multilevel approach is also stressed in the contributions of Lerner (Chapter 1), Markovsky (Chapter 2), and Emler (Chapter 5). According to Markovsky, theories of justice operate at one of two levels. One level focuses on cognitive processes, interpersonal comparisons, and individual responses to distribution of rewards. The other level is concerned with justice on the aggregate and collective level. Markovsky defends the position that the two levels can be bridged theoretically, providing a richer understanding of processes at each level. New theoretical and research developments are discussed, highlighting the effects of social–structural and contextual factors on individual judgments. So, parallel to a societal development of justice norms, one can distinguish a psychological development of norms and motives. In this respect, one may refer to the works of Elias (1969), who phrased it as follows:

> The specific process of psychic education in the Western societies is nothing more than the individual civilization process to which in civilized societies each upgrowing individual, given the age-long societal civilization process, has been subjected. Therefore the psychogenesis of a habitus of adults cannot be understood without a sociogenesis of civilization. (p. 23).

Young individuals are taught the structure of society and the moral codes operating in it. The growing complexities of the relationships between individuals, the increasing complexities of the division of labor, and the like are accompanied by an increasing complexity of the cognitive representations of these relationships in the human mind.

Emler (Chapter 5) proposes improvement of the cognitive development theory of moral behavior by paying attention to processes of socialization: that is, of becoming a member of society. Membership can express itself in three different orders: the structural order, the categorical order, and the personal order. Being or becoming a member of a certain order influences the development of moral insight. The way society solves problems of experienced injustice by applying legal procedures influences the development of procedural justice in the child. In his contribution, Lerner (Chapter 1) presents a preliminary statement of a theoretical framework integrating psychological and societal determinants of justice. It is proposed that the societal structure provides the rules of entitlement and decision making that regulate the course of routine social interaction. These socially based norms are representable in people's conscious thought processes. By contrast, the psychological-generated rules of entitlement typically contradict conventionally accepted rules of thought and discourse and thus remain "unconscious." The major part of Lerner's contribution considers the motivationally important circumstances that engage the unconscious psychologically compelling determinants and how their appearance in behavior is both shaped and legitimized by the situationally prevailing normative context. Billig (Chapter 7) stresses the importance of ideology to account for indvidual attitudes about justice and the discrepancies between these attitudes. According to Billig, individual-level models are too closely linked to perceptual models, resulting in a neglect of the role of language, with its faculty of negation. At the ideological level, it is important to study the contradictory and ambivalent aspects in order to situate psychological processes in a wider context.

Validity of Justice Rules

In the short history of empirical justice research, several studies have been carried out using different subjects, different methods, and different situations. Research findings could show that frequently gender differences exist in allocation behavior (for a review, see Major & Deaux, 1981). The equality rule seems to be more popular among women than among men. So the standards for what is to be considered just may differ between groups and social aggregates, even within one society. We may expect that differences in opinions and norms about just behavior may be even larger when we compare different countries with large differences in culture and sociohistorical context. Up to now there have been some studies that pay attention to the relation between nationalities and conceptions of justice. To mention only a few, Mikula (1974) found no differences in reward allocation by Austrian and American students; Mann, Radford, and Kanagawa (1985) could show some differences between Japanese and Australian children in allocation behavior.

Miner (1984) apparently demonstrated some disdain for one of the best-known theories of justice, that is, equity theory. In evaluating various theories in organizational psychology according to their usefulness, he rated equity theory in the bottom category (not so useful) because of its lack of specific applications.

Equity theory is not the only theory of justice. Miner's critique, however, draws attention to the relationship between basic and applied research in the area of justice. Applying different methods in justice research is becoming more and more popular. This trend can be seen in the reader edited by Bierhoff, Cohen, and Greenberg (1986), in which a section was devoted to applications of justice research. The growing interest in applied research has called attention to the need to carry out field studies next to laboratory studies. The growing interest in the "mixed approach" is not the only reason for the trend of more varity in research methods. Some "internal" developments within a certain research domain also accelerated the interest in other research methods. There is now not a generally agreed answer to the question of whether findings of justice research can be generalized over persons, methods, and situations. But one of the aims of a conference on social justice in human relations was to give a more definite answer to the question whether data from subjects in different cultures are more or less the same. In this respect, the contribution of ter Laak and Aleva (Chapter 6) is of some importance because, in their studies on the cognitive development of children, the data may be compared with data from studies in North America. Based on a comparison of these data with the data from several North American studies, one may conclude that cross-cultural differences are minimal, although one should keep in mind that there probably are no large differences between both cultures.

The study of Deutsch (Chapter 8) is also important because he compares the findings from laboratory studies with those from naturalistic case studies. Deutsch poses the question of whether economic efficiency and equality of reward allocation covary. Experiments on cooperation and competition show that equal distribution of resources between group members has more positive effects on productivity, friendliness of relationships, and self-esteem than an unequal distribution of resources. Using different methods and settings, Deutsch could corroborate the findings from laboratory studies.

In order to get adequate data from research on social dilemmas, researchers, according to Grzelak (Chapter 9), should circumvent some fallacies, such as the numerical fallacy and the monetary fallacy. Research on social dilemmas has until now too much concentrated on money as the resource to be allocated. Grzelak asserts that the use of money in our Western culture is strongly related to happiness and unhappiness and that the use of numerical scores triggers a cognitive schema that may be different from the one using nonnumerical data.

The data from the study of Törnblom *et al.* show that the application of the equality principle is quite different for subjects who are anonymous or who are not. Vogelaar and Vermunt could show that the equity rule is used differently, depending on the type of input criteria to be evaluated, on the socioeconomic status of the subjects and on their political party preference.

Universality of Justice Rules

Justice researchers are constructing theories in which justice rules have universal application. Walster, and Walster and Berscheid (1978) start from the assumption that all individuals strive to increase their self-interest. In their aspiration to get more, individuals are thwarted by others. In the Hobbesian struggle for a greater share of scarce goods, individuals are forced to compromise in order to prevent a war of all against all. In allocating resources, individuals try, therefore, to find a compromise in terms of an outcome in which the individual and the other have their share—an equitable outcome. An allocation in which the other receives all will be accepted only if other interests are at stake.

As Lerner (1981) shows, individuals also behave in an altruistic or unselfish way when no other interests are at stake, only because they want to behave according to some moral code. Lerner assumes that the norms and values in our society prescribe egoistical behavior. Psychologically generated rules of entitlement contradict the accepted rules of thought and discourse. In this view, egoistical as well as altruistical behavior can be shown, dependent on the way society prescribes the kind of behavior to be salient. An equitable allocation is not a compromise in the struggle to get more and more but a compromise to prevent deterioration of one's own position. Because Lerner does not rely on human nature to explain justice behavior but on interaction between prescribed norms and psychologically generated rules of entitlement, his view offers possibilities to arrive at universal rules of justice.

Not only do individuals have a relationship with society at large, they are also members of groups and categories. The membership of groups shapes the individuals thoughts and feelings, and the individual makes use of his or her membership group to influence the social and physical environment. Different groups offer different rules of entitlement and deserving, depending on the kind of group and the position of the group within society.

Individuals may have different types of relationship with groups.

It may be one of conflict, independence, and dependence (Sherif & Sherif, 1969). Deutsch (Chapter 8) has shown with data from laboratory studies and field studies the influence of cooperation and competition on preference for an equal or unequal distribution of resources. The influence of groups on individuals is large because groups may offer a positive social identity to the individual. In Tajfel's view (Tajfel, 1978), individuals strive for a positive social identity, which they achieve by increasing the social worth of the group to which they belong. Individuals favor the group that offers them a positive social identity. Starting from this assumption of ingroup favoritism, the allocation behavior of individuals is easy to explain: Individuals allocate outcomes in favor of one's own group members and not in favor of members of outgroups. This favoritism is present even when the difference between in- and outgroup is based on irrelevant input criteria, such as having different colors of caps.

The findings from Tajfel and others suggest only a modification of Walster, Berschield, and Walster's assumption of the important role of self-interest in the allocation of outcomes. Tajfel provides a group perspective of the individual's self-interest motivation. It is questionable, however, whether the group-level explanation of justice behavior may be reduced to the individual level, as Tajfel seems to do. Three studies in the present volume handle this issue extensively.

In his contribution, Cohen (Chapter 10) tries to bridge the gap between group-level explanation of justice behavior and individual-level explanation. Cohen asserts that distribution of resources is preceded by processes of defining membership of groups. Important aspects to define membership are aspects such as the nature of the boundaries of group membership and the relative size of a group. Defining someone as belonging to the ingroup or to the outgroup has tremendous effects on the distribution of resources between individuals. Individuals who belong to the outgroup are assumed to be allocated less than individuals who belong to the ingroup. Cohen assumes, however, that individuals who are motivated to care for others are not inclined to exclude others from a distribution. In the same way, belonging to social networks decreases the tendency to exclude others.

Syroit (Chapter 11) compares interindividual with social injustice. To define intergroup injustice, Syroit takes into account the definition of group, derived from Tajfel (1978), who defines a group in terms of the common definition of its members. In elaborating a model of intergroup injustice, some prerequisites must be met: A person must define himself or herself psychologically as a member of a group or category; the person must act in terms of self–other identifications based on group membership; and the person must adhere to a social change structure of belief.

That there are marked differences between individual and group reactions on experienced injustice has been shown in the study of Rabbie and Lodewijkx (Chapter 12). In an ingenious experiment, the authors could show that groups react more aggressively to norm violations of another party than individuals do.

From the studies cited here, one may conclude that rules of justice have tremendous impact on the lives of individuals. But at the same time, one has to admit that justice rules are more salient in some situations than in other ones. To search for regularities in conditions under which justice rules are salient or not is the most important task of justice research. In the present volume, you can find some results of the endeavor.

References

Bierhoff, H. W., Cohen, R. L., & Greenberg, J. (1986). *Justice in social relations.* New York: Plenum Press.

Elias, N. (1969). *Uber den Prozess der Zivilization [The process of civilization].* Bern: Francke Verlag.

Lerner, M. J. (1975). The justice motive in social behavior: Introduction. *Journal of Social Issues, 31*(3), 1–19.

Lerner, M. J. (1981). The justice motive in human relations. In M. J. Lerner & S. C. Lerner (Eds.), *The justice motive in social behavior* (pp. 11–36). New York: Plenum Press.

Major, B. & Deaux, K. (1981). Individual differences in justice behavior. In J. Greenberg & R. L. Cohen (Eds.), *Equity and justice in social behavior* (pp. 43–76). New York: Academic Press.

Mann, L., Radford, M., & Kanagawa, C. (1985). Cross-cultural differences in children's use of decision rules: A comparison between Japan and Australia. *Journal of Personality and Social Psychology, 49*(6), 1557–1564.

Mikula, G. (1974). Nationality, performance, and sex as determinants of reward allocation. *Journal of Personality and Social Psychology, 29*(4), 435–440.

Miner, J. B. (1984). The upaved road over the mountains: from theory to applications. *The Industrial-Organizational Psychologist, 21*(2), 9–20.

Moore, B., Jr. (1978). *Injustice. The social bases of obedience and revolt.* White Plains, NY: M. E. Sharp.

Sherif, M., & Sherif, C. W. (1969). *Social Psychology.* New York: Harper & Row.

Tajfel, H. (1978). *Differentiation between social groups. Studies in the social psychology of intergroup relations.* London: Academic Press.

Walster, E., Walster, G. W., & Berscheid, E. (1978). *Equity theory and research.* Boston: Allyn & Bacon.

I

Justice
Societal and Developmental Processes

1

Integrating Societal and Psychological Rules of Entitlement
The Basic Task of Each Social Actor and Fundamental Problem for the Social Sciences

Melvin J. Lerner

The Social Psychological Theory

The Integrating Experience of Entitlement

This social psychological theory of justice began to take shape and direction with the assumption that the experience of entitlement is the essential psychological ingredient of an entire family of human events associated with social justice: issues of equity, deserving, rights, fairness, and the justice of procedures, distribution and retributive acts (Hogan & Emler, 1981; Karniol & Miller, 1981; Walster, Walster & Berscheid, 1978). The cognitive component of this generic event is the judgment, often tacit, that someone, or some category of people, is entitled to a particular set of outcomes by virtue of who they are or what they have done. The "entitled to" is experienced affectively and motivationally as an imperative, a sense of requiredness between the

Melvin J. Lerner • Department of Psychology, University of Waterloo, Waterloo, Ontario, Canada N2L 3G1.

actor's perceived outcomes and the person's attributes or acts (Asch, 1952).

The easily recognizable differences among these justice-related concepts can be attributed to two main sources. Some may be best described as simply language conventions associated with particular social settings, for example, procedural and legal justice. Others, however, may reflect important social psychological differences in the judgments of entitlement. For example, deserving most often refers to the relations between an actor and his or her fate (Lerner, Miller, & Holmes, 1976), whereas fairness judgments typically imply a comparison of two or more actors' outcomes in that situation (Messick & Sentis, 1983). This distinction is often vividly apparent in situations of insufficient resources where the most fair distribution among the participants requires that they all must settle for considerably less than they each deserve by virtue of their prior acts or attributes (S.C. Lerner, 1979).

Entitlement Provided by the Social Structure

An extremely important consequence of recognizing the centrality of the experience of entitlement is that it leads very naturally to the most visibly prevalent source of entitlement in people's lives: the social structure. The sociocultural factors located in that structure generate the experience and expression of entitlement in various ways.

One is very directly through more or less explicit normative prescriptions defining who is entitled to what from whom. These may take the form of generally agreed-upon rules of living that apply to all members of a society. Gouldner's description of the norm of reciprocity (Gouldner, 1960) is a good example of a generally applicable standard of entitlement: "Anyone who gives you x is entitled to x from you." Someone who does you a kindness is entitled to and so forth. Anyone who acts cruelly, who violates others' entitlements deserves and so forth. These general rules not only define entitlements but also create evaluative standards for judging someone's worth as a good or not-so-good person or citizen.

Much more elaborate systems of entitlements and obligations appear in the status–role-based expectations of the social institutions that provide the structural bases of virtually all social endeavors (Blau, 1964; Homans, 1961). Fathers are entitled to "x" from their children, children are entitled to "y" from their parents–mothers. Each of these status-roles in our complex society has rather elaborated subsets of relations with various relevant actors—professors vis-à-vis graduate students, undergraduates, professors of equal rank, secretaries, and so forth. It is important to recognize that activities in these social contexts are framed in terms of elaborate rules of entitlement and obligation.

In addition to general and institutional norms, other sociocultural factors have a less direct but considerable importance in shaping judgments of entitlement. For example, the social concepts and stereotypes that describe categories of people include not only their characteristics and general social ranking but also the value of their personal attributes potentially generalizable to virtually any social context (Berger, Fisek, Norman, & Zelditch, 1977).

The common social reality also includes assumptions about how people plan their lives and make decisions (Heider, 1958; Nisbet & Ross, 1980). In our society, some version of a more or less enlightened "economic model" of social motivation is most widely accepted (Lerner, 1982; Sampson, 1975). The commonly held view is that, by and large, most people want to be decent and to treat others fairly, but we all live in a world where we must look out for our own interests and protect those who depend upon us. In meeting those obligations, people believe they are required to compete for relatively scarce or highly desired resources—job, promotion, social status (Blau, 1964; Schelling, 1978; Thibaut & Kelley, 1959). Within the rules of fair competition and general decency, it is expected that they will use their intelligence and other resources to make the best deal for themselves. There is evidence that these norms of competitive self-interest pervade even the most intimate of relationships (Berscheid & Campbell, 1981).

The Psychological Origins of Entitlement

Those are some of the more important structural components establishing the social reality in which people function. But that is not the only way they appear in their lives. The normative rules of entitlement and models of human decision making are all incorporated within the person's psychological structure. As a consequence, people's conceptions of their world, what they and others want or are entitled to, are to some extent fairly direct representations of that publicly available reality. However, although the process of learning and internalizing this social reality is occurring, there is reason to believe that other psychological processes are also generating rules of entitlement of considerable importance.

The observations of developmental psychologists suggest that the child continually performs two related basic tasks. One is the construction of a stable environment including objects and ways of acting or paths. The other is the formulation of the evaluative worth of the events that occur. The earliest cognitive constructions of this personal environment are characterized by concrete operations or even more primitive constructions of sensory inputs that create a world of people, events, and ways of acting. At the same time, evaluative characteristics such as desirable/undesirable, good/bad, become attached to the various cognitive elements by simple association. At this level of cognitive functioning (preformal operations), there appears to be an "oughtness" or requiredness that is generated between the value of an act, the person, and the outcome: "Good things happen to good people" (Flavell, 1977; Heider, 1958; Piaget, 1965).

An additional source of requiredness may be created by the child's objectifying, giving impersonal and evaluative status to ways of operating on the environment, ways of getting from "here" to "there." The early script that is generated can be paraphrased as "valued outcomes require special abilities and efforts." That requiredness appears as the usually tacit but firm expectation that anyone who performs the appropriate acts is entitled to the inevitable desired endstate.

A basic assumption of the theory presented here is that although conventional rules of thought and evaluation gradually dominate the maturing child's conscious cognitive processes, the initial constructions of evaluated objects and ways of operating on the environment endure and provide the rather crude templates and scripts for the preconscious organization of all later experiences (Lerner, 1981; Shweder & Miller, 1985; Werner, 1948). In effect, I am proposing, as have Gestalt theorists before me, that a sense of requiredness or directional imperative permeates people's cognitive construction of events that take place in their world (Asch, 1952). This requiredness is directed toward generating an appropriate correspondence between the perceived worth of the person, the value of his or her acts and outcomes. The unconscious search for the appropriate fit seems to be elicited by the perception of any of these elements—actor, act, or outcome. A state of tension is then created and continued until the required construction is completed. That can be accomplished either by inferring the past virtue of actors from their present fate or by creating the appropriate future outcome in fantasy or reality.[1]

Much, if not all, of this may appear overly cognitive with no more affective or motivational involvement than states of cognitive imbal-

---

[1]It is also possible that if appropriate closure can not be achieved, temporary, possibly even permanent alterations may be sustained in the self-system of some aspect of the objective world (Kruglanski, 1980).

ance (Heider, 1958) or dissonance (Festinger, 1957). However, that certainly does not seem to be the case with the perception of violated entitlements. Most often, the participant's reactions resemble those that are generated by events that are "unthinkable," "impossible," "outrageous." These cognitively based emotional reactions have been identified as the essential ingredient that transforms frustrations or disappointments into anger and outrage (Cook, Crosby, & Hennigan, 1977; Crosby, 1976). This is quite understandable when one considers that not only do people construct and maintain a stable environment but that these constructions provide the framework for all the important activities in their lives. It should be no surprise then that events threatening the integrity of that construction elicit overdetermined, multiply motivated reactions.

Unconscious Entitlement Demands in Social Behavior

Basic to the theory presented here is the proposition that adults' judgments of entitlements can be shaped by unconscious processes originating in the earliest and most primitive stages of cognitive organization. When people are fully engaged participants in an encounter, their entitlement judgments and associated emotional reactions often reveal a direct matching of the perception of people's fates and their worth. This association of the evaluative worth of acts, attributes, and outcomes is remarkably different from the formal operational thought consciously performed upon sets of symbolic representations of reality. "Rational decision making," according to conventional rules of mature thought, appears primarily when people are reacting dispassionately in relatively routine or nonthreatening circumstances.

What evidence is there that these early cognitive processes and scripted associations such as "good people—good outcomes" unconsciously continue to influence adults' reactions to important events in their lives?

The fact that people often assign blame and culpability for clearly unintentional, unpredictable, or accidental outcomes has been easy to document in controlled laboratory settings. For example, in a series of well-known experiments, people were made to feel guilty for inadvertently leaning on the edge of a table or pulling out the only chair available on which they could sit, when those simple, innocent acts were associated with very regrettable consequences. The consequences in these cases usually involved an event such as the spilling and the resultant disorganization of file cards representing months of a student's efforts (Carlsmith & Gross, 1969; Freedman, 1970).

At the anecdotal level, anyone who has inadvertently spilled a stain-producing liquid can recall the experiences associated with hurting someone or damaging another's property accidentally. Though to all concerned, even the victim, the harm was obviously unintentional and the event almost certainly unavoidable in any realistic sense, we feel guilty and foolish. According to many developmental theories, people should have grown beyond this primitive level of moral reasoning by the age of 8 or 10 (Piaget, 1965; Simmons, 1981). Yet, reasonably mature adults do often appear to reason backwards, associating the value of the outcome with the worth of the person who "caused" the action: bad outcome, bad person.

Considerably more serious and tragic manifestations of this primitive blaming process appear in people's reactions to members of society who have been victimized by forces over which they have no control. It has been repeatedly shown that victims of crime, crippling diseases, social discrimination, and poverty are at serious risk of being found blameworthy by virtue of their assumed irresponsible behavior or their generally undesirable character (Lerner & Miller, 1978; Ryan, 1971). Even more remarkable, from an objective analysis, is the extent to which the victims are prone to blame themselves beyond any conventionally acceptable rules for the assignment of culpability (Lerner & Miller, 1978).

Though certainly prevalent, reasoning "backwards" from victims' fates to their merit may not be the most common or dramatic manifestation of people's unconscious, entitlement-driven construction of reality. At the very conscious public level, most religious institutions in our society promise the believer there is a governing force in the universe insuring that ultimately they will have what they deserve. Public expressions of this faith in a justice delivering power may appear among people who are in seemingly hopeless conditions of deprivation or suffering (Lerner, 1980). It may also be employed unconsciously as a coping strategy when anticipating a crisis (Kubler-Ross, 1969). Zuckerman (1975), in an ingenious experiment, revealed that a predictable subset of university students facing important examinations were especially eager to be virtuous and helpful in ways that had no direct logical or realistic relation to the examination. Though they would not admit it to themselves, much less others, their actions indicated they were glad for any opportunity to do something "good" so they would then be rewarded in the future with a good grade on the examination. Similarly, others have described how many Britons in anticipation of bombing attacks went through virtually obsessive-compulsive rituals to prove themselves "good," worthy people, with the typically unarticulated expectation they would be judged worthy to be saved.

Ellard (1983) has provided perhaps the clearest experimental demonstration of this "unconscious" belief in a force that ensures the future will balance out present injustices. In pursuing this hypothesis, he focused upon the future expectations of bright, educated people, who, on a standard scale (Rubin & Peplau, 1975), explicitly disavowed the belief they lived in a just world where people eventually get what they deserve. Ellard, nevertheless, was able to alter their future expectation by inducing the feeling that they were either especially privileged or very deprived people at this time in their lives. This was done by the simple, but effective, device of having students answer questions that focused exclusively on how deprived, stressful, and demanding their lives were presently. As predicted, the "deprived" students revealed, subsequently, an increased confidence that their future would be comparatively free of common disastrous events. On the other hand, having a comparable group respond to a series of questions that focused their attention on how especially privileged they were at this time in their lives generated a more pessimistic view of their future. In comparison with a control group that had no such prior induction, those people who were made to feel overbenefitted believed they were significantly more likely to face disastrous events: divorce, major illness, unemployment, and the like.

In essence, Ellard demonstrated that these intelligent adults altered temporarily their overall feelings about what the future held for them in ways that revealed their assumption that a justice-creating force was in control of their lives. They expected future events to balance the inequities of the present. Those undergoing deprivation thought they would be compensated eventually, whereas the overbenefitted anticipated being appropriately deprived. But by whom? By what? It is important to remember for our purposes that these were people who had previously described such beliefs in a "just world" as superstitions and fairly tales with no relation to what happens in the real world.

The Integrating Propositions

In summary, I have proposed that people's judgments of their own and others' entitlements develop out of two rather distinct processes. On the one hand, people adopt and reflect in their conscious thought processes the publicly available normative systems located in the social structure. These include both general and very specific rules of entitlement and the conventionally accepted ways of applying them in specific interactions, that is, by rationally self-interested but responsible decisions concerning the acquisition and allocation of resources.

On the other hand, as a natural consequence of the interaction of human psychological processes with physical and social reality, people develop a construction of their world that includes personally compelling imperatives concerning the entitlements of kinds of people, outcomes, and acts (i.e., good things must happen to good people, if not now then eventually). These entitlements appear to follow rules that typically contradict conventional ways of thinking and are thus not directly represented in the person's inner or public dialogues.[2]

If one accepts the possibility that in the normal course of development people acquire two bases for evaluating entitlements, the consciously representable normative, and the unconsciously held evaluative scripts and rules of association, the next important question must address when and how they appear in people's lives.

Proposition 1. On most occasions, people automatically follow the normatively structured prescriptions of entitlement and obligation of their salient status roles with relatively minor individual or subcultural variations (Langer, 1978). If, in the course of acting out these socially scripted scenarios, they are required to make a conscious decision, they attempt to employ the conventionally accepted process of rationally considering the alternatives and selecting that option most likely to promote their own best self-interest.

Proposition 2. When events appear to contain the possibility of violating the psychologically based rules of entitlement, when they become "hotter" affectively and seriously engaging motivationally, then the "unconscious," primitive rules of entitlement and information processing become a compelling determinant of the person's reactions.

Proposition 3. These psychologically central rules of entitlement will be experienced and expressed by the actor in forms that are appropriate to the normative context. For example, even those people

---

[2]It may be worth nothing at this point that the assumption of two levels of cognitive processes, one that is representable consciously in conventional thought forms and a second with its own rules of organization that are not accessible to conscious representation, is consistent with recent developments in cognitive psychology (Nisbet & Ross, 1980).

who merit Kohlberg's (1969) designation of postconventional morality frame their reaction in language and rules that are designed to make them appear both understandable and acceptable according to normatively appropriate standards.

These propositions assume that some aspect of the person as social actor is continually monitoring and responsive to cues in the environment concerning everyone's outcomes and entitlements and that information is processed simultaneously at two levels of consciousness. One is the publicly available normatively conventional level; the other, the typically consciously nonretrievable level of scripts and agendas that are organized by rules of association. Also assumed is a psychological process or structure that performs a gate-keeping or integrating function, determining when and how the consequences of the information processed at these two levels appear in the person's reactions. As it happens, various independent sources of contemporary psychological inquiry are generating support for such theoretical assumptions (Bowers & Meichenbaum,1984).

Research Relevant to the Theoretical Proposition

The Central Hypothesis

A major implication of what I propose here is that the most important conflicts people face are not those arising from discrepancies between what people want and what they believe is fair but those emerging from the competing demands of various entitlements (Lerner, et al,1976). The difference becomes most evident in the prediction that in important encounters people will not be initially and preeminently concerned with what they want and then implement rules of deserving to achieve or justify those preferred outcomes (Messick & Senitis, 1983; Walster & Walster, 1975). Instead, they will be constrained to express or meet the experienced entitlement-based requirements in a manner that does not violate the normative expectations in that situation.

Let us turn now to some data that speak fairly directly to these issues.

Incentives for Work: Maximizing Profit and Meeting Entitlements

To what extent would a prospective employee's desire to work be enhanced or diminished by the opportunity to help innocent victims?

To examine this issue, Dale Miller (1975, 1977) provided young men with the opportunity for temporary employment. In the critical experimental condition, the prospective employees learned that if they accepted the job offer one-third of their pay would be deducted from their earnings and given to a family in desperate need. That offer proved to be a much greater incentive for them to work than the opportunity to keep the entire pay for themselves. But, that was true only when their remaining share of pay fell within the range of what was considered to be fair for that work. As expected, when their now deserving was not threatened, the opportunity to help the victimized family was of considerably greater value to them than keeping that additional third of the pay for themselves.

That finding, though interesting in its own right, takes on particular theoretical significance when compared with the role-playing reactions of similar young men (Miller, 1975). When they were presented with the essential features of the situation and asked to predict how they or their friends would react to one of the various incentive conditions, their predictions revealed a consistent profit-maximizing strategy. If any of their pay was to be given to the family, they would be much less willing to work, regardless of the remaining share. Their consensually supported view was that they, as everyone else, worked to earn money, not to do social work.

What do these findings mean? It is safe to assume that the role-playing subjects were describing the normative expectations for people involved in gainful employment. In effect, these norms insist that you owe it to yourself and those directly dependent upon you to earn as much money as you can or at least get a fair pay for your work. To do otherwise would be to act irresponsibly. As a result, when actually confronted with the opportunity to help the innocent suffering family in the experiment, the young men could not act upon the impulse to help until that normative rule was met. Allowing them to meet their obligation to themselves by keeping a fair amount resulted in the clear behavioral expression of the desire to eliminate the innocent family's deprivation.

The Economic Exchange Required to Legitimize Caring for Victims

These findings are consistent with the general hypothesis that people feel impelled to eliminate undeserved suffering but that this urge must be expressed in normatively acceptable ways. So, for example, by custom and social convention people donate to worthy charities in specially controlled ways on specifiable occasions. But are there not other normatively legitimizing contexts that would allow the expression of the desire to help victims?

To pursue one possible answer to that query, John Holmes had students go door to door soliciting funds on behalf of two charitable causes (see Lerner et al, 1976). As expected, they found very little willingness to donate money directly either to provide critically needed help for emotionally handicapped children or to buy athletic equipment for the neighborhood children's organized sports activities —bats, balls, uniforms, and the like. However, in the theoretically important conditions, they couched their solicitation in terms of an economic exchange—"would you like to buy this rather nice decorator candle? (also rather expensive). By the way, the proceeds of this sale will go to help," then they described either of the two beneficiaries.

When the proceeds were destined to enhance the pleasure of the neighborhood children's sports activities, the public was rather unmoved. This appeal created no measurable incentive for buying the candles. There was, however, a great response if the people were informed that the profit was to help the innocently victimized children. People who would otherwise have donated very little directly to help those children and who had no intrinsic interest in buying these expensive candles suddenly found themselves in great need of them. Or at least, they bought them at a remarkable rate. Apparently the economic exchange context legitimized their acting upon the impulse to help the innocent, suffering children. The working assumption was that the internal demand had to be normatively legitimized by opportunity to exchange their money for candles. We anticipated with some success that in our society making a purchase would provide that opportunity.

Normative License for Incurring the Costs of Retributive Justice

This analysis also implies that it should be possible to change the normative context in ways that would make it appropriate for people to meet the entitlements of others, even in preference to legitimately maximizing their own profit. Using a common understanding of the norms in our society, Jim Meindl and I constructed the following set of experimental conditions to test this hypothesis.

The situation we used (Meindl & Lerner, 1983) employed young men who believed they were participating in a study assessing the interest value of various new parlor games. In the initial phase of the experiment, either they, or their partner, or a third party with whom they had no particular relation, was the target of an unprovoked verbal assault from another participant, who denigrated the victim's intelligence and personal integrity.

Subsequently, the subject had to choose between playing either a game against "the villain" involving the infliction of increasing mutual economic costs or an alternative game with yet another participant in which inevitably both would greatly increase their earnings. The subject was convinced that no one but himself would know of his choice. To preclude anticipated gratitude or indebtedness, they also understood that all participants would remain anonymous to one another both during and after the study.

One reasonably mature response to the verbal assault would have been to avoid any further contact with the obviously deranged harm doer while pursuing the legitimate opportunity to earn additional money for oneself. Most subjects did that when a third party with whom they had no particular relation in the experiment was the assaulted victim. They were somewhat more likely to elect confronting the villain in the costly encounter if he had insulted them personally. But the strongest reaction, by far, occurred when their experimentally designated "partners," whom they had not met and could not expect to meet, were the victims of the villain's unprovoked verbal assault. Virtually all the men in that critical condition chose to punish the villain even at considerable economic cost to themselves. Additional data supported the inference that these young men were able to legitimize their impulse to correct an injustice—the undeserved verbal assault—by referring to the norms that require people to protect those uniquely dependent upon them—in this case, their "partner."

Summary and Implications. It is important to emphasize that in these experiments we were able to make predictions based on an understanding of the normative expectations that apply to people functioning in acquisition and allocation contexts. But second, we also had theoretically based reasons to expect that people would be very responsive to issues of their own and others' entitlement deserving. When alternative normative expectations are situationally applicable, they will attend to those norms that sanction their impulse to rectify injustices, even when that is the economically more costly alternative.

Where Does the Theory Lead Us? Some Implications for the Social Sciences

In its present relatively crude form, this social psychological theory of entitlement, nevertheless, points to some potentially important methodological, theoretical, and social policy issues.

Methodological Implications: Inferring Human Motives from the Enactment of Normative Expectations

One of the important tasks of the theory presented here is to provide a systematic understanding of the observation that, in emotionally or motivationally uninvolving situations, people generally adhere to the normative expectations associated with various status roles, whereas in motivationally critical encounters, they are often influenced by rules of entitlement that reflect more primitive scripted associations—for example terrible outcomes, bad people.

The methodological implications of these observations and theoretical propositions become apparent when one considers that the vast majority of the available research findings in the areas of social exchange, equity, fairness, allocation behavior, and distributive and procedural justice have been generated in situations with two common characteristics. One of these is that the subjects–respondents are led to believe they are involved in a simulation of some aspect of the world of commerce or legal competition. This, of course, establishes the normative context appropriate to the situation. Secondly, the subjects–respondents either deal with trivial outcomes in an experimental simulation or are asked to play a particular role—supervisor, employee, litigant—in a hypothetical situation. In either case, the subjects must rely almost exclusively upon their understanding of the normative expectations appropriate to those contexts in order to generate a response. Not represented in their reactions are those processes and rules of entitlement that are elicited when people are fully engaged, motivationally involved, in an encounter.

It is not at all surprising, then, that the overwhelming weight of the research findings in these important areas of inquiry confirms the "economic" model of human motivation: People will naturally, inevitably, try to maximize their own normatively justifiable profits within the constraints of general rules of decency. However, if the theory presented here is valid, this form of enlightened self-interest is what one would expect to find when, in the absence of serious personal concerns, people are expressing only the generally understood norms that apply to economic–competitive encounters.

To reiterate for purposes of emphasis: There is considerable evidence that people's behavior may deviate from the normative expectations in predictable ways when their affective–motivational processes are fully engaged. In addition to the evidence presented earlier in this chapter, consider, for example, Milgram's research on obedience (Milgram, 1974). That program of research dramatized the systematic discrepancies between the extent of harm-producing obedience exhibited by fully engaged participants and the predictions made by role-playing subjects, including experts in the study of human behavior. Their predictions closely followed the normative expectations. Similarly, repeated careful documentation has shown that whereas emotionally detached observers predict and manifest compassion for innocent victims, those more fully involved as witnesses or victims primarily attempt to eliminate the experienced injustice— including at times blaming and derogating the victims themselves (Lerner & Miller, 1978; Ryan, 1971; Simons & Piliavin, 1972). These important reactions are rarely, if ever, represented in the normative predictions.

One way to capture the essence of the methodological and theoretical issues here is by referring to the "fundamental attribution error" (Ross, 1977) that people often commit in explaining their own and others' behavior. This error is the serious underestimation of the influence that situational constraints and determinants have on people's behavior. As a result, people too readily believe that acts reveal the actor's internal dispositions—motives, abilities, personal preferences. In minimally engaging situations, such an error may involve the attribution by the investigators of subjects' reactions to personal motives rather than to the influence of the normative demands created by the investigators in their economic simulations and hypothetical situations.

We now have both evidence and theoretical reasons to question the inferences that have been generated from the almost exclusive reliance on minimally engaging situations. One clear implication of this analysis is the need for more compelling contexts in which to test our theories of human motivation.

Theoretical Implications: Social Change and Rules of Entitlement

The theory I have described assumes a normative status quo, a more or less stable social structure. But as societies and their institutions change, so do societally structured bases of entitlement judgments. This suggests two directions for important theoretical elaborative efforts. One is an integration of this social psychological framework with those social sciences that provide an understanding of the societal, economic, political, historical factors that account for changes in normative structure. The other direction is to generate a theory to explain how people create meaningful definitions of the situation, including issues of entitlement, when the normative context is ambiguous or conflicted. That may seem equivalent to the question (by now very familiar to social psychologists) of when do people apply a particular justice rule, that is of equality, equity, need, winner-takes-all, and so forth. Much more elaborate models have attempted to describe the processes that determine situationally generated definitions of entitlement (Deutsch, 1982; Folger, 1984; Greenberg & Cohen, 1982; Lerner, 1981).

Social Policy Implications: Maximizing Profit as a Defensive Strategy

The policy implications of this theory become evident when considering the familiar problem of gaining and insuring sufficient cooperative efforts to avoid destructive conflicts over insufficient and/or diminishing resources. The social dilemma in these situations derives from the apparent or real conflict between each member's interest and the collective good. If each participant acts rationally to maximize personal gain, the result will be the destruction of the desired resources or other equally great losses accruing to the collectivity. That is obviously an important issue in a society (world) where increasing demands and powerful technology escalate both the probability and potentially destructive consequences of such conflicts.

It is generally thought that the solution to the dilemma lies in each member, or a sufficiently large subset of members, tailoring their activities to promote the welfare of all concerned, while voluntarily incurring some costs or losses, at least on a short-term basis. That is usually translated into the question of how to convince people it is to their advantage, their short or long-term self-interest, to cooperate in ways that will promote the common good. The most obvious way of gaining such cooperation is to establish social devices for the detection and punishment of exploitative behavior and rewarding cooperative acts, that is, altering the external payoffs in the situation; in some situations this may indeed be the most sensible strategy.

However, by resorting to external payoffs and sanctions, we may be precluding other very important sources of cooperation. There is reason to believe, for example, that people will be more satisfied with their fair share than with a maximal amount of the commonly desired resource. The prevalence of profit-maximizing strategies in economic encounters occurs primarily as a response to normative demands, rather than as an inherent and inevitable manifestation of human motivation (Lerner, 1980). If this is the case, it should be possible to elicit alternative norms that would allow people to cooperate rather than compete as they try to provide for themselves and those dependent upon them.

Rather than assessing the relevant processes by presenting people with a series of vignettes, or placing them in a laboratory simulation, we felt it was essential to examine these issues in a field experiment in which respondents could be fully engaged while we maintained the careful control provided by random assignment to experimental conditions. Fortunately, we were able to obtain sufficient funding to establish a survey research center that used a number of part-time employees to do telephone interviewing, coding, and the like. Unknown to them, however, these employees were also our experimental subjects.

In the basic experimental situation, each employee, after having previously been trained at various tasks, arrived at work and was required to decide how to divide his or her time that evening at the center. In the privacy of their own work room and with complete confidence they could not be held accountable to others, they were able to divide their efforts between two jobs of equal importance and priority for their employer. Although the specific tasks were varied experimentally, it was always the case that one of the jobs paid the employees directly on the basis of their individual productivity, whereas the other paid each worker an equal share of what had been earned by the combined productivity of all four workers that evening. It was arranged so that all the employees realized they could be most confident of maximizing their own pay by working exclusively at the job for which they would be paid directly on the basis of their own productivity because they were assured a share of the work completed by any of the other three workers at the second job.

By systematically alternating the method of payment associated with a specific task (e.g., making telephone appointments), we were able to quantify, by simply counting the number produced under each condition, the extent of free riding or the incentive to avoid exploitation. In general, we found considerably greater productivity at whatever task was associated with direct payment of one's own efforts. We also found that the employees thought this was an entirely legitimate way to act. By having some conditions where the workers expected to complete their pay slips at the end of the evening in one another's company, we were able to show that when thus accountable to the others, the employees were no more likely to work at the cooperative task. Apparently, they were not at all ashamed of trying to maximize their profit as individual employees.

But then, how could one alter that self-interested pattern while maintaining the basic ecological validity of an actual job? That turned out to be relatively easy, if all four employees that evening were women. Without prior discussions or opportunity to communicate with one another, most of the women worked predominantly on the cooperative group's shared task. Because most of them spontaneously chose to work at the group task, their average total earnings were approximately equal to that earned by the self-oriented men. It was very significant, though not surprising in retrospect, that the self-interested strategy reappeared among the women when they learned that two of the four employees involved were men. Apparently, those women were aware of the male-appropriate work norms and adopted the self-interested norms as a "defensive" strategy.

Given that the women's preference for a cooperative response disappeared when male employees were present, it became of central importance to pursue the problem of how men might escape the normative trap of having to compete in order to maximize their earnings. As one possible solution, we resorted to familiar male norms that can legitimize cooperation: being members of the same team.

To test this hypothesis, male employees were given clothing and confronted with other props that identified them as members of the "Blue Team." That procedure led to only a minimal reduction in the self-maximizing strategy when they were allowed to remain unaccountable to the others for their behavior. However, if they expected to meet their team members at the end of the evening's work, a significantly large number chose to work at the cooperative pay task. This finding is important mainly because the expectation of being accountable to other employees did not induce cooperation when they were operating under the typical workplace norms. As predicted by the theory, public accountability had to be associated with another normative context: one that promised they would not be violating the powerful norms to compete and look out for their private interests. It appear that being defined as a member of a "team" provided that opportunity.

These findings alone are not able to distinguish clearly between an intrinsically preferred versus defensive strategy explanation for the men's increased cooperative behavior. However, they are sufficiently encouraging, especially when combined with related findings (Kidder, Belletrie, & Cohn, 1977), to merit more serious efforts to find ways of facilitating free cooperation among men in the marketplace.

Summary

The theoretical framework I have presented here can be summarized rather briefly. In our society, most of the time, we act out, in a rather "mindless fashion" (Langer, 1978), the highly scripted sequences of activities and interactions that are regulated by socially based rules concerning "who" is entitled to "what" from "whom." On those occasions when we dispassionately consider alternative courses of action, our decisions reveal rationally self-interested efforts to make our way in a world where everyone is thought to be similarly self-interested. When matters become serious in terms of the magnitude of actual or anticipated consequences, we become primarily invested in maintaining the belief we are good people living in a just word.

These theoretical notions provide an alternative to the prevailing models of social motivation. Hopefully, they are sufficiently intriguing to stimulate further research.

Acknowledgments. This article is based upon an address given at the International Conference on Social Justice in Human Relations held in Leiden, The Netherlands, July 1986. The research and theory presented in this article were made possible by a series of grants and fellowships initially from the National Science Foundation, United States, but primarily the Canada Council and then the Social Sciences and Humanities Council of Canada. I owe special thanks to my colleagues and students Monique Gignac, John Holmes, Mike Naccarato, Mike Ross, and Mark Zanna, who commented on earlier drafts of this manuscript.

References

Asch, S. E. (1952). *Social psychology.* New York: Prentice-Hall.

Beger, J., Fisek, M. H., Norman, R. Z, & Zelditch, M., Jr. (1977). *Status characteristics and social interaction: An expectation states approach.* New York: Elsevier.

Berscheid, E., & Cambell, B.(1981). The changing longevity of heterosexual close relationships: A commentary and forecast. In M. J. Lerner & S. C. Lerner (Eds.), *The justice motive in social behavior* (pp. 209–234). New York. Plenum Press.

Blau, P. M. (1964). *Exchange and power in social life.* New York: Wiley.

Bowers, K. S., & Meichenbaum, D. (1984). *The unconscious reconsidered.* New York: John Wiley & Sons.

Carlsmith, J. M, & Gross, A. E. (1969). Some effects of guilt on compliance. *Journal of Personality and Social Psychology, 11,* 232–239.

Cook, T D., Crosby F., & Hennigan, K. M. (1977). The construct validity of relative deprivation. In J. M. Suls, & R. M. Miller, (Eds.), *Social comparison processes: Theoretical and empirical perspectives.* Washington DC: Hemisphere Corp.

Crosby, F. (1976). A model of egotistical relative deprivation. *Psychological Review, 83,* 85–113.

Deutsch, M (1982). Interdependence and psychological orientation. In V. J. Derlega & J.Grzelak (Eds.), *Cooperation and helping behavior.* New York: Academic Press.

Ellard, J. M. (1983). An exploratory study of the "Existential Charade." Unpublished MA thesis, University of Waterloo, Waterloo, Ontario, Canada.

Festinger, L. L. (1957). A theory of cognitive dissonance. Evanston, IL: Row, Peterson.

Flavell, J. H. (1977). Cognitive development. Englewood Cliffs, NJ: Prentice-Hall.

Folger, R. (1984). Emerging issues in the social psychology of justice. In R. Folger (Ed.), The sense of injustice: Social psychological perspectives (pp. 3–24). New York: Plenum Press.

Freedman, J. L. (1970). Transgression, compliance, and guilt. In J. Macaulay & L. Berkowitz (Eds). Altruism and helping behavior. New York: Academic Press.

Gouldner, A. W. (1960) The norm of reciprocity: A preliminary statement. American Sociological Review, 25, 161, 178.

Greenberg, J., & Cohen, R. L. (1982).Why justice: Normative and instrumental interpretations. In J. Greenberg, & R. L. Cohen (Eds.), Equity and justice in social behavior (pp. 437–470). New York: Academic Press.

Heider, F. (1958). The psychology of interpersonal relations. New York: Wiley.

Hogan, R., & Emler, N. P. (1981). Retributive justice. In M. J. Lerner & S. C. Lerner (Eds.), The justice motive in social behavior (pp. 125–143). New York: Plenum Press.

Homans, G. C. (1961). Social behavior: Its elementary forms. New York: Harcourt, Brace & World.

Karniol, R., & Miller, D. T. (1981). Morality and the development of conceptions of justice. In M. J. Lerner, & S. C. Lerner, (Eds.), The justice motive in social behavior (pp. 73–89). New York: Plenum Press.

Kidder, L. H., Belletrie, G., & Cohn, S. E. (1977). Secret ambitions and public performances. Journal of Experimental Social Psychology, 13, 7080.

Kohlberg, L. (1969). Stage and sequence: The cognitive-developmental approach to socialization. In D. Goslin (Ed.), Handbook of socialization theory and research. New York: Rand McNally.

Kruglanski, A. (1980). Lay epistemo-logic-process and contents: Another look at attribution theory. Psychological Review, 87, 70–87.

Kubler-Ross, E. (1969). On death and dying. New York: Macmillan.

Langer, E. J. (1973). Rethinking the role of thought in social interaction. In J. Harvey, W. Ickes, & R. Kidd (Eds.), New directions in attribution theory (Vol. 2). Hillsdale, NJ: Erlbaum.

Lerner, M. J. (1977). The justice motive: Some hypotheses as to its origins and forms. Journal of Personality, 45, 1–52.

Lerner, M. J. (1980). The belief in a just world: A fundamental delusion. New York: Plenum Press.

Lerner, M. J. (1981). Justice motive in human relations: Some thoughts on what we know and need to know about justice. In M. J. Lerner, & S. C. Lerner, (Eds.), The justice motive in social behavior: Adapting to times of scarcity and change (pp. 11–35). New York: Plenum Press.

Lerner, M.J. (1982). Justice motive in human relations and the economic model of man. In V. Derlega & J. Grzelak (Eds.), Cooperation and helping behavior. New York: Academic Press.

Lerner, M. J., & Miller, D. T. (1978). Just world research and the attribution process: Looking back and ahead. Psychological Bulletin, 82, 1030–1051.

Lerner, M. J., Miller, D. T., & Holmes, J. G. (1976). Deserving vs. justice: A contemporary dilemma. In L. Berkowitz (Ed.), Advances in experimental social psychology (Vol. 9) New York: Academic Press.

Lerner, S. C. (1979). Behavior in the crunch. Alternatives, 8, 2.

Meindl, J. R., & Lerner, M. J. (1983). The heroic motive: Some experimental demonstrations. Journal of Experimental Social Psychology, 19, 1–20.

Meindl, J. R., & Lerner, M. J. (1984). Exacerbation of extreme responses to an outgroup. *Journal of Personality and Social Psychology, 47,* 71–84.

Messick, D. M., & Sentis, K. (1983). Fairness, preference, and fairness biases. In D. M. Messick, & K. S. Cook, (Eds.), *Equity theory: Psychological and sociological perspectives.* New York: Praeger.

Milgram, S. (1974). *Obedience to authority.* New York: Harper & Row.

Miller, D. T. (1975). *Personal deserving versus justice for others: An exploration of the justice motive.* Unpublished doctoral disseration, University of Waterloo, Waterloo, Ontario, Canada.

Miller, D. T. (1977). Personal deserving versus justice for others. *Journal of Experimental Social Psychology, 13,* 1–13.

Nisbett, R. E., & Ross, L. (1980). *Human inference: Strategies and shortcomings of social judgment.* Englewood Cliffs, NJ: Prentice-hall.

Piaget, J. (1965). *The moral judgment of the child.* New York: Free Press.

Ross, L. D. (1977). The intuitive psychologist and his shortcomings. In L. Berkowitz (Ed.), *Advances in experimental social psychology* (Vol. 10) New York: Academic Press.

Rubin, Z. & Peplau, A. (1975). Who believes in a just world? *Journal of Social Issues, 13* 65–89.

Ryan, W. (1971). *Blaming the victim.* New York: Pantheon Press.

Sampson, E. (1975). On justice as equality. *Journal of Social Issues, 31,* 45–64.

Schelling, T. (1978.) *Micromotives and macrobehavior.* New York: Norton.

Shweder, R. A., & Miller, J. G. (1985). The social construction of the person: How is it possible? In K. J. Gergen & K. E. Davis (Eds.), *The social construction of the person.* New York: Springer-Verlag.

Simmons, C. H. (1981). Theoretical issues in the development of social justice. In M. J. Lerner, & S. C. Lerner (Eds.), *Justice motive in social behavior* (pp. 41–55). New York: Plenum Press.

Simmons, C. H., & Piliavin, J. A. (1972). The effect of deception on reactions to a victim. *Journal of Personality and Social Psychology, 21,* 56–60.

Thibaut, J., & Kelley, H. H. (1959). *The social psychology of groups.* New York: John Wiley & Sons.

Walster, E., & Walster, G. W. (1975). Equity and social justice. *Journal of Social Issues, 31,* 21–44.

Walster, E, Walster, G. W., & Berscheid, E. (1978). *Equity: Theory and research.* Boston: Allyn & Bacon.

Werner, H. (1948). *Comparative psychology of mental development.* New York: International Press.

Zuckerman, M. (1975). Belief in a just world and altruistic behavior. *Journal of Personality and Social Psychology, 31,* 972–976.

2

Prospects for a Cognitive–Structural Justice Theory

Barry Markovsky

Introduction

Who agrees on the meaning of "justice"? By various accounts, it is a societal condition, a feeling inside, a cognition, a guideline for administering rewards, a guideline for administering punishments, the unattainable perfect condition of an ideal social system, a goal that may be reached through legislation. Can it really be all of these things?

In a sense, justice certainly is all of these things. Fortunately, however, for the purposes of formulating scientific theories of justice, one need only state what justice means in the context of that theory. This presumes that justice has no true or "essential" nature—or that if it does, it is not relevant to whatever it is that the given theory is attempting to explain. Although such an approach rankles many social scientists, philosophers, administrators, lawmakers, law enforcers, and most everyone else for that matter, it does have certain advantages. After millennia of searching for the true and essential meaning of justice, after hundreds, perhaps thousands of impassioned if conflicting solutions, a different perspective is warranted. This alternative perspective could be called a *social constructionist* approach: Assume that there is no true or essential justice beyond its socially constructed meanings. Then explain the causes and consequences of those meanings.

Barry Markovsky • Department of Sociology, University of Iowa, Iowa City, Iowa 52242.

One result of this view is that the study of justice in human relations can benefit by the integration of previously distinct approaches. It would be legitimate, for example, to suppose that justice has both cognitive and social structural components. More than one justice may exist without creating theoretical cleavages *if* we are willing to supply provisional definitions for justice as it is used in particular theoretical contexts. Furthermore, it is possible to construct justice theories with an eye toward integrating previously disparate conceptions. As discussed later, this means that justice theories aimed at apparently divergent domains may be made more powerful through bridges constructed between them.

This approach places heavy emphasis on the evaluations and behaviors of individuals. Whether it is the worker assessing her pay, the legislator assessing economic distributions, labor union members making wage and benefit demands, or the social psychologist constructing a theory, justice ideas are filtered through perceptions, evaluations, and communications. (Even if there is a pure and essential meaning for justice, I doubt that it could survive this series of filters and obstacles unscathed.) Still, however, this is not a reductionist position. Justice evaluations are determined as much by information provided by social structures and contexts as by the individual who gathers and processes the information.

Philosophical approaches part ways with this social scientific approach in several crucial respects. Philosophical approaches seek unconditional, universal prescriptions for justice—to answer questions such as "what is the nature of justice?" and "how can justice be achieved in a social system?" Philosophical solutions are prescriptive: "Justice exists only if x is true," or "only if a society creates conditions a, b, and c." In contrast, scientific approaches are designed to be descriptive and explanatory. They address a different set of questions: "Under what conditions is justice or injustice perceived?" and "how do people and/or groups respond to perceived injustices?" Scientific solutions are of the form "x is perceived as just (or unjust) under conditions a, b, and c," and "if x is perceived as unjust, the perceiver will behave as follows."

Furthermore, justice for the philosopher is an idealized, ever-possible, systemwide arrangement of valued things. Social scientific approaches, in contrast, do not require—and often do not presume— the existence or universal nature of justice. Instead, they focus on the conditions that promote the creation or adoption of justice principles, how they become manifested at the level of the individual or what interest conflicts they entail.

For as long as it has posed unyielding philosophical problems, justice has been a pressing social policy issue. Today, policy debates do gather input from the social science literatures. However, these social sciences usually include the fields of political science and economics. On occasion, data that have been gathered in sociological surveys is examined. In general, however, there is little input from sociological and psychological justice theories. Arguments rage over what political/economic system is most just, ignoring the complex cognitive factors that play on perceptions of justice and ignoring the complex social factors that play on such cognitions. Without belittling attempts at formulating social policy prescriptions, it must be recognized that the success of any such attempt is contingent upon understanding the cognitive and social structural factors that lead a society's members and policymakers to form their evaluations of a given state of affairs. Without such knowledge, there is every chance that policy-induced interventions will produce redistributions perceived as even more unjust than the original.

This view goes against commonsense thinking about justice. It asks the social observer to suspend, at least provisionally, any philosophical or religious belief he or she may have concerning the existence of a true, ideal, if unrealized state of justice. The view implies that justice is more a way of perceiving than an objective state of affairs. It is therefore not surprising that debates about the true nature of justice have never approached settlement. This view holds that it is not the nature of justice that is at issue but rather the question of how people and groups adopt, apply, and enforce their particular justice standards.

In the following discussion, justice is taken to be a socially and cognitively constructed phenomenon. The implications of this general approach for the study of behavior at several levels of analysis will be examined, including the physiological, bioecological, psychological, and social structural levels. The intention is to provide a metatheoretical framework around which existing knowledge may be woven and further knowledge may be integrated. Although most of the examples will deal with judgments of distributive justice, the approach is equally applicable to any situation where some type of result is evaluated with regard to actions performed or characteristics possessed that are deemed relevant to that result.

Psychophysiological and Bioecological Perspectives on Justice

Justice evaluations are not reducible to the interactions of chemicals in brains and bodies. However, there is undoubtedly a physiological component. Injustice is not merely an observation that people make. Notwithstanding the electrochemical processes at the core of all brain activity, we know that at a higher level of processing, justice evaluations sometimes carry a potent emotional impact. To the extent that we understand the intimate and complex relationship between physiology and emotion, we learn something about the impact of justice issues upon individuals. It is probably safe to assert the following: The more intense an individual's physiological response to injustices in a social situation, the more motivated that individual will be to enact changes in either the situation or in his/her evaluation of one or more components of the situation.

What then is the nature of this physiological response, and what is its likely source? I believe that the physiological component of the emotional response to perceived injustice is a stress response. This means that injustices are social stressors and, as such, touch us in a very deep and primitive way. The neurophysiology of stress and subsequent arousal responses is very complicated and includes a variety of brain and brain stem structures. However, quite a lot is known about stress, and for decades it has been an extremely active area in psychology. A great deal has been learned (see Appley & Trumbull, 1967; Selye, 1976; Cox, 1978; Hassett, 1978; Fazio & Cooper, 1983).

For example, externally induced stress in the form of threats induces a battery of responses in the parasympathetic nervous system—the so-called fight or flight reaction. Two of these responses include heart rate increases and heightened sweat-gland activity in the palms of the hands. Both of these responses are easily measured using noninvasive electrocardiograph (EKG) and galvanic skin response (GSR) measures. In a recent study (Markovsky, 1988a), heart rate and skin conductance data were collected in a simple pay-for-work situation. Relative to what they were led to expect for their work quality, subjects were either underpaid, overpaid, or paid justly. The results provided evidence for the predicted arousal responses corresponding to the onset of both beneficial and harmful injustices. If small, transient injustices do consistently produce arousal, it is certainly worth examining whether larger, chronic injustices in natural settings are linked to stress-related health factors and behaviors such as turnover and absenteeism.

Another angle from which we may view justice evaluations and responses stems from the theory of natural selection. Sociobiology (Dawkins, 1976; Wilson, 1975, 1978;) and evolutionary ecology (Pianka, 1978; Smith, 1983) represent two areas of relatively recent development with important implications for human populations. Sociobiology is a highly controversial field that most biological and social scientists either love or hate, corresponding to uncritical acceptance or unconditional rejection, respectively. Evolutionary ecology is less known, less controversial, and relaxes sociobiology's adherence to evolutionary genetics.

Evolutionary thinking has the potential to provide tentative, even testable statements about the nature and development of justice concerns in human social systems. Sociobiology would assert that humans are genetically predisposed to formulate justice standards applicable to members of the groups they form. Evolutionary ecology may further assert that the standards themselves evolve through a trial and error process such that those standards having the greatest survival value to the group persist, and those of lower value extinguish along with the groups that employ them.

Of course, sociobiology has been justly criticized for positing a genetic basis for anything that you would care to explain, placing it on shaky epistemological ground. However, we can circumvent that problem by supposing, in accord with evolutionary ecological thinking, that justice norms are passed along culturally rather than genetically transmitted. It then becomes much easier to imagine scenarios for the evolution of justice norms.

A hypothetical example: A tribe leader had a vision while under the influence of an hallucinogenic fungus. In this vision a great beast told the leader that he must convince the tribal members to pool their resources and skills. Then, whoever contributes the most will be permitted to take the most. If these orders are not instituted, the beast will destroy the world. In previous visions, the great beast told the leader to have tribe members tie their children's wrists to trees during each day's dusk and to wash between all toes before eating. The tribe members, fearing the leader's power to sanction, obeyed his word. However, although wrist tying and toe washing eventually could have changed from obeyed commands to benign customs, perhaps changing in character or even disappearing, the resource allocation system may have an inherent stability in that it can reduce intragroup conflict. If so, it is likely to be transmitted through time to new generations of tribe members and to other tribes through intermarriage and other forms of cultural diffusion. It fosters a healthy competition among the tribe members, and each contributor knows that he or she may expect a return in kind for any resources rendered. Those tribes that split away and adopt other resource-utilization strategies may not fare so well. The point is that a wholly "rational" system of justice can be selected from among competing systems, whereas its meaning and appearance to the individuals in the system may bear no resemblance to its actual operation.

Although this scenario surely contains my own cultural biases, the main point should not be obscured: Some groups manage to produce workable, self-perpetuating justice norms. These norms may emerge by mutual agreement, decree, or chance, and assert equity, need, or equality principles. Once generated, these norms provide the group a mechanism for mediating conflicts over valued resources. A group whose members spend their time enthusiastically gathering and exchanging resources may well have a competitive advantage over the group whose members are distrustful, backbiting, and uncooperative.

Thus justice may have an ecological aspect. It is capable of promoting the survival of reproductive groups that adopt justice principles for the distribution of resources that are capable of increasing survival chances.

Information Processing

Information processing, judgment, and decision making are major areas in cognitive psychology. Because equity is also a major area, it is surprising that there is little work linking the two areas. One exception is provided by Norman Anderson. His "information integration" approach uses simple algebraic models to represent cognitive manipulations of information (Anderson, 1981, 1982). In tests of several alternative models, Anderson and Farkas (1975) found that the following model best described their results:

$$\frac{R_A}{R_A + R_B} - \frac{I_A}{I_A + I_B} = 0$$

Where R is an amount of reward, I is a level of investment, and actor A is comparing his or her rewards and investments to those of B. However, this model is somewhat limited in that it requires exactly two actors and precise knowledge of each actor's and the total rewards and investments in the situation. Further, the model does not address the psychological impact of departures from the equitable state that it defines. Tests of the model always provide three of the four pieces of information required by the model and ask subjects to provide the fourth. Although it is important that equity models provide this service, it would also be desirable for them to model the intensity of feelings of injustice for given configurations of rewards and invest-ments.

Anderson's statistical methods are intimately connected to his theoretical models. He uses the method of functional measurement to test the algebraic theoretical models with analysis of variance tech-niques. The ANOVA methods assume that stimuli and response variables are interval scaled. Interval scales have no zero points and are not valid under ratio transformations (Fararo, 1978). They assume that equal intervals are equally valued, for example, that the difference between 15 and 20 degrees Celsius on the temperature scale is the same as the difference between 5 and 10 degrees.

If we can make even stronger assumptions about the scaling of stimulus and response variables in justice evaluations, then we can construct even more refined models. One potentially fruitful direction utilizes psychophysical scaling methods. These methods assume that people can make ratio scale judgments about the elements of the evaluation. More accurately, the methods permit ratio transformations of power functions of the measured variables.

For example, we know that monetary reward scales usually have a clear zero point, that they often have decreasing marginal utility, and that this utility curve is nicely represented using a power function. That is, the *subjective values* of reward levels are given by a power transformation of the objective reward levels: The objective value is raised to a power less than 1 and multiplied by a scaling constant. Equivalently, we may say that subjective reward values are log-linearly related to objective rewards.

Many researchers have claimed to test mathematical models that relate rewards and investments to states of justice or equity or to degrees of injustice or inequity experience (e.g., Harris, 1976, 1983; Harris *et al.*, 1981; Messick & Sentis, 1979; Moschetti, 1979; Alessio, 1980). However, the usual procedure is to simply take the objective measures of rewards and investments and plug them into the mathe-matical model. This completely ignores the possibility that respon-dents may not evaluate rewards and investments in a way that corresponds to their face values.

For example, using a pay scale ranging from 0–100 cents, I found that subjects' evaluations of the monetary amounts were typically described by a power function with an exponent of .85. That is, there was diminishing marginal value for money even on this restricted range of values. For performance scales ranging from 0–100 points, the power function representing the evaluations had an exponent of 1.1. This means that to double the *subjective value* of a given amount of money takes more than twice that amount and to double the subjective evaluation of a given performance score takes less than double that score.

As a result of these marginal effects, justice models that require one to "plug in" face values of reward and investment levels are incorrectly specified. In fact, in tests of a variety of specifications for justice evaluation formulas, I have found that the following "subjective difference" model works quite well:

$$J = k|R_s - R_s^*|$$

where the justice evaluation (J) is assumed to vary according to the absolute difference between subjective evaluations of actual reward (R_s) and expected rewards (R_s^*), the latter given on the basis of an actual performance and an explicit distribution standard. A scaling parameter (k) can account for the influence of individual variations in responsiveness or other factors such as clarity of information, identification with the reward recipient, or the perceived legitimacy of the distribution standard (Markovsky, 1985a). In a study utilizing psychophysical scaling of subjective evaluations of pay, performance, and injustice, this model explained over twice the variation in justice evaluation responses as its nearest competitor (Markovsky, Ford, & Choe, 1987).

The area of psychophysics (Lodge, 1981; Stevens, 1972, 1975) provides methods of measuring and validating magnitude estimations of physical and social stimuli. This means that all of the elements of a justice evaluation can be mapped onto ratio-level subjective scales and used to test whatever mathematical model of justice we choose. Further, because respondents make magnitude estimations of degrees of injustice, models that relate degrees of objective over-or underreward to degrees of injustice experience can be accurately tested. Initial analyses indicate that this method provides a very promising direction for increasingly refined tests of justice evaluation theories (Markovsky et al., 1987).

Another important area in cognitive psychology is judgment heuristics research (see Kahneman et al., 1982; Beyth-Marom et al., 1985). This research attempts to answer the question, "How do we make decisions under conditions of uncertainty?" The answer takes the form of a menu of judgment heuristics or simplifying methods from which we select the most appropriate, depending upon the type of judgment demanded of us. One heuristic that is especially relevant to justice evaluations is "anchoring" (Markovsky, 1988b).

Anchoring works in the following way. Suppose you distribute slips of paper to everyone in a classroom. On the paper is a statement and a question. It reads: "How many cities and towns are there in

Holland?'' Then half of the slips state: "Obviously there are more than 50. But if you had to guess, how many would you say there are?'' The other half state: "Obviously there are fewer than 100,000. But if you had to guess, how many would you say there are?'' When the results are tallied you will find that those responding to the question framed by the low "anchor" of 50 produce much lower estimates than those with the high anchor of 100,000. It is as if the anchor is used as a starting point, and then respondents move conservatively up or down the scale from the low or high anchor, respectively.

For justice evaluations, I have found two types of anchoring (Markovsky, 1988b). First, in cases where we attempt to determine fair reward levels, estimates of this amount are biased by extraneous anchor information such as knowledge of a minimum wage or of a conceivable maximum wage (Markovsky, 1984a). This was also true for estimates of the amount of punishment deemed just for various crimes (Markovsky, 1984b). Depending upon extreme sentences that were mentioned, respondents estimated imprisonment periods under high anchor conditions that were more than twice the length of sentences estimated under low anchor conditions.

Second, evaluations of the fairness of a given reward were biased by comparisons to previous justice evaluations. For example, a moderate underpayment seems less unjust following a more extreme underpayment than when it follows a less extreme underpayment. This is most certainly one of the mechanisms underlying the process of accommodation to unjust rewards. More important, the anchoring extension to the distributive justice theory allows applications to more realistic situations than previous models. Anchors are most salient when there is some uncertainty as to the standards, rewards, or investments in a justice evaluation, and I believe that such uncertainty is far more prevalent than the certainty implicit and required by other justice models.

Bridging to Groups

Next we will begin to connect the processing and the elements of justice evaluations to group-level phenomena. First, however, we must established a meaning for the term group and for several related terms such as category, collectivity, and aggregate.

For Tajfel (1981), whether a set of actors forms a group depends on certain shared beliefs. A group is a body of people who see themselves as a group. In contrast, "category" members share one or more characteristics but do not possess feelings of "groupness." This is very much in the spirit of the social constructionist approach in this chapter. However, it will be useful to modify this so that nonmembers may also believe in the existence of a group: A group is a body of people whose members are *believed* to feel that they are a group. That is, from the standpoint of an observer, whether a member or not, a set of people is a group when the observer believes that they are a group, whatever the actual sentiments are among members of the set. Tajfel has a long-standing research agenda aimed at identifying factors that determine whether or not sets of actors are seen (or see themselves) as groups. He has found, for example, that attributes of others that have been made salient through repetition become the basis for perceptions of social categories.

Merton (1968) and Merton and Rossi (1968) attempted to define the terms *category*, *collectivity*, and *group* on the basis of objective properties that are unique to each. Groups have established interaction patterns among actors; all actors view themselves as members; and all members are recognized as such by nonmembers. Collectivities are comprised of "people who have a sense of solidarity by virtue of sharing common values and who have acquired a sense of moral obligation to fulfill role expectations." A category is an aggregate sharing a particular social status but lacking any normative structure and regularized interaction patterns. Although such properties may provide a useful objective basis for distinguishing the different types of sets that actors may comprise, these are also the types of properties that are potentially salient to observers. Therefore, we can link these subjective and objective definitions by assuming that the more grouplike a set of actors in the sense that Merton and Rossi describe, then the more grouplike it will appear to an observer.

As a general rule, we may expect that any aspect of justice evaluations that are affected by perceptions of others will be heightened to the extent that those others are perceived as forming a category rather than an aggregate, a collectivity rather than a category or aggregate, or a group rather than a collectivity, category, or aggregate. This will be assumed in the discussions to follow, where the term *group* will be used for the sake of brevity.

There are several ways that groups can enter into justice evaluations. First, an individual can make justice evaluations on behalf of a group. Second, a group can provide a standard against which the rewards and investments of individuals or other groups are compared. Third, justice evaluations may be made regarding the shape of the distribution of rewards across the members of a group relative to some ideal distribution. Fourth, group structures may affect justice processes in various ways. Each of these will be discussed next.

Evaluation of Group Rewards

First, we have already assumed that individuals gather ii
their rewards and investments, process this informatio
some type of justice assessment. It is then but a small th
to allow that individuals may do the same with respect to   ᵤᵣ
a family's situation. Justice evaluations can be made on others' behalf,
and real feelings of injustice experienced, as long as (1) the evaluator
cares about the well-being of the target of the evaluation and (2) the
evaluator has in mind some standard against which the target's
rewards may be compared. In fact, humans are renowned for their
ability to formulate stereotypes about groups on the basis of very little
information. Nothing prevents us from using selective knowledge of a
group's rewards and investments, gathered through a variety of possible channels, to form stereotyped conceptions of what the group as a
whole has invested and received.

For whites in the United States who view black economic disadvantages as stemming from a simple lack of education, effort, or
intrinsic capacities relative to whites, discrepancies in economic
well-being are just. For those who consider blacks to be equally capable
as whites of making reward-relevant investments but as having been
denied opportunity to do so, the economic discrepancies are unjust.
The point is that we have no trouble handling aggregated information
in the formation of justice evaluations for groups.

In testing my own theoretical model of justice evaluations, I have
found that the extent to which group (and, theoretically, collective,
categorical, and aggregate) reward discrepancies produce feelings of
injustice depends, at least in part, upon how strongly the evaluator
identifies with the group whose rewards are being evaluated (Markovsky, 1985a). Thus, although a white American may be aware of the
economic plight of American blacks, this will have no emotional
impact on the white person unless she or he identifies with blacks.
Identification could arise through, for example, the belief that there are
more similarities between the two groups than differences. With
greater identification, the evaluator's experience becomes entwined
with the experience of the subject of the evaluation. In experimental
research (Markovsky, 1985a), identification conditions have been
shown to make the difference between self-interested and group-
interested responses to injustice.

Group-Provided Reward Standards

A group may either passively or actively provide norms, laws, customs, suggestions, and the like that provide standards against which

the rewards and investments of individuals or other groups are compared. The status-value theory of distributive justice (Berger *et al.*, 1972, 1983) assumes passive standards. The relevant groups are actually sets of "generalized others" (e.g., occupational categories, status classes) that are seen to possess particular levels of valued characteristics and receive particular levels of valued rewards. Actors in actual situations compare their own and others' relative rewards and investments with those possessed by the generalized others. Injustice is experienced when there is a lack of correspondence between the "local" and "referential" elements of the comparison.

For example, to decide whether your salary is fair, you first assess the characteristics you possess and/or investments you have made that are relevant to that salary. Then you obtain (remember, concoct, request, etc.) information on generalized others like yourself. You next attempt to determine the pay received by these generalized others. If that pay matches your own, you perceive justice. Otherwise, you perceive injustice.

Groups also actively create justice standards and may invest tremendous collective resources in attempting to promote and enforce them. In this sense, justice norms are subject to the same tests of legitimation as group authority figures and, once accepted, can become as real as the resources whose distribution they influence.

For example, there are movements in certain U.S. industries to create "comparable worth" standards that attempt to establish shared values for various individual skills and characteristics. Also, we are all familiar with ongoing attempts by black South African leaders to establish new standards for the relative treatment of whites and blacks in that country. Furthermore, all state judicial systems are as actively engaged in deciding upon the sanction levels appropriate for various transgressions as they are in the more abstract task of administering justice.

Evaluating Aggregate Distributions

Justice philosophies, economic policy decisions, and wage structures frequently take into account the overall shape of the distribution of rewards in social aggregates. In other words, although it may be the case that all members of a social aggregate are justly rewarded for their investments at rates agreeable with widely shared standards, the shape of the reward distribution entailed by those justice standards may itself appear unjust relative to some idealized shape. As it is possible to collapse a group's levels of reward and investment into single values and compare them with those of another group or standard, so too may we examine properties of the *shape* of the distribution of goods across a group's members and compare this with some other group's or with some idealized standard.

In order to accomplish this, the justice evaluator's standard of comparison must no longer be simply an ordered pair of investment and reward levels or a function describing their relation. To evaluate the distribution, knowledge is required on at least some of the various parameters of the distribution—minimum and maximum values, the extent and direction of any asymmetry, how peaked or flat it is, the location of the mean and mode, the proportion of the population falling above, below, or between certain percentiles, whether the cumulative distribution function is strictly increasing, the ratio of the positive tail length to the negative tail, and so on. Then whatever parameters are deemed relevant will be compared to some reference parameters from the distribution for another population, real or ideal.

For example, a given political ideology may entail a meritocracy, with the proviso that all of the state's governed be guaranteed a particular unconditional minimum level of well-being. Following Jasso (1983), it is clear that in the ideal, the actual reward distribution will be determined by the distribution of investments and the just reward distribution function that has been adopted. The resulting distribution of rewards will be just with respect to the meritocracy principle but not necessarily according to the minimum reward proviso. If any portion of the left tail of the reward distribution falls below the minimum permissible level, then the state must adopt policies— such as a system of taxation—that redistribute sufficient resources to the members of the subminimum group. On the small-group scale, interpersonal pressures could even evoke an informal system of direct redistribution.

As an example of concerns with the shape of the aggregate distribution, in some academic departments, salary committees are allotted a lump sum to allocate among members of the department. In such a case, fairness criteria for the distribution of pay may include, in addition to such factors as merit and seniority, the extent to which the shape of this year's distribution is similar to the shape of last year's. A "peak" or "trough" in the new distribution that was not present on last year's may create justice concerns and lead to debates and discussion of alternatives. As I have described it, this type of issue is separate from whether or not the individuals comprising the anomalous segment in the distribution are justly paid, for we are assuming that they have been. This evaluation raises what may be called a higher order justice issue.

Next, a personal example in which pressure was exerted for the modification of a just distribution of rewards. For a time in college I worked as a busboy in a restaurant where all of the waiters' tips were pooled. Fifteen percent of the tip pool was divided among the busboys who were on duty. On busy nights, waiters earned $12 to $15/hour, busboys around $6 to $7/hour. For each busboy this meant, among other duties, setting, clearing, and resetting approximately 50 tables.

One day disaster struck. I was on duty on a very busy Sunday, and the second busboy failed to show up for work. In addition, the dishwashing machine broke down. Because busboys worked most directly with the person washing dishes, I had to take on additional responsibilities, helping to hand-wash dishes when I could. By the end of the night, I had worked a very exhausting 10 hours, reset 110 tables, and received around $120 from my share of the tips—$12/hour.

These events took place in the late 1970s and so for an impoverished college student, this payment was a pot of gold—but a pot whose bounty I surely deserved. There was a full contingent of waiters that night, and they received their expected $15/hour. Before I left, however, my manager pulled me aside for a talk. He said that no busboy had ever earned anywhere near this amount in one day, that everyone had to work extra to compensate for the missing busboy and the broken dishwasher, and that perhaps I would be willing to turn over some of my money to one of the waiters who had an especially long and difficult shift.

In spite of the redistribution pressure, I found it easy to rationalize that my excessive reward was fair compensation for an excessive effort and that every waiter was already receiving more pay per hour than I. I did not yield, and I did not feel guilty. Clearly this was a case where there was a disagreement on the ideal distribution of rewards in the group, and where there was pressure toward redistributing rewards in accord with one of the ideal distributions, but in conflict with the other.

Group Structural Effects

There are a number of ways that group structures affect justice processes. If justice evaluations require key bits of information (e.g., reward and investment levels, referential specifications), then one of the most obvious ways that group structures affect justice evaluations is by restricting the flow of such information. That is, group members at certain positions in group structures may be denied access to information or be given false or ambiguous information on the rewards or investments of specific or generalized others.

Informational barriers may arise through purposive construction or as unintended artifacts of the group structure. For example, informational barriers may be built by the owner of a small business who keeps information on her own excessive salary hidden from workers. Or a worker who has received a raise may misreport its magnitude to a coworker or distort information on what he did to deserve the raise in order to avoid angering the coworker.

In deeply hierarchical structures, the tenuousness of communication patterns—apart from any purposive actions of group members—can serve as barriers to justice-relevant information. I just read about the annual salary of the president of my university. It sounded quite high to me, but my initial reaction was not an experience of injustice; I have little conception of either the investments expected of university presidents, or whether my university president lives up to them.

Finally, another way that structures can affect justice processes is through the formation of differentiated subgroups. The same investments may be highly valued in one subgroup but worth little in another. Thus the distribution of justice evaluations in the larger group will be conditional upon the distribution of investment valuations among subgroups, as well as upon the actual distribution of investments.

An article by Gartrell (1985) points to an interesting consequence of group structures: justice evaluations of actors in various parts of the structure made with regard to members of other parts of the structure may themselves form a pattern. So if we constructed a matrix of group substructures such as occupational categories in an organization or industry and if we let the elements of that matrix represent the justice evaluation of occupation x with respect to occupation y, mathematical algorithms such as cluster analysis or blockmodeling may be used to look for sets of subgroups that tend to evaluate the pay of another set of subgroups in a similar manner. As it stands, these are exploratory methods, and there is no theory that predicts particular clusters independent of knowledge of perceived rewards and investments (Markovsky & Ford, 1987). However, the power of these methods opens the way for some sophisticated theorizing in this area.

For example, assume that we are interested in understanding and predicting the likelihood and strength of collective responses to injustice, such as riots, strikes, and revolts. Using clustering methods applied to survey data, we could measure—from the perspective of an evaluating cluster—the extensiveness of clusters of unjustly rewarded categories and the degree of unanimity of those perceptions within the evaluating cluster. This method can give a far more detailed picture of how members and groups in a social system regard themselves and each other than more simplistic pairwise comparison methods implied in most justice, equity, and relative deprivation theories.

Collective Justice Evaluations

To this point we have only considered the justice evaluations made by individuals. In this brief section, it will be shown that it is a fairly simple matter to expand justice theories to incorporate the idea of collective justice evaluations. For analytical purposes, it may be useful to conceive of this phenomenon as comprised of a combination of individual dispositions and certain types of relations among certain of these individuals. That is, injustice experience is "collectivized" not as a simple summation of individual experiences but by also taking account of particular types of relations among individuals in a collectivity.

In other work (Markovsky, 1985a,b), I made the distinction between *incongruence* and *injustice experience* at the individual level. Incongruence is simply the realization that a reward expectation has been violated. Injustice experience is the emotional response to that realization and is affected by such factors as perceived accuracy of the information, the legitimacy of the comparison standard, and the degree of identification with the subject of the justice evaluation.

At the group level, *collective incongruence* may be defined as the amount of negative injustice experience in a group, weighted by the proportion of the group in this state (Markovsky, 1985c). In order for collective injustice to exist for the group, however, something more is required than the presence of a number of disgruntled group members. The members who experience injustice must further experience these injustices in shared social contexts. Collective injustice experience may then be defined as collective incongruence existing within a shared social context, where the actors in that context assume that other participants in that context share the same belief. It is then possible to treat collective injustice as a factor in its own right. Depending upon one's theoretical perspective, it may be deemed a consequence of types of economic systems, state policies, historical circumstances, and so forth. Or it could be treated as a determining factor in theories of social movements, organizational turnover, employer–employee relations, and so on.

Jasso's (1980) theory presents a number of predictions about collective behavior contingent only on statistical parameters of a group's distribution of justice evaluations. The parameters included the Gini's mean difference—a measure of variance for the distribution—the arithmetic mean, the lower extreme value, the arithmetic mean of the negative segment of the distribution, and so on. The collective behaviors linked to these parameters include propensity for the aggregate to dissolve, propensities for violent revolutionary conflict, the degree of concord or discord, and rates of crime, mental illness, and emigration. The utility of such collective approaches for explaining human behavior remains to be determined. However, the fact that we have a method for conceptualizing something so complex as the relation between individual judgments and collective behavior is itself noteworthy.

There is a fascinating type of justice evaluation not previously discussed that has both individual and collective aspects. Whenever individuals employ a given standard for a justice evaluation, the potential exists—especially in group settings—for alternative standards to be brought to the attention of the evaluator. The evaluator is then called upon to make a justice metaevaluation, that is, to evaluate the appropriateness of the first standard in light of the second. The justice evaluation is now made on behalf of the first standard with reference to the second, much the same way that justice may be judged on behalf of one person with reference to another person, group, or standard. The two processes are essentially identical except that now a norm or standard is the object of evaluation and a higher order principle serves as the point reference. In a similar way, judgments of "procedural justice" (for example, Folger, 1986) are simply justice evaluations formed about an allocation method with reference to some other real or idealized method.

The importance of metaevaluations cannot be overemphasized. We know that groups may select from a variety of justice norms against which actual reward distributions may be assessed. For example, Deutsch (1985) and several chapters in Mikula (1980) suggest various social conditions that may generate distribution norms based on need, performance, equality, and so on. It follows that conflicts are certain to occur when group members or subgroups disagree about which norm is appropriate.

In order to evaluate alternative distribution norms or justice principles, actors must evaluate the anticipated consequences of those alternatives against one another or against the existing distribution of rewards. These evaluations may concern the actor's own potential rewards relative to his or her present rewards, or they may concern potential subgroup rewards. In either case, it will be necessary that given a fixed amount of rewards to allocate, any alternative justice principle will result in an improvement in some members' conditions and a deterioration in the conditions of others.

If an alternative principle is presented as "more just," if it would benefit a particular subgroup, and if the subgroup has the resources and coordination to act collectively, then that subgroup will attempt to have the alternative justice principle adopted by the larger group and to reallocate rewards accordingly. Whenever individuals and groups begin to seriously question existing justice principles through comparisons to alternatives, there arises the potential for major social reorganization. The alternative justice principle can serve as the rallying point around which collective action is organized. If successful, new dimensions of group stratification may be defined, old ones eliminated, and large scale shifts in the actual incumbents of various strata will occur.

A Justice Scenario

The justice norms that we spontaneously apply in natural settings and the standards actually held by social actors probably agree quite often. However, most natural settings are sufficiently complex so as to permit a variety of types and layers of justice standards, each with the capability of modifying evaluations made with reference to the others. Anyone interested in intervening in the justice evaluation process, such as employers attempting to promote a sense of equity and harmony through manipulations of wage structures, must therefore take great care in uncovering the justice standards that are actually operating and resist imputing those which merely seem likely.

Social justice concerns often become social policy concerns. Laws governing taxation, business practices, and judiciary decisions are all policy decisions with implicit justice evaluations. However, participants in policy debates generally have limited theoretical understanding of the bases of the positions they and their opponents hold. Lacking such understanding, policies aimed at redistributing social rewards are worse than impotent: They become sources of new, unforeseen injustices.

The following extended hypothetical example is intended to demonstrate the types of multilayered justice evaluations that group members and social researchers are capable of making, and the implications for interventions aimed at correcting injustice at each evaluative layer. The example is not intended to represent a real situation but to tease out the roles played by various types of information that may enter into real situations. In short, it exemplifies some of the cognitive-structural processes described and demonstrates how apparent injustices that may at first seem discriminatory can disappear in light of new information.

Let us take the perspective of a hypothetical justice evaluator who is concerned with pay in the company in which he is employed. A personnel director is informed by a report that men in this company receive an average wage of $6.00/hour and women receive an average wage of $10.00/hour (Table 1). Upon reading this report, his face reddens, his hands tense, and the little hairs on the back of his neck stand up. He considers the information in the report and perhaps, too, his physical reaction to it, and concludes that the situation is profoundly unjust.

The evaluator is forming an assessment on behalf of the group with which he strongly identifies—men—with respect to another group—women. This could even be a collective injustice, assuming that most or all of the company's men reach the same conclusion and that they all believe that the others share this evaluation. To rectify the injustice, men and women in the company would have to receive the same average wage. This may be achieved through a pay policy that multiplies each man's present wage by 5/3 or each woman's by 3/5.

What can we say about the basis of our hypothetical evaluator's judgment? Clearly, it suggests the use of a very simple justice principle: The investments of "male" and "female" should imply no differential rewards in this company. Because men and women receive differential rewards, the situation is unjust.

Of course, this position is potentially ill-informed and erroneous. When our evaluator is pressed, he may agree that some bases for differential rewards are legitimate, for example, position in the company. He must then admit that his initial assessment of the sex-based wage inequality would not be unjust if sex is highly correlated with this legitimate basis for differential reward. His initial reaction may involve a spurious correlation. That is, although sex and wages are highly correlated, occupational status and not sex may be the true basis for pay differences. Our evaluator should conclude that more information is needed.

If a sex-equalizing pay policy is instituted at this point, the results could be disastrous. Although equalizing the pay of men and women,

Table 1. Mean Pay for Men and Women in a Hypothetical Company

Men	Women
$6.00	$10.00

Table 2. Mean Pay for Men and Women by Occupational Level

	Mean	
	Men	Women
Low level	$4.46	$4.46
High level	$19.82	$19.82

the intervention may also equalize the pay of employees of different occupational status levels, some of whom have legitimate claims to higher pay.

Suppose that the additional information takes the form of a more detailed report showing a breakdown of mean wages by sex and by, for simplicity, two occupational levels (Table 2). It is found that male and female low-level workers both average $4.46/hour and that high-level men and women both average $19.82/hour. Thus there are no sex differences in pay once we control for occupational level. Our evaluator must conclude that sex is not the basis for the differential pay. The intervention would have created far more injustice than it eliminated.

What, then, is the basis for differential pay across the sexes if it is not sex itself? Our justice evaluator soon realizes that for the ratio of male to female wage rates to equal .60, there must be many more males in low-level positions than females. In fact, of the 1,000 men in the company, 900 (or 90%) are in low-level positions. Of the 520 women in the company, 500 (or 96%) are in high-level positions (Table 3). Our evaluator makes another justice judgment: The distribution of men and women across low-and high-level positions is unjust. At the same time, an implicit justice evaluation is made: The *justice standard* specifying equal pay for men and women is itself unjust when assessed against the higher order principle relating rewards to occupational levels.

What type of intervention policy would solve this problem? Apparently one that equalizes the proportion of men and women within each occupational level. Calculating expected cell counts will tell us what those proportions should be (Table 4). There should be

Table 3. Frequencies and Proportions of Men and Women at Each Occupational Level

	Frequencies				Proportions	
	Men	Women			Men	Women
Low level	900	20	(920)	Low level	.90	.04
High level	100	500	(600)	High level	.10	.96
	(1000)	(520)	(1520)		(1.00)	(1.00)

Table 4. Expected Frequencies and Proportions of Men and Women at Each Occupational Level

	Expected frequencies				Expected proportions	
	Men	Women			Men	Women
Low level	605	315	(920)	Low level	.605	.605
High level	395	205	(600)	High level	.395	.395
	(1000)	(520)	(1520)		(1.00)	(1.00)

60.5% of each sex in the low-level positions and 39.5% of each sex in the high-level positions.

This justice evaluation assumes that the just condition is one in which occupational status is now the reward, sex the investment, and because sexes are presumed equally valued, occupational status should be equivalent. However, this evaluation is analogous to the earlier one deemed "potentially ill-informed and erroneous." If pressed, the evaluator would probably concede that there are legitimate bases for differentiating low-and high-level workers, bases such as skill. Assume that skill may be accurately measured. What, then, would the evaluator make of the finding that low-level men and women both average "low" on skill measures whereas high-level men and women both average "high" on skill (Table 5)? All appears just.

Again, the perceived correlation is spurious. The relationship between sex and occupational level is due to the correlation of skill with sex. And now, of course, it is company policy that appears to be unjust; a policy that permits the selective hiring and/or promotion of skilled women and unskilled men.

This involves still another justice judgment: Is it just for company policies to guide hiring and promotion by sex? Our evaluator has found it unjust for his company to have done so. Can this injustice be invalidated by further information? Most definitely. Having gained access to the personnel department's job application files, our justice evaluator discovers that the company's distribution of skill levels by sex closely reflects the corresponding distributions among all 2,000 job

Table 5. Skill-Level Frequencies for Low- and High-level Employees

		Occupational Level		
		Low	High	
Skill	Low	920	0	(920)
	High	0	600	(600)

Table 6. Frequencies and Proportions of Male and Female Applicants at Each Skill Level

		Frequencies					Proportions	
		Men	Women				Men	Women
Skill	Low	1185	25	(1210)	Skill	Low	.90	.04
	High	130	660	(790)		High	.10	.96
		(1315)	(685)	(2000)			(1.00)	(1.00)

applicants in the files (Table 6). The female applicants are significantly more skilled than the male applicants. This means that the company policy is not the least bit discriminatory. The company is indeed hiring solely on the basis of skill and experience regardless of sex. It just so happens that the company's candidate pool has disproportionately high numbers of skilled women and unskilled men. Whatever the source of this problem, our probing evaluator will no doubt find the situation unjust.

In sum, the evaluator has made a series of "nested" justice evaluations, as shown in the upper part of Table 7. We could imagine the pattern continuing as shown in the bottom of the table. If the world was organized in such a way that differences in socialization cause men to place lower emphasis on their education, which produces lower skills, which results in lower occupational status, and so on, the issue arises as to whether men and women should be socialized the same way.

Put another way, at the bottom of this series of justice evaluations will eventually lie a question that cannot be answered by some type of

Table 7. Nested Justice Evaluations

Evaluated social reward	Observed basis of differentation	Resulting evaluation
Pay	Sex	Unjust
Pay	Occupational level	Just
Occupational level	Sex	Unjust
Occupational level	Skill level	Just
Skill level	Sex	Unjust
Skill level	Education	Just
Education	Sex	Unjust
Education	Socialization	Just
Socialization	Sex	•
•	•	•
•	•	•
•	•	•

survey or data analysis. That question can only be circumvented by a decision about values but with the realization that the decision *is* a decision and not a fact. In the example, there are arguments for both sides, whether we like them or not. To some, a socialization process that benefits some at the expense of others is unjust. To others, sex-related pay differences are an acceptable consequence of a process that produces differentiated social roles.

Conclusions

Two points in particular distinguish the scenario from what actually occurs in natural settings. First, it is unrealistic to suppose that a single individual would probe so deeply into the bases of his perceived injustices. The evaluator would not only have to be aware of all of the justice standards employed but would probably also have to subscribe to multiple normative systems in order to have been made aware in the first place. On the other hand, we can imagine that over time, evaluators in this type of position could probe for and gather such information, resulting in a comparable series of evaluations. However—and this is the second point—it is unrealistic to imagine that none of the observed inequalities were produced by discriminatory practices.

Discrimination may even be viewed as the conflict of justice principles. One group views another as inferior and treats them accordingly. What could be more fair—at least from the perspective of the "superior" group? But another group, using another standard, views the basis of the assessment of the mistreated group as invalid. To rectify an apparent injustice—such as the widespread inferiority of women's wages in the United States—it will never be sufficient to assume the injustice is self-evident in the inequality. Always, some justification, some alternative self-serving principle, can be dredged up.

The comparable worth strategy in the United States represents an attempt to move one level below the surface fact of sex-differentiated pay. It holds, essentially, that the differentiation is in large part due to the existence of male-dominated and female-dominated jobs and occupations, with male-dominated jobs and occupations the more favorably compensated. If compensation is made to reflect not the sex dominance of a job, but its value to an employer, it is claimed that sex-based pay differentiation will be alleviated.

I don't think so. As our justice evaluator found, there are just too many other ways to justify a group's lower earnings. Any remedy will fail to the degree that it neglects not only deeper forms of differentiation but also outright discriminatory processes taking place at those deeper levels. For example, the same sex role socialization that helps to create undercompensated female-dominated professions will also promote the underevaluation of those professions. Both critics and advocates of comparable worth remedies are aware of such biases. Advocates hold that knowledge of these biases permits the development of unbiased rating systems. This would be useful, but the product remains to be seen (Gold, 1983; Trieman & Hartmann, 1981).

There is no simple solution. However, the study of justice at the level of physiology, bioecology, information processing, or collective behavior at least helps to identify and clarify the problems. Studying justice tells us how solutions to justice problems lie as much in intangible feelings and abstract points of reference as in the thing being evaluated. We understand how it is that the same social data can be processed in different ways by different people and produce different conclusions, and why what one social movement finds to be incontrovertibly unjust may appear as perfectly just to another. The key is to not take justice for granted.

References

Alessio, John C. (1980). Another folly for equity theory. *Social Psychology Quarterly, 43,* 336–340.

Anderson, Norman H. (1981). *Foundations of information integration theory.* New York: Academic Press.

Anderson, Norman H. (1982). *Methods of information integration theory.* New York: Academic Press.

Anderson, Norman H., & Farkas, Arthur J. (1975). Information integration theory applied to models of inequity. *Personality and Social Psychology Bulletin,* 1: 588–591.

Appley, Mortimer H., & Trumbull Richard. (Eds.). (1967). *Psychological stress.* New York: Appleton-Century-Crofts.

Berger, Joseph, Zelditch, Jr., Morris, Anderson, Bo, & Cohen, Bernard P. (1972). "Structural aspects of distributive justice: A status-value approach. In Joseph Berger, Morris Zelditch, Jr., & Bo Anderson (Eds.), *Sociological theories in progress,* Vol. 2 (pp.119–146). Boston: Houghton Mifflin

Berger, Joseph, Fisek,M. Hamit, Anderson, Bo, and Wagner, David G., (1985). Formation of reward expectations in status situations. In Joseph Berger & Morris Zelditch, Jr. (Eds.), *Status, rewards, and influence* (pp.215–261). San Francisco:Jossey Bass.

Beyth-Marom, Ruth, Dekel, Shlomith, Gombo, Ruth, & Shaked, Moshe. (1985). *An elementary approach to thinking under uncertainty.* Hillsdale, NJ: Lawrence Erlbaum Associates.

Cox, Tom. (1978). *Stress.* Baltimore: University Park Press.

Dawkins, Richard. (1976). *The selfish gene.* New York: Oxford University Press.

Deutsch, Morton. (1985). *Distributive justice.* New Haven, CT: Yale University Press.

Fararo, Thomas J. (1978). *Mathematical sociology.* Huntington, NY: Kreiger.

Fazio, Russell H., & Cooper, Joel. (1983). Arousal in the dissonance process In John T. Caccioppo & Richard E. Petty (Eds.), *Social psychophysiology*. (pp. 122–152) New York: Guildford Press.

Folger, Robert. (1986). A referent cognitions theory of relative deprivation. In James M. Olson, C. Peter Herman, & Mark P. Zanna, (Eds.), *Relative deprivation and social comparison*. Hillsdale, NJ: Lawrence Erlbaum.

Gartrell, C. David. (1985). Relational and distributional models of collective justice sentiments. *Social Forces, 64,*: 64–83.

Gold, Michael Evan. (1983). *A dialogue on comparable worth*. Ithaca, NY: IRL press.

Harris, Richard J. (1976). Handling negative inputs: On the plausible equity formulae. *Journal of Experimental Social Psychology, 12:* 194–209.

Harris, Richard J. (1983). Pinning down the equity formula. In David M. Messick & Karen S. Cook (Eds.), *Equity theory: Psychological and sociological perspectives*. New York: Praeger.

Harris, Richard J., Messick, David M., & Sentis, Keith P. (1981). Proportionality, linearity, and parameter constancy: Messick and Sentis reconsidered. *Journal of Experimental Social Psychology, 17:* 210–225.

Hassett, James. (1978). *A primer of psychophysiology*. San Francisco: W. H. Freeman and Company.

Jasso, Guillermina. (1980). A new theory of distributive justice. *American Sociological Review, 45:* 3–32.

Jasso, Guillermina. (1983). Fairness of individual rewards and fairness of the reward distribution: Specifying the conflict between the micro and macro principles of justice. *Social Psychology Quarterly, 46:* 185–199.

Kahneman, Daniel, Slovic, Paul, & Tversky, Amos. (1982). *Judgment under uncertainty: Heuristics and biases*. New York: Cambridge University Press.

Lodge, Milton. (1981). *Magnitude scaling: Quantitative measurement of opinions*. Beverly Hills: Sage.

Markovsky, Barry. (1984a). *Anchoring justice judgments*. Paper presented at the annual meetings of the American Sociological Association, San Antonio, TX.

Markovsky, Barry. (1984b). *Modeling criminal justice judgments*. Paper presented at the annual meeting of the Midwest Sociological Society, Chicago, IL.

Markovsky, Barry. (1985a). Toward a multilevel distributive justice theory. *American Sociological Review, 50:* 822–839.

Markovsky, Barry. (1985b). Evaluating theories of justice and equity. In Edward J. Lawler (Ed.), *Advances in group processes* (Vol. 2, pp. 197–226). Greenwich, CT: JAI Press.

Markovsky, Barry. (1985c). *Multilevel justice theory*. Sociology Working Paper Series, The University of Iowa.

Markovsky, Barry (1988a). Injustice and arousal. *Social Justice Research, 2:* 223-233.

Markovsky, Barry (1988b). Anchoring justice. *Social Psychology Quarterly, 51:* 213-224.

Markovsky, Barry, & Ford, Thomas W. (1987). Testing justice theories with blockmodels. *Social Forces, 65:* 1143–1149.

Markovsky, Barry, Ford, Thomas W., and Choe, Joon-Young. (1987). *Justice evaluations: Scaling issues and model tests*. Presented at the annual meetings of the American Sociological Association, Chicago.

Merton, Robert K. (1968). Continuities in the theory of reference groups and social structure. In Robert K. Merton, *Social theory and social structure* (Enlarged ed., pp. 335-440), (original edition, 1957). New York: Free Press.

Merton, Robert K., & Rossi, Alice S. (1968). Contributions to the theory of reference group behavior. In Robert K. Merton, *Social theory and social Structure* (Enlarged ed.; pp. 215–248). (original edition, 1957). New York: Free Press.

Messick, David M., & Sentis, Keith P. (1979). Fairness and preference. *Journal of Experimental Social Psychology, 15:* 416–434.

Mikula, Gerold (Ed.). (1980). *Justice and social interaction.* New York: Springer-Verlag.

Moschetti, G. J. (1979). Calculating equity: Ordinal and ratio criteria. *Social Psychology Quarterly, 42,:* 172–175.

Pianka, E. R. (1978). *Evolutionary ecology (2nd ed.)* New York: Harper & Row.

Selye, Hans. (1976). *The stress of life.* New York: McGraw-Hill.

Smith, Eric Alden. (1983). Evolutionary ecology and the analysis of human social behavior. In R. Dyson-Hudson & M. A. Little (Eds.), *Rethinking human adaptation: Biological and cultural models* (pp. 23–40). Boulder, CO: Westview Press.

Stevens, S. S. (1972). *Psychophysics and social scaling.* Morristown, NJ: General Learning Press.

Stevens, S. S. 1975. *Psychophysics: Introduction to its perceptual, neural and social prospects.* New York: John Wiley.

Tajfel, Henri. (1981). *Human groups and social categories.* Cambridge, England: Cambridge University Press.

Trieman, Donald J. & Hartmann, Heidi I. (Eds.). (1981). *Women, work and wages: Equal pay for jobs of equal value.* Washington, DC: National Academy Press.

Wilson, Edward O. (1975). *Sociobiology.* Cambridge, MA: Harvard University Press.

Wilson, Edward O. (1978). *On human nature.* Cambridge, MA: Harvard University Press.

3

The Allocation of Positive and Negative Outcomes
When Is the Equality Principle Fair for Both?

Kjell Y. Törnblom, Solveig M. Mühlhausen,
and Dan R. Jonsson

Many researchers concerned with the social psychology of distributive justice seem to assume that the allocation of positive and negative resources tends to follow the same principles of justice (e.g., Deutsch, 1975; Lerner, 1974, 1975, 1977, 1981, Leventhal, 1976a, b; Greenberg & Cohen, 1982). Perhaps for this reason and because it may frequently be less difficult and less ethically questionable to expose people to positive rather than to negative outcomes, we do find a theoretically unmotivated emphasis of experimental studies on the allocation of positive to the neglect of negative resources. The latter reason, of course, does not explain why issues concerning fairness or justice in the allocation of negative outcomes are only rarely approached also by means of other methods than the experimental.

The need to fill the gaps in our knowledge about justice in the allocation of negative outcomes has been voiced by a number of researchers (e.g., Rothbart, 1968; Greenberg, Mark, & Lehman, 1985; Griffith, 1989; Hamilton & Rytina, 1980; Kayser & Lamm, 1980; Lamm,

Kjell Y. Törnblom • Department of Sociology, University of Colorado at Denver, Denver Colorado 80217-3364.   Solveig M. Mühlhausen and Dan R. Jonsson • Department of Sociology, University of Göteborg, Göteborg, Sweden.

Kayser, & Schanz, 1983; Deutsch, 1983; Cook & Hegtvedt, Törnblom, 1988). However, the simple question, "Does the allocation of positive and negative outcomes follow the same rules of justice?," will not carry us very far, as it is unreasonable to expect a universally valid affirmative or negative answer. In this study we ask: *Under what conditions and to what extent* does the allocation of positive and negative outcomes follow the same or different justice rules? More explicitly, under what conditions and to what extent is it likely that a person who considers rule x as just (or unjust) for the allocation of positive outcomes in a given context also considers rule x as just (or unjust) for the allocation of negative outcomes?

In the present study, we are concerned with the justice of *equality* (in the form of *equality of treatment*, in which case all involved receive equal outcomes at all occasions), in the allocation of (undeserved) reward and punishment. We wanted to examine, in a number of conditions, whether or not an individual's justice rating of the equality rule in the allocation of positive outcomes would correspond to his/her rating of equality in the allocation of negative outcomes. As a given individual may rate the equality principle as either just (+) or unjust(−) in each case, she or he may be described in terms of one of four possible "response patterns." [+ +], [− −], [+ −] or [− +]. The first sign in each pair indicates the rating of equality for *positive* and the second for *negative* outcomes. The first two pairs designate those who are *consistent* in their ratings of equality in positive and negative outcome allocation, whereas the last two pairs designate the *inconsistent* persons. A number of interesting issues emerge on the basis of this categorization. We will return to these in a later section, in which we will also present our study in greater detail. Let us first, however, briefly examine how much existing research can tell us about the relationship between justice in positive and justice in negative outcome allocation. We will confine our review to findings relevant to the equality principle.

Previous Research on Justice in the Allocation of Positive and Negative Outcomes[1]

Most of the studies briefly described have several common denominators. All but three report their findings in terms of frequencies by

---

[1]Since this chapter was written additional research has been produced e.g., Griffith, 1989; Griffith and Sell, 1988; Meeker and Elliot, 1987; Elliot and Meeker, 1984, 1986; Törnblom, 1988.

which subjects chose equality in the allocation of positive as compared to negative outcomes. (Mean justice ratings of the equality rule are reported in Schmitt & Montada, 1982; Törnblom & Jonsson, 1985, 1987.) Money constituted the positive as well as the negative outcomes allocated in all studies but one (Hassebrauck, 1985). All studies but three (Schmitt & Montada, 1982; Törnblom & Jonsson, 1985, 1987) were concerned with dyads, and usually both participants were responsible in various degrees for the conduct, that resulted in the positive and negative outcomes that were allocated to them. All but one (Hassebrauck, 1985) were questionnaire studies, and subjects responded in the capacity of outside observers.

Data from three Dutch studies concerned with behavior in a work setting (Steensma, von Grumbkow, & Wilke, 1977; von Grumbkow, 1977; von Grumbkow, in prep.) consistently showed that allocations of positive outcomes (in the form of bonuses) conformed more closely to the equality rule than did the allocation of negative outcomes (in the form of fines). Comparable findings emerged from a study by Hassebrauck (1985), in which equality was more frequently endorsed for positive than for negative outcomes. This study was conducted in Germany, and subjects were 4- to 8- year-old children who watched a puppet show in which the actors received rubber berries as rewards and chore assignments (separating rice and bird seed) as punishment.

Lamm and his associates (Kayser & Lamm, 1980; Lamm & Kayser, 1978; Lamm, Kayser, & Schanz, 1983) obtained results in the opposite direction of these four studies. Gains and losses were divided between two partners of a joint venture. The partners were described to subjects in different conditions as similar, casually acquainted, friends, or nonfriends. Equality was more frequently endorsed for the allocation of losses than for the allocation of gains. In addition, equality was favored in both positive and negative outcome allocations when the actors were described as nonfriends (but not when described as friends).

In a study by German psychologists Schmitt and Montada (1982), equality was, in general, considered about equally just for positive and negative outcome allocations by subjects. Goods, symbols, privileges and rights, and positions were presented or withdrawn in social-relations-oriented, economically-oriented, and welfare-oriented contexts. Overall, the equality principle received positive justice ratings for both positive and negative outcome allocations.

Mixed findings were obtained in a study by Törnblom and Jonsson (1987). When fictitious actors were described as a soccer team, the equality-of-treatment rule received higher justice ratings for positive outcome allocation (presentation of monetary awards and bonuses) than for negative outcome allocation (withholding monetary compensations and bonuses). However, the reverse held true for individually competing runners (nonteam conditions), that is, equality was judged as more just for the allocation of negative than for the allocation of positive outcomes. In all conditions of positive and negative outcome allocation, the equality-of-treatment rule received positive justice ratings. Törnblom and Jonsson (1985) reported data for two additional rules of equality: equality of results and equality of opportunity. With one exception, these two "subrules" of equality were considered unjust for both positive and negative outcome allocation. Equality of results was judged equally unjust for the allocation of positive and negative outcomes in nonteam conditions as well as in those team conditions in which there was only one recipient. It was considered less unjust in negative than in positive outcome allocation in team conditions in which there were several recipients. Equality of opportunity was viewed as equally unjust for both positive and negative outcome allocations when there were several recipients in team and nonteam conditions. In cases involving a single recipient, equality of opportunity was considered less unjust for the allocation of positive outcomes than for negative (for teams as well as for non-teams).

Evidently, the results from the studies reviewed here are far from consistent. In some cases, equality was considered more just for the allocation of positive than for negative outcomes; in other cases the reverse held true, and in still others, equality was viewed as equally just (or unjust) for both. These divergent findings are difficult to explain unequivocally, as the studies are not directly comparable.

Different Types of Positive and Negative Outcomes

Apart from the many possible methodological differences and biases, there are several factors, of course, that might account for findings in the above studies that (perhaps deceptively) are contradictory. One of the most challenging and important of these is likely to be the different kinds of phenomena that may be encompassed by the terms *positive* and *negative outcomes*. For example, in those of the studies cited where equality was found to be more frequently endorsed for positive than for negative outcome allocation, the former was operationalized in terms of resources being presented and the latter in terms of fines and chores being imposed, in both cases effected by a third party (an authority figure). On the other hand, in studies where the opposite relationship was found, outcomes were represented by self-administered sharing of gains and losses from a joint venture. Thus it seems quite plausible that *different types* of positive and negative outcome allocation differentially affect the way we judge the justice of allocation rules. The imposition of an equal division of punishment, for instance, certainly seems more unjust than a self-administered equal sharing of joint losses—especially in cases when the recipients have contributed unequal amounts of negative inputs.

A systematic exploration of the effects that different types of positive and negative outcomes might have on the perceived fairness of allocation rules would first of all require a taxonomy for each of the two. Different kinds of negative outcomes, for example, like punishment, retribution, retaliation, revenge, costs, losses, burdens, deprivations, may certainly evoke different kinds of responses. This applies to victims, and to perpetrators, as well as to outside observers. Conceptualized in another way, presenting negative (or positive) outcomes versus withholding versus taking away positive (or negative) ones will probably elicit different cognitive, emotional, and/or behavioral reactions.

Different Ways of Producing Outcomes

Of course, the significance of outcome allocation, per se, may frequently be rather obscure, and its relationship to justice evaluations of allocation principles may not make much sense, unless the way in which the outcomes to be allocated were produced (i.e., the "input" side) is considered. For example, there would surely be a "difference between dividing a pie that" a person "has baked and dividing a pie that has drifted gently down from the sky" (Wolff, 1977, p. 207). And the presentation, withholding, and taking away of positive and negative outcomes each have different implications depending upon whether the outcomes were produced by means of positive or negative commission (i.e., "doing good" or "doing bad") or through positive or negative omission (i.e., "not doing bad" or "not doing good"). The combination of these four "behavioral modalities" (see Törnblom & Jonsson, 1987, for a fuller discussion and an empirical test involving these distinctions) with the previously mentioned six "modes of outcome allocation" (i.e., the presentation, withholding, and taking away of positive and negative outcomes) generates a 4 × 6 typology that might contribute to a more systematic inquiry.

The studies reviewed bring to the fore another aspect of outcome production that has clear implications for the way these outcomes are allocated. In some studies, outcomes were collectively produced by two or more group members, whereas other studies dealt with persons who were independently engaged in resource acquisition. In general, one would expect the equality principle to be considered more appropriate and just than other distribution rules for the allocation of collectively produced outcomes whereas equal distribution appears less likely when independently acquired resources are to be justly allocated. But is there any reason to believe, in any of these two instances, that the allocation of positive and negative outcomes would *not* follow the same principle?

Do Existing Models Distinguish between Justice in Positive and in Negative Outcome Allocation?

The theoretical models proposed by Lerner (1974, 1975, 1977, 1981), Deutsch (1975), Leventhal (1976a,b), and Greenberg and Cohen (1982), for example, either seem to assume that their component propositions are equally relevant and valid for positive and negative outcome allocation, or else they simply avoid facing the issue squarely. Attribution theory would also make the same predictions for positive and negative outcome allocation: If the acquisition of (positive or negative) outcome is attributed to external factors, equal allocation would be considered fair; if internal factors are seen as responsible, equitable allocation would be the most just solution to the distribution problem. In any case, it appears safe to maintain that these frameworks are incapable, at their present stage of elaboration, to generate propositions that make different predictions with regard to justice in positive and in negative outcome allocation. Neither do they offer sufficient (if any) reasons as to why there should be no differences between the two.

Lerner (1981), for instance, proposed that justice is synonymous with the equality principle when the social relationship is focal for participants in a unit relation with convergent goals. In a similar vein, Deutsch (1975) suggested that equality will be the dominant justice principle "in cooperative relations in which the fostering or maintenance of enjoyable social relations is a primary emphasis" (p. 146). It is not unreasonable to suggest that the validity of these propositions is contingent on additional factors. The *perspective* from which a situation is viewed appears to be among the most important ones. For example, in a cooperative or unit relationship (with a given primary emphasis or convergent goal), participants may have contributed in equal or unequal amounts. (The extreme case of the latter is when one person is responsible for all contributions.) If the perspective from which a situation is perceived is a crucial factor, Lerner's and Deutsch's propositions appear to be valid only under an assumption that all able participants make equal contributions, or that the version of equality involved is equality of results (i.e., that although participants may be unequally treated at any given occasion, they will end up with equal total amounts of outcome in the long run).

Only if equality is interpreted as equality of results (which is based on a long-term temporal perspective of the relationship), or if all (or most) actors make similar total contributions, then a distinction among actor perspectives may not necessarily be crucial. This is because the actors would know that although everyone will be treated inappropriately at some occasions and appropriately at others, they will all come out approximately equal with regard to total outcomes in the long run. It is not at all clear, however, which version(s) of the equality principle these models are meant to encompass. It seems a bit farfetched to posit that the typical person who makes, say, all of a group's positive contributions, or consistently more than the other group members, would find a relationship enjoyable or fair in the long run if she or he receives no more outcomes than they do.[2] As Simpson (1976, p. 6) has argued, "Any plausible theory of justice must assume a limit on the strength of social and altruistic motivation and suppose that, while individuals are prepared to act justly, they are not prepared to abandon their interests." A similar objection is made by Leventhal, Karuza, and Fry (1980, p. 182): "It may be necessary to modify the assumption that persons concerned about preserving harmony always prefer equal distributions. When there are sizable differences in performance, they may reject total equality and prefer a distribution that gives somewhat greater reward to better performers." Nor is it particularly plausible to think that a person would believe that the others would find a relationship with him or her enjoyable or just, if they had to share the consequences of his or her negative contributions. If the others (i.e., those who are not responsible for contributions) are sufficiently much solidarity oriented, they might not mind sharing the negative consequences incurred by one or a few fellow group members. On the other hand, they might feel embarrassed to accept positive outcomes for which they are not responsible (and which they may need less than the person who produced them).

Thus it seems reasonable to suggest, even for unit relationships when the social relation, per se, is salient that (1) predictions may be too

---

[2]Although studies have shown that high contributors may divide their outcomes equally with people who contribute less (e.g., Shapiro, 1975; Schwinger, 1980), it seems doubtful that this would continue to happen repeatedly in the long run. In addition, even though high contributors are observed to apply the equality principle, this does not necessarily mean that they consider their own behavior as just. Self-presentational purposes or concern for others' welfare, rather than fairness motives, may be the immediate determinant of such conduct.

general and meaningless if the perspective from which a situation is viewed is ignored, (2) the relative contributions of participants may not always (especially in the long run) be of little or no importance, (3) therefore, equality (especially in its equality of treatment version) may not always be considered the most appropriate or just allocation principle, and (4) an allocation rule considered just for positive outcome allocation may be viewed as unjust for negative outcomes, or vice versa.

The Present Study

The main focus of this study is the extent to which people are believed to be consistent or inconsistent in their justice evaluations of the equality principle as applied to the allocation of positive and negative outcomes. More specifically, in subjects' minds, do the same persons who consider equality as just (or as unjust) in positive outcome allocation also consider it as just (or as unjust) in negative outcome allocation? Or, do they believe people to consider equality as just in one and as unjust in the other? Or, as a third possibility, do subjects believe that people's justice evaluations in the two cases are unrelated?

Some people may be see as *consistent* in that they consider equal allocation just or unjust for both positive and negative outcomes. These two patterns are designated [+ +] and [− −], respectively. Here the first sign refers to the evaluation of equality in positive and the second in negative outcome allocation. Others may be seen as *inconsistent*, viewing the justice of equality in one way for positive and in another way for negative outcomes. These patterns are designated [+ −] or [− +].

In each type of the fictitious stimulus situations chosen for this study four persons were involved. Only one of them was responsible for either praiseworthy or blameful conduct. However, subsequent positive or negative outcomes (in the form of reward or punishment) were imposed in equal amounts on all four individuals by a third party. Under such circumstances we argued that subjects would think that a person responsible for outcomes and those who are not responsible would view the situation differently, partly due to the fact that a given response pattern has different implications as seen from these two perspectives.

Equal Allocation from the Perspectives of Responsible and Nonresponsible Recipients

To consider equality as just in both positive and negative outcome allocation and acting accordingly (i.e., the positively consistent pattern [+ +]) would be to the nonresponsible person's advantage in that she or he receives "undeserved" positive outcomes. On the other hand, the receipt of undeserved negative outcomes would be to his/her disadvantage. The responsible person would be advantaged and disadvantaged in an opposite manner. She or he would receive less positive and negative outcomes than deserved (except in the "total-for-all" condition—see later discussion), the former of which is disadvantageous and the latter advantageous. To take another and more extreme example, the [+ −] pattern would be maximally advantageous to a nonresponsible but maximally disadvantageous to a responsible person. It is obvious, then, that the meaning and consequences of a given response pattern may vary significantly as a function of the perspective from which it is viewed. This may certainly include the evaluations of a response pattern in terms of relative justice.

When evaluating the justice of the equality principle, we asked half of our subjects to take the role of the person responsible for positive or negative outcomes and the other half the role of the nonresponsible persons. The performance of this task probably involved several (conscious or unconscious) ideas on the part of our subjects. First, they might have certain assumptions about people's major motivations. For example, do they think that most people are motivated to give higher priority to their own than to other people's interests, or vice versa? In the first case, it would be reasonable to make the following predictions with regard to how the four response patterns would be rated in relation to one another. From a nonresponsible person's perspective [+ −] would be preferable to [+ +] and [− −] whereas [− +] would be considered outright unjust. For a responsible person, [− +] would be the most and [+ −] the least preferred pattern. However, if subjects assumed that most people are more oriented toward the welfare of others, the rank orders attributed to the nonresponsible and the responsible persons would be the reverse of those given here.

Second subjects may have some beliefs about the extent to which people's justice evaluations and behaviors are tempered by norms and values of the social system to which they belong. Thus, even though subjects might believe people to be basically selfish in their orientations, for example, they are also likely to recognize the existence of external forces acting as constraints in the opposite direction. Thus, a number of factors operating on different levels (the individual, the group, the societal, and/or the cultural) are likely to come into play when people attempt to predict the evaluations and behavior of others. Consequently, although a dimension of considerable significance, the perspective from which a situation is viewed will not by itself be a sufficient explanatory factor. In the same manner would an account of a group's dominant goal (e.g., Deutsch, 1975) or of the prevailing social relationship (e.g., Lerner, 1981) be inadequate as the sole predictors without a specification of the focal perspective.

Lacking information about at least some of the crucial factors, predictions about subjects' attributions about responsible and nonresponsible persons' justice evaluations (i.e., whether they are believed to be consistent or inconsistent in their evaluations of equality in positive and negative outcome allocations, and what type of consistency or inconsistency they would exhibit) appear rather meaningless. Therefore, a study of exploratory nature (rather than a hypothesis testing study) in which subjects are given the opportunity to comment on their justice ratings attributed to responsible and nonresponsible actors seemed to be well motivated at this stage.

Meaningful predictions about whether or not a person considers an allocation rule (like equality) to be just in the allocation of positive and/or negative outcomes would require an assessment of those factors that are activated in the particular situation at hand. Lansberg (1984) has suggested an interesting approach to integrating institutional, situational, and individual factors affecting the choice of allocation principles by way of examining the degree of congruency among those factors. Furthermore, given certain valent goal states (emanating from internal and/or external conditions), our assumption is that people in general are likely to consider that allocation rule most just that is most conducive to the attainment of those goals. It appears difficult, in other words, to conceive of absolute standards of justice in isolation from their consequences.

A secondary interest in the present study was to examine the effects of two types of social relationships (group vs. nongroup) among the responsible and nonresponsible actors and the effects of knowledge about the identity of the responsible person (known vs. unknown) on the relative frequency by which the four response patterns are believed to be exhibited. Here, a few hypotheses appeared more straightforward to generate than in the context of rank ordering the four patterns of justice evaluations

The Social Relationship among Recipients: Group versus Nongroup

There are, of course, a number of variables that may modify the differences between the nonresponsible and responsible perspectives with regard to fairness evaluations of the equality principle. Among those variables the type of social relationship that prevails among actors has been shown to be of considerable significance. Indeed, several empirical studies have documented its effects on justice evaluations and behavior (e.g., Mikula & Schwinger, 1973; Mikula, 1974; Lerner, 1974; Lamm & Kayser, 1978; Austin, 1980; Lamm, Kayser, & Schanz, 1983). A second factor that may modify the effect of focal perspective on justice conceptions is the identity of the person who is responsible for the conduct resulting in positive or negative outcome allocation. There are, of course, a variety of ways in which a person's identity may be described, for example, in terms of status, power, gender, social class, physical attributes, behavioral characteristics, and so on. In the present study we were simply interested to see whether or not our subjects would attach importance to the responsible person's identifiability, that is, to compare a situation in which she or he is known with a situation in which she or he is unknown. We will now turn to the effects of social relationship and save the discussion of identifiability for the next section.

One may assume that one's sense of moral community commonly extends to one's own (membership) group in a greater extent than to outsiders. The scope of an individual's conception of this group may, of course, range from very narrow (e.g., a dyad) to very broad (e.g., all living creatures). A common presumption is that all members of the group constituting one's moral community have a moral right to be treated equally. Anderson (1969) has distinguished between what he calls exclusive and inclusive criteria of evaluation in the context of resource allocation. *Exclusive* criteria refer to those characteristics that are relevant to a differential evaluation of people with regard to their contributions and costs. *Inclusive* criteria are those characteristics that are shared by all within a given social system (e.g., membership of a society or a group), on the basis of which each individual has a right to obtain an equal share of resources. However, Goode (1978) has suggested that situations in which equality is considered are those in which "the people involved see each other as members of the group or community [original emphasis removed] *and are socially defined as equals with reference to that particular situation* [emphasis added]" (p. 352).

Two comments appear to be warranted in this context. First, it seems that the notion of "equality," as hinted at by Goode and Anderson (also see Deutsch, 1985:195, pp. 36–37), might frequently be conditional upon specific qualifications (e.g., being a group member). Membership would then constitute a relevant "input" meriting appropriate (i.e., equitable) treatment—equal treatment of equals, but not of unequals. If so, the equity rule is phrased as, and mistaken for, an equality rule.

Second, as Goode seems to imply, membership, per se, might be a necessary but not sufficient characteristic required for equal treatment. Additional requirements relevant for a given situation may also have to be met in order for an individual to qualify for equal treatment. In other words, pure situations of equality might be less real than situations in which both inclusive and exclusive criteria apply. Thus inclusive criteria of evaluation may be tempered (modified) by the simultaneous consideration of exclusive ones. This argument is supported in a study by Debusschere and van Avermaet (1984) on compromises between equity and equality.

In the present study, for example, we suspected that the legitimacy of equality (as a dominating principle when the membership group is made salient as a representation of a moral community) might vary (1) with the perspective from which the situation is perceived (perhaps especially so in cases like the one involved in this instance, where only one person is responsible for the outcomes to be equally shared by the nonresponsible actors as well) and (2) with sign of outcome allocation (i.e., positive vs. negative).

It seems plausible, then that the majority of individuals who are responsible for conduct leading to negative outcomes would consider it less just (or more unjust) to share them equally with members of their own group (moral community) than with outsiders. Nonresponsible (i.e., innocent) persons, in turn, would be less likely to consider the imposition of undeserved negative outcomes as just, when the person responsible for those outcomes is an outsider than when she or he is a fellow group member.

On the other hand, a person who is responsible for conduct resulting in positive outcomes would be inclined to consider it more just to share them equally with his/her group mates than with outsiders. Nonresponsible persons, in turn, would be likely to regard it as more just to share positive outcomes equally when the person who is responsible for those outcomes is an outsider than when she or he is defined as a member of one's own group.

If these propositions are taken seriously, we would expect a greater proportion of our subjects to believe the [+ −] pattern to be exhibited among nonresponsible actors when the person responsible for outcomes is not a group member than when she or he is. The opposite would be likely for the [− +] pattern, that is, a greater proportion of subjects would believe it to be exhibited in cases where the responsible person is a group member than when she or he is not.

These predictions would be reversed for subjects assuming the role of the person who is *responsible* for conduct leading to positive and negative outcome allocation. (Predictions with regard to the remaining two response patterns, [+ +] and [− −], cannot be made merely on the basis of the present and rough distinction between two types of social relationship.)

It is fairly obvious that the [+ −] pattern may be characterized as the most "selfish" one for nonresponsible recipients (as undeserved positive but not negative outcomes are shared and accepted), and as the most "unselfish" pattern for a *responsible* actor (because she or he is willing to share his/her positive outcomes with others but unwilling to impose his/her negative ones on them). Endorsement of the [− +] pattern would represent the most "unselfish" one for a *nonresponsible* but the most "selfish" one for a *responsible* actor.

With these, and those previously mentioned, interpretations is mind, the following predictions seem obvious with regard to the effect of "social relationship" on the relative frequencies by which the [+ −] and [− +] patterns are believed to be exhibited by persons responsible and not responsible for positive and negative outcomes:

1. Endorsement of the [+ −] pattern among nonresponsible recipients: nongroup > group
2. Endorsement of the [− +] pattern among nonresponsible recipients: group > nongroup
3. Endorsement of the [+ −] pattern by the responsible recipient: group > nongroup
4. Endorsement of the [− +] pattern by the responsible recipient: nongroup > group.

Identifiability of the Person Responsible for Outcomes: Known versus Unknown

It is tempting to assume that if the person responsible for the resources to be allocated is *not* identifiable (i.e., is unknown), no allocation rule other than equality would be appropriate, acceptable, and just. If no person can be considered responsible, there is no obvious reason why some should receive more outcomes than others. As Brickman et al. (1981, pp. 196–197) have suggested, "macrojustice principles in general [e.g., equality] will be more salient and more acceptable when their microjustice alternatives [e.g., equity] are perceived to be biased, invalid, or corrupt." And even if some of the participants would be opposed to equality, the negotiations required for a consensus about another allocation principle may become too costly an alternative (cf. Walster & Walster, 1975).

However, it seems rather counterintuitive to suggest that equality will always be considered the most just principle, when the person who is responsible for the production of outcomes is unknown to the nonresponsible persons. This becomes rather obvious if the allocation of positive and negative outcomes is viewed from the different perspectives of responsible and nonresponsible recipients.

If the identity of the person who is responsible for the outcomes to be equally allocated is known, the nonresponsible persons are probably more likely to be willing, and to consider it just, to share his/her negative outcomes (i.e., to ease his/her burden) than when she or he is not known. (Why make sacrifices when the beneficiary is not identifiable?) When positive outcomes are to be shared equally among the responsible and nonresponsible person, the latter are less likely to feel reluctant, and more likely to consider it just, to do so when the responsible person's identity is unknown to them. In general, as evidenced by studies on deindividuation, people are more likely to feel indifferent to or deprive people they know nothing about as compared to people who are individuated.

A person who is responsible for conduct resulting in positive outcomes is more likely when she or he is known than when she/he is unknown to consider it just to share those outcomes equally with others. There are usually fewer constraints (at least external ones) against being egoistic in private than in public conditions. For the same reason, is it more likely that a person who is responsible for negative outcomes would hesitate less, and consider it more just, to share them equally with nonresponsible persons when she or he is unknown.

By way of these considerations we arrive at the following predictions about the effect of the responsible person's identifiability on the relative frequency by which the [+ −] and [− +] response patterns are believed to be exhibited by recipients responsible and not responsible for conduct resulting in positive and negative outcome allocation:

5. Endorsement of the [+-] pattern among nonresponsible recipients: unknown > known.
6. Endorsement of the [-+] pattern among nonresponsible recipients: known > unknown.
7. Endorsement of the [+-] pattern by the responsible recipient: known > unknown.
8. Endorsement of the [-+] pattern by the responsible recipient: unknown > known.

Method

Overview

Each subject responded anonymously to one of eight questionnaires, each of which contained four vignettes describing different fictitious-situations. Two situations involved undesirable conduct by four army draftees, whereby the action of one of them directly caused material damages. The remaining two vignettes described desirable conduct where, in a similar manner, only one of the four draftees was directly responsible for the positive consequences.

The study encompassed a total of 32 conditions generated on the basis of a 2 × 2 × 2 × 4 design: *sign of outcome allocation* (positive vs. negative) × *social relationship* (group of four friends vs. non-group, i.e., four nonacquainted persons) × *identifiability of the responsible actor* (known vs. unknown) × *amount of outcome* (smaller total vs. same total vs. higher total vs. total for all).[3] As our study encompassed 32 different conditions, each one of the 8 versions of the questionnaire contained 4 different conditions (vignettes). For each condition subjects responded to 8 questions.

Subjects

A total of 154 Swedish male army draftees (mean age = 20.0 years) volunteered to participate in the study during regular class meetings. Eight classes (one per version of the questionnaire) were involved, varying in size from 17 to 21 persons. Each subject was asked to respond to the questionnaire by making a total of 32 ratings (i.e., 8 for

---

[3]The theoretical basis and results pertaining to this variable (amount of outcome) will be discussed and presented elsewhere (Törnblom & Mühlhausen, in prep). However, a brief description of the four conditions of the variable is warranted in this context. If the responsible person would be rewarded or punished alone, he would receive a given amount of outcome (in this case a total of 4 days of leave or confinement to the base, respectively). In the "smaller total" condition, each of the four persons (including the responsible one) received half a day each (i.e., a total of 2 days); in the "same total" condition each one received 1 day (i.e., a total of 4 days, in which case all of them shared the same total amount the responsible person would have received if rewarded-/punished alone); in the "higher total" condition each person received a day and a half (i.e., a total of 6 days); and in the "total for all" or "collective reward/punishment" condition each one received 4 days (i.e., a total of 16 days, whereby each person received the same amount of outcome as the responsible person would have received alone).

each of the 4 conditions). In addition, they were encouraged to motivate their ratings by replying to open-ended questions.

The Questionnaire

For all four conditions included in each questionnaire two variables were held *constant* ("amount of outcome" and "identifiability of responsible actor") whereas two were *varied* ("sign of outcome allocation" and "social relationship"). See Table 1 for an overview of the design and an account of the four conditions covered by each version of the questionnaire.

Each vignette (describing desirable or undesirable conduct—see illustrative examples) was followed by a set of eight questions. Two of them concerned the *justice* of, two the *desirability* of, and two the *acceptability* of an equal division of the reward/punishment among the four actors described in the scenarios. Subjects were required to take the perspective of the three nonresponsible persons for one set of the three questions and the responsible person's point of view for the other set. [When the identity of the responsible person was unknown, the question was phrased according to the following pattern: "If one of them *believed* himself to be responsible, how just (or desirable, or acceptable) would he, in your opinion, consider the fact that each one of the other three persons received as long a leave/confinement to the base as himself?" rather than "according to your opinion, how just (or desirable, or acceptable) would the responsible person consider?", as phrased in the cases where his identity was known]. The two final questions required subjects to state their beliefs about the effectivity and the size of the reward/punishment. The answer to each question (except the one concerning size of outcome) was given along a 4 point scale, that is 1 = entirely unjust, 2 = moderately unjust, 3 = moderately just, 4 = entirely just. Outcome size (question 8) was rated along a 5 point scale ranging from 1 (far too small) through 3 (just about right) to 5 (far too large). In addition, subjects were asked to motivate each of their ratings (except for question 8) in an open-ended fashion. In the context of the present chapter we only report findings pertaining to the ratings of fairness.

To illustrate the fashion in which scenarios were presented to the subjects, one vignette describing the "Negative outcome—Nongroup—Unknown—Total for all" is reproduced here:

> Boris, Pontus, Niklas, and Göran belong to the same military company but
> do not know each other. When they were at the canteen one evening they

Table 1. Design of the Study[a]

Sign of outcome allocation	Positive				Negative			
Social relationship	Group		Nongroup		Group		Nongroup	
Identifiability of responsible actor	Known	Unknown	Known	Unknown	Known	Unknown	Known	Unknown
Amount of outcomes								
Smaller total (½ day)	1	2	1	2	1	2	1	2
Same total (1 day)	3	4	3	4	3	4	3	4
Higher total (1½ days)	5	6	5	6	5	6	5	6
Total for all (4 days)	7	8	7	8	7	8	7	8

[a]Numbers 1–8 refer to versions of the questionnaire. Each number's different positions indicate the conditions covered by that particular questionnaire.

happened to be seated at the same table. On the suggestion of one of them they engaged in a game of poker. Suddenly, they got involved in a fight with some other draftees, whereby one of the four persons at the poker table pushed an adversary into a glass showcase in which sandwiches were displayed. The glass broke, and the sandwiches were ruined.

The next day Boris, Pontus, Niklas, and Göran were called to the commanding officer to be held accountable for the desolation at the canteen. Normally, the person responsible for the damages would have received 4 days of confinement to the base as punishment. However, as no one was entirely clear about which one of the four was guilty, the commanding officer decided that all four of them would each receive a penalty of four days.

Results

Consistency and Inconsistency of Justice Evaluations of Equality in Positive and Negative Outcome Allocations

One may express the degree of consistency between a person's justice evaluations of equality in positive and negative outcome allocation in terms of their intercorrelation. A correlation score approaching $+1$ would indicate that equality is similarly evaluated for both positive and negative outcome allocation. A zero correlation indicates that the way in which equality is evaluated for positive outcomes is statistically unrelated to how equality is evaluated for negative outcomes. Finally, if those subjects rating equality as just for positive outcomes would tend to rate it as unjust for negative ones, and vice versa, the score would approach -1.

The attributed fairness ratings of positive and negative outcome allocations were correlated by means of Yule's Q for the responsible and for the nonresponsible recipients, respectively, resulting in a score of $-.05$ for the former and $.32$ for the latter. Thus there was a relatively strong tendency for subjects to believe that recipients who are *not responsible* for outcomes would be consistent in their justice evaluations, that is, that they would rate equality in the same way for both positive and negative outcome allocation. On the other hand, they believed that the way in which a *responsible* actor–recipient would view equality in positive outcome allocation is not related to how equality would be evaluated for negative outcomes.

We may also examine the differences between the evaluations attributed to responsible and nonresponsible actors by comparing the two proportions of consistent and inconsistent response patterns. [4] In the case of nonresponsible recipients (see Table 2) we obtained 176 (57.3%) consistent (i.e., the [+ +] and [− −] patterns) and 131 (42.7%) inconsistent responses (i.e., the [+ −] and the [− +] patterns). The corresponding figures for the responsible actor–recipient were 142 (46.4%) and 164 (53.6%). (The reader should, perhaps, be reminded that each subject made two ratings for both positive and negative outcome allocation, which explains why the total number of responses for (attributions to) each of the actors exceeds 300, although the number of subjects only amount to 154.) Thus the consistent patterns were more frequently exhibited than the inconsistent ones when the perspective of the nonresponsible recipients was focal. The reverse was true when subjects assumed the role of the responsible actor, although the difference between the number of consistent and inconsistent responses is less than half of what it is for the nonresponsible recipients, that is, -22 (7.2%) vs. 45 (14.6%), respectively, the latter of which is statistically significant ($t = 2.60$; $p < .01$) whereas the former is not ($t = -1.26$) [5]

Types of Consistent Pattern Attributed to Responsible and Nonresponsible Recipients. What types of consistency ([+ +] or [− −]) and inconsistency ([+ −] or [− +]) were found among the justice evaluations attributed to the responsible and nonresponsible recipients? Did we find a pattern that was dominating in each case? The distribution of endorsements [6] of the four response patterns is shown in Tables 3 and 4. The [+ +] pattern strongly dominated the [− −] pattern in the case of nonresponsible recipients (41.7% vs. 15.6% $t = 6.77$; $p < .001$), whereas the difference between these two consistent

---

[4]An analysis of variance with justice evaluation of the equality principle as the dependent variable and sign of outcome, social relationship, responsibility, and identifiability as independent variables is not included here because it would not be directly relevant, given the purpose of the study. Such an analysis might show, for instance, that the justice principle is more favorably evaluated for positive than for negative outcomes, or that the equality principle is more favorably evaluated for the group than for the nongroup condition. In this study, however, we are not concerned with the evaluation of the equality principle, per se, but with the consistency in justice evaluations of the equality principle for positive and negative outcome allocations.

[5]The statistical significance of differences between proportions was tested as described in Chou (1963), for example, using a testing statistic with the standard normal distribution. This is equivalent to a distribution with an "infinite" number of degrees of freedom.

[6]It should be noted that subjects did not attribute "endorsement" of response patterns, per se, as justice evaluations of positive and negative outcome allocations were made separately rather than pairwise.

Table 2. Consistent and Inconsistent Justice Evaluations of Equality in Positive and Negative Outcome Allocation, as Attributed to Nonresponsible and Responsible Recipients

	Nonresponsible recipients	Responsible actor	Difference	t
Consistent evaluations (+ + and − −)	176 (57.3%)	142 (46.4%)	34	1.92*
Inconsistent evaluations (+ − and − +)	131 (42.7%)	164 (53.6%)	−33	−1.93*
Total	307 (100%)	306 (100%)		
Difference	45 (14.6%)	−22 (7.2%)		
t	2.60**	−1.26		

*p < .05, **p < .01, ***p < .001.

Table 3. Justice Evaluations of Equality in Positive and Negative Outcome Allocation, as Attributed to Recipients Not Responsible for Outcomes[a]

		Nonresponsible recipients	
		Evaluation of equality for negative outcome allocation	
Evaluation of equality for positive outcome allocation		−	+
	+	101 (32.9%)	128 (41.7%)
	−	48 (15.6%)	30 (9.8%)

[a]Yule's Q = .32; [+ +] vs. [+ −]: t = 1.80; [+ +] vs. [− +]: t = 9.94; p < .001; [+ +] vs. [− −]: t = 6.77; p < .001; [+ −] vs. [− +]: t = 7.38; p < .001; [+ −] vs. [− −]: t = 4.65; p < .001; [− +] vs. [− −]: t = 2.10; p < .05.

patterns was not statistically significant for the *responsible* actor (24.5% vs. 21.9%; T = .67). Thus, a majority of subjects believed that *nonresponsible* recipients would consider the equality principle *just* (rather than unjust) for both positive and negative outcome allocation, whereas the proportion of subjects who believed that *responsible* actors would positively evaluate equality for both is about equally large as the proportion who believed they would consider equality as unjust for both.

Types of Inconsistent Pattern Attributed to Responsible and Nonresponsible Recipients. With regard to the two inconsistent response patterns, the [+ −] greatly outnumbers the [− +] pattern for the nonresponsible recipients (32.9% vs. 9.8%; $t = 7.38$; $p < .001$) as well as for the *responsible* actor (37.6% vs. 16.0%; $t = 5.63$; $p < .001$). In other words, the attributions for nonresponsible and responsible actors were in agreement; most subjects believed that both categories of recipients would consider equality as just for positive but as unjust for negative outcome allocation, rather that the other way around.

Rank Order among Response Patterns for Responsible and Nonresponsible Recipients. Overall, there was no statistically significant difference between the dominating consistent [+ +] and the dominating inconsistent response pattern [+ −] for the *nonresponsible* recipients ($t = 1.80$). However, the endorsements of these two patterns (see Table 3) were significantly greater than of the remaining two patterns [− −] and [− +], the former of which was exhibited to a significantly greater extent than the latter ($t = 2.10$; $p < .05$). Thus, the rank order among endorsements of the four response patterns attributed to the nonresponsible recipients was [(+ +) = (+ −)] > (− −) > (− +).

The picture is a bit more complicated with regard to the *responsible* actor. The endorsement was significantly greater for the [+ −] pattern than for all three remaining response patterns (see Table 4), of which [+ +] = [− −] and [− −] = [− +], whereas the consistent positive pattern [+ +] was believed to dominate the [− +] pattern ($t = 2.39$; $p < .02$). Thus the rank order among endorsements of the four response patterns attributed to the responsible actor was (+ −) > {[(+ +) > (− +)] = (− −)}.

Nonresponsible versus Responsible Recipients: The Justice of Equality in Positive and Negative Outcome Allocation. As shown in Figure 1, the proportion of subjects attributing a consistent positive evaluation of equality in positive and negative outcome allocation (i.e., the [+ +] pattern) to the nonresponsible recipients was larger than that for the responsible actor ($t = 4.52$; $p < .001$). The reverse was true for the [− −] and the [− +] patterns. A larger proportion of our subjects attributed endorsement of these patterns to the responsible actor than to the nonresponsible ones ($t = -1.99$; $p < .05$; and $t = -2.31$; $p < .05$, respectively). There was no significant difference between attributed endorsements of the [+ −] pattern ($t = -1.21$).

The Effect of Social Relationship

We predicted that a larger proportion of subjects would attribute endorsements of the [+ −] pattern to *nonresponsible* recipients in

Table 4. Justice Evaluations of Equality in Positive and Negative Outcome Allocation, as Attributed to Actor Responsible for Outcomes[a]

		Responsible recipients	
		Evaluation of equality for negative outcome allocation	
Evaluation of equality for positive outcome allocation		−	+
	+	115 (37.6%)	75 (24.5%)
	−	67 (21.9%)	49 (16.0%)

[a]Yule's Q = −.05; [+ +] vs. [+ −]: $t = -2.97$; $p < .01$; [+ +] vs. [− +]: $t = 2.39$; $p < .02$; [+ +] vs. [− −]: $t = .67$; [+ −] vs. [− +]: $t = 5.63$; $p < .001$; [+ −] vs. [− −]: $t = 3.69$; $p < .001$; [− +] vs. [− −]: $t = 1.69$.

nongroup than in group conditions, whereas the reverse was expected for the [− +] pattern. These hypotheses (1 and 2) were not supported. We obtained the following distributions of our subjects: 32.0% in the nongroup and 33.8% in the group condition for the [+ −] pattern, whereas the figures for the [− +] pattern were 9.8% in both conditions. Neither were the differences between the endorsement rates for the [+ +] and [− −] patterns, respectively, in the group and nongroup conditions large enough to reach statistical significance (42.2% and 14.3% respectively, in the group condition, and 41.2% and 17%, respectively, in the nongroup condition).

We may note, however, that the correlation score (Yule's Q) for the four response patterns was .29 in the group and .34 in the nongroup condition. Thus, there was a tendency to believe that equality would, in both conditions, be positively evaluated by nonresponsible recipients for both positive and negative outcome allocations. (This was not the case for the perspective of the responsible actor, as we shall see.)

Predictions exactly opposite to these were made for subjects' attributions to the *responsible* actor (see Hypotheses 3 and 4). Again, no significant differences were obtained. The relevant figures were 40.5% versus 34.6% in the group and nongroup conditions, respectively, for the [+ −] pattern and 15.7% versus 16.3% in the nongroup and group conditions, respectively, for the [− +] pattern. In addition, the differences for the [+ +] and [− −] patterns were not significant. (The figures were 23.5% and 19.6%, respectively, in the group condition, and 25.5% and 24.2%, respectively, in the non-group condition.)

The correlation score for the four response patterns was −.18 in the group and .06 in the nongroup condition. Thus the way responsible actors were believed to evaluate equality for positive outcome alloca-

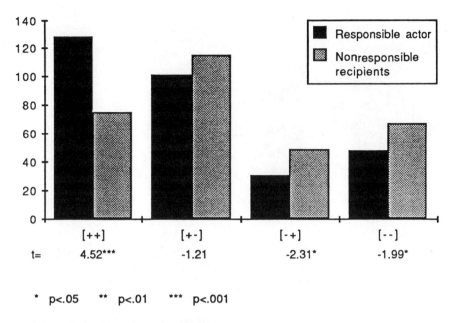

Figure 1. Justice evaluations of equality in positive and negative outcome allocations as attributed to responsible and nonresponsible recipients

tion was not statistically related to how they were believed to evaluate equality for negative outcome allocation.

The Effect of Identifiability of the Actor Responsible for Outcomes

We predicted that a larger proportion of subjects would attribute endorsements of the [+ −] pattern to nonresponsible recipients when the responsible actor was unknown than when he was known, whereas the reverse was expected for the [− +] pattern (see Hypotheses 5 and 6). As shown in Figure 2, the obtained results are directly opposite in their direction, although not statistically significant (30.8% vs. 35.1% for the unknown vs. the known condition in the case of the [+ −] pattern and 6.6% vs. 12.8% for the known vs. the unknown condition with regard to the [− +] pattern). Neither were the differences significant between the endorsement rates for the [+ +] and [− −] patterns, respectively, in any of two conditions.

The correlation score for the four response patterns was .51 in the known and .14 in the unknown condition. Thus when the responsible

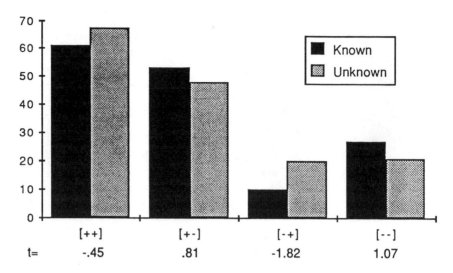

Figure 2. Justice evaluations of equality in positive and negative outcome allocations as attributed to *nonresponsible* recipients in known and unknown conditions.

actor was *known*, subjects had a tendency to believe that equality would be positively evaluated by nonresponsible recipients for both positive and negative outcome allocation. In the *unknown* condition, the evaluation of equality in positive and negative outcome allocation was believed to be unrelated. (The opposite was true for the perspective of the responsible actor, as we shall see.)

Predictions opposite to these were made for subjects' attributions to the *responsible* actor–recipient (see Hypotheses 7 and 8). Again, we obtained results in opposite directions to those predicted (see Figure 3). The difference between the condition in which the responsible actor thought he was known and the condition in which he believed he was unknown was significant for the [+ −] pattern ($t = -2.92$; $p < .01$) but not for the [− +] pattern (14.1% in the unknown condition, which was not significantly different from 18% in the known condition). In addition, the attributed endorsement rate for the [+ +] pattern was significantly higher for a responsible actor who believed himself to be known as compared to unknown ($t = 3.78$; $p < .001$). No statistically significant difference was obtained for the [− −] pattern.

The correlation score for the four response patterns was .09 in the known but − .25 in the unknown condition. Thus, when the responsible actor believed himself to be *unknown*, subjects had a tendency to think that equality would be positively evaluated by the responsible actor for positive outcomes but negatively evaluated for negative

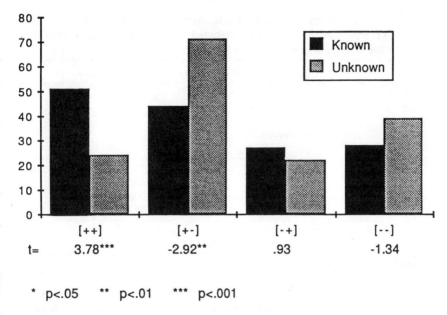

* p<.05   ** p<.01   *** p<.001

Figure 3. Justice evaluations of equality in positive and negative outcome allocations as attributed to the *responsible* actor in known and unknown conditions.

outcomes. In the *known* condition, the evaluation of equality in positive and negative outcome allocation was believed to be unrelated.

Nonresponsible versus Responsible Recipients: The Justice of Equality in Positive and Negative Outcome Allocation When the Responsible Actor Is Known and Unknown. Table 5 shows that the proportion of subjects attributing a consistent positive evaluation of equality in positive and negative outcome allocation (i.e., the [++]pattern) was larger than for each of the three other patterns, when the actor who is responsible for outcomes was *known*. This was true for subjects taking the perspective of the responsible as well as the nonresponsible recipients, and there was no statistically significant difference between the two. Neither were there any significant differ-- ences between the proportions of subjects focalizing the two perspectives with regard to attributed endorsements of either the [+ −] or the [− −] response patterns. However, the endorsement of the inconsistent [-+] pattern attributed to the responsible actor was significantly larger than the endorsement attributed to the nonresponsible recipients (18.0% vs. 6.6%; t = 3.01; p < .01).

When the actor responsible for outcomes was *unknown*, the proportions of subjects attributing endorsement by the responsible vs. the

Table 5. A Comparison of Justice Evaluations of Equality in Positive and Negative Outcome Allocations as Attributed to Nonresponsible versus Responsible Recipients When the Latter Is Known

Evaluation of equality for positive and negative outcomes	Responsible actor known		
	Nonresponsible recipients	Responsible actor	t
[− −]	27 (17.9%)	28 (18.7%)	−.18
[− +]	10 (6.6%)	27 (18.0%)	−3.01**
[+ −]	53 (35.1%)	44 (29.3%)	1.07
[+ +]	61 (40.4%)	51 (34.0%)	1.15
Total	151 (100%)	150 (100%)	
Yule's Q	.51	.09	

*p < .05; **p < .01; ***p < .001.

nonresponsible recipients differed significantly for all but one (i.e., [− +]) response patterns. As shown by Table 6 endorsements attributed to the responsible actor were higher than those ascribed to the nonresponsible recipients for the [− −] and [+ −] patterns, but the other way around for the [+ +] pattern. No significant difference was obtained for the [− +] pattern

The reader may note that the rank orders among response patterns attributed to nonresponsible and responsible actors coincide, when the responsible actor is known. Furthermore, these rank orders, as well as

Table 6. A Comparison of Justice Evaluations of Equality in Positive and Negative Outcome Allocations as Attributed to Nonresponsible versus Responsible Recipients When the Latter Is Unknown

Evaluation of equality for positive and negative outcomes	Responsible actor unknown		
	Nonresponsible recipients	Responsible actor	t
[− −]	21 (13.5%)	39 (25.0%)	−2.59**
[− +]	20 (12.8%)	22 (14.1%)	−.33
[+ −]	48 (30.8%)	71 (45.5%)	−2.68*
[+ +]	67 (42.9%)	24 (15.4%)	5.36***
Total	156 (100%)	156 (100%)	
Yule's Q	.14	−.25	

*p < .05; **p < .01; ***p < .001.

the one for the nonresponsible recipients in the unknown condition, are identical to the "total" order attributed to the nonresponsible recipients (as described earlier). It seems rather curious that the rank orders attributed to the responsible actor in the known and unknown conditions both differ from the "total" (uncollapsed) order.

Correlations among attributed justice ratings of positive and negative outcome allocations by nonresponsible and responsible recipients in known and unknown conditions gave the following results: .51 in the known and .14 in the unknown condition for *nonresponsible* recipients and .09 in the known and − .25 in the unknown condition for the *responsible* actor.

Thus there was a strong tendency for subjects to believe that recipients who are *not responsible* for outcomes would be consistent in their justice evaluations of equality for positive and negative outcome allocation when the responsible actor is known, whereas evaluations were believed to be unrelated when he is unknown. The *responsible* actor, however, was assumed to be relatively inconsistent in the unknown condition, as opposed to the known condition in which evaluations were believed to be unrelated.

Summary of Major Findings

The following is an overview of the main results of this study in which justice evaluations of the equality principle in positive and negative outcome allocation were attributed by male subjects to male actors who were responsible or not responsible for conduct resulting in collective reward and punishment.

1. 57.3% of the subjects believed that *nonresponsible recipients* would evaluate equality in the same way (i.e., consistently) for both positive and negative outcomes. The consistent [+ +] pattern received higher endorsement than [− −], the inconsistent [+ −] higher than [− +] whereas there was no statistically significant difference between the endorsements for the [+ +] and [+ −] patterns. The total rank order among response patterns was [(+ +) = (+ −)] > (− −) > (− +). In the known condition, equality was evaluated consistently (as just) for both positive and negative outcome allocation whereas in the unknown condition, the way equality was believed to be evaluated for positive outcome allocation was unrelated to the way it was believed to be evaluated for negative outcome allocation.

2. The evaluation of equality attributed to the *responsible actor* in positive outcome allocation was believed to be unrelated to his evaluation of equality in negative outcome allocation. 46.4% of the subjects believed that equality would be consistently and 53.6%

inconsistently evaluated. The consistent [+ +] and [- -] patterns received equally high endorsements, the inconsistent [+ -] higher than the [- +], and the total rank order was (+ -) > {[(+ +) > (- +)] = (- -)}. In the known condition the way in which equality was believed to be evaluated for positive outcomes was unrelated to the way it was believed to be evaluated for negative outcomes whereas, in the unknown condition, equality was believed to be evaluated inconsistently for positive and negative outcome allocations (i.e., as just for positive and as unjust for negative outcomes).

3. *Social relationship* (i.e., group vs. nongroup) had no effect on attributed justice evaluations. In both group and nongroup conditions, equality was believed to be consistently evaluated by nonresponsible recipients, whereas evaluations by the responsible actor were believed to be unrelated.

Discussion

The major impetus for the study was an interest to extend our knowledge about the conditions under which the allocation of positive and negative outcomes may or may not follow the same justice principle(s). We confined our investigation to the equality-of-treatment rule and examined whether role-playing subjects would consider equality to be just (or unjust) in *both* positive and negative outcome allocations, or if they would view equality as just in one and as unjust in the other.

Half of our subjects were assigned the perspective of an actor–recipient responsible for praiseworthy or blameful conduct resulting in positive or negative outcomes, respectively. The other half of our subjects were asked to take the perspective of outcome recipients who were not responsible for such conduct. Outcomes were allocated to responsible and nonresponsible persons in equal amounts, however. The responsible actor was known in half and unknown in the other half of the conditions to which our subjects were exposed. In addition, two types of social relationships (group and nongroup) were said to prevail among the responsible and nonresponsible recipients.

Consistency versus Inconsistency in Justice Evaluations

Attributions to nonresponsible recipients. According to our data (see Figure 1 and Table 3), a majority of subjects taking the perspective of the *nonresponsible* recipients believed that they would evaluate the justice of equality in the same way for both positive and negative outcome allocation (Yule's Q = .32). More specifically, most of these subjects believed that nonresponsible recipients would consider it just (rather than unjust) to share equally the rewards as well as punishment resulting from the acts of another person (i.e., attributed endorsement was higher for the [+ +] than for the [− −] pattern).

It is interesting to note (see Figure 2), that the tendency to attribute consistency in the evaluation of equality in positive and negative outcome allocation was even stronger for subjects in the condition where the responsible actor was *known* (Yule's Q = .51, and the proportion of consistent is significantly larger than the proportion of inconsistent endorsements). However, this tendency disappears almost entirely in the condition where he is unknown (in which a correlation score of .14 indicates that the evaluations of equality in positive and negative outcome allocation are largely unrelated). In sum, subjects believed that *nonresponsible* recipients would consider equality as just in both positive and negative outcome allocations (i.e., [+ +]) but *only* when the responsible actor was *known*.

These findings prompt the question why the majority of subjects believed that the three persons who were not entitled to outcomes would consider it just to share equally the entitled person's positive as well as negative outcomes only when he was known. An examination of the qualitative data (i.e., subjects' commentaries to their attributed justice ratings in the open-ended questions) appeared to give a clue to at least a partial explanation. When the responsible actor was *known*, subjects emphasized *the collectivity* of actors to a much greater extent than when he was anonymous (unknown). All four recipients were seen as equally much "involved" in the situation (even though only one of them was directly responsible for the particular act that resulted in reward or punishment). When the responsible actor was known, 86%[7] of the comments emphasized "equal involvement" in the situation resulting in positive outcomes and 97% in the situation

---

[7]In the *unknown* condition, we obtained 107 out of 154 possible comments in the open-ended question where the fairness rating was to be motivated (i.e., 70%) in the context of positive and 76% in the context of negative outcome allocation. The corresponding figures in the *known* condition were 60% and 44%. On the basis of these proportions, we computed the proportion of comments to *positive ratings* of the fairness of equality. In the *unknown* condition, 56% comments were made for positive ratings of equality in negative and 82% in positive outcome allocation. The corresponding figures for the *known* condition were 52 and 83. Out of these, 56% in the *unknown* condition emphasized that "all four actors were involved or present" in the situation resulting in negative outcome allocation and 63% in the situation resulting in positive outcome allocation. The figures for the *known* condition were 97% and 86%, respectively.

resulting in negative outcomes. The corresponding figures for the condition in which the responsible actor was anonymous (unknown) were 63% and 56%. Thus there was a good reason why no one should receive more outcomes than the others in the known condition. Why, then, would equal involvement (or the presence of all actors) be more salient in the known condition? It may be easier to experience the one-for-all and all-for-one feeling when all involved are known, than when one or more are unknown. A number of subjects pointed out that the responsible actor would not have dared to act in the way he did, unless the other three persons had been present. This comment is not made in the unknown condition, however.

Attributions to the Responsible Actor–Recipient. Subjects who took the perspective of the actor who was *responsible* for outcomes believed that his evaluations of equality in positive and negative outcome allocation would not necessarily be consistent. The proportion of subjects attributing endorsements of the consistent positive and negative patterns, [+ +] and [− −], was as large as the proportion attributing endorsements of the inconsistent patterns, [+ −] and [− +]. In addition, the proportions of attributed endorsement of the [+ +] and [− −] patterns were (statistically) equally large.

In this context, it is interesting to note that subjects assigned to the condition in which the responsible actor was *unknown* had a tendency to believe that he would evaluate equality in one way for positive and in another for negative outcome allocation (Yule's $Q = -.25$, and the proportion of inconsistent endorsement is significantly larger than the proportion of consistent). Attributed endorsements remained unrelated in the *known* condition, however. In sum, subjects believed that the responsible actor would evaluate equality in opposite ways for positive and negative outcome allocations *only* when he was unknown. More specifically, the [+ −] pattern obtained significantly higher endorsements than the [− +] pattern (which was also the case for the perspective of nonresponsible recipients). In other words, when unknown, the responsible actor was believed to evaluate equality as just in the allocation of positive but as unjust in the allocation of negative outcomes. Unfortunately, our qualitative data did not provide any clues toward a meaningful explanation of this finding.

Differences in Justice Evaluations between the Known and Unknown Conditions

Attributions to Nonresponsible Recipients. Our hypotheses that attributed endorsements would be higher for the [+ −] ("selfish") pattern in the unknown than in the known condition and that the reverse would be the case for the [− +] ("unselfish") pattern were not supported. In fact, no significant differences between the known and unknown conditions were obtained for any of the four patterns (see Figure 2). One would have expected subjects to attribute more selfishness to the nonresponsible recipients (i.e., endorsement of the [+ −] pattern) when the responsible actor was anonymous than when he was known to them. One would also have expected subjects to attribute more unselfishness to the nonresponsible recipients (i.e., endorsement of the [− +] pattern) when the responsible actor was known to them than when he was anonymous.

Attributions to the Responsible Actor. With regard to subjects' attributions for the responsible actor, we hypothesized that endorsements would be higher for the [+ −] ("unselfish") pattern when he was known than when he was anonymous and that the reverse would be the case for the [− +] "selfish") pattern. However, opposite to our prediction a significantly larger proportion of subjects attributed endorsement of the [+ −] pattern in the unknown than in the known condition (see Figure 3). It may seem curious that subjects believed unselfishness to be more frequently exhibited in private (unknown) than in public (known) conditions, or at least that unselfishness would be considered more *just* in the former than in the latter case. It may seem equally curious that selfishness is not believed to be more common in private than in public conditions. However, as the *justice* of selfishness (i.e., the [− +] pattern) was the issue, our results pertaining to both responsible and nonresponsible recipients are quite logical: Selfishness is usually considered unfair, whether or not the subject person is identifiable or not.

The facts that a larger proportion of our subjects believed that responsible actors would consider it just to share both positive and negative outcomes (i.e., the [+ +] pattern) when he was known than when he was unknown and that there was no difference between the conditions in which he was assumed to consider it most just to keep both types of outcomes for himself (i.e., the [− −] pattern) are not readily explainable on the basis of the available data.

Rank Orders among the Four Response Patterns for Responsible and Nonresponsible Recipients

It is surprising that most subjects (37.6%) believed that the actor *responsible* for (or entitled to) outcomes would consider it *just* to share his *positive* outcomes equally with nonentitled people but *unjust* to share his *negative* outcomes with them (the [+-] pattern received higher endorsement than each of the other three patterns). After all, this is maximally disadvantageous for him, indicating a totally unselfish (altruistic) orientation. It seems rather unlikely that subjects would attribute the endorsement of the [+-] pattern to self-presentational motives on the part of the responsible actor or to some norm of politeness, as they were simply asked what they thought about the responsible actor's *private* justice evaluations rather than his likely public behavior. Furthermore, self-presentational motives appear out of the question as an explanation due to the fact that attributed endorsement of the [+-] pattern was significantly higher for the unknown than for the known responsible actor (rather than the other way around).

As far as the nonresponsible recipients are concerned, subjects attributed the higher endorsements of the [+ +] and the [+ −] patterns (41.7% of the former and 32.9% of the latter, with no statistically significant difference between the two). There was no significant difference between the proportions of subjects attributing endorsement of the [+ −] pattern by the responsible and the nonresponsible recipients. (see Figure 1). Contrary to what was the case for the responsible actor (to whom this pattern is maximally disadvantageous), receiving undeserved rewards but not punishment is, of course, maximally advantageous to the nonresponsible recipients. Thus most subjects taking the role of the responsible actor believed that he would be primarily oriented towards the interests of nonresponsible others, whereas many of those assigned to the perspective of the nonresponsible recipients believed them to be self-oriented. *However*, an equally large proportion of subjects in the latter condition attributed endorsement of the [+ +] pattern, in which case equality for undeserved negative outcomes was also seen as just. In this case, nonresponsible recipients were seen as both self-and other oriented, in the former case for positive and in the latter for negative outcome allocation.

Although the "selfish" pattern [+ −] ranked first (together with the [+ +] pattern) for *nonresponsible* recipients, the "unselfish" (or "other-oriented") pattern [− +] received the lowest relative rank (32.9% vs. 9.8%). The opposite was true for the *responsible* actor. For him [+ −] constitutes the "other-oriented" pattern, that ranked first, whereas the "selfish" pattern [− +] ranked last (37.6% vs. 16%). Would this be true also in "real-life" situations, and if rewards and punishment were self-administered rather than imposed by a third party?

These findings are not fully consistent with predictions on the basis of attribution theory. Research on "attribution bias" has shown that people have a tendency to attribute personal responsibility to their own positive outcomes (i.e., as caused by internal factors, such as their own effort and/or ability), whereas others' positive outcomes are ascribed to external causes (such as task difficulty or luck). On the other hand, one's negative outcomes are attributed to external causes, whereas others' negative outcomes are attributed to internal factors. Consequently, and directly opposite to our findings, subjects should have attributed the highest endorsement for the [− +] pattern to the responsible actor, and for the [+ −] pattern to the nonresponsible persons (which is in partial agreement with our findings).

What problems might occur in a society where people (whether or not they are responsible for positive and/or negative conduct) would be willing, and consider it just, to share equally positive but not negative circumstances with each other, whereas an authority (e.g., a government) in charge insists on pushing equality as an overriding social policy? And what kind of social climate can be expected to prevail, if people would not hesitate to reap the fruits of others' efforts while objecting to alleviate each other's burdens?

Maybe such gloomy questions should not be asked at this stage, however. After all, the results of this study cannot, without further evidence, be taken as a description of the actual state of affairs with regard to the justice conceptions harbored by people who are and are not responsible for the generation of positive and negative outcomes. At most, our results are only indicative of people's beliefs about others' justice evaluations. However, if the well-known dictum "If men define situations as real, they are real in their consequences" (Thomas & Thomas, 1928, p. 572) is taken seriously, then we must not underestimate the possibility that people might treat others in consistency with their assumptions about them and that one's subjective reality may push one's own justice conceptions into congruency with what is perceived as the official morality. If so, a person who believes that exclusive criteria are commonly applied for negative but inclusive for positive outcomes is likely to be a highly vulnerable individual. This person would have a highly idealized picture of other's, believing that people who are guilty of misconduct are against imposing resulting aversive consequences on others, whereas those who have managed to produce favorable circumstances wish to share them with others less fortunate. The gullibility of such a person may invite exploitation and violation of simple human rights. Defining negative outcomes as a matter of personal responsibility may easily result in a generalized conviction that justice requires the individual to endure and find remedies to suffering unassisted by others. Indeed, this orientation may be exemplified by the reluctance and refusal of many eligible recipients to accept needed social welfare. Similarly, by defining one's hard-earned positive outcomes as "common property" the individual may not resist or react with moral indignation when (part of) what has been gained is taken away by others. The view that emerges of people who have not been instrumental to the accomplishment of outcomes is one of "free riders." That is, they are seen as people who wish to share others' positive outcomes (whereas subjects were equally divided with respect to what they thought about people's willingness to share negative outcomes.)

In one sense, the fact the [+ −] pattern was seen as more frequently exhibited than, in particular, the [− +] pattern for both responsible and nonresponsible recipients is, of course, simply a consequence of the overall attributed evaluation of equality in positive and negative outcome allocation. For both responsible and nonresponsible recipients, attributed justice evaluations of equality in positive outcome allocation were predominantly positive (62.1% for responsible and 74.6% for nonresponsible recipients). For negative outcome allocation, however, preferences leaned slightly toward the negative side (40.5% positive evaluations for responsible and 51.5% for nonresponsible recipients).

The total positive attributed evaluation of equality of treatment in positive outcome allocation found in this study of Swedish draftees is entirely consistent with previous findings. For instance, in a study by Törnblom, Jonsson, and Foa (1985), Swedes were found to express stronger preferences for equality in positive outcome allocation than did Americans, whereas the latter expressed stronger preferences than Swedes for allocations according to contributions. Similarly, results from a study by Törnblom and Jonsson (1985) showed that Swedes expressed particularly strong preferences for the equality-of-treatment rule.

Swedish society seems to be very equality oriented, at least as far as positive outcomes are concerned, as exemplified by the strong emphasis on economic equality. One may argue, however, that the problem of justice in the allocation of *negative* outcomes has not received as much attention as justice in positive outcome allocation, This may, perhaps, be partly due to the simple facts that Sweden is an "affluent society" and that a source of suffering like war has not been part of the Swedish experience for more than 150 years. This relative neglect of "negative" (as opposed to "positive") equality might account for the fact that attributed evaluations of the equality rule are much more evenly divided (between positive and negative) for negative than for positive outcome allocation. Whatever the reasons, this imbalance between positive and negative equality, leading to a predominance of the [+ −] over the [− +] pattern, may result in highly debatable consequences, as noted. Furthermore, these adverse effects will probably be aggravated in a situation of economic scarcity, or a political or military crisis.

Justice Evaluations Attributed to Responsible versus Nonresponsible Recipients

It is interesting to note the relatively small proportions of subjects who believed that the [− −] pattern (i.e., that equality is viewed as unjust for both positive and negative outcome allocation) would be exhibited. This pattern was ranked third among the four for responsible and nonresponsible recipients alike. According to equity theory, one would expect this pattern to be the most highly endorsed one: The person who is responsible for the outcomes, and thus entitled to them, would consider it just *not* to share them with others, whereas those not responsible for these outcomes would feel unjustly (over) rewarded if they (despite being nonentitled) received a share of them. Obviously, the contribution principle would not receive precedence by our subjects, contrary to what one would expect on the basis of equity theory.

Overall, a larger proportion of subjects attributed endorsement of the [− −] pattern to the responsible than to the nonresponsible recipients (see Figure 1). However, this difference was obtained only for subjects in the *unknown* condition (see Tables 5 and 6). One might speculate, regarding public (known) conditions, that people of both categories (i.e., responsible and nonresponsible for outcomes) would be equally interested/disinterested to uphold people's rights and obligations with regard to entitlements (as our data might indicate). An anonymous responsible person, however, might be less constrained to make claims to all rewards when he does not have to encounter the other persons involved. His conscience might at the same time forbid him to be so selfish as to deny others some of his rewards while imposing some of his burdens.

With regard to the [− +] pattern, the overall difference between the responsible and nonresponsible recipients remains the same as for the [− −]pattern. However, in this case, the difference remains only for subjects in the *known* condition. Why, then, was it only in the known condition that the proportion of subjects who attributed the [− +] pattern to the nonresponsible recipients was larger than the proportion of subjects who attributed this pattern to the responsible actor? When considering that the [− +] pattern is the most "unself-ish" one for nonresponsible recipients but the most "selfish" one for the responsible actor, it seems natural to expect different results. That is, nonresponsible recipients should be less inclined to be unselfish when they do not know for whom they make sacrifices, whereas a responsible actor should find it less difficult to be selfish when she or he is anonymous. Similarly, nonresponsible recipients should be more motivated to be unselfish when they know who the responsible actor is whereas a responsible actor should feel constrained to be selfish when known. Finally, we may recall that a larger proportion of subjects attributed endorsement of the [+ +] pattern to the nonresponsible recipients than to the responsible actor. This difference disappeared in the known but remained and was magnified in the unknown condition. We did not gain any clues to these results from subjects' commentaries; neither can we think of any unequivocal explanations to the observed differences between the two conditions.

Social Relationship and Justice Evaluations

Although previous studies have shown that different types of social relationship among actors seem to affect justice conceptions and behavior in different ways, the present study did not. As the reader might recall, our stimulus situations involved four recipients in a military setting. In the "group" condition, they shared the same room and knew each other well, whereas in the "nongroup" condition they merely belonged to the same military company and did not know each other.

There is a possibility that our subjects might have have perceived two "levels" of group formation: a subunit represented by the informal group of actors sharing the same room, and a larger encompassing group identified as the formal group of draftees belonging to the military company as a whole. It is possible, then, that subjects might have defined the actors' social relationship as a group in both condi-tions, rather than as a group in the former and as a nongroup in the latter, as intended.

Another possible explanation to the lack of differences in justice evaluation between the group and nongroup conditions may be gath-ered from subjects' commentaries in the open-ended questions. A common interpretation was that group solidarity (automatically) emerged in the nongroup condition, due to the events that placed the four actors "on the same side," being more or less dependent upon each other. They were, in other words, perceived by subjects as a unit, responding in unison to external opponents.

Generalizations to Other Institutional Settings and Resource (or Outcome) Classes

Our study is not only limited in terms of the particular social relationship(s) perceived by subjects to exist (or develop) among the actors but also in terms of the *institutional setting* in which events took place (a military setting) and with regard to the transacted *resource*, that is the allocated outcome (length of confinement or leave, which possibly could be classified as "status," possibly in combination with love in terms of Foa's, 1971, classification system).

As much as two individuals may evaluate the justice of a particular allocation rule in opposite ways for the same situation, a given individual may as well evaluate a particular rule in opposite ways for two different situations. In the same way, a given allocation principle may be just for the allocation of one resource but unjust for another. For instance, the need rule may be considered unjust for transactions within economically oriented institutions but just for allocations within the family. Similarly, an allocation principle considered just for the allocation of money may be deemed unjust for another resource like affection. Yuchtman (1972), for example, found that pay and possessions are often equally distributed in the Israeli kibbutz, whereas power and authority are equitably allocated. A respectable number of studies could be cited in these contexts (e.g., Kayser, Schwinger, & Cohen, 1984; Törnblom, Jonsson, & Foa, 1985). Due to the close connection between context (or institutional setting) and resource type transacted, it is frequently difficult to sort out the effects of one from the other. (Törnblom & Foa, 1983, have summarized studies concerned with the effect of resource and institutional setting on choice of distribution principle.)

Summary and Conclusions

This study might, hopefully, have provided some preliminary information related to the question under what conditions and to what extent the allocation of positive and negative outcomes follow the same or different justice rules. That our results are to be taken as both preliminary and as covering only a limited aspect of this topic is, perhaps, needless to point out. Our study only dealt with rewards and punishment that were *imposed* on recipients by a third party; the situation at issue involved *four recipients of whom only one was responsible* for the production of outcomes; only *one type of positive (reward) and one type of negative (punishment) outcome* were examined; the actors were *collectively sanctioned; females were not included* in the study, neither as subjects nor as actors; scenarios were confined to a *military setting*; only *two types of social relationship* were included; only *one type of allocated resource (status?)* was involved; actors only exhibited *two types of behavioral modality* (positive and negative commission); and the *equality principle* was the only justice principle examined. In addition, our study dealt with *justice evaluations as attributed to others.* It would also be desirable to observe the "real" behavior of the object persons.

With these limitations in mind, we may summarize those findings of the present study that pertain to our major research question: (1) Only those *recipients who were not responsible* for conduct resulting in the outcomes to be allocated were believed to be *positively consistent,* that is to consider the equality-of-treatment rule as just in the allocation of rewards as well as punishment. In other words, they were believed to consider it just to receive equally much of those positive and negative outcomes as the person who had produced them received. However, this held true *only when the responsible actor was known.* (The attributed evaluations of equality for positive and negative outcome allocations were unrelated when the responsible actor was anonymous.) Furthermore, the positively consistent [+ +] and the inconsistent [+ −] patterns received equally high endorsements, higher than the [− −] and [− +] patterns. Thus subjects were divided with regard to the sharing of negative outcomes. (2) The *recipient who was responsible* for the conduct resulting in the outcomes to be allocated was believed to exhibit the inconsistent [+ −] pattern, that is, to consider the equality-of-treatment rule as just in the allocation of rewards but as unjust in the allocation of punishment. In other words, he was believed to consider it just to give each one of those who were not responsible for the outcomes as much reward as he received himself but unjust to impose equal amounts of punishment on them. However, this was the case *only when he was anonymous.* (The attributed evaluations of equality for positive and negative outcome allocations were unrelated when he was known.)

An observation seems warranted with regard to the fact that the [+ −] pattern was believed to be considered the most just one (along with the [+ +] pattern for nonresponsible recipients). As Deutsch (1985, p. 247) has argued, "To be successfully egalitarian, a cooperative community must avoid *invidious* distinctions among its members even as it recognizes and responds to their individuality; lack of distinctions, as well as invidious ones, lead to alienation and the breakdown of cooperation" (original emphasis). The objection (attributed by our subjects to the innocent and guilty alike) to equal sharing of negative outcomes perhaps indicates a preference for invidious distinctions, particularly in cases where the guilty person has acted intentionally. In such a case, the opposite may not be conducive to a spirit of cooperation. Unless aversive conditions were brought about by external causes, egalitarian systems might not be particularly well served by avoiding invidious distinctions in the context of negative outcomes.

If our results are taken seriously, one may ponder a crucial question for social systems (like Sweden) in which equality is heavily emphasized as an official ideology: Are people equally prone to subject themselves to equality with regard to aversive circumstances (i.e., negative outcomes) as they might be with regard to desirable conditions (i.e., positive outcomes)—even in cases when they may not perceive themselves as responsible for the production of the negative outcomes to be equally shared? Our findings suggest that equality as a dominant ideology may be more problematic to institutionalize in the domain of aversive than in the domain of desirable circumstances. If so, this is a formidable problem that warrants a prominent place in current debates. After all, a fundamental aspect of a "moral community" consists in people's willingness to alleviate the burdens of the less fortunate, especially in cases where the victims of aversive conditions cannot be held personally responsible for their occurrence.

Acknowledgment. The preparation of this chapter was facilitated by a grant (83/20) from the Bank of Sweden Tercentenary Foundation to the senior author.

References

Anderson, B. (1969). Teoretiska synpunkter på rättvisa och jämlikhet. *Sociologisk Forskning, 6*, 27–40.

Austin, W. (1980). Friendship and fairness: Effects of type of relationship and task performance on choice of distribution rules. *Personality and Social Psychology Bulletin, 6*, 402–407.

Brickman, P., Folger, R., Goode, E. & Schul, Y. (1981). Microjustice and macrojustice. In M.J. Lerner & S.C. Lerner (Eds.), *The justice motive in social behavior* (pp. 173–202). New York: Plenum Press.

Chou, Y. (1963). *Statistical analysis.* New York: Holt, Rinehart & Winston.

Cook, K. S. & Hegtvedt, K. A. (1983). Distributive justice, equity, and equality. *Annual Review of Sociology, 9*, 217–241.

Debusschere, M. & Avermaet, E. van. (1984). Compromising between equity and equality: The effects of situational ambiguity and computational complexity. *European Journal of Social Psychology, 14,* 323–333.

Deutsch, M. (1975). Equity, equality and need: What determines which value will be used as the basis of distributive justice? *Journal of Social Issues, 31,* 137–150.

Deutsch, M. (1983). Current social psychological perspectives on justice. *European Journal of Social Psychology, 13,* 305–319.

Deutsch, M. (1985). *Distributive justice: A social-psychological perspective,* New Haven: Yale University Press.

Elliot, G. C. and Meeker, B. F. (1984). Modifiers of the equity effect: Group outcome and causes for individual performance. *Journal of Personality and Social Psychology, 46:* 586–597.

Elliot, G. C. and Meeker, B. F. (1986). Achieving fairness in the face of competing concerns: The different effects of individual and group characteristics. *Journal of Personality and Social Psychology, 1986, 50:* 754–760.

Foa, U. G. (1971). Interpersonal and economic resources. *Science, 171,* 345–351.

Goode, W. J. (1978). *The celebration of heroes. Prestige as a control system.* Berkeley, CA: University of California Press.

Greenberg, J. & Cohen, R. L. (1982). Why justice? Normative and instrumental interpretations. In J. Greenberg and R. L. Cohen (Eds.), *Equity and justice in social behavior* (pp. 437–469) New York: Academic Press.

Greenberg, J., Mark, M. M., & Lehman, D. R. (1985). Justice in sports and games. *Journal of Sport Behavior, 8,* 18–33.

Griffith, W. I. (1989). The allocation of negative outcomes: Examining the issues. In E. E. Lawler and B. Markovsky (Eds.), *Advances in group processes,* Vol. 6. Greenwich, Conn.: JAI Press.

Griffith, W. I. and Sell, J.(1988). The effects of competition on allocators' preferences for contributive and retributive justice rules. *European Journal of Social Psychology, 18:* 443–455.

Grumbkow, J. von. (1977). Verdeling van positieve en negatieve beloningen. *Mens en Onderneming, 31,* 285–294.

Grumbkow, J. von. (1990). *Power strategies and the equitable allocation of positive and negative sanctions.* In preparation.

Hamilton, V. L. & Rytina, S. (1980). Social consensus on norms of justice: Should the punishment fit the crime? *American Journal of Sociology, 85,* 1117–1144.

Hassebrauck, M. (1985). Retributive und distributive Gerechtigkeit im Aufteilungsverhalten von Kindern. *Zeitschrift für Entwicklungspsychologie und Pädagogische Psychologie, 17,* 164–171.

Kayser, E. & Lamm, H. (1980). Input integration and input weighting in decisions on allocations of gains and losses. *European Journal of Social Psychology, 10,* 1–15.

Kayser, E., Schwinger, T. & Cohen, R. L. (1984). Laypersons' conceptions of social relationships: A test of contract theory. *Journal of Social and Personal Relationships. 1,* 433–458.

Lamm, H. & Kayser, E. (1978). The allocation of monetary gain and loss following dyadic performance: The weight given to effort and ability under conditions of low and high intra-dyadic attraction. *European Journal of Social Psychology, 8,* 275–278.

Lamm, H., Kayser, E. & Schanz, V. (1983). An attributional analysis of interpersonal justice: Ability and effort as inputs in the allocation of gain and loss. *The Journal of Social Psychology, 119,* 269–281.

Lansberg, I. (1984). Hierarchy as a mediator of fairness: A contingency approach to distributive justice in organizations. *Journal of Applied Social Psychology, 14,* 124–135.

Lerner, M. J. (1974). The justice motive: "Equity" and "parity" among children. *Journal of Personality and Social Psychology, 29*, 538–550.

Lerner, M. J. (1975). The justice motive in social behavior: Introduction. *The Journal of Social Issues, 31*, 1–19.

Lerner, M. J. (1977). The justice motive: Some hypotheses as to its origins and forms. *Journal of Personality, 45*, 1–52.

Lerner, M. J. (1981). The justice motive in human relations. Some thoughts on what we know and need to know about justice. In M. J. Lerner & S. C. Lerner (Eds.), *The justice motive in social behavior* (pp. 11–35). New York: Plenum Press.

Leventhal, G. S. (1976a) Fairness in social relationships. In J. W. Thibaut, J. T. Spence, & R. C. Carson (Eds.), *Contemporary topics in social psychology*. Morristown, NJ: General Learning Press.

Leventhal, G. S. (1976b). The distribution of rewards and resources in groups and organizations. In L. Berkowitz & E. Walster (Eds.), *Advances in experimental social psychology* (Vol. 9; pp. 91–131). New York: Academic Press.

Leventhal, G. S., Karuza, J. Jr. & Fry, W. R. (1980). Beyond fairness: A theory of allocation preferences. In G. Mikula (Ed.). *Justice and social interaction* (pp. 167–218). New York: Springer-Verlag.

Meeker, B. F. and Elliot, G. C. (1987). Counting the costs: Equality and the allocation of negative group products. *Social Psychology Quarterly, 50*:7-15.

Mikula, G. (1974). Individuelle Entscheidungen und Gruppenentscheidungen über die Aufteilung gemeinsam erzielter Gewinne: Eine Untersuchung zum Einfluss der sozialen Verantwortung. *Psychologische Beiträge, 16*, 338–364.

Mikula, G. & Schwinger, T. (1973). Sympathie zum Partner und Bedürfnis nach sozialer Anerkennung als Determinanten der Aufteilung gemeinsam erzielter Gewinne. *Psychologishe Beiträge, 15*, 396–407.

Rothbart, M. (1968). Effects of motivation, equity, and compliance on the use of reward and punishment. *Journal of Personality and Social Psychology, 9*, 353–362.

Schmitt, M. & Montada, L. (1982). Determinanten erlebter Gerechtigkeit. *Zeitschrift für Sozialpsychologie, 13*, 32–44.

Schwinger, T. (1980). Just allocation of goods: Decisions among three principles. In G. Mikula (Ed.), *Justice and social interaction* (pp. 95–125). New York: Springer-Verlag.

Shapiro, E. G. (1975). The effect of expectations of future interaction on reward allocations in dyads: Equity or equality. *Journal of Personality and Social Psychology, 31*, 873–880.

Simpson, E. (1976). Socialist justice. *Ethics, 87*, 1–17.

Steensma, H., von Grumbkow, J., & Wilke, H. (1977). Boete, beloning en billijkheid. *Nederlands Tijdschrift voor de Psychologie, 32*, 519–526.

Thomas, W. I. & Thomas, D. S. (1928). *The child in America: Behavior problems and programs.* New York: Knopf.

Törnblom, K. Y. & Foa, U. G. (1983). Choice of a distribution principle: Crosscultural evidence on the effects of resources. *Acta Sociologica, 26*, 161–173.

Törnblom, K. Y. & Jonsson, D. R. (1985). Subrules of the equality and contribution principles: Their perceived fairness in distribution and retribution. *Social Psychology Quarterly, 48*, 249–261.

Törnblom, K. Y. & Jonsson, D. R. (1990). Distribution vs. retribution: The perceived justice of the contribution and equality principles for cooperative and competitive relationships. *Acta Sociologica 1987, 30*, 25–52.

Törnblom, K. Y., Jonsson, D. R., & Foa, U. G. (1985). Nationality, resource class, and preferences among three allocation rules: Sweden vs. USA. *International Journal of Intercultural Relations, 9*, 51–77.

Törnblom, K. Y. (1988). Positive and negative allocations: A typology and a model for conflicting justice principles. In E. E. Lawler and B. Markovsky (Eds.), *Advances in group processes*, Vol. 5. Greenwich, Conn.: JAI Press.

Törnblom, K. Y. The social psychology of distributive justice. In K. Scherer (Ed.), *Justice: The state of the art in theory and research*. Cambridge: Cambridge University Press, in press.

Törnblom, K. Y., & Mühlhausen, S. M. *Sharing equally the rewards and punishments deserved by one person: Perceived justice as a function of the amount of outcomes.* In preparation.

Walster, E., & Walster, G. W. (1975). Equity and social justice. *Journal of Social Issues, 31,* 21–43.

Wolff, R. P. (1977). *Understanding Rawls.* Princeton, NJ: Princeton University Press.

Yuchtman, E. (1972). Reward distribution and work-role attractiveness in the Kibbutz— Reflections on equity theory. *American Sociological Review, 37,* 581–595.

4

Allocation Standards
Equity, Equality, and Asymmetry

Ad L. W. Vogelaar and Riël Vermunt

Introduction

It is generally agreed that people are rewarded differently for different types of contributions. Fairy tales are a fine example of the difference in reward allocation. Historians as well as philosophers conceive of fairy tales as stories that have come to us through both oral and written traditions with generally strong normative tendencies. In our view, the normative tendency in fairy tales especially concerns aspects of justice: If you behave well, which means according to a certain standard of justice, you will be rewarded accordingly. If you do not behave well, you will be punished. In order to receive rewards or punishments, heroes and nonheroes of fairy tales must perform various activities. Cinderella, for instance, must wash dishes and clothes and do dirty work for her stepmother and sisters. She is rewarded for these inconveniences, not with money or things one can buy for money, but by marriage to a (rich) prince. Tom Thumb had to suffer discomfort—he is sent to a dark forest and has to fight a giant, but he mainly receives his reward because he offers intelligent contributions—he uses pebbles and small pieces of bread to find the way back home; he also uses the giant's boots. He is rewarded with wealth.

Ad L. W. Vogelaar and Riël Vermunt • Department of Social and Organizational Psychology, University of Leiden, 2333 AK Leiden, The Netherlands.

Equity

If both children and adults are questioned on just or unjust treatment of characters in fairy tales, they will be capable of judging inputs and rewards in terms of justice, however different these may be.

In a preliminary study, Vermunt (1985) was able to show that students, evaluating justice of rewards and punishments in fairy tales, were rather accurately capable of evaluating characters' inputs in terms of rewards and punishments. The relationship between different types of input (contributions, inconveniences, and attributes; Cook & Yamagishi, 1983) and outcomes (material as well as nonmaterial rewards) proved to be fairly equitable. This finding does not, in our view, show that the equity model is ubiquitous, but rather that, from early childhood on, adults are acquainted with combining different types of input with different types of outcomes to evaluate the fairness of rewards and punishments. Various authors have shown this capability of subjects in experiments that were set up in a more rigorous way (Anderson, 1976; Cook & Yamagishi, 1983; Farkas & Anderson 1979).

Although these findings show that equity is used in the allocation of rewards, these results do not imply that the equity model is equally well suited for various inputs or outcomes (Van Kreveld, Vermunt & De Vries, 1987) or for positive versus negative inputs (see Törnblom et al, Chapter 3 in this volume). The types of input we would like to focus on in the present study are *inconveniences* in the work setting (e.g., dirty work, noise, moisture), *contributions* (e.g., quality of work), and *attributes* (e.g., age, status). The type of outcome studied is the amount of money subjects are willing to pay in return for varying levels of input.

Contributions are inputs over which a person is considered to have control. It will be probable, therefore, that a person is rewarded with more or less money according to the level of the contribution. *Inconveniences*, on the other hand, are seldom self-chosen and cannot be directly attributed to the person. In the evaluation of inconveniences, the amount of harm they may cause is important, and harm can easily be expressed in terms of extra rewards, especially when harmdoing is attributed to external circumstances. *Attributes* are given entities, and, in the short term, a person has little control over his or her position on them.

Equality

Authors have different views on equality. Some authors see equality as a special instance of equity (Anderson, 1976; Walster & Walster, 1975).

Others assume that equality is essentially different from equity (e.g., Lerner, 1975). In this study, we adopt the view that equality and equity are not related. Following Harris (1983), we assume that persons allocate rewards perfectly equitably when they use the same, small or large, differences in outcome for equal differences in input level. Equality is considered as the degree to which different levels of input lead to minor or no differences at all in outcome allocation.

This reasoning leads to the conclusion that there is high equality as well as high equity when people use the same small differences in outcome level for equal differences in input; there is low equality and high equity when people use the same large differences in outcome level for equal differences in input; and finally there is high equality and low equity when people use irregular but small differences or no differences at all for equal differences in input.

In our opinion, not all types of input are judged equally relevant in the given situation. Therefore, it seems likely that subjects make small or large distinctions between outcomes, dependent on the relevance of the input. Highly relevant inputs result in large outcome differences, whereas low relevant inputs result in minor outcome differences. With inputs of little relevance, an equal allocation of outcomes is more appropriate than with highly relevant inputs. We assume that attributes such as age, need, and the like are less relevant for the work situation presented than inconveniences and contributions. Reis (1983) concludes that males rely more on equity, females more on equality. Equality judgments are also related to the value system of respondents. Left-wing voters are assumed to allocate more equally than right-wing voters.

Asymmetry

The asymmetry phenomenon is not well known in justice literature. It was described by Tversky (1977), Codol (1984, 1985) and Extra and Vermunt (1989). In short, asymmetry can be described as a phenomenon in which the evaluation of (dis)similarity between objects depends on the point of reference of the comparison. Thus a person may compare two objects by taking one object as the reference point of the comparison and the other as the comparison object. The asymmetry hypothesis states that an object of a certain category is judged as more similar to a prototypical object of that category than the prototypical object from the nonprototypical object. In other words, a prototype is judged as more dissimilar from a nonprototype than a nonprototype from a prototype (Tversky, 1977). Codol (1984) has shown that the asymmetry hypothesis does hold for social objects as well. In one of the experiments (Codol, 1984), Codol asked his subjects to compare a high-status person with a low-status person on several personal attributes. Three groups of subjects were formed. One third of the subjects were asked to compare the low-status person (object) with the high-status person (reference point), and vice versa for another one-third. The remaining subjects were not given any reference point in the comparison. The confirmed hypothesis was that the high-status stimulus person (prototype) was evaluated as less similar to the low-stimulus person than the reverse. Applied to the present situation, this finding leads to the following assumption: In our hierarchical society, with people striving for upward mobility, high-status persons are seen as the main representatives of successful people.

In the research reported here, a fictitious person A, with average inputs and average outcomes as a reference point, is compared with a fictitious person B, whose input differs from the input of A. In the case that B's input is higher than that of A, B is the prototype; in the case that B's input is lower than that of A, A is the prototype. When it concerns inconveniences, we think the opposite will be the case: To undergo less inconvenience implies a higher status. A is always the reference point. Following this line of reasoning and applying it to our data, we expect that B will receive a higher reward for more input, rather than a lesser reward for less input. For inconveniences, we expect that B will be rewarded less for fewer inconveniences than more for more inconveniences. Therefore, the distribution of rewards will be skewed.

We assume that the amount of asymmetry mainly depends on the relevance of attributes of objects for the situation. In our view, the relevance of attributes is influenced by subjective factors. Subjective factors are related to values, attitudes, and experiences of subjects. In The Netherlands, for instance, there is a considerable difference between left-wing and right-wing ideology with regard to many issues. Left-wing party members and voters are convinced that inconveniences in work should be considerably compensated, whereas right-wing voters are more inclined to compensate for more contribution and for a number of attributes, such as skill, experience, and the like. We therefore expect that, with respect to inconvenience, the asymmetry phenomenon will be stronger for left-wing voters and, with respect to contributions and a number of attributes, it will be stronger for right-wing voters.

Research Questions

In the Introduction, we described three types of allocation standards: equity, equality, and asymmetry. We also mentioned three types of input: contributions, attributes, and inconveniences in the work situation. Next we mentioned the fact that subjects of different ideology or of different gender seem to differ in their use of allocation standards. In this chapter, two questions will be discussed:

1. Which standards of allocation (equity, equality, and asymmetry) are used for various types of input?
2. In what way do different types of persons differ in the allocation of rewards?

Method

The study is based on a reanalysis of data of Vermunt and Van Kreveld (1981), who selected from earlier studies (Vermunt & Midden, 1976; see Lijftogt, 1966) 19 job classification items. About half of these items are person-related characteristics, some of them *contributions*, for instance, "number of hours worked"; others *attributes*, for example, "status." The other half of the items concern *characteristics related to the work situation*, for instance, "amount of noise." For the sake of convenience, in this chapter, all of these items will be named "job classification items." For an overview of all job classification items used, see Table 1.

For all 19 items, the following situations have been presented in a questionnaire:

Person A is an average worker in an industrial plant who earns 100 Dutch guilders for one working day. Another person B contributes:

- Much less than A, say 50% less
- A little less than A, say 10% less
- A little more than A, say 10% more
- Much more than A, say 50% more

For each of the 19 job classification items, the respondents were asked to indicate the amount of money they would allocate to person B in each of the four situations. The four situations were presented at the same time.

Respondents

The questionnaire was sent to a random sample of 167 respondents in Leiden, The Netherlands. Of all respondents, 117 (67%) returned their questionnaires. Of those, 111 could be used for further analysis.

Analysis

Each respondent allocated an amount of money to all four situations of all 19 job classification items. The question to be answered is, do we know what kinds of allocation standards people use in allocating rewards?

The standards that were used in the analysis are

1. *Equality*. Do people allocate rewards irrespective of level of input? In that case, person B will get the same amount of money in all four situations.
2. *Equity*. Do people allocate rewards exactly proportional in relation to the level of input?
3. *Asymmetry*. Do people allocate rewards to levels of input above the standard of person A differently from levels of input below the standard?

It is hardly to be expected that all individuals allocate rewards using only one of the standards. Therefore, a formula for each standard was developed to measure the degree to which each of the standards is used by respondents:[1]

Indexes for equality were calculated in the following way:

$$R(0) = \frac{1}{S(Y)} \tag{1}$$

or

$$R(0) = S(Y) \tag{2}$$

$S(Y)$ is the standard deviation of the outcomes. With respect to research question 1, $S(Y)$ in (1) is calculated for every job classification item over all respondents. With respect to research question 2, $S(Y)$ is calculated for every respondent within every job classification item. This results in zero in a number of cases. Therefore, (1) cannot be used and (2), a measure of "unequality," is used in the analyses.

$S(Y)$ is an indication of the degree in which different inputs of person B are rewarded without taking the specific level of input into account. The less distinction there is between the given amounts of money, the smaller is $S(Y)$.

For equity and asymmetry dummy variables have been created that represent respectively linear and quadratic functions.

---

[1]For his contribution in the development of the formulas we wish to thank John van de Geer, Department of Datatheory, University of Leiden.

	Inputs				
	-50%	-10%	10%	50%	
Equity	-50	-10	10	50	X1
Asymmetry	1	-1	-1	1	X2

The dummy variables X1 and X2 may be seen as ideal models as to how rewards should be allocated according to the specific standard. The correlation coefficient calculated between a dummy variable and the given amounts of money indicates the degree in which the specific standard is used. A correlation coefficient of 1 between the dummy variable of equity and the allocated amounts indicates perfect equity.

The equity index and the asymmetry index of each job classification item were calculated by correlating X1 respectively X2 with the four amounts of money. In case of research question 1, one measure of equity and of asymmetry was calculated for each job classification item over all respondents. In case of research question 2, measures were calculated separately for each job classification item for each respondent. In the instances in which $S(Y)$ is zero, $S(X1Y)$ and $S(X2Y)$ will be zero as well. In these cases $R(1)$ and $R(2)$ were defined as zero.

Equity:

$$\text{In formula: } R(1) = \frac{S(X1Y)}{S(X1) \times S(Y)} \tag{3}$$

Formula (3) will result in an index value with maximum 1, only if differences in rewards for various levels of input are exactly linear in comparison to the differences in levels of input. In this way a maximum of 1 will be reached not only when rewards of exactly "50 90 110 150" are given but also when these reward figures are "95 99 101 105" or "100 104 106 110." Any series that has other proportions in rewards will produce a lower index.

It can be concluded from (3) that the input of the hypothetical person A has not been taken into account in calculating the index of equity. The index value depends only on the input of person B. Person A functions as a reference point only.

The rationale for this formulation of equity is that all four situations were presented at the same time, so that respondents were able to compare B's inputs, and no instruction was given for use of 100 as a mean outcome.

Asymmetry:

In formula: $R(2) = \dfrac{S(X2Y)}{S(X2) \times S(Y)}$ (4)

In (4), the index value will result in zero when there is perfect symmetry. Positively skewed series such as "95 95 110 150" result in a positive index value; negatively skewed series such as "50 90 105 105" result in a negative index value.

Research Question 1

Do people use different standards of allocation (equity, equality, or asymmetry) for different types of input?

Values of the allocation standards of all 19 items over all respondents are presented in Table 1. Also shown is the mean difference from 100 for every job classification item.

Table 1 shows that equity explains the variance far more than asymmetry. The absolute indexes of equality, on the one hand, and equity and asymmetry, on the other, cannot be compared.

Table 1. Calculated Standards for All Job Classification Items

	Difference from 100	Equity	Asymmetry	Equality
Effort	− 1.00	.71	− .01	1.07
Dirty work	2.38	.66	.12	1.58
Responsibility	1.18	.79	.05	1.06
Experience	− .05	.74	.01	1.30
Danger	5.80	.71	.10	.85
Supervision	− .35	.19	− .01	2.46
Quality	− .61	.80	.01	1.00
Status	1.16	.35	.06	1.57
Age	− .88	.55	− .06	1.55
Number of hours	.22	.88	.02	.72
Draught	1.50	.52	.10	2.13
Occupational disease	5.33	.65	.09	.92
Moisture	2.18	.55	.11	1.74
Skill	.21	.75	.02	1.23
Noise	3.00	.57	.11	1.41
Need	.74	.35	.05	2.73
Quantity of work	− .21	.75	.02	1.17
Monotony	1.62	.35	.11	2.21
Temperature	3.87	.58	.15	1.49

The highest mean rewards are allocated to danger and occupational disease, and next highest to inconveniences in the work situation, that is, dirty work, moisture, noise, and temperature.

Items that are rewarded most equitably are number of hours and, to a somewhat lesser degree, effort, responsibility, experience, quality, and skill. Also, high index values result for quantity of work and danger. Most of these items have low index values on equality.

Age is the only item that has a relatively high negative index on asymmetry. Age is an item in which the difference between allocation of rewards in case of lower-than-standard input (younger age) is larger than the difference between the allocation of rewards in case of higher-than-standard inputs. Inconveniences in the work situation result in relatively high positive indexes, which implies that differences between allocations in case of higher-than-standard input are greater than differences between allocations of rewards in case of lower-than-standard inputs. The other items are approximately symmetrical.

When the 19 indexes of the three standards are correlated, we see that equity has a highly negative correlation with equality (Pearson correlation coefficient-.87). Correlations with asymmetry are not significant. The more equitable the allocation, the less equal the allocation seems to be.

In order to obtain a good insight into the relationship between allocation standards, on the one hand, and job classification items, on the other, we analyzed the indexes by means of SMACOF3, an unfolding technique developed by the Department of Datatheory in Leiden (Heiser, 1981). For this purpose, the index values of the job classification items for every allocation standard were standardized. After this standardization, a constant of 3 was added to every value. To use SMACOF3, the indexes were considered as preference data. To be specific, a high index value on equity for a specific job classification item was treated as a high preference of that item for equity, and a low index value as a low preference. In SMACOF3, both standards and job classification items are plotted in such a way that less distance between these two classes points to greater preferences for each other. As there are several items and several standards that have to be fitted into the same plot, concessions will have to be made in the final solution.

The SMACOF3 analysis resulted in Figure 1. Figure 1 shows two dimensions, an equity versus equality dimension and an asymmetry dimension. On this second dimension, in the lower part, the items with a positive asymmetry are located. Age is situated in the higher part, which is an item for which asymmetry is negative. After having drawn large circles of the same size around the three standards, we see that the following clusters of items are apparent:

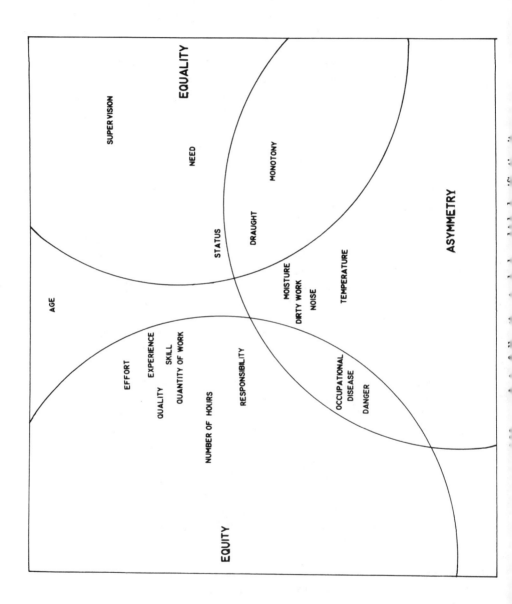

1. The contributions: number of hours, effort, quality, and responsibility are situated close to the equity point. Attributes such as experience and skill are also located in this circle, as are quantity of work (which is related to the job but is not an inconvenience), and the inconveniences occupational disease and danger.

2. Equality is surrounded by the attributes need and status. Also situated within the circle are three job-related items: draught and monotony (which can be classified as inconveniences) and supervision. Further analysis shows that, for these items, the largest percentage of the respondents does not allocate different outcomes as a result of different inputs. In the case of status, need, and supervision, more than 70% of the respondents allocate perfectly equally.

3. In the circle around asymmetry are situated danger and occupational disease (both are situated halfway between equity and asymmetry), draught and monotony (situated where the circles around asymmetry and equality do overlap), and dirty work, moisture, noise, and temperature. All these items can be classified as inconveniences, related to the work situation. The more dangerous types of items are situated near equity, the less dangerous types near equality. Further analysis shows that for most of the items that belong to this cluster, about 40% or more of the respondents allocate rewards positively asymmetrical. Monotony is an exception, with 30% of the respondents using this standard. With respect to the other items, few respondents use this allocation standard.

4. Situated somewhere between equity and equality and far from asymmetry, age is the only item that was not included in one of the circles. Age is the only item for which more than 20% of the respondents use negative asymmetry as an allocation standard.

Research Question 2

In what way do people differ in the allocation of rewards?

As we have shown before, allocation behavior of subjects depends on the allocation standards subjects use, as well as on the type of input to be judged. Different subjects use different standards for different types of input. Thus, what we want to know is this: In what way do different subjects use different standards for different types of input? We require a method of analysis that enables us to handle three sets of variables (modes) at the same time.

Classical methods of analysis show only the relationships between two modes at a time, such as for instance, persons and job classification items, or persons and allocation standards, or allocation standards and job classification items, but not the same three modes simultaneously.

TUCKALS (Kroonenberg, 1983) is a method developed specifically for this purpose. TUCKALS3 analyzes relationships between persons, job classification items, and allocation standards simultaneously.

Compared to a two-dimensional solution, three dimensions in the TUCKALS-analysis did not explain much extra variance. Therefore, we chose to describe the two-dimensional solution for each mode $(2 \times 2 \times 2)$. This implies that two independent dimensions resulted for each mode. In the solution, these dimensions are drawn in a way that the dimensions of different modes correlate as highly as possible. The fitted proportion of the total sum of squares gives an indication as to the goodness of fit of the solution. This measure is .26, which leaves the residual proportion at .74. Thus the fit is not very good, and we will have to be careful in drawing conclusions.

The following personal characteristics have been taken into analysis: age, gender, occupation, salary, political preference, and education. Inspection of the person-mode shows us the following two dimensions. The first dimension points to a distinction between two groups: (1) older people, those earning between 1,500 and 2,000 guilders per month, people who have a political preference for the Socialist Labor Party, and skilled laborers (in summary: older working-class people) on the one (positive) side of the dimension: and (2) younger people, earning between 2,000 and 3,000 guilders per month, those who have a political preference for the Democratic (D66) Party (younger middle-class people) on the other (negative) side of the dimension. The second dimension shows a distinction between two other groups: (1) People who have a political preference for the Christian Democratic Party, unskilled laborers or unemployed, those who earn less than 1,500 or more than 3,000 guilders per month (Christian Democratic Party voters with high or low income) on the one (positive) side of the dimension; and (2) those with a political preference for the Progressive Radical Party, older high-school-educated persons, and workers earning between 2,000 and 3,000 guilders per month (older middle-class progressives) on the other (negative) side of the dimension. Gender does not seem to be an important variable in the present research. No distinction has been found between males and females in the allocation of rewards.

The relationships between job classification items and standards for person dimension 1 (older working-class people versus younger middle-class) are shown in Figure 2, and for person dimension 2

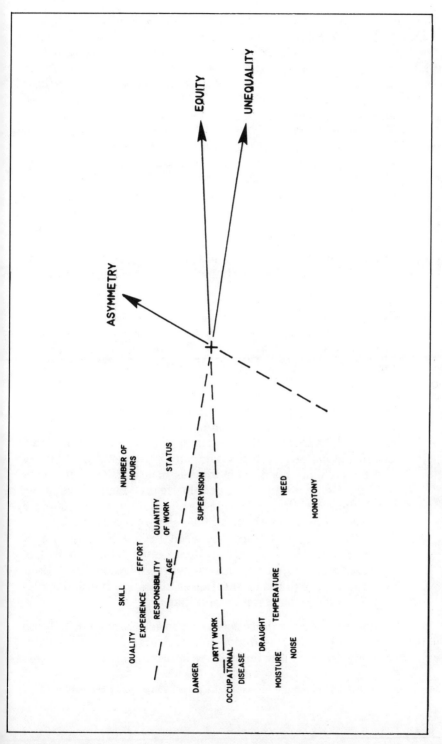

Figure 2. Relationships between job classification items and allocation standards for older working-class people.

(Christian Democratic Party voters with high or low income versus older middle-class progressives) in Figure 3.

The relation between job classification items and standards can be established by drawing the variables of one mode as vectors from the origin and by projecting the variables of the other mode on these vectors. Projections on the "head" side of the vector point to a positive relationship between job classification items and allocation standards: projections on the "tail" side point to a negative relationship and projections near the origin point to no relationship at all.

These relationships are applicable for people who are situated on the positive side of person dimension 1, in this case older working-class people. For people situated on the negative side of dimension 1, younger middle-class people, the opposite relationship between job classification items and standards are applicable.

Knowing that older working-class people are located on the positive side of person dimension 1 and younger middle-class people on the negative side, we may conclude the following from Figure 2:

1. There is a high negative relationship between equity and "unequality" [2] on the one hand, and all job classification items except supervision, number of hours, need, monotony, and status on the other hand. This implies that older working-class people make less use of the standard of equity and more use of the standard of equality than others. Especially younger middle-class people do apply the standard of equity more often than others and make less use of the standard of equality.

2. A highly negative relationship has been found between asymmetry and the inconveniences danger, dirty work, occupational disease, monotony, draught, temperature, moisture, and noise and the attribute need. This implies that, in case of inconveniences, older working-class people use this standard less often than others do. Young middle-class people use this standard relatively often where inconveniences are present.

3. No differences were found between people in their use of standards for job classification items supervision, number of hours, and status. This indicates that there are no distinctions between people in the application of allocation standards with respect to these job classification items.

Figure 3 shows the distinctions between subjects varying widely on person dimension 2. On this dimension, Christian Democratic Party voters, with high or with low income, are situated on the positive side

---

[2] As we have explained before, the inverse of the measure of equality is used.

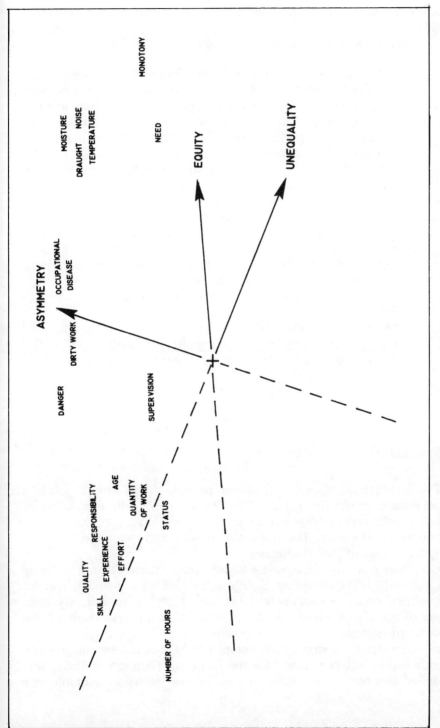

Figure 3. Relationships between job classification items and allocation standards for Christian Democratic Party voters with low or high income.

of the dimension and older middle-class progressives on the negative side.

Figure 3 shows the following results:

1. A strong positive relationship was found between asymmetry and the inconvenience danger, occupational disease, moisture, noise, draught, dirty work, monotony and temperature and the attribute need. This finding shows that older middle-class progressives apply this standard less often than do other people in cases of inconvenience. In this case, Christian Democratic Party voters, in high or low income brackets, make relatively more use of this standard.
2. There is a negative relationship between equity and unequality, on the one hand, and status, number of hours, experience, responsibility, quality, effort, skill, quantity of work and age, on the other hand. This implies that, with respect to these items, older middle-class progressives more often use equity and less equality. Christian Democratic Party voters, with high or with low income, make little use of equity and more of equality.
3. Christian Democratic Party voters, in high or in low income brackets, use equity more and equality less with respect to the inconveniences moisture, draught, noise, temperature, monotony, and the attribute need. For older middle-class progressives, the opposite was found.

Summary

The younger middle-class (younger people, those with a political preference for the Democratic (D66) Party, people who earn between 2,000 and 3,000 guilders per month) relatively often apply the allocation standard equity. The same was found for the standard of asymmetry in case of inconveniences.

Older working-class people (older people, those earning between 1,500 and 2,000 guilders per month, skilled laborers, people who have a political preference for the Socialist Labor Party) make relatively often use of the allocation standard equality. Little use was made of the standard asymmetry in cases of inconvenience.

Christian Democratic Party voters with high or low income (people with a political preference for the Christian Democratic Party, unskilled laborers or unemployed, low-income earners, or employees earning more than 3,000 guilders per month) relatively often apply the allocation standard equality where contributions and the attributes skill, experience, age, and status are involved. The allocation standard equity was used relatively often with respect to a number of inconveniences and the attribute need, as was the allocation standard asymmetry for inconveniences.

Older middle-class progressives (with a political preference for the Progressive Radical Party, older people, the high-school educated, those earning between 2,000 and 3,000 guilders per month) relatively often use the allocation standard equality with respect to a number of inconveniences and the attribute need. They often apply the allocation standard of equity with respect to contributions and the attributes skill, experience, age, and status. They do not often use the allocation standard asymmetry where inconveniences are involved.

With respect to their judgments, males and females react similarly.

Conclusions and Discussion

Figure 1 shows clear differences in reward allocation with respect to inconveniences, attributes or contributions. Inconveniences were separated from other job classification items because, in this case, higher-than-standard input was more clearly distinguished than lower-than-standard input when allocating rewards. In respect to the other items, excluding age, there is no difference between higher-than-standard and lower-than-standard input. Therefore, it is considered as fair that, for most contributions and a number of attributes, a certain increase in input should be accompanied by an equal increase in outcome, whatever the specific level of input. This is not the case for inconveniences: In case of high original levels of input, the increase in outcome was estimated considerably higher than if original levels were low.

The results show an asymmetry phenomenon that is antithetical to the asymmetry that we formulated earlier and in which the prototype is the person who has fewer inconveniences to contend with. In this study, we found that the difference in outcome between the prototype (B, less inconvenience than A) and the nonprototype A, is less than the difference in outcome between the nonprototype (B, more inconvenience than A) and the prototype A.

What could be the explanation for the fact that this asymmetry is contrary to our expectations? Underlying assumptions of our expectations were that less inconvenience is related to more status and that comparison of higher status persons with lower status persons leads to greater differences in reward than comparison of lower-status persons with higher-status persons. A possible explanation for our findings is that status is not a relevant criterion for comparison and that, in this case, the "lamentable" person, the one for whom pity is felt, is the prototype.

Another important question is why a certain type of asymmetry occurs only in case of inconveniences and not in case of attributes or contributions. Is it because we are more capable of thinking in terms of linear relationships between inputs and outcomes when dealing with attributes or contributions? Or is it because we are better able to handle differences in input with respect to contributions and attributes than with respect to inconveniences (work is either dirty or not)?

This finding may have consequences for the practice of job classification. Evidently, the scale we use for other items should not be applied when measuring inconveniences in regard to justice. For inconveniences, differences on the lower parts of the scale appear to be smaller than for other items. This finding should be expressed in numbers attached to scale values that are used to obtain a score on which salary is based.

At this stage one should bear in mind that from Figure 1, it may be inferred that all three standards have the same prominence. With the exception of equity and asymmetry, however, it is impossible to compare the prominence of the three standards. Equality was derived from the amount of variance of the given rewards, whereas equity and asymmetry were attempts to explain this same total amount of variance. The results show that equity is by far a more important standard than asymmetry. This implies that if results had not been standardized, all items would have a greater distance to asymmetry than to equity. With respect to equality and equity, there is no way at all to conclude which of these standards is more important for allocating rewards. What can be compared is the relative distance between an item and a standard. Items that have a greater distance from a standard than other items may be considered to have less preference in regard to this standard.

The results show a highly negative correlation between equity and equality. One could conclude that these two allocation standards are poles on one dimension. Before drawing a firm conclusion, however, we must consider the fact that two related problems could account for this finding:

1. The equity measure $R(1)$. The equity score for individuals approaches 1 whenever persons allocate larger outcomes for larger inputs, whatever the magnitude of the difference.

2. Equity is 0 and equality maximum when persons do not make distinctions in outcome level for different inputs.

In most cases, equity will therefore be either 0 or approaching 1. Thus, if a large number of persons allocate equal outcomes for different input levels, the equality score will be high and the equity score low. If a lesser number allocate equal outcomes, the equality score will be much lower and the equity score will be high.

From Figure 1, we are also able to conclude which items are most prominent for this particular situation (the work situation). The distance from equality indicates this prominence. If items are located near equality, large differences in input lead to only small differences in outcome, a result that shows that, in a work situation, people attach little value to differences concerning these inputs. Our conclusion is that differences in level of need, status, draught, monotony, and supervision are not important in the reward allocation.

To our knowledge, no research has as yet been done to relate different categories of people to different inputs and to different allocation standards simultaneously. What has been done is research as to which standards different subjects prefer (Hermkens, 1983; Reis, 1983; Törnblom et al., Chapter 3 in this volume) but not in relation to different types of input.

The line of research we set out in this chapter seems promising. At this moment, however, it leaves us with results that should be treated as far from conclusive, especially because the fit of the solution is not really good.

Gender did not seem to be a distinguishing variable in this research. We did not find confirmation of findings in other studies (e.g., Reis, 1983) that males and females differ in their use of the standards of equity and equality. Perhaps the work situation is an instance in which males and females use allocation standards in the same degree. We did not find confirmation for the expectation that left-wing voters are more inclined to compensate for inconveniences than right-wing voters.

Younger people, people with a political preference for the Democratic (D66) Party, those earning between 2,000 and 3,000 guilders per month have a relatively strong inclination to use the asymmetry standard when evaluating inconveniences, whereas older people, those earning between 1,500 and 2,000 guilders per month, skilled laborers, people with a political preference for the Socialist Labor Party make relatively little use of this standard. From salary, age, and kind of work, one may conclude that the latter group of respondents was more experienced in undergoing inconveniences at work. This could lead to the assumption that the latter group would be inclined to plead for better compensation in case of inconveniences because of their experience. Why then is it that the former group wishes to compensate more than the latter group? Perhaps this can be explained by assuming that older people are used to the fact that inconveniences were not well compensated for in the past and the former group grew up with the idea that compensation for inconveniences is a matter of justice.

References

Anderson, N. H. (1976). Equity judgments as information integration.Journal of Personality and Social Psychology, 33, 291–299.

Codol, J. P. (1984). Social differentiation and non-differentiation.In H. Tajfel (Ed.), The social dimension: European developments in social psychology; (vol. 1, pp.314–337). Cambridge: Cambridge University Press.

Codol, J. P. (1985). L' estimation des distances physique entre personnes: Suis-je aussi loin de vous que vous êtes de moi? L' Annee Psychologique, 85, 517–534.

Cook, K. S., & Yamagishi, T. (1983). Social determinants of equity judgments: The problem of multidimensional input. In D. Messick & K. S. Cook (Eds), Equity theory. Psychological and sociological perspectives (pp. 95–126). New York: Praeger Publishers.

Extra, J., & Vermunt, R. (1989). Asymmetrie in de vergelijking van personen. In A. Van Knippenberg (Ed.), Fundamentele Sociale Psychologie. Deel 3. Tilburg: Tilburg University Press.

Farkas, A. J., & Anderson, N. H. (1979). Multidimensional inputs in equity theory. Journal of Personality and Social Psychology, 37,876–896.

Harris, R. J. (1983). Pinning down the equity formula. In D. Messick, & K. S. Cook (Eds.), Equity theory. Psychological and sociological perspectives (pp. 207–241). New York: Praeger Publishers.

Heiser, W. J. (1981). Unfolding analysis of proximity data. Dissertatie, Leiden.

Hermkens, P. J. (1983). Oordelen over de rechtvaardigheid van inkomens. Dissertatie, Utrecht.

Kroonenberg, P. M. (1983). Three-mode principal component analysis. Leiden: DSWO-Press.

Lerner, M. J. (1975). The justice motive in social behavior. Journal of Social Issues, 31(3), 1–19.

Lijftogt, S. G. (1966). De genormaliseerde methode van werkclassificatie. Dissertatie, Utrecht.

Reis, H. T. (1983). The multidimensionality of justice. In R. Folger, (Ed.), The sense of injustice: Social psychological perspectives. New York: Plenum Press.

Tversky, A. (1977). Features of similarity. Psychological Review, 84, 327–352.

Van Kreveld, D., Vermunt, R., & De Vries, H. (1987). How much of what does a person deserve for what? Recognition and pay for devotion, working circumstances and production. Utrecht: Vakgroep Sociale- en Organisatiepsychologie.

Vermunt, R. (1985). Rechtvaardigheid in sprookjes. Leiden:Vakgroep Sociale- en Organisatiepsychologie, Intern Rapport.

Vermunt, R., & Midden, K. (1976). *Determinanten van arbeidssatisfactie*, Intern rapport, Vakgroep Sociale en Organisatiepsychologie, Leiden.

Vermunt, R., & Van Kreveld, D. (1981). Vergelijkbare betalingen. De invloed van diverse vergelijkingscriteria op wenselijk geachte betalingsverhoudingen. *Gedrag, 9,* 125–142.

Walster, E., & Walster, G. W. (1975). Equity and social justice. *Journal of Social Issues, 31*(3), 21–43.

5

What Do Children Care about Justice?
The Influence of Culture and Cognitive Development

Nicholas Emler

La justice est la sanction des injustices establies.
—ANATOLE FRANCE

Introduction

This chapter is concerned with the acquisition in childhood of commitment to standards of justice. All who have studied the question agree that even in early childhood there is some sense of what is fair and what is unfair. That is, children react to the treatment they get not simply in terms of how intrinsically pleasant or aversive it is but according to whether it is deserved. Many would go further and argue that young children are guided by such notions of fairness in the treatment they mete out to others. The issue developmental psychologists have addressed is how these notions originate and how they change as the child grows older.

The best known, most thoroughly elaborated and, in the opinion of many, the most successful treatment of this development is that supplied by work in what has become known as the cognitive developmental tradition (cf. Damon, 1977; Kohlberg, 1976; Piaget, 1932). Almost everyone currently writing on this topic refers to or makes use

Nicholas Emler • Department of Psychology, University of Dundee, Dundee, DD1 4HN, Scotland.

of some version of cognitive–developmental theory and, even if there is substantial disagreement about details, most of these writers appear to accept its basic assumptions.

My ambition in this chapter is not to enumerate the very real achievements of the cognitive–developmental approach (interested readers should consult the articles by Damon, 1981; Emler & Hogan, 1981; Karniol & Miller, 1981; Simmons, 1981), but to convince you that a cognitive–developmental analysis by itself is insufficient to account for the standards of justice to which individuals become committed in the course of their development or the stances they adopt with respect to different standards of justice.

In the extant literature on children's notions of justice, there are two features to which I would like to draw attention. The first is that orientations to justice, in the sense both of caring about justice and the particular standards an individual cares about, are regarded as consequences of intellectual development. The second is that the research evidence indicates children do, to what might be regarded as a surprising degree, care about and act on the basis of what is fair. Let us consider the background to and implications of the first of these features.

Justice and Problem Solving

To understand the type of analysis that cognitive developmental theory offers, it is helpful to consider the research strategy with which it is associated. Since Binet's pioneering work on intellectual development at the turn of the century, that strategy has been to give individual children problems or puzzles to solve and so to discover each child's problem-solving capacities and procedures. Behind this strategy lie the more general assumptions that the natural or material environment constantly presents individuals with such problems and puzzles and that human intelligence operates as a system for solving them more or less adequately.

Piaget's great contribution to the psychology of intellectual development included two key insights. The first was that the mental resources children bring to problem solving undergo qualitative changes over time. Younger children do not merely fail to solve the problems that older children can manage; they think about the problems in quite different ways, applying to them quite different mental frameworks. The second was that the constantly repeated activity of problem solving is itself the source of qualitative change and development of the more adequate, successful, or sophisticated procedures characteristic of older children.

The same kind of analysis that Piaget made of the developing child's relations with the material world could, he supposed, be applied to the child's relations with the social world, at least up to a point. This world likewise constantly presents the individual child with problems and puzzles; the child tries to solve these and in the process gradually transforms the capacities he or she has available for their solution.

What are the problems with which social life presents us? Developmental psychologists interested in children's notions of justice have principally been concerned with problems posed by the allocation of limited resources among multiple claimants. Though Piaget's own interests were more general than this, his research into children's moral judgments (Piaget. 1932) accorded an important place to the question of distributive justice. The children he questioned revealed at least three distinct strategies for resolving distribution problems. A common strategy among the youngest children questioned, 6-year-olds, was to defer to adult authority; whatever any adult in the situation demanded took priority as a fair solution. But some children at this age and an increasing proportion at later ages preferred a strict equality of treatment and believed even adult wishes should be subordinate to this requirement. Finally, among some of the oldest children questioned, mainly the 11-and 12-year-olds, another approach was sometimes found. They would modify a rigid equality of treatment to take into account or make allowance for differences in circumstances such as age, special needs, or previous services rendered. Piaget called this conception *equity* though his interpretation is broader than current usage; it also subsumes the justice of need.

Piaget found that the same three principles characterized children's varying views about the distribution of burdens and the use of unequal distributions as a form of punishment. Damon's (1977) work has suggested some modifications to this sequence, at least insofar as pure positive justice problems are concerned. Following Piaget, one of the most influential figures in the study of moral reasoning in recent times has been Lawrence Kohlberg, though Kohlberg (1976) went considerably further than Piaget in drawing direct parallels between cognitive development and the development of capacities for the analysis of moral and social conflicts. Kohlberg insisted that all moral conflicts, whether they arise over issues of authority, law, civil rights, property rights, punishment, or the value of human life are basically questions of justice. He regarded all moral reasoning as fundamentally a search for just solutions to conflicts of interest. In other words, individuals are naturally inclined to regard the best solution to any dilemma as one that meets the requirements of justice, and they are naturally disposed to try and discover this solution. The way in which the ideal or just solution is defined and the powers for discovering it in any situation undergo gradual and qualitative change over the course of development. Like Piaget, Kohlberg viewed development as an intrinsic disposition of the individual's intellectual system; the individual's capacity to determine the just solution to any conflict of interests evolves as a consequence of having such problems to solve or, put in Kohlberg's own terms, development depends on the density and variety of an individual's "role-taking opportunities."

Kohlberg described six general stages in the development of an individual's capacity to resolve moral conflicts. He argued these are true developmental stages in the same sense as those Piaget defined for the development of logical operations but furthermore that they are functionally related to stages of logical thinking; to each level of moral reasoning there is a corresponding level of logical operations that is necessary to its achievement. This point has been echoed in a more general way by Damon (1981).

> In reasoning about positive justice, children call on their abilities to categorize the world, to order the world, to establish reciprocal relations between events in the world, to quantify goods and rewards. In this manner, children's logical reasoning is reflected in their justice reasoning. (p. 62)

However, Damon shares with Turiel (1983) the opinion that in other respects, Kohlberg's theory of general stages of moral reasoning is too ambitious. They incline instead to the view that there are several relatively independent strands to the development of moral insight, each with its own sequence of changes, and that notions of distributive justice represent just one of these strands. Thus Damon's research strategy has been closer to Piaget's than to Kohlberg's, asking children specifically about reward distribution problems and attempting to describe the strategies that are specific to this class of problem. Damon has suggested that at least six qualitatively distinct types of response can be found in the age range 6 to 10 and that they represent a developmental sequence.

Perhaps the apotheosis of the problem-solving perspective on children's notions of distributive justice is to be found in the review by Hook and Cook (1979). They examine studies in which children have been presented with allocation problems. In these studies, children are typically requested to distribute a fixed sum of money or other readily quantifiable reward among a set of claimants. The latter differ from one another in various respects but most conspicuously in their relative contributions or the amount of work they have done. Hook and Cook (1979) specify a number of different distribution rules—principally *equality, ordinal equity* (rank ordering outcome to correspond to the rank order of inputs), and *proportional* equity (or to each in direct proportion to his or her quantified contribution)—and attempt to identify the rule that is most predominant at different ages. They claim that equality is the earliest distribution rule to be widely applied; it is then displaced by ordinal equity which is in turn displaced but only among the oldest subjects in the studies reviewed, those in their teens and adulthood, by proportional equity. The authors then map these changes in rule use onto changes in the capacity for logical thought, pointing out that the concept of ratios upon which proportional equity logically depends is only available to children who have reached what Piaget called the level of formal operations in intellectual development (Inhelder & Piaget, 1958), a level normally achieved after 12 years of age and often considerably later. In effect, the problem of what is a fair distribution becomes a computational problem to which there is a determinate solution, as there are for problems in mathematics, logic, or geometry. And as the child's intellectual resources become more sophisticated, so they become capable of solving more complex distribution problems.

Hook and Cook's (1979) analysis epitomizes what Flavell (1972) has called a displacement model of sequences in developmental change; at each stage a new rule or principle displaces the one previously applied. Once the child is capable of understanding the new rule, he or she applies it in preference to the previous one. The work of Enright and his colleagues (e.g., Enright, Enright, Manheim, & Harris, 1980; Enright, Franklin, & Manheim, 1980; Enright, Enright, & Lapsley, 1981; Enright et al., 1984) is similar in approach. In this case the sequence starts with self-interest that is then displaced by distribution on the basis of external characteristics (e.g., relative size or age), equal distribution, distribution according to relative contributions, and finally distribution according to relative needs.

A rather different multiprinciple view has been put forward by Lerner and others (Lerner, 1977; Mikula, 1984). It is that people have a range of justice principles on which they can draw, and they select from these principles as the occasion demands. Lerner argues that children are like adults in this respect and will regard parity or equality as appropriate in one situation, equity in another, and need in a third. Lerner has not examined the use over age of different distribution rules in any systematic way but claims that even young children, 5-and 6-year-olds, are, for example, able to discriminate the situational appropriateness of equity and parity rules (Lerner, 1974).

Lerner (1977; Lerner & Simmons, 1966; Long & Lerner, 1974) also accords a somewhat different role to intellectual development. He is less concerned with the role of the child's intellectual resources in solving specific problems than with his or her contribution to the achievement of a more general and enduring conclusion about the social world, namely that people's outcomes generally match what they deserve, this in turn producing commitment to a "personal contract." The personal contract is a renunciation of immediate gratifications for the sake of greater long-term benefits, based on the confidence or trust that these benefits, if deserved, will indeed be forthcoming. The child's growing intellectual awareness subsequently gives rise to a "social contract" as another general conclusion is drawn: Others are equivalent to the self in that they also make personal contracts and if any is to have his or her contract honored then all must have their contracts honored. This seems to contain two ideas: first, that individuals depend on one another to get what they each deserve; second, they all inhabit the same environment and if that environment is so unreliable as to threaten others' personal contracts, if others appear not to get what they deserve, then one's own contract is at risk. In other words, if individuals are to feel secure in their personal contracts they need to believe that the world is a just place, in which people as a whole generally get what they deserve. Inevitably, however, this results in a degree of cognitive distortion, for all outcomes, good or bad, must be regarded as deserved.

What is less clear in this analysis is how children decide what people deserve. Are children assumed naturally to possess an intuition of what is fair and what is not in different situations? From whence does the intuition come that a justice of need is appropriate in one context, parity in another, and equity in a third? Do these also have a basis in intellectual development, in the child's autonomous capacity for logical or rational analysis, or are the distinctions cultural in origin? Lerner's analysis leaves this question open; the cognitive–developmental approach quite definitely does not.

Cognitive Constructivism versus Cultural Determinism

Researchers in the cognitive–developmental tradition suppose that they are and should be studying the basic cognitive attributes of the "class of organisms called 'people' " (Flavell & Ross, 1981, p. 307); in other words features common to a species, and this is as true of those studying moral reasoning and concepts of justice as it is of those more concerned with mathematical or logical operations. The relevant phenomena are therefore decidedly not the products of membership of a particular culture or social group or historical epoch. In the particular case of justice, the desire for justice and the standards of justice an individual believes to be relevant are not matters of local or historically relative convention or customary practice. Neither are they implanted in the child by the particular society into which it is born.

The explanation for the form and content of cognition, and indeed for the occurrence and direction of cognitive development is to be found in the nature of the species and the properties of the environment to which this species adapts. Following Piaget, it is widely accepted that the course of intellectual development is dictated by the internal logic of thought itself and by the imperatives of biological functioning—conservation of internal organization in the process of accommodating to the invariant properties of the material environment. Thus all cognition is a more or less adequate, adapted, or accurate representation of the objective properties of the environment. And so also with concepts of justice. If people believe equity to be an appropriate standard in particular circumstances, then it is a natural inclination of the species and, moreover, a rational and nonarbitrary choice.

In practice, when cognitive developmentalists have considered the possibility of cultural influences upon thinking or moral norms, they have done so in terms of a particular dichotomy (Gibbs, 1985). Either the child is an active and autonomous problem solver that constantly constructs and reconstructs its own problem-solving capacities in the direction of increasingly adapted, coherent, and rational strategies, or the child's beliefs are passive reproductions of culturally determined, irrational and arbitrary standards. The culture imposes patterns of thought upon the child. Cognitive developmentalists then argue that because children clearly do "construct systematic, non-arbitrary social concepts" (Turiel, 1983, p. 217), the cultural determinist interpretation must be in error.

Some attempt has been made to compare these models more directly by studying the views of children from different cultural or social backgrounds. The assumption is that if the constructivist model is in error, then different styles of reasoning or different developmental sequences should be found in different cultural and social milieux. Kohlberg claims that no such differences have been found so far as his stages are concerned (see Snarey, 1985, for a recent review). More specifically, with respect to justice notions, Enright, Enright, Manheim, and Harris (1980) and Enright *et al.* (1984) respectively compared the responses of children from different social classes and different cultures and in both cases reported no differences in developmental sequences. Setting aside the doubt that the research strategies used would or could reveal cultural differences if they existed, the fact remains that some form of social or cultural influence on development is very strong. The same evidence (Enright, Enright, Manheim, & Harris 1980; Snarey, 1985) shows that rates of development and even the final level achieved vary considerably from one social group to another. This observation has attracted little comment, yet its implications are surely profound.

The idea that culture and society play no constructive part in shaping commitments to justice is one that I wish to challenge in this chapter. But as a preliminary to developing this challenge, there is a second feature of the developmental work on justice to consider.

From Decent Children to Beastly Adults

One of the great problems with the cognitive–developmental analysis of socialization and one others have commented upon (e.g., Brown & Herrnstein, 1975) is that it does not seem to account for the way that adults actually behave. It is hard to reconcile the thoroughly decent, humane, and reasonable children that the work of Damon, Lerner, and others reveals to us with the adults we know they become. These children seem entirely consistent with the theoretical model of human nature cognitive development psychology offers. Like Edmund Burke, they appear to do what humanity, reason, and justice tell them they ought to do; they do all seem to care about justice. And yet as adults many will be thoroughly beastly to others, manipulating, cheating, and dispossessing their fellows, denying them their rights, depriving them of their just desserts. At the same time, many more remain their passive victims, apparently acquiescing to the injustices done to them. Finally, many children will grow into adults who will silently tolerate the injustices done to others.

Perhaps some dramatic change occurs after childhood; perhaps they suffer moral amnesia or intellectual regression. But this seems unlikely. Kohlberg, who did more than anyone to promote the study of moral reasoning beyond the childhood years, concluded that if any changes occur at all they are in the direction of even more coherent and rational standards of justice, and an even more thorough commitment to achieving just solutions to conflicts. As Brown and Herrnstein (1975) observe, the kinds of mature, adult members of the human species predicted by this development theory bear little resemblance to those revealed in the experimental social psychology of Milgram, Zimbardo, Latane, and others. So, what is missing?

Socialization

Part of what is missing I believe is acknowledgment that the social development of the child is also a process of socialization, by which I mean a process of becoming a member of society, but not just any society or human society in the most general terms, and not just any member. It is a process of becoming a member of a particular society, for example, the society that exists in Dundee in the 1980s and becoming an occupant of a particular position within that society, especially an occupant of a status within a hierarchical structure.

It is my argument that the specific society and culture in which a child grows up and the position or positions the child comes to occupy in that social system have an influence on the standards of justice or fairness that child comes to care about.

One of the great, if unrecognized, obstacles to progress in social and developmental psychology in the past has been the absence of a serviceable model of society and social life, or of the kinds of problems with which social life actually confronts people, or of the manner in which such problems are normally solved. So much work has been predicated on the simplest of all possible models, one in which society consists merely of other people, anonymous, undifferentiated, and interchangeable (Doise, 1980; Emler & Fisher, 1981).

A perfect model has yet to be found, but I believe that a useful starting point is provided by the anthropologist, J. Clyde Mitchell (1969). He has suggested that, analytically, social life can be regarded as ordered in three ways.

First, there is a *structural* order of interrelated and more or less formally defined offices and positions that individuals may periodically or more permanently occupy with respect to one another. These positions normally entail powers, duties, and obligations that are regarded as impersonal and are often defined by statute or regulation. This is the order made familiar to us by the classical social theorists in their analyses of role relationships within formal organisations and bureaucracies. Second, there is a *categorical* order based on divisions of people into broad social categories—male–female, middle class–working class, Protestant–Catholic, adult–child, citizen–foreigner—and upon shared stereotypes or images of the typical members of these categories. Frequently the categorical order also entails important power relations.

Finally, and Mitchell believes most basic of all, there is a *personal order* defined by networks of relationships, ties, loyalies, and obligations existing between specific individuals. Although these orders may be distinguished analytically, in everyday practice they are likely to interpenetrate. The advantage in distinguishing them is that each involves different issues of justice and injustice. It might be argued that children are not to begin with involved in or touched by issues of justice at the level of structural or categorical orders, or even at the level of the complex web of personal relationships with which adults contend. I disagree and hope that the grounds for my disagreement will become clearer in the course of the chapter.

The Personal Order

One of the most basic rules at the level of personal relations between individuals appears to be the rule of reciprocity (cf. Gouldner, 1960): return favors and do not hurt those who have helped you. There is good evidence that very early in life children have grasped, even if only intuitively, this basic rule (e.g., Berndt, 1977; Levitt *et al.*, 1985; Staub & Sherk, 1970).

But there are a couple of things that are perhaps less well recognized about this rule as it applies and is applied in the personal order. The first is that reciprocation of favors should not be immediate or precisely equivalent. Brown (1986) has commented on this in terms of a distinction between economic and social exchange. (Holmes, 1981, has made similar points regarding the differences between commercial and close personal relationships.) In the former, the equivalency of mutual exchanges is precise and quantifiable and usually is defined on a monetary scale. ''Reciprocation'' is also usually immediate unless alternative conditions are specifically agreed upon in advance. If we are party to an exchange in which the other does not meet these conditions, then we tend to feel aggrieved.

Matters are very different in social exchange. Favors are not paid off precisely and those who exchange favors are careful to be imprecise or vague about the value of what is exchanged (see Boissevain, 1984; also Mars, 1982). Moreover explicit conditions about a time limit for the return of favors would be regarded as bad form. The imprecise value of such personal favors helps to maintain relations of credit and debt between individuals and so contribute to the persistence of a personal relationship between them. This may actually be the object of this favor giving. Or rather, there are advantages in maintaining relationships with people from whom favors may be sought when unforeseen needs arise in the future. To quantify favors and require immediate and precisely equivalent reciprocation would be to reduce social relations to the commercial relations of buying and selling, a series of isolated, one-off transactions. But in this system of social exchange when if ever do we feel aggrieved? When we request a favor in return and it is refused. Our sense of grievance may not produce reactions as extreme as those of Don Corleone in Mario Puzo's novel (who, it will be recalled assassinates an acquaintance who fails to respond when a "small" favor is requested in return for an earlier one), but the underlying sentiments are the same.

One need not postulate a sense of fairness as the motivation behind the reciprocation of favors. The personal order implies something else that is not, so far as one can judge, widely recognized in social psychology: People dwell in social worlds populated by acquaintances; they are embedded in communities. Within these communities, they are known and known about. They are under constant observation and constantly discussed. As a result, they have *reputations* based on their past dealings with the community's other members. People can be expected to uphold reciprocation rules to the extent that they care about and need to care about their reputations (including reputations for not returning favors, borrowed lawnmowers, and other concrete and less tangible kindnesses). Not to do so would undermine their chances of securing future favors. None but a hermit can afford to be entirely indifferent to reputation.

We do not yet know much about how these concerns and understandings are developed in childhood, but we might expect intellectual development, together with certain social experiences, to be involved in appreciating the contingencies of reputation management. We might expect individual differences in the degree to which individuals are sensitive to or successful in shaping their reputations within their communities, but there is little in these proposals that could not be accommodated within a cognitive–developmental analysis. For such an analysis, therefore, so far so good.

One observation that social anthropologists have frequently made of small face-to-face communities is the pervasiveness within them of the intense and often bitter competition for status that occurs between (social) equals (Bailey, 1971). I do not know whether competition for status is a human universal, though some have cogently argued that this is likely to be the case (Hogan, 1983), but there are well-documented cultural differences in the emphasis given to status competition (e.g., Benedict, 1935; Harris, 1971).

Evidence has also emerged recently of cultural and subcultural variations in the extent to which children apply the contributions (or equity) rule in allocating resources (e.g., Mann *et al.*, 1985; Nisan, 1984). Taking these observations together casts a concern with equity as an appropriate standard of distributive justice in a different light, different that is from the position found to underpin the cognitive–developmental analysis.

That position is well described by Nisan (1984): "the inner logic of the equity principle—the benefit expected to the community from encouraging one's contribution and the reciprocity that is the cornerstone of the principle" (p. 1026), a logic the recognition of which is dependent on sufficient cognitive maturity.

But organizational and industrial psychologists point out that the equity or contributions principle is also a competitive principle that is competition inducing (Deutsch, 1985; Leventhal, 1976), and in part the competition involved is for an inherently scarce resource—relative status. It seems at least plausible that members of a society oriented toward competition for individual status would endorse the contributions rule because differential reward or remuneration operates as a public marker of status (and as Homans once observed, in the pursuit of status, the *public* nature of the differential is everything). Thus children growing up in such a society may be expected to argue for application of the contributions rule when they are engaged in a competition for status. Where an equitable allocation would benefit them, they will want the rule applied as a public confirmation of their superiority over their rivals. Presumably status competition is less appropriate between team members, and so in this case the contributions rule would not be applied, as Lerner (1974) has shown. But why might children apply the contributions rule when acting as disinterested third parties? Possibly they will do so when they think they are judging a competition and when they believe that they and the claimants share the norms of status competition.

When an individual is personally disadvantaged by application of the contributions rule (in the sense of losing status), he or she might be expected to favor an alternative, such as parity, something indicated in research carried out by Mikula (1980).

Retributive Justice

This brings me to retributive justice in personal relations and particularly to retaliation and revenge. The inclination to revenge seems strong and pervasive. Certainly Shylock in Shakespeare's *Merchant of*

Venice regarded it as a natural human reaction. There are many arguments and explanations for the basis of this inclination, several of them examined by Hogan and Emler (1981). Thus there is the view that social living imposes burdens on community members; all have to renounce a degree of freedom and suffer a share of the misery. This produces a strong inclination to punish cheats, people who seem to be trying to evade their share of this misery.

But I think a case can be made for revenge often having a more personal focus. We know that children regard acts of aggression committed in retaliation for some deliberate attack as less blameworthy than unprovoked attacks (e.g., Berndt, 1977; Shantz & Voyandorf, 1973); they accept retaliation as a legitimate mitigating plea.

But why should individuals feel it necessary to retaliate, beyond considerations of immediate self-defense? I think the answer can again be found in the conditions of human communal existence and the fact that under these conditions individuals have reputations. Individuals retaliate to protect their status and reputation within communities of acquaintances. Not to do so would be to acknowledge publicly the lower status an unanswered attack or insult implies. Not to do so may result in a reputation for weakness, cowardice, and disinclination to defend oneself or one's property, leading to further attacks on oneself or one's dependents (cf. Furer-Haimendorf, 1967). This interpretation is consistent with Felson's (1978) observation that retaliation is more likely when an audience, especially of acquaintances, witnesses the original insult or attack. It also suggests that much aggression is a response to perceived slights and insults, something confirmed in research by Dodge and others (e.g., Dodge & Frame, 1982), and an attempt to protect one's reputation by asserting that one's dignity is not something to be trifled with.

In his studies of children's moral judgments, Piaget (1932) included some inquiries into views about retaliation. In this area of judgment, he found a remarkably strong sex difference in views, a finding seldom mentioned in contemporary reviews of his work. Boys appeared to believe in returning blow for blow in equal measure if not more; girls believed in returning no more than the number of blows received and in many cases less. It is, of course, speculation, but perhaps these boys were becoming socialized into a society that allowed and expected them to compete for statuses from which girls were excluded.

What contemporary reviews record of Piaget's observations is that as children grow older, they grow out of approval for direct retaliation (Lickona, 1969). As one model of reasonableness observed at the tender age of 10: "there is no end" to revenge (Piaget, 1932, p. 323).

Forgiveness, the Judeo–Christian ethic of mercy advocated by Shylock's adversary, takes precedence. So is rejection of retaliation in preference for turning the other cheek, loving one's enemies, or practicing the golden rule, a natural emergent of growing intellectual insight?

It should be said that Piaget's own data do not support this conclusion; 95% of the oldest children questioned, 12-year-olds, thought it right to retaliate. Durkin (1961), on the other hand, found that a majority of children, and especially older (13-year-olds) as compared to younger (7-year-olds), rejected retaliation. The kinds of justifications they gave suggested either that nonretalitation would somehow reform the culprit, shaming him or her into behaving more decently next time or, more simply, that it is better to be nice.

Should we see these reactions as rational, developmentally more sophisticated and mature, or as self-presentations that accord with a pervasive ethic of forgiveness? First, it is not clear that these children would feel the same way about a culprit who proves himself or herself impervious to reform by good example. Second, it is not clear that turning the other cheek is a rational long-term strategy. Computer simulations of repeated prisoner's dilemma games indicate that under these conditions retaliation against a partner who defects from cooperation is the more rational strategy (Axelrod, 1984). Finally, it is not clear who has ever practiced, as distinct from preaching, endless forgiveness. On the basis of a number of ethnographic studies of village communities in Europe, Bailey (1971) observed that the very few individuals who did consistently turn the other cheek were universally regarded as foolish and naive by their fellows.

Now it is true that disapproval of the principle of direct retaliation by the victim is frequently voiced in adult society, and very much for the reasons Piaget's 10-year-old gave. But this disapproval does not ultimately appear to rest upon a rejection of retaliation itself. Rather it derives from a concern with the socially destructive repercussions of direct retaliation by victims. Many long-dead communities have left us with vivid echoes of their preoccupation with these anxieties. Icelandic sagas from the tenth century speak of the tragedy of endless revenge, of wounds kept green and grievances pursued generation after generation. In a later century, the Shakespearean dramas that stirred the public imagination were not tales of distributive justice but of revenge. In all of Shakespeare's great tragedies, what motivates the action is desire for vengeance. Today, the popular fiction of comic strips and Westerns demands that villains get their comeuppance and the hero his revenge as the only satisfactory conclusion. But the insight of the sagas and great drama is that there is no satisfactory conclusion; revenge breeds further revenge.

It is not hard to see how cycles of revenge develop—for the same reason that other kinds of debt are seldom settled in personal relationships—injuries are difficult to quantify. (And competition, like cooperation, has no end in personal relationships. The first blow may be regarded not just as an attack on one's status but announcement of an intention to compete; once competition is initiated, the restoration of equality ceases to be an option). Blows may be counted, but even in this case numerical reciprocation will not avoid disputes. How many children do you know who will agree about the relative force or malice of each blow. Hurt and shame make it difficult for victims to be objective about the injury done to them or the circumstances that motivated it. Given the scope for misunderstanding between people, we should perhaps be surprised that there is not more vengeance in everyday life.

Communities and cultures have evolved procedures for containing revenge not by supressing it but by providing a substitute. So, if children come to reject personal retaliation as a legitimate means of settling grievances, this is perhaps because they have come to share in culturally supported priorities for other means of delivering justice. In other words, the conclusion reached by Piaget's 10-year-old is unlikely to be one he would have arrived at unaided by his culture.

Procedural Justice and Structural Order

When people say they want justice, what they are usually appealing for is not an equal distribution of the spoils but punishment for someone who has offended them. Why appeal to others? Either, as already suggested, because the community disapproves or forbids direct retaliation or because one lacks the power to retaliate successfully oneself. Electra appealed to her brother to revenge her upon the uncle who had killed her father. Her modern-day counterpart would probably appeal to the courts. Courts provide formalized *procedures* for delivering justice, and these procedures in turn raise questions of fairness. For developmental psychology, the question concerns the childhood origins of commitment to these procedures as fair and appropriate. As yet, very little developmental research has been directly concerned with procedural justice (see Demetriou & Charitides, 1986; Fry & Corfield, 1983; Gold et al., 1984; Torney-Purta, 1983). However, Piaget (1932) can be regarded as having made an early attempt to study children's orientations to certain elementary forms of procedural justice.

Piaget introduced his work on children's moral judgment with the proposition that morality consists of a system of rules; the basic question concerns the individual's respect for rules. Rules in turn, or at least some rules, may be thought of as social devices for regulating conflicts, by providing solutions for recurrent problems. Piaget (1932) examined children's understanding of procedures for creating and revising rules by questioning them about a very simple case, that of the rules of their own games. The youngest children he questioned could not envisage such procedures; they imagined social rules to be brute facts of existence. But between 6 and 12 years, children came to recognize the functions of rules in preventing or resolving disagreements. More significantly, though, older children's respect for rules lay in the procedures by which they had been established. Piaget's older informants believed that the fairest way to create or alter rules is to allow each individual who is to be bound by them to have an equal say in the form they should take. Rules should be established by mutual agreement, by consensus or a majority vote. In other words, these children arrived at an attitude of respect for democratic procedure. This is not an aspect of Piaget's work that has received much attention subsequently, though a study by Solomon et al. (1972) produced comparable results. They found that among 7- to 13-year-olds, only the oldest expressed a preference for equality of representation in group decision making.

The problem yet again is whether these and other preferences are the spontaneous products of individual cognitive growth, the rational insights of an active intelligence, independently arrived at. Gold et al. (1984), studying certain other aspects of procedural justice, apparently believe they are.

> One is struck by the degree to which the pattern of children's moral judgments approximates what one would intuitively regard as a sensible, mature pattern of judgments about procedural justice. (p. 1758)

One should be wary of such intuitions.

Historically there have been many procedures for establishing justice and each at the time has surely seemed eminently sensible and mature to those who made use of them. Medieval knights thought it sensible to submit their competing claims to the judgment of God (Howard, 1976), which in practice meant that the one who succeeded in bludgeoning or hacking the other to death with axe, sword, or club had been adjudged by the deity to have had the more just claim. A little later, in the sixteenth and seventeenth centuries, the procedures for trying people accused of witchcraft—for example, pricking their bodies all over with a metal spike to discover whether the devil had touched them (his touch was supposed to leave a spot insensitive to pain)—were regarded as entirely reasonable and mature.

I am not about to argue that the procedures currently preferred in countries that formerly tried witches in this way, America, France, or Britain, for example, are not more reasonable. But arriving at the current procedures has been a long, laborious *historical* process (and nobody in the business supposes they are incapable of further improvement); they are not procedures that would have or did spontaneously occur to individuals, armed only with their intellects and unaided by several hundred years of accumulated collective wisdom. My point is that such institutions are cultural and collective inventions. Individuals may recognize the inherent logic and advantages of these inventions (and many may not). It may even be possible to identify stages in the development of such recognition (cf. Demetriou & Charitides, 1986). But the procedures are collective products, evolved on a historical time scale, not the inventions of individuals. What we regard as common sense today is more often an achievement of collective trial and error than individual logical deduction.

There is a quite direct connection between procedural justice and the structural order. The legal system in contemporary societies is typically a highly bureaucratized set of procedures in the sense defined by Weber (1947). That is, it consists of a rational organization of offices in which office holders, appointed by virtue of technical competence, have defined powers, responsibilities, and spheres of jurisdiction and are expected to administer the rules and execute the decisions that fall within their responsibilities in an impartial and disinterested fashion. As Weber foresaw, the same principles of social organization have come to underlie all political and economic organization in contemporary Western industrialized society. We are immersed in such impersonal and formal organizations; the structural or institutional order pervades every detail of our public lives. Two hundred years ago, such organization was far less commonplace.

Let us now pull some of this together and derive some further observations about justice and the structural order. First, although developmental research has dealt primarily with the informal procedures that parents might apply or that children might devise amongst themselves (Fry & Corfield, 1983; Gold et al., 1984; Piaget, 1932; Solomon et al., 1972), the structural order has become the model for many of the most significant forms of procedural justice in contemporary life. Second, a key feature of this kind of procedure and indeed of structural order generally is the relation of formal or, in Weber's terms, legal–rational authority it assumes between certain people; a person or persons are formally empowered to make specified classes of decisions and interpret specified sets of rules with respect to specified categories of others.

Roberts (1979) describes many of the less formal precursors to this arrangement, the use of mediators, arbitrators, umpires, and referees to help settle conflicts. Indeed, throughout human history, putting someone in charge and granting him or her authority over certain matters has been a common solution to the problem of maintaining community cohesion in the face of conflicts between community members. But, as Weber realized, formal authority has special features that distinguish it from, for example, the traditional authority of a village elder or chieftain or the charismatic authority of a prophet or a messiah. Among others, these features include a formal definition of powers, usually recorded in written form, and the requirement that authority be exercised impartially.

Third, therefore, a structural order entails standards for behavior that are quite different from those that would be applicable in the personal order. Fourth, the widespread conduct of human affairs in accordance with these standards is a relatively recent innovation in terms of the natural history of the species. Therefore, insofar as children accommodate to the peculiarities of this style of social organization, this must be regarded as a process of socialization and not simply of cognitive development. It is something that only happens because a child grows up in an industrialized, urbanized, centrally administered and literate society, all conditions favoring the proliferation of structural order.

What do we know about children's acquisition of orientations toward a structural order or formalized procedural justice? Do they recognize a difference between the structural and personal orders, and do they judge action that occurs within the framework of the former according to different standards? If so, what is the source of these insights and inclinations? We have begun to find answers to some of these questions in a preliminary study (e.g., Emler, Ohana, & Moscovici, 1987).

There are grounds for believing that an important contribution to children's learning about the structural order and its principles of operation is their experience of formal schooling. The school is likely to be the first formal organization most children encounter on an extended basis. It is therefore likely to be in this context that reactions specific to such an order will first be apparent. We found that even young children and certainly most 8- and 9-year-olds were applying distinctions that acknowledged the special requirements of formal order. These children are well aware, for example, that personal loyalties and preferences, acceptable at the level of the personal order, are not supposed to operate in an institutional context; individuals must be treated in terms of what their formal status formally entitles them to. Hence these children judge it unfair for teachers to discriminate on the basis of personal preferences. They also recognize that the relevant question in an institutional context is not *whether* rules can be modified, Piaget's 1932 question, but *who* has the authority to do so. Yet again, however, there is no universal consensus as to the proper limits of institution-specific obligations and constraints, suggesting that in different societies different priorities may emerge. We found, for example, that Scottish children believed it was reasonable to invoke an institutional rule to justify an action even though the rule itself was judged unfair, whereas French children rejected this justification for action.

Much research remains to be done on children's understanding of formal organization; our own work has only begun to scratch the surface. But understanding how such organization is supposed to work is not everything. The criminal justice system supposedly acts as a source of constraint upon members of society—it requires of them certain duties and renunciations. But in principle, it is also supposed to serve as a source of protection for their own rights and redress for their grievances. Though recognizing these principles, many young people appear to believe that the principles are subverted by the individuals charged with their execution. That is, the law is not in practice administered impartially or evenhandedly. In particular, many young people suspect that the system will not deal sympathetically with their own grievances or offer them any meaningful protection. For some reason, these beliefs are more prevalent among boys than girls (Emler & Reicher, 1987) and become more widespread with age. And these beliefs have predictable behavioral consequences. Black (1983) has suggested that many criminal acts have their origins in a desire to right perceived injustices. Crime is self-help justice. Black also notes that those most likely to find the formal system an imperfect substitute for direct retaliation are those with a low status in society. Our disenchanted adolescents were particularly inclined to suspect the formal system of partiality and bias against the poor and the disadvantaged, which brings us to the categorical order.

The Categorical Order

In common with the other forms of social ordering I have considered, there is little developmental research directly concerned with the impact of the categorical order on standards of justice. But there is some nondevelopmental research that indicates the kinds of question we should perhaps be considering.

Tajfel (1984) has pointed out that issues of social justice and injustice arise most acutely with respect to relations between social groups, and his own work provides some indications as to why this might be. For example, Tajfel and others (e.g., Tajfel et al., 1971) have provided powerful demonstrations of the impact of categorization and category membership on resource distribution. When recipients can be categorized into ingroup and outgroup members, the requirements of equality or equity are overwhelmed by a potent norm of ingroup favoritism. Many other theorists have had occasion to comment on the power of ingroup loyalty as a moral imperative; we reserve the greatest moral outrage for those who fail to demonstrate this loyalty (see Levine & Campbell, 1972). Moreover, the standards of fairness that people believe they should extend to fellow members of their community are not always regarded as binding in dealings with outsiders (Furer-Haimendorf, 1967). As yet, most of what we know about children's notions of ingroup loyalty and favoritism comes from studies of the development of racial attitudes and identifications (Milner, 1975).

However, it is important to recognize that intercategory relations vary along at least one important dimension. At one end are relations between politically and economically autonomous, sharply bounded groups, prototypically the nation-state. At the other are relations between individuals holding contrasting category memberships but belonging to the same political and economic system, such as relations between male and female. Toward this latter end are most of the cases in which issues of social justice arise. Within social systems, social categories seem above all to be associated with established and persisting inequalities, and the most significant division is that based on differences of political and economic power.

How do people react to gross differences in wealth and power? There are two kinds of answer to this, the theoretical and the empirical. Let us briefly consider each in turn. The position of Marxist social theory is that one's attitude to social inequalities will be conditioned by one's position in the socioeconomic structure. Those who benefit from the status quo will regard it as just, whereas those who belong to social categories disadvantaged by it will not.

Most other theories predict that everyone, whatever their own position in the system of inequalities, will regard them as legitimate. Such a prediction would be made from the Just World theory, which implies not that justice is at work in society producing deserved inequalities but that people need to believe this is the case. Equity

#3

theory implies on the contrary that a consensus about the legitimí
inequalities could rise from people perceiving matters objective
people's contributions differ, then their outcomes should differ. Therefore, if people believe that the world is a just place, or more modestly
that in their own society people generally get what they deserve, this
may be because they are right and not because they have confused the
operation of fate with the workings of justice (as the Just World theory
assumes).

Functionalist social theory assumes that social system survival
requires generalized consensus about the legitimacy of social arrangements and if these include inequalities of wealth, then this, too, should
be widely accepted as justified. In other words, belief in a just society
is a functional requirement of social systems rather than a psychologically required distortion or an objective deduction.

Cognitive–developmental theory is not quite so straightforward. If
a commitment to the logic of equity is taken to be the natural end point
of development (cf. Hook & Cook, 1979), then a consensual acceptance
of social inequalities might be expected. If, on the other hand,
naturally emerging concepts of justice place need above relative
contributions, then development should lead to rejection of the status
quo.

What does developmental research actually show? Connell (1977)
has reported that young children are more likely to criticize inequalities in wealth as unfair, whereas older children appear to regard
inequalities as justified, and commonly their justifications appeal to
considerations of equity (see Leahy, 1983). In other words, findings
appear consistent with the developmental literature on children's
allocation decisions (Hook & Cook, 1979). So are these children acting
like the scrutineers of equity theory, examining the inputs and outcomes of different individuals in society, estimating what they deserve, and then comparing this with the status quo and concluding that
the status quo does after all agree with what is just? This does not seem
likely, for several reasons. First, it is inappropriate to generalize from
research on allocation decisions to beliefs about social inequalities.
The former presents problems in which inputs and outcomes are
precise, simple, quantified, and known. In the latter case, none of these
will necessarily apply. But the former also presents *problems*. In the
latter case, the child's role is quite different. Indeed, it is arguable that
allocation problems place children in an unrealistic position because
they are seldom able or required to decide *independently* what others
should receive. Damon (1981) has ingeniously shown that when
children must agree jointly on a fair distribution of some reward, their
decisions differ from those they make independently. Decision making

about allocations is a power holder's role and, what is more, justice may not even be the prime issue for allocators (see Leventhal, 1976). With respect to wealth and social inequalities, children realistically have even less scope for decision making. They are confronted with established practices and entrenched positions and can do no more than offer a judgment on what is already being done. But in another important respect, this is not like problem solving in allocation tasks for there is no problem to solve.

Kohlberg once observed that if you wish to study an individual's moral reasoning, you must give him or her problems to reason about; these must in effect be unsolved cases, unfamiliar and unusual situations for which therefore no answer has already been worked out. But social inequality is not an unfamiliar case; it is a condition people have been living with for millennia. It would be surprising if explanations and justifications had not been thoroughly worked out and disseminated within any social system in which social inequalities were well established. Thus if one asks children about, for example, wealth and poverty, it is unlikely that they will be consulting various autonomously developed internal standards of justice or revealing a process of independent moral reasoning. It is more likely, surely, that their responses will reveal their knowledge of and commitment to those explanations and justifications of inequality, those social representations (cf. Moscovici, 1983) that circulate within the communities to which they belong.

There is no obvious decisive test of this claim, at least none that has occurred to me so far, but it does seem to provide a more plausible interpretation of some data we have collected on children's views about economic inequalities (Emler & Dickinson, 1985; Emler & Luce, 1985).

We examined children's perceptions of the connections between occupation and income. Comparing children in Scotland and America, we found that quite different kinds of justifications were offered for income inequalities. In Scotland, a common justification was to refer to the relative demands made by different kinds of work (job difficulty, amount of work done). No mention was made, as it was very frequently in America, of the higher qualifications and greater investment in education required for certain jobs. In each case, therefore, children made reference to differential inputs, as equity theory predicts, but the inputs selected were quite different. Conceivably the children in each country were identifying the inputs that do actually differentiate the job holders in their respective countries. But it is more likely, I would suggest, that in these two countries, inequalities are supported by different ideologies, and children have become more or less committed to the ideologies that prevail in their respective societies.

The degree of this commitment, however, does seem to be a function of the child's own position in the socioeconomic system. In both countries, middle- and upper-middle-class children, compared to working-class children, appeared to possess a more extensive and detailed justification for inequalities of income and to be more committed to it. Thus, for example, in both countries, the former were more likely to reject the idea of equalizing incomes across occupations. Interestingly, middle- and upper-middle-class children also appeared to have a more differentiated representation of income inequalities— they perceived greater inequalities than did the working-class children—and their knowledge of income differences appeared to a greater degree to be organized in terms of social class categories—they perceived a greater difference between middle- and working-class occupations. It seems that knowledge, like wealth, is unequally distributed in society.

This work supports conclusions derived from studies of adults' views of social inequalities (Mann, 1970). The latter also indicate that disadvantaged groups seldom have a coherent ideology that is critical of the status quo; they merely fail to share as fully in the dominant ideology that supports it.

Concluding Remarks

I hope by now to have convinced you that there is at least a prima facie case for cultural influences on children's notions of justice. In particular I believe the following two conclusions can be drawn.

First, society provides an ordered, nonrandom set of social arrangements—which can be thought of in terms of personal, structural, and categorical orders. Children must come to terms with these established arrangements and make some sense of them. They do not have the option of reconstructing society from first principles. Furthermore, the social arrangements into which they are born will not be universal; other children at other times and in other places will be confronted with different arrangements.

Second, this society will embody a stock of accumulated explanations and justifications for existing social arrangements, and of solutions for common problems, often in the form of rule systems and authority structures. Children will, to some degree and depending on the position they occupy in society, come to share in these explanations and justifications and prefer these solutions. This is not to say that conflict is alien to social systems or that established practices and beliefs are not subject to constant renegotiation and change, for to do so would be to forget their origins in human social interaction. But equally, it would be foolish to ignore the inertia of convention or to imagine that the child is free to ignore it.

Where does this leave the cognitive–developmental approach? It is undoubtedly true that children's intellectual resources expand as they grow older, and their capacities for analyzing and interpreting the world become more complex and sophisticated as a result. It is likely therefore that older children will be better able to penetrate the ideological structures and understand the principles underpinning the social arrangements with which their culture presents them. But social worlds come prestructured and preinterpreted so far as each new generation is concerned.

Given another chapter, I would want to go much further and ask about the origins of children's cognitive capacities. In such a chapter, I would argue that children's cognitive capacities are structured by their societies as much as by any inherent developmental tendency of the organism. To this end, I would point first of all to the wide differences across cultures in rates of cognitive development and levels finally achieved. I would recall Piaget's observation that the development of thought depends on confrontation with the thought of others. In other words, the principal source of the problems the child has to resolve is not the material environment but the need to find a basis for agreement with others. This insight has subsequently been ably illustrated by Doise and Mugny (1984) and Perret-Clermont (1980), whereas Damon (1981) has shown that the requirement of agreeing with others can also be an important stimulus to the development of justice concepts.

But finally I would want to ask whether a capacity for independent problem solving, based on consultation of internal standards, is what the world demands of the child. A study by Walton (1985) casts serious doubt on this view. Her observations of the problems children actually face in their relations with others show these are most commonly resolved through negotiation. In matters of justice as in others, the human response is a collective, not a solitary, search for answers.

Acknowledgments. Research referred to in this chapter was supported by ESRC grants HG11/24/11 and IO1230013 to the author and CNRS grant No. 95 5218 to Professor S. Moscovici.

References

Axelrod, R. (1984). *The evolution of cooperation.* New York: Basic Books.

Bailey, R. (1971). *Gifts and poison: The politics of reputation.* Oxford: Blackwell.

Benedict, R. (1935). *Patterns of culture.* Boston: Houghton Mifflin.

Berndt, T. (1977). The effect of reciprocity norms on moral judgement and causal attribution. *Child development, 48,* 1322–1330.

Black, D. (1983). Crime as social control. *American Sociological Review, 48,* 34–45.

Boissevain, J. (1984). *Friends of friends: Networks, manipulators and coalitions.* Oxford: Blackwell.

Box, S. (1983). *Power, crime and mystification.* London: Tavistock.

Brown, R. (1986). *Social psychology: The second edition.* New York: Free Press.

Brown, R., & Herrnstein, R. (1975). *Psychology.* Boston: Little, Brown.

Connell, R. W. (1977). *Ruling class, ruling culture.* Melbourne: Cambridge University Press.

Damon, W. (1977). *The social world of the child.* San Francisco: Jossey Bass.

Damon, W. (1981). The development of justice and self-interest during childhood. In M. Lerner & S. Lerner (Eds.), *The justice motive in social behavior* (pp. 57–72). New York: Plenum Press.

Demetriou, A., & Charitides, L. (1986). The adolescent's construction of procedural justice as a function of age, formal thought and sex. *International Journal of Psychology, 21,* 333–353.

Deutsch, M. (1985). *Distributive justice: A social psychological perspective.* New Haven: Yale University Press.

Dodge, K., & Frame, C. L. (1982). Social and cognitive biases and deficits in aggressive boys. *Child Development, 53,* 620–635.

Doise, W. (1980). Levels of explanation in the European Journal of Social Psychology. *European Journal of Social Psychology, 10,* 213–231.

Doise, W., & Mugny, G. (1984). *The social development of the intellect.* Oxford: Pergamon.

Durkin, D. (1961). The specificity of children's moral judgements. *Journal of Genetic Psychology, 98,* 3–14.

Emler, N., & Dickinson, J. (1985). Children's representations of economic inequalities. The effects of social class. *British Journal of Developmental Psychology, 3,* 191–198.

Emler, N., & Fisher, S. (1981, September). *Gossip and the nature of the social environment.* Paper presented at the Annual Conference of the British Psychological Society, Social Psychology Section, Oxford.

Emler, N., & Hogan, R. (1981). Developing attitudes to law and justice. In S. S. Brehm, S. M. Kassin, & F. X. Gibbons (Eds.), *Developmental social psychology* (pp. 298–314). New York: Oxford 1981.

Emler, N., & Luce, T. (1985). *Social class background and perception of occupation-related income differences in middle childhood.* Unpublished, University of Dundee.

Emler, N., & Reicher, S. (1987). Orientations to institutional authority in adolescence. *Journal of Moral Education, 16,* 108–116.

Emler, N., Ohana, J., & Moscovici, S. (1987). Children's beliefs about institution roles: A cross-national study of representations of the teacher's role. *British Journal of Educational Psychology, 57,* 26–37.

Enright, R., Enright, W., & Lapsley, D. (1981). Distributive justice development and social class: A replication study. *Developmental Psychology, 17,* 826–832.

Enright, R., Enright, W., Manheim, L., & Harris, B. E. (1980). Distributive justice development and social class. *Developmental Psychology, 16,* 555–563.

Enright, R., Franklin, C., & Manheim, L. (1980). Children's distributive justice reasoning: A standardised and objective scale. *Developmental Psychology, 16,* 193–203.

Enright, R., et al. (1984). Distributive justice development: Cross-cultural, contextual and longitudinal evaluations. *Child Development, 55,* 1737–1751.

Felson, R. (1978). Aggression as impression management. *Social Psychology, 41,* 205–213.

Flavell, J. (1972). An analysis of cognitive developmental sequences. *Genetic Psychology Monographs, 86,* 279–350.

Flavell, J., & Ross, L. (1981). *Social cognitive development: Frontiers and possible futures.* Cambridge: Cambridge University Press.

Fry, P. S., & Corfield, V. K. (1983). Children's judgements of authority figures with respect to outcome and procedural fairness. *Journal of Genetic Psychology, 143,* 241–250.

Furer-Haimendorf, C. von. (1967). *Morals and merit: A study of values and social controls in South Asian societies.* London: Weidenfeld & Nicholson.

Gibbs, J. (1985). Moral development "versus" socialization: A critique. *American Psychologist, 40,* 1071–1080.

Gold, L. J., Darley, J. M., Hilton, J. L., & Zanna, M. P. (1984). Children's perceptions of procedural justice. *Child Development, 55,* 1752–1759.

Gouldner, A., (1960). The norm of reciprocity: A preliminary statement. *American Sociological Review, 25,* 161–178.

Hamilton, V. L., & Sanders, J. (1983). Universals in judging wrongdoings: Japanese and Americans compared. *American Sociological Review, 48,* 199–211.

Harris, M. (1971). *Culture, man and nature: An introduction to general anthropology.* New York. Crowell.

Hogan, R. (1983). A socioanalytic theory of personality. In M. Page (Ed.), *Nebraska Symposium on Motivation 1982.* (pp. 55–89) Lincoln: University of Nebraska Press.

Hogan, R., & Emler, N. (1981). Retributive justice. In M. Lerner & S. Lerner (Eds.), *The justice motive in social behavior.* (pp. 125–143) New York: Plenum Press.

Holmes, R. (1981). The exchange process in close relationships: Microbehavior and macromotives. In M. Lerner & S. Lerner (Eds.), *The justice motive in social behavior* (pp. 261–284). New York: Plenum Press.

Hook, J., & Cook, T. (1979). Equity theory and the cognitive ability of children. *Psychological Bulletin, 86,* 429–445.

Howard, M. (1976). *War in European history.* Oxford: Oxford University Press.

Inhelder, B., & Piaget, J. (1958). *The growth of logical thinking from childhood to adolescence.* New York: Basic Books.

Karniol, R., & Miller, D. T. (1981). Morality and the development of conceptions of justice. In M. Lerner & S. Lerner (Eds.), *The justice motive in social behavior* (pp. 31–53) New York: Plenum Press.

Kohlberg, L. (1976). Moral stages and moralization: The cognitive development approach. In T. Lickona (Ed.), *Moral development and behavior: Theory, research and social issues* (pp. 31–53). New York: Holt, Rinehart & Winston.

Leahy, R. (1983). Development of the conception of economic inequality: II. Explanations, justifications, and concepts of social mobility and change. *Developmental Psychology, 19,* 111–125.

Lerner, M. (1974). The justice motive: "Equity" and "parity" among children. *Journal of Personality and Social Psychology, 29,* 539–

Lerner, M. (1977). The justice motive in social behaviour: Some hypotheses as to its origins and forms. *Journal of Personality, 45,* 1–52.

Lerner, M., & Simmons, C. (1966). The observer's reaction to the "innocent victim": Compassion or rejection? *Journal of Personality and Social Psychology, 4,* 203–210.

Leventhal, G. (1976). The distribution of rewards and resources in groups and organizations. In L. Berkowitz & E. Walster (Eds.), *Advances in experimental social psychology* (vol. 9). New York: Academic Press.

Levine, R. A., & Campbell, D. T. (1972). *Ethnocentrism: Theories of conflict, ethnic attitudes and group behavior.* New York: Wiley.

Levitt, M. J., Weber, R. A., Clark, M. C., & McDonnell, P. (1985). Reciprocity of exchange in toddler sharing behavior. *Developmental Psychology, 21,* 122–123.

Lickona, T. (1969). Piaget misunderstood: A critique of the criticisms of his theory of moral development. *Merrill-Palmer Quarterly, 16,* 337–350.

Long, G., & Lerner, M. (1974). Deserving, the "Personal contract" and altruistic behaviour by children. *Journal of Personality and Social Psychology, 29,* 551–556.

Mann, L., Radford, M., & Kanagawa, C. (1985). Cross-cultural differences in children's use of decision rules: A comparison between Japan and Australia. *Journal of Personality and Social Psychology, 49,* 1557–1564.

Mann, M. (1970). The social cohesion of liberal democracy. *American Sociological Review, 35,* 423–439.

Mars, G. (1982). *Cheats at work. An anthropology of work-place crime.* London: Allen & Unwen.

Mikula, G. (1980). On the role of justice in allocation decisions. In G. Mikula (Ed.) *Justice and social interaction.* New York: Springer.

Mikula, G. (1984). Justice and fairness in interpersonal relations: Thoughts and suggestions. In H. Tajfel (Ed.), *The social dimension* (Vol. 1; pp. 206–221). Cambridge: Cambridge University Press.

Milner, D. (1975). *Children and race.* Harmondsworth: Penguin.

Mitchell, J. C. (1969). *Social networks in urban situations.* Manchester: Manchester University Press.

Moscovici, S. (1983). The phenomenon of social representations. In R. Farr & S. Moscovici (Eds.), *Social representations* (pp. 3–69). Cambridge: Cambridge University Press.

Nisan, M. (1984). Distributive justice and social norms. *Child Development, 55,* 1020–1029.

Perret-Clermont, A-N. (1980). *Social interaction and cognitive development in children.* London: Academic Press.

Piaget, J. (1932). *The moral judgement of the child.* London: Routledge & Kegan Paul.

Roberts, S. (1979). *Order and dispute: an introduction to legal anthropology.* Harmondsworth: Penguin.

Shantz, D. W., & Voydanoff, D. A. (1973). Situational effects on retaliatory aggression at three age levels. *Child Development, 44,* 149–153.

Simmons, C. (1981). Theoretical issues in the development of social justice. In M. Lerner & S. Lerner (Eds.), *The justice motive in social behavior* (pp. 41–55). New York: Plenum Press.

Snarey, J. (1985). The cross-cultural universality of socio-moral development: A critical review of Kohlbergian research. *Psychological Bulletin, 97,* 202–232.

Solomon, D., Ali, F-A., Kfir, D., Houlihan, K. A., & Yaeger, J. (1972). The development of democratic values and behaviour among Mexican-American children. *Child Development, 43,* 625–638.

Staub, E., & Sherk, L. (1970). Need for approval, children's sharing bahaviour, and reciprocity in sharing. *Child Development, 41,* 243–252.

Tajfel, H. (1984). Intergroup relations, social myths and social justice in social psychology. In H. Tajfel (Ed.), *The social dimension* (Vol. 2; pp. 679–715). Cambridge: Cambridge University Press.

Tajfel, H., Billig, M., Bundy, R. P., & Flament, C. (1971). Social categorization and intergroup behaviour. *European Journal of Social Psychology, 1,* 149–178.

Torney-Purta, J. (1983). The development of views about the role of social institutions in redressing inequality and promoting human rights. In R. Leahy (Ed.), *The child's construction of social inequality* (pp. 287–310). New York: Academic Press.

Turiel, E. (1983). *The development of social knowledge.* Cambridge: Cambridge University Press.

Walton, M. (1985). Negotiation of responsibility: Judgements of blameworthiness in a natural setting. *Developmental Psychology, 21,* 725–736.

Weber, M. (1947). *The theory of social and economic organizations.* (A. M. Henderson & T. Parsons Eds. and trans). New York: Free Press.

6

Distributive Justice in Children
Social Psychological and Developmental Psychological Perspectives

Jan ter Laak and Liesbeth Aleva

Introduction

Distributive justice refers to the fairness of distributing or allocating resources to individuals and groups. Resources may be material, like money, food, and goods, or immaterial, like status, attention, and punishment. Empirical study of distributive justice originated in social psychology. This discipline offers two essential elements: a set of theoretical statements about distributive justice and an experimental paradigm to study reactions to (unfair) allocation and allocation behavior itself. This paradigm was mainly used to determine if and when children behaved like adults when allocating resources.

In this chapter, we briefly mention the classical and recent theoretical statements on distributive justice. Next, we review empirical studies on allocation behavior of children. We interpret the results of these studies developmentally. Then we review some developmental theoretical statements about allocation and distributive justice and we summarize characteristics and results of our own research. Our

Jan ter Laak • Department of Child Studies, University of Utrecht, 3508 TC Utrecht, The Netherlands   Liesbeth Aleva • Department of Developmental Psychology, University of Leiden, 2333 AK Leiden, The Netherlands.

conclusion is that a developmental perspective enriches the experimental social psychological analyses of allocation behavior and distributive justice rules.

Classical and Recent Theoretical Statements on Distributive Justice

Homans (1961) formulated the initial theoretical statement on distributive justice. He regarded the proportional relationship between cost or investment and reward or profit as fundamental. This is the equity or proportionality principle, which states that each person's share is proportional to his or her contribution or cost. According to Homans, people develop this principle gradually through observation of the environment and experiences in exchange situations, ultimately resulting in normative expectations. Blau (1964) also applied the equity rule but added preexisting social norms as bases for the rule. Adams (1965) agreed with Homans and Blau but emphasized causes and consequences of lack of equity for individuals.

Adams' statements were based on employer–employee relationships and in fact most research was conducted in this field including reactions to overpayment and underpayment as well as allocation behavior of employers in varying circumstances.

These three classical statements were developed in the context of social exchange approaches toward behavior. The equity rule of justice dominated. People acquire this principle by experiencing direct social exchanges, thus creating expectations of (un) fair exchanges. Homans and Adams emphasized individual expectations. Blau also mentioned social norms.

Other theoretical statements on distributive justice comprehend extensions and comments on the equity rule. Walster, Berscheid, and Walster (1973), for example, extended the "equity theory" to other domains. It was also applied in exploitative relationships between harmdoers and victims and in helping situations and intimate relationships. They also distinguished "actual" and "psychological" equity. The major purpose of their work was to predict when individuals feel themselves unjustly treated and how they will react to such feelings. Lerner (1975) developed the concept of *deservingness*, which related a person to his or her outcomes. Certain violations of the equity rule could be explained with the statement: "These people get what they deserve." Like others, he criticized the monopoly of the equity rule as the single justice rule. He added several other rules that are appropriate in different situations. We will confine ourselves to describing rules on distributive justice predominant in justice literature. Beside the rule of equity or proportionality, equality (i.e., all persons should be rewarded equally) and need (i.e. resources are allocated according to needs) are distinguished. Leventhal (1976) also distinguished these three rules. In his research, attention was given to active allocation of rewards in different circumstances not merely to reactions of employees on unfair allocation in mainly industrial settings.

Other theoretical statements do not emphasize the acquisition of rules, probably assuming that justice principles are acquired just like any other set of norms and values. An exception to the idea that acquisition of the concept of justice depends on socialization agents only is Lerner's (1975, 1981) suggestion that the concept of justice originates in the interaction of developing cognitive structures and experiences in childhood. But little research has been undertaken to investigate this hypothesis.

Why do people care for justice? According to some theorists, pursuit of justice is an instrument to reach goals like economic productivity, social order, peace, and rewards for fair allocators. Other theorists also indicate the fact that people may stick to justice principles because they are prescribed by social norms and customs. In Kohlberg's (1958) developmental theory the previously mentioned motives are developmental levels. The highest level is adherence to ethical principles, that is, justice for the sake of justice.

Allocation by Children

Working with children, application of the allocation paradigm was easy. Sometimes developmental hypotheses were of interest. For example, at what age do children use the equity rule? Developmental questions concerning the genesis of rules or processes of acquiring justice principles were seldom asked. Most of the empirical research dealt with situational variables influencing allocation by children. To a lesser extent, individual and cultural differences were investigated.

The most frequently investigated variable in allocation behavior of children is achievement. Four-year-olds, for example, seemed to use the equity principle if they were explicitly asked to distribute candy in proportion to achievement (Nelson & Dweck, 1977). Without explicit instruction, they were inclined to use the equality principle. Six-year-olds, however, used the equity principle even without explicit instructions to give everyone according to achievement (Lerner, 1974). Four-year-olds were perceptive of the needs of recipients as well. Apparently needy recipients were rewarded more than others (Anderson & Butzin, 1978; Gerling & Wender, 1982). Seven-year-olds were influenced by the status of recipients, that is, physical size and age. Taller and older recipients were rewarded better than smaller and younger children. This factor did not influence the allocations of 9-year-olds (Graziano, 1978).

Another important factor is the perceived value of rewards: 9- and 10-year-olds were made to believe that they received more than they deserved. In the next allocation, they were inclined to allocate a greater part of their rewards to "orphans" than children who believed that they got exactly what they deserved (Long & Lerner, 1974; Miller & Smith, 1977).

Furthermore, the kind of instruction received was a significant factor in the allocation. The instruction to allocate in such a way that "everyone is satisfied" made the use of the equality principle probable in 4- and 5-year-old children. The instruction to give to everyone, according to achievement, however, resulted in a more frequent use of the equity principle (Gerling & Wender, 1982; Nelson & Dweck, 1977). Variations in social relations between recipients were sometimes related to the allocation of rewards. Allocators relinquished less to friends than to nonfriends, if they thought they were entitled to get the rewards themselves. Moreover, friends asked for fewer rewards if they thought that the allocator had a right to the rewards (Staub & Noerenberg, 1981). The instruction to cooperate in a team sometimes yielded a more equal distribution than competitive or individualistic instruction in 6- to 12-year-olds (Barnett & Andrews, 1977; Lerner, 1974). This result, however, was not replicated in studies of Tompkins and Olejnik (1978) and Nisan (1984). Four- to 6-year-old allocators tended to favor friends above strangers (Tolan & Kranz, 1981). Other children's previous allocations also influenced allocation: 10- to 12-year-olds allocated rewards more equally if they were given an equal amount on an earlier occasion but not if they were rewarded according to achievement (Barnett, Howard, & Andrews, 1978). When 14- and 15-year-old subjects were rewarded according to chance, they allocated equally afterwards. If however, the allocation, was intentionally unequal, they also rewarded unequally. (Garrett & Libby, 1973). Seven-year-olds were either not affected by previously received rewards or imitated earlier allocation (Dreman, 1976).

The study of individual differences is almost confined completely to gender differences. The results are contradictory. If differences between girls and boys were found, they occurred mainly in allocation tasks where emphasis was laid on competition between participants (e.g., Barnett & Andrews, 1977; Barnett, Howard, & Andrews, 1978; Graziano, Musser, Rosen, & Shaffer, 1982; Leventhal, Popp, & Sawyer,

1973). In general, girls more often than boys divided equally and paid less attention to the achievements of participants.

Cultural differences were mostly absent (Furby, 1979; Graziano Musser, Rosen, & Shaffer, 1982). In a study by Nisan (1984), however, it was found that Kibbutz children 6 to 12 years old preferred equal allocation, whereas children from cities preferred "equity" allocation. Children of both groups regarded effort as the relevant factor. Kibbutz children assumed that the efforts of all participants were equal. Children from cities, however, deduced the amount of effort from actual achievement.

Age Differences and Developmental Interpretations

Most of the previously mentioned studies did not intend to demonstrate age differences. These differences, however, were apparent sometimes. The handling of differences was twofold. Some authors, emphasizing the very young age at which children used allocation rules, consequently paid little attention to age differences. Others interpreted age differences as preferences, or consequences of a general cognitive development.

Nelson & Dweck (1977) were impressed by the young age at which children used the equity rule: 4 years and older. It was also apparent that 6-year-olds used the rule more easily, that is, without explicit reference to the act of dividing proportionally. In Anderson and Butzin's (1978) view, the capacity of 4-year-olds to integrate information from 2 two-valued dimensions was salient and this was a serious argument against the Piagetian claim that only children of about 7 would be able to decenter and consider two dimensions at a time. The authors also admitted that integration was better when children were older.

Keil and McClintock (1983) wondered whether there was a relation between age and preference for certain allocation rules. In a metastudy, they distinguished three rules: self-interest, equality, and proportionality or equity. The authors indicated that certain task conditions made certain principles more prominent. Equality was prominent when achievement was equal and the relation between participants was cooperative. Equity suited well when achievement was unequal and the participants were competitive. Equality and equity were applied both when achievement was unequal and the relation between participants was cooperative. The authors took the salience of the principles into account. For example, a clear indication for self-interest was the situation in which the equity or equality principle was prominent and the allocator kept most of the rewards to himself, even if he contributed the same or less than the other recipient. Children of 4 to 8 years old appeared to prefer self-interest (Hook, 1978; Lane & Coon, 1972; Mikula, 1972). Keil and McClintock (1983) also described a more sophisticated behavior in pursuit of self without violating the allocation principles. This behavior occurs when people apply equity rules for high achievement of their own. This allocation behavior was found in 5-to 9-year-olds (e.g., Streater & Chertkoff, 1976; Leventhal & Anderson, 1970 [boys]; Lerner, 1974; Nelson & Dweck 1977; Ter Laak & Weber, 1985 . Preference for equality was found in 5-to-12 year olds (e.g. Gerling & Wender,1982; Lerner, 1974 [boys]; Leventhal & Anderson, 1970 [girls]; Mikula, 1972; Nisan, 1984; Ter Laak & Weber, 1985; Streaker & Chertkoff, 1976). Children of 11 years and older seem to prefer the equity rule (Mikula, 1972; Nisan, 1984). However, in some studies, 5-year-olds seemed to prefer an equitable distribution (Lerner, 1974; Nisan, 1984). Self-interest decreased between 7 and 13 years (Keil & McClintock, 1983). Most children in this age group preferred equal allocation. For example, in 9- and 10-year-olds, 60% of all allocations were equal. Preference for proportionality was found mostly in 12- to 14-year-olds.

In their review, Keil and McClintock concluded that a relation between age and preferences exists. It was clear that almost all children were able to use all three rules. Which rule was applied depended on the situation. Moreover, the children showed preferences related to age. A straightforward developmental interpretation of the application of the proportionality principle by children of different ages was formulated by Hook and Cook (1979). Their review study investigated at what age exactly the proportionality rule was applied. Although they found, for children younger than 13, a relation between achievement and the amount allocated, the subjects did not allocate exactly proportionally. For example, in Lerner's (1974) study, participants contributed 4 and 2 units respectively. The 11-year-olds, however, allocated 3.55 and 2.45 units, respectively. Studies by Hook (1978) and by Tompkins and Olejnik (1978) confirmed the relation between cognitive–numerical development and the correct application of the proportionality rule. Hook and Cook eventually distinguished three stages in allocation behavior. These stages ran parallel to Piagetian stages of cognitive development. The first one is self-interest or equality (children younger than 6 years old). Only one dimension, the amount of goods to be allocated, is involved in the allocation. The second one is ordinal equity (children between 6 and 13 years old). Two dimensions are involved, both the amount of goods and achievement of recipients, but the values on the dimensions cannot be computed exactly. The third one is equity (from 13 years old). Everyone is rewarded proportionally to achievement.

Montada (1980) made some critical remarks about this kind of developmental interpretation of justice rules. In his opinion, development is about changing structures and not about content, like preferences, for example. Concerning the integration of 2 two-valued dimensions (Anderson & Butzin, 1978), the author wondered whether the integration was really about justice rules. Although he did not mention it, the same can be said of cognitive–numerical development. We suggest considering both the ability to decenter and the cognitive–numerical ability as necessary but not as sufficient prerequisites for understanding and correct application of the equity principle.

Developmental Theoretical Statements about Distributive Justice

In his annual review chapter in 1981, Masters remarked that developmental psychology concerns every aspect of psychology. One only had to add: "The development of . . .". This may be true, but it neglects the developmental tradition in psychology.

Generally, development refers to partly internal changes in the individual, as opposed to behaviorism. It also contains irreversible changes and involves the acquisition of more adequate control structures. The changes are directional over time. Fischer and Silvern (1985) tried to define empirical criteria for the existence of developmental change. They mentioned structural change, relations of performance to age, qualitative change, discontinuous change, and the fact that what can be learned is limited by the developmental level of the individual.

The development of distributive justice and allocation behavior was also studied within this tradition. In a sense it is possible, as Montada (1980) did, to consider Piaget's (1932) distinction between heteronomous and autonomous morality as an aspect of the development of justice rules. Likewise, it is possible to consider Kohlberg's (1958) famous stages of moral development as linked to distributive justice and allocation behavior. In this section, however, we prefer to confine discussion of the development of distributive justice rules to studies that refer more directly to the development of allocation behavior and distributive justice.

Moessinger (1975) studied the structural development of insight in sharing and property by 4- to 15-year-old children. Two subjects were asked to imagine themselves owners of a piece of land with two and five trees respectively and to divide another three trees among them.

The author used the Piagetian clinical interview in order to assess the underlying thought structures. Moessinger found three structurally different stages in the 4-to 15-year-old subjects: Subjects up to 6 to 7 years proceeded by alternating give-and-take actions. They paid attention neither to the already existing differences in possession (two and five trees) nor to the other three trees that had to be divided. Between 7 and 12 years, the subjects predominantly divided equally, that is, eventually both got the same amount. Answers to the interview questions pointed to the fact that initial possessions, two or five trees, and the amount to be shared, three trees, were treated as if they were of the same kind. From 12 years on, the initial possessions and the set to be shared were considered as different types of property.

Damon (1977, 1981) was interested in the organizing principles of the social world of children. One aspect was the concept of distributive justice. He confronted children between 4 and 12 years with hypothetical and real situations in which rewards earned by small groups had to be divided among the members. For example a small group of children made drawings, the members each making a different number. The drawings were sold. How should the earned money be divided between group members?

On the basis of interviews, Damon distinguished six developmental levels. First, children confused their own desires or wishes with justice. Second, self-interested wishes were justified by irrelevant external features of the recipients. For example, "she got most because she runs fast." Third, the equality rule was used as a justification for the allocation. The reason was that unequal allocation might result in quarrels, screaming, and conflicts. Fourth, the allocation was justified by referring to relevant features of recipients. For example, "he is very smart, he is best in sports." Fifth, children acknowledged that more and different justifications at one time were possible. They tried to make a quantitative compromise. Sixth, children were able to coordinate considerations of equality, reciprocity, and merit of the recipients. They deliberated extensively and were determined about their decisions.

Damon investigated the relation between justifications in hypothetical situations and in real allocation behavior. In real situations, children's justifications and allocations lagged one or two levels. Simons and Klaassen (1979) confirmed this relation in their study. Enright, Franklin, and Manheim (1980) did a good job in developing a standardized instrument instead of Damon's laborious interview. The developmental–theoretical statements supposed structurally different levels, which were assessed with the help of justifications and allocation behavior. The sequence of the levels is determined by assessing dimensions, values on dimensions and the coordination of two or more dimensions and their respective values.

Some Characteristics and Results of Our Research

It is clear that social psychological and developmental perspectives do not coincide or cooperate. Graziano (1984) called them two "paradigms" in the sense of Kuhn. By this, he meant that the perspectives could not be reduced to each other and were incommensurable. It is also clear that most research is done from the social psychological perspective.

In our research, we tried to emphasize the developmental aspect while using the experimental social psychological paradigm. This means that age differences were developmentally interpreted. Theoretical statements like the aforementioned can be helpful, for they can be extended by the information integration approach applied with children of different ages (Anderson & Butzin, 1977), the information-processing analysis (Knight, Dubro, & Chao 1985), and general cognitive levels (Case, 1985). The age groups were not chosen to discover at which age children use principles or to generalize over ages. On the contrary, they were chosen to discover developmental trends.

The experimental tasks were borrowed from social psychology. There were additions, however. Subjects were asked to explain their allocation to make sure that they behave "justly" in their own opinion and to get insight into their motives. The selection of elements of information and (non)integration was left to the subjects. Therefore, our subjects were not asked to repeat all elements of the allocation tasks, unlike what occurs in much social psychological research with children. The hypothesis was that, by making them repeat the elements that were not salient in the first place, these elements would be made salient artificially. Instead, all elements were presented in pictures that accompanied the allocation tasks. Also a choice concerning content is made. Much attention will be paid to the influence of (the understanding of) social relations between participants on allocation behavior and the use of distributive justice principles.

The Integration of Achievement, Need and Status in 8-, 10-, and 12-Year-Old Children*

In this study, we investigated whether and how 8-, 10-, and 12-year-olds integrated 2 two-valued dimensions in an allocation situation. The pairs of dimensions were achievement and need, achievement and status, and need and status. Integration of information refers to the weighting of different factors.

---

*The three complete studies are published in Dutch. Summaries are available on request.

Piaget suggested that children up to 7 or 8 years centered only on one dimension in a two-dimensional situation like the conservation tasks. Anderson and Butzin (1978), on the contrary, found that even 4-year-old children were able to absorb four pieces of information, that is, two values on two dimensions.

Integration of different pieces of information that point in the same direction will result in a strong response. For example, if recipient A's achievement and needs are higher than recipient B's, A will receive more rewards compared to the situation of equal achievement or equal need. If the values on the dimensions foster a contradictory allocation, a compromise will be reached (Leventhal, 1976). The factor of the two that got more weight can be deduced from the number of rewards. For example, if achievement got more weight than need, then the rewards are divided more unequally; if achievement is unequal and need is equal, than achievement is equal and need is unequal.

With the help of hypothetical stories, two values at a time (high, low) were varied on two dimensions (achievement and need, need and status, and achievement and status). The subjects were asked to divide 16 dimes between the two main characters of the stories. Achievement was varied by means of the number of tasks performed. Need was varied by the amount of wanted but lacked goods or money. Status was varied by differences in age (4 years) and body length (with the help of drawings).

The results showed a significant interaction effect of age and the variations on achievement and need. When achievement and need of the recipient were both high, 12-year-olds allocated more to this recipient than 10- and 8-year-olds. Moreover, when achievement was high and need low, 12- and 10-year-olds allocated more than the 8-year-olds. From the rank of the amounts of rewards, it seemed probable that the 12- and 10-year-old subjects took in the information on achievement and need into account. For example, the difference in allocated dimes between story characters marked by high achievement/high need and low achievement/low need was much bigger than that between story characters marked by high achievement/low need and low achievement/high need. The last situation more often caused equal allocations. Moreover, it appeared that 12-year-olds put more weight on the achievement dimension than on the need dimension. In the situation of high achievement/equal need (equal = a high or low value for both story characters), the recipient got higher rewards than in the situation of equal achievement/high need. Ten-year-olds, on the contrary, seemed to weight achievement and need equally. Rewards allocated in the situations of high achievement/equal need and equal achievement/high need were almost the same.

The allocation of 8-year-old subjects differed from those of older children. They hardly made any difference between situations of high achievement/high need, high achievement/equal need, and low achievement/high need. It seems plausible that the 8-year-olds, unlike the 12- and 10-year-olds, did not or did not consistently take in the information on both the achievement and need dimensions. It seems possible that 8-year-olds based their allocation on one dimension only. If dimensions were the same for recipients (high achievement/equal need or equal achievement/ high need), subjects based their allocation on the unequal dimension. In situations of uneven information (high achievement/low need), allocation was alternately based on achievement or need. It was striking that a high achievement/equal need recipient got less than an equal achievement/high need recipient. Probably, they ascribed in this allocation situation more weight to the need dimension than to the achievement dimension.

Combination of values on the dimensions need and status hardly produced any age differences. Subjects of all ages took in the information on need and status.

We concluded that 12- and 10-year-old subjects integrated the values on the dimensions. This was not consistent in 8-year-olds. Moreover, the kind of dimension did matter. Eight-year-olds, for example, integrated better on the need and status and on the achievement and status dimensions than on the achievement and need dimension.

Finally, the explanations and justifications of the children were analyzed. As age increased, the number of arguments for achievement, status, achievement and status, and achievement and need also increased. In contrast, the number of arguments for need and equality decreased when age increased. Explanations of 12-year-olds held significantly more achievement and status arguments than those of 10-and 8-year-olds. They also more often used two appropriately combined arguments. Subjects of 8 and 10 years old more often mentioned need as an argument than 12-year-olds.

We concluded that, in this embedded situation of 2 two-valued dimensions, the Piagetian claim that young subjects are not consistent in combining these dimensions may be supported. Moreover, it was apparent that the kind of dimension is not neutral.

The Integration of Sociometric Position, Need, and Status in 7-, 9-, and 10-Year-Old Children

Need and status were operationalized and varied in the same way as in the previously mentioned study. The sociometric position was varied in two values. A high position was for a boy or girl who was liked very well, with whom everyone wanted to play, and who seldom quarreled with other children. A low position was the opposite.

The results showed no interaction effects of age and need/status and sociometric position/need dimensions. There was, however, an age effect for the sociometric position/status dimension. The sociometric position was weighted more by the 7-year-olds than by the 9- and 11-year-olds. In this study, the children integrated values and dimensions better than in the previously mentioned study. In the first study, however, lack of integration was predominantly found in the combination of achievement and need.

Combination of the results of the two studies reinforced the idea that integration is not free of content and context. In some domains or contexts, young children probably integrate information more spontaneously than in other domains and contexts.

The Effect of Previous Allocation by Others on the Allocation of 7-, 9-, and 11-Year-Old Children

Allocations are mainly done by people who know each other. Their previous behavior and relations probably influence their allocation behavior. The purpose of this study was to investigate the effect of previous allocation on the choice of one of four allocation rules. Subjects of 7, 9 and 11 years of age allocated rewards to another hypothetical person, who had previously allocated rewards. These allocations were either altruistic, equal, or individualistic (self-interest). In their allocation, subjects had to allocate in one of four alternative ways: altruistic, equal, individualistic, and competitive. In the last one, the benefits of the other were minimalized even at the cost of the subject's own benefits. Each subject had to make a choice in six hypothetical situations.

The number of equal allocations increased with increasing age. The number of individualistic choices, however, decreased with increasing age. Older children were more inclined to choose the altruistic alternative than younger children. The competitive choice was hardly ever made. The modal choice of 7-year-olds was individualism, whereas 9- and 11-year-olds mainly allocated equally. Previous allocation clearly influenced choices of 9- and 11-year-old children. The youngest group more often neglected the previous allocations.

The differences between the age groups, that is, a trend from individualistic to equal allocation, can be explained by differences in information-processing skills. Knight, Dubro, and Chao (1985) and Chao, Knight, and Dubro (1986) explained these age differences by referring to complex and simple social values. Equality was considered as a complex value, whereas individualism, altruism, and competition (rivalry) were regarded as simple ones. The older children were able to understand and act according to the complex values.

The 7-year-olds were hardly affected by previous allocations. A possible explanation is that these subjects could not integrate previous allocations in their choices. An alternative explanation is their defective perspective-taking ability (Damon, 1977).

This study showed age differences that are possibly well explained by increasing information-processing capacities and perspective-taking abilities. The distinction between complex and simple values may be considered as a first step in analyzing task structures. The level of task difficulty usually interacts with the cognitive developmental level of the subject.

In our current research, this approach is continued, although we try to conduct more ecologically valid research by using real allocation situations and real persons. In order to embed allocation behavior and insight in distributive justice rules in a more general social cognitive framework, several measurements are done with 6-, 8-, and 10-year-old children like social-perspective taking, sharing behavior, and distributive justice.

Concluding Remarks

Although Graziano (1984) is justified in saying that social psychological and developmental–psychological frameworks are different paradigms, there are some links. The topics of allocation behavior and understanding of distributive justice rules are possibly enriched by combination of the perspectives.

Clearly, there are age differences in allocation behavior and use of justice rules. It is also clear that allocation and justice rules are social phenomena, that is, they are affected by a host of social psychological variables. The effect of these variables, however, is not the same for subjects of different ages. A developmental perspective should explain and predict these differences. The developmental perspective on allocation behavior should be more specific. Until now, relatively general and almost content-free and context-free frameworks were used (e.g., general cognitive development, information integration, structure of arguments, etc). Specific task analyses have to be added. On the other hand, the framework should not become too specific, e.g., by confining to only one task, for example, allocation of money. Time will tell if this equilibrium will be achieved.

References

Adams, J. S. (1965). Inequity in social exchange. In L. Berkowitz (Ed.). *Advances in experimental social psychology*, Vol.2; pp. 267–299. New York, Academic Press.
Aleva, A. E (1986a). *Eerlijk zullen we alles delen. Onderzoek naar rechtvaardig verdelen.* [Let's share. Investigation of fair allocation] Doctoraalscriptie, Leiden. [Doctoral study, Leiden]
Aleva, A.E. (1986b). De invloed van het verdeelgdrag van een ander op de voorkeur voor verdeelregels bij 7-,9- en11-jarigen. [The Influence of Allocation Behavior of Others on the Preference for Distributive Rules in 7-, 9- and 11-year olds]. Leiden: *Psychological Reports* DEV-86-01.
Anderson, N., & Butzin, C. (1978). Integration theory appliedto children's judgments of equity. *Developmental Psychology*, 14, 593–606.
Barnett, M. A, & Andrews, A. J. (1977). Sex differences in children's reward allocation under competitive and cooperative instructional sets. *Developmental Psychology*, 13, 85–86.
Barnett, M. A., Howard, J., & Andrews, A. J. (1978). The role of imitation and sex differences in children's reward allocation behavior. *Journal of Genetic Psychology*, 133, 299–300.
Blau, P. M. (1964). *Exchange and power in social life*. New York: Wiley.
Case, R. (1985). *Intellectual development*. New York: Academic Press.
Chao, C. C., Knight, G. P., & Dubro, A. F. (1986). Information processing and age differences in social decision-making. *Developmental Psychology*, 22, 500–508.
Damon, W. (1977). *The social world of the child*. San Francisco: Jossey-Bass.
Damon, W. (1981). The development of justice and self-interest during childhood. In Lerner M. J. and S. Lerner (Eds.).*The justice motive in social behavior*. New York: Plenum Press.
Dreman, S. B. (1976). Sharing behavior in Israeli school-children: Cognitive and social learning factors. *Child Development*, 47, 86–194.
Enright, R. D., Franklin, C. C., & Manheim, L. A. (1980). Children's distributive justice reasoning: A standardized and objective scale. *Developmental Psychology*, 16 193–202.
Fischer, K. W., & Silvern, L. (1985). Stages and individual differences in cognitive development. *Annual Review of Psychology*, 36, 613–648.
Furby, L. (1979). Equalities in personal possessions: Explanations for and judgments about unequal distribution. *Human Development*, 22, 180–202.
Garrett, J., & Libby W. (1973). Role of intentionality in mediating responses to inequity in the dyad. *Journal of Personality and Social Psychology*, 28, 21–27.
Gerling, M., & Wender, J. (1982). Gerechtigkeitsvorstellungen von Kindern in Aufteilungssituationen: Die Bedürfnisberücksichtigung als Prinzip distributiver Gerechtigkeit. *Psychologische Beitrage*, 24, 242–252.
Graziano, W. G. (1978). Standards of fair play in same-age and mixed-age groups of children. *Developmental Psychology*, 14, 524–530.
Graziano, W. G. (1984). A developmental approach to social exchange processes. In: J. Masters & L. Yarkin (Eds.), *Boundary areas in social and developmental psychology* (pp.161–193). New York: Academic Press.
Graziano, W. G., Musser, L., Rosen, S., & Schaffer, D. (1982).The development of

fair-play standards in same-race and mixed race situations. *Child Development, 53,* 938–947.

Homans, G. C. (1961). *Social behavior: Its elementry forms.* New York: Harcourt, Brace & World.

Hook, J. (1978). Development of equity and logico-mathematical thinking. *Child Development, 49,* 1035–1044.

Hook, J. G., & Cook, T. D. (1979). Equity theory and the cognitive ability of children. *Psychological Bulletin, 86,* 429—475.

Keil, L. J., & McClintock, C. G. (1983). A developmental perspective on distributive justice. In D. M. Messick & K. S. Cook (Eds.), *Equity theory. Psychological and sociological perspectives* (pp. 13–46). New York: Praeger Publishers.

Knight, G., Dubro, A., & Chao, C. C. (1985). Information processing and the development of cooperative, competitive and individualistic social values. *Developmental Psychology, 21,* 87–45.

Kohlberg, L. (1958). *The development of modes of moral thinking and choice in the years ten to sixteen.* Unpublished Ph. D. thesis, University of Chicago.

Laak ter, J. J. F., & Weber, M. (1985). Eerlijk zullen we alles delen. [Share it all fairly] *Pedagogisch Tijdschrift, 10,* 413–419.

Lane, I. M., & Coon, R. C. (1972). Reward allocation in preschool children. *Child Development, 43,* 1382–1389.

Lerner, M. J. (1974). The justice motive: "Equity" and "parity" among children. *Journal of Personality and Social Psychology, 29,* 539–550.

Lerner, M. J. (1975). The justice motive in social behavior: Introduction. *The Journal of Social Issues, 31,* 1–20.

Lerner, M. J. (1981). The justice motive in human relations: some thoughts on what we know and need to know about justice. In M. J. Lerner & S. Lerner. (Eds.), *The justice motive in social behavior* (pp. 11-35). New York: Plenum Press.

Leventhal, G. S. (1976). The distribution of rewards and resources in groups and organizations. In L. Berkowitz and E. Walster (Eds.), *Advances in experimental social psychology* (Vol.9, pp. 91–131). New York: Academic Press.

Leventhal, G. S., & Anderson, D. (1970). Self-interest and the maintenance of equity. *Journal of Personality and Social Psychology, 15,* 57–62.

Leventhal, G. S., Popp, A. L., & Sawyer, L. (1973). Equity or equality in children's allocation of reward to other persons? *Child Development, 44,* 753–763.

Long, G., & Lerner, J. M. (1974). Deserving, the "personal contract" and altruistic behavior by children. *Journal of Personality and Social Psycholgy, 29,* 551–556.

Major, B., & Deaux, K. (1982). Individual differences in justice behavior. In J. Greenberg & R. L. Cohen. (Eds.), *Equity and justice in social behavior* (pp. 43–76). New York: Academic Press.

Masters, J. C. (1981). Developmental psychology. *Annual Review of Psychology, 32,* 117–151.

Mikula, G. (1972). Die Entwicklung des Gewinnaufteilungsverhal tens bei Kindern und Jugendlichen. Eine Untersuchung an 5-, 7-, 9- und 11-jahrigen. *Zeitschrft für Entwicklungspsychologie und Pädagogische Psychologie, 4,* 141–164.

Miller, D. T., & Smith, J. (1977). The effects of own deservingness and deservingness of other on children's helping behavior. *Child Development, 48,* 617–620.

Moessinger, P. (1975). Developmental study of fair division and property. *European Journal of Social Psychology, 5,* 385–394.

Montada, L. (1980). Developmental changes in concepts of justice. In G. Mikula (Ed.), *Justice and social interaction* (pp. 257–282). New York: Springer-Verlag.

Nelson, S. A., & Dweck, C. S. (1977). Motivation and competence as determinants of young children's reward allocation. *Developmental Psychology, 13,* 192–197.

Nisan, M. (1984). Distributive justice and social norms. *Child Development, 55,* 1020–1029.

Piaget, J. (1932). *The moral judgment of the child.* New York: Harcourt Brace.

Selman, R. (1971). The relation of role-taking to the development of moral judgement in children. *Child Development, 42,* 79–91.

Simons, R., & Klaassen, M. (1979). Children's conceptions and use of rules of distributive justice. *International Journal of Behavioral Development, 2,* 225–267.

Staub, E., & Noerenberg, H. (1981). Property rights, deservingness, reciprocity, friendship: The transactional character of children's sharing behavior. *Journal of Personality and Social Psychology, 40,* 271–289.

Streater, A. L., & Chertkoff, J. M. (1976). Distribution of rewards in a triad: A developmental test of equity theory. *Child Development, 47,* 800–805.

Tolan, K., & Krantz, M. (1981). Reward allocation and friendship in preschool children. *Journal of Genetic Psychology, 138,* 207–217.

Tompkins, B. M., & Olejnik, A. B. (1978). Children's reward allocations: The impact of situational and cognitive factors. *Child Development, 49,* 526–529.

Walster, E., Berscheid, E., & Walster, G. W. (1973). New directions in equity research. *Journal of Personality and Social Psychology, 25,* 151–176.

II

Justice in Intragroup and Intergroup Relations

7

Consistency and Group Ideology
Toward a Rhetorical Approach to the Study of Justice

Michael Billig

> Each group nourishes its own pride and vanity, boast itself superior, exalts
> its own divinities, and looks with contempt on outsiders. Each group thinks
> its own folkways the only right ones, and if it observes that other groups
> have other folkways, these excite its scorn.

So wrote Sumner (1906, p.12) in his classic introduction to the concept
of *ethnocentrism*. He was asserting, as a general law of social relations,
that every group perceives differences between itself and other social
groups and also that groups add moral evaluations to the perception of
these differences. It is not merely that other groups are seen to possess
different customs from one's own but that the customs of others are felt
to be morally inferior. For example, outgroups' concepts of justice are
held to be fundamentally unjust by ingroups. Sumner, of course, was
not the first to comment upon the moral diversity, which exists in the
world, and the fact that the diversity is not tolerated. The anonymous
Greek author of *Dissoi Logoi* presented pairs of opposing customs:

> To the Spartans it is seemly that young girls should do athletics and go
> about with bare arms and no tunics, but to the Ionians it is disgraceful. And
> to the former it is seemly for their children not to learn music and letters,
> but to the Ionians it is disgraceful not to know these things. (II, 9–10, full
> text in translation in Sprague, 1972)

Michael Billig • Department of Social Science, University of Loughborough, Loughborough, Leicestershire, LE11 3TU, England.

The author of *Dissoi Logoi* was describing the intolerance of moral diversity but was not offering any form of explanation. However, it was Sumner's contribution, not merely to coin the term *ethnocentrism* as a handy description of the phenomenon, but also to treat the phenomenon as a puzzle in need of a psychological answer. Cultural chauvinism needed to be explained, and, even if Sumner's own preference for an evolutionary explanation is no longer fashionable in current social psychological theorizing, the issue continues to be a basic one. Instead of the phenomenon being linked to hypothesised processes of evolution, it is now closely associated with the psychology of justification. The linkage is not a recent one. Many of the ideas of contemporary social psychologists can be found in Vilfredo Pareto's *Mind and Society* (1935). In this rambling and ironic work, there is an assumption of general ethnocentrism: "every sect, every party, accuses its adversaries of immoral acts, while it fails to see its own" (p. 1269). Pareto links this universal moralism to the psychological motivation for justification and to the desire to paint a coat of logical varnish over our conduct. Thus ideological justifications can be created, in order to set a group's interests in a moral discourse. For example, "a family, or some other ethnic group, occupies a piece of land, comes to own flocks, and so on." The mere fact of possession is not sufficient to satisfy the moralizing instincts of humans, but "man, being a logical animal, had to discover the 'why' of the fact" (pp. 175–176). In consequence, justifications are produced, and these give reasons why the group justly possesses what it does and why it would be unjust for any other group to aspire to such possession. In this way the logical veneer is a moralizing veneer, which justifies the ingroup, and in so doing, casts implicit or explicit aspersions on the justifications of the outgroup.

Consistency and Bias

Although social psychologists have shown limited interest in Pareto's work, many of the issues in contemporary social psychological theory are similar to those discussed in *Mind and Society* (see Billig, 1982, and Taylor & Moghaddan, 1986, for recent discussions connecting Pareto's ideas to those of modern social psychology; for early critical reactions to Pareto's work by psychologists, see McDougall, 1935; Murchison, 1935). In particular, much recent social psychological work has been devoted to issues concerning justification. Like Pareto, modern social psychologists assume that people are motivated to find reasons that justify why they act as they do. Pareto, in common with many modern theorists, assumed that people, and indeed groups, seek to make their attitudes consonant with their behavior. The construction of a group ideology to justify possession is one such example. On a more individual level, it was Pareto's notion that people do not tend so much to act in ways that conform to their beliefs, but that, more often, they construct their attitudes to match their behavior (see, *Mind and Society*, 1935, pp. 179–180).

Similar views surface in modern social psychology, principally in dissonance theories, which stress how attitudes are brought into line with behavior. The classic dissonance experiments showed that, once people had been induced to behave in a way that was discrepant with their attitudes, they were likely to alter the attitudes, in order to make them consonant with the behavior (Festinger, 1957; Wicklund & Brehm, 1976; Wicklund & Frey, 1981). Even some of the critics of dissonance theory, nevertheless, formulated alternative positions, which were still in keeping with the spirit of Pareto. For instance, Bem (1970) interpreted the results of the classic dissonance experiments in terms of "self-persuasion." He argued for reversing the assumption that attitudes cause behavior and suggested that "the cause-effect sequence most often appears to be 'behavior first, then attitudes'" (p. 68). Bem's proposed sequence is, of course, similar to Pareto's hypothesized calender of events, in which the group first secures its possessions and then formulates its myths to show that the possession is in accord with the principles of justice.

A similar sequence can be found in the formulations of equity theory. This theory assumes that people are motivated to believe that their relations with others are equitable. If people find themselves behaving inequitably with others, then they are liable to derogate their victims, thereby justifying their own actions. Thus victims of aggression are liable to be held to deserve punishment, solely for the reason that they are being aggressed against. For example, Walster, Berscheid, and Walster (1976) write: "An obvious way in which a person who has harmed another can persuade himself that his act was equitable is by devaluing the victim's outputs" (p. 10; see also, Austin, Walster, & Ure, 1976; Adams & Freeman, 1976). It is no coincidence that "one of the grandfather's of equity theory," to use the words of Tajfel (1984, p. 696), should be George Homans. It was Homans, who was instrumental in introducing the work of Pareto to an English-speaking audience, although he was later to write that Pareto provides "a poor foundation for a sociology, for he was not much interested in what we should now call social structure and commanded an inadequate psychology, though few when he wrote commanded a better" (Homans, 1983, p. 2).

Pareto's psychology, like that of dissonance theory, was based upon motivational assumptions. Both sorts of psychologies assumed that discrepancies between actions and beliefs, or the absence of justificatory beliefs, produce a motivation to formulate justifications. Balance theorists were somewhat imprecise about the psychological status of the motivation to restore consonance. For example, this imprecision is revealed in McGuire's (1966) comment that "we view consistency as a tendency, a drive, a motive" (p. 33), without further specification, and Singer (1966) wrote that "few, if any of the theorists discuss the motivational bases underlying their theories in any detail" (p. 52). Similarly, Pareto was imprecise about the nature of the motivations he assumed to underlie "nonlogical" justifications. He employed psychological terms like *residues, sentiments,* and *instincts* confusingly without clear reference to psychological processes. Both Pareto's psychology and that of modern theorists assume that the hypothesized motivations can operate at the level of individual excuses and at the level of group ideology. Although much of equity theory limits itself to the individual level of explanation, nevertheless extensions can be made to the group level (see, Doise, 1982, for a discussion of levels of explanation in social psychology in general and of equity theory in particular). For example, Lerner's extension of equity theory assumes that social groups, as well as individuals, are motivated to believe that the world is, at root, a just place (e.g., Lerner, Miller, & Holmes, 1976; Lerner, 1977; see Taylor & Moghaddan, 1987, Chapter 4 for a discussion of the relations between equity theory and beliefs about racial inequality).

In the last 15 years, motivational theories in social psychology have tended to give way to cognitive ones. Instead of examining the motivational states that might give rise to the creation of justifications, social psychologists have tended to concentrate upon cognitive processes. This has not led to an abandonment of questions about justification and consistency, rather to an awareness of some of the subtle processes of thought, which lead to the production of self-serving, internally consistent attitudes. The change can be illustrated by the title of an article by Greenwald (1980): "The Totalitarian Ego" that described the ways in which people's thought processes (the "ego," as opposed to the "id" of motivational theories) fabricate conscious experience, so that unpleasant, or psychologically threatening, thoughts are repelled from conscious awareness. The metaphor of *totalitarianism* was deliberately employed by Greenwald, to suggest that the individual mind operates, and, indeed, must operate, in a way akin to totalitarian authorities that censor all information thought to be critical of the state.

If Freud in *Five Lectures on Psycho-Analysis* (1962) also drew a similar analogy between the mental processes of the individual and state censorship, then there is a difference between the "id censor" of psychoanalytic theory and the "ego censor" of cognitive social psychology. The psychoanalytic description concentrates upon deeply hidden, and rather shameful, motivations, whereas modern cognitive social psychology emphasizes how information is twisted and repressed by normal processes of thinking. Moreover, it has been argued by cognitive social psychologists that normal processes of the ego, rather than the abnormal motivations of the id, lie at the root of intergroup prejudices (for cognitive accounts of prejudice and stereotyping, see, for example, Ashmore & Del Boca, 1981; Hamilton, 1979; Rothbart, 1981; Tajfel 1981; Turner, 1982).

A number of cognitive social psychologists have suggested that stereotyping emerges from the need to process and categorize information. Billig (1985), in a critical discussion of this work, has pointed to a number of assumptions made by cognitive social psychologists, which, when taken together, imply that prejudice is a normal, and indeed an inevitable, cognitive process. It is assumed that our senses are bombarded by too many stimuli at any one time, and, therefore, our senses must be selective, in determining which information is attended to. The processes of selection are not random, but we are equipped with mental schemata, which sort incoming information according to preset principles. In consequence, the processes of information reduction operate according to bias, just as the state censor can prevent certain material reaching the pages of the state-owned newspapers. Cognitive social psychologists have focused upon the role of categorization in the way that information is processed. In order for stimuli to be processed meaningfully, they must be categorized. Thus cognitive social psychologists, such as Cantor, Mischel, and Schwartz (1982), tend to assume that categorization is the basic cognitive process, "the fundamental quality of cognition," which allows "us to structure and give coherence to our general knowledge about people and the social world" (p. 34). However, it is also assumed that the categorizing of information is a process of simplification, which reduces the potential information of a stimulus. The unique features of particulars are reduced as they are slotted into the relevant categories. As Rosch (1978) and Morris and Rosch (1981) stress, categories enable us to treat objectively different stimuli as being similar. However, it is also assumed that stereotyping occurs when members of social groups are treated as being equivalent, and the sense of individuality is lost. Individuals are treated merely as being members of a category, whose essential features have been determined in advance (see, for example, Allport's, 1958, classic discussion of stereotypes). Because the act of categorization is considered a basic cognitive process, then the categorizing, or stereotyping, of individuals seems to be inevitable, when the social perceiver thinks about social groups. As Taylor (1981) has suggested, "stereotyping is the outgrowth of normal cognitive processes," and Hamilton (1979) has written that "it seems almost inherent in us" to use stereotypes, when we think about people as members of social groups. In consequence, stereotyping is explained in terms of normal processes of thinking, and group prejudice, based upon stereotyping, becomes, according to the assumptions of cognitive social psychology, an inevitability. Hamilton (1979) has called this a "depressing dilemma" (p. 55).

Not only do cognitive social psychologists suggest that categorization leads to a simplification of information but also that it is inevitable that the schemata, which determine how information selectivity operates, contain certain biases. If prejudice involves making prejudgements about members of social groups on the basis of their group membership, then, according to many cognitive social psychologists, normal thinking and information processing is akin to prejudice: It involves sorting information according to certain preset biases. In this way, cognitive social psychologists have discussed how the "totalitarian ego" arranges incoming information in such a way that prior presuppositions are confirmed. For example, Bruner (1957) suggested that people generally see what they expect to see. Duncan (1976) showed how the processes of perceptual selection and biased interpretation can operate in an intergroup situation. White subjects were likely to interpret an aggressive action by a white person as being "playful," but the same action, performed by a black, was more likely to be seen as "aggressive." In this way, without the unconscious motivations of an authoritarian personality (Adorno et al., 1950), the prejudiced person is regularly "seeing with their own eyes" information that confirms the initial prejudices. Rothbart (1981) has suggested that we tend to remember things that are consonant with our preconceptions, whereas it is the awkward facts that are likely to be consigned to the dustbins of memory. Snyder (1981) has provided evidence about the self-fulfilling nature of stereotypes: Having formed a view about an individual or group, we are liable to be motivated to search for, and notice, information that confirms the bias. Hewstone and Brown (1986) discuss how these cognitive biases can operate in situations of intergroup contact. Such processes of normal thought ensure that contact between groups, far from breaking down presuppositions, can sometimes provide opportunities for the mutual reinforcement of presuppositions (see, also, Amir, 1969; Cook, 1984).

There are also a number of other cognitive biases, which supposedly predispose perceivers to prejudiced perceptions and judgments. Peterson (1985), in a discussion of the ways in which the biases of information processing affect political judgments, writes that "people make mistakes due to a faulty understanding of what is typical or representative" (p. 500). For example, people tend to overgeneralize from small samples and to treat certain examples as being representative of a whole class of stimuli (Nisbett & Ross, 1980). Anderson (1980) has connected this bias to racial stereotyping, as a few instances, which confirm the stereotypes, are held to represent the whole social group, about which the perceiver holds biased presuppositions. Similarly, biases in attribution can lead to the continual protection of presuppositions from disconfirming evidence. Hewstone and Jaspars (1984) argue that people have different styles of explaining behavior that contradicts stereotyped assumptions, depending whether the behavior is displayed by ingroup or outgroup members. For example, negative behavior by the ingroup, or positive behavior by an outgroup, is explained away in terms situational pressures, rather than by the characteristics of the persons involved. Behavior that confirms the stereotype, by contrast, is liable to be seen as being produced by the characters, or inner natures, of the persons (Taylor & Jaggi, 1974).

In consequence, it can be seen that cognitive social psychology has produced a similar picture to that of dissonance theory and that of Pareto. All three approaches show how individuals, and groups, possess consistently self-serving and distorted images of the world. The motivational theories concentrate upon the dramatic crises, which lead to the creation of individual or ideological justifications. The individual is caught behaving in a surprising way, or the group has neglected to provide a justificatory myth for itself, and both sorts of situations provide a crisis to be resolved. On the other hand, the approach from cognitive social psychology concentrates upon the more mundane events, which presumably are happening throughout waking life. Unthinkingly people are presumed to arrange incoming information in ways which bolster their self-serving prejudices. The result is a consciousness, which is nourished by consistently confirming information. On a group level, the result is a group ideology, that generally provides the members of the group with positive information about themselves; if a crisis should occur, then steps to reduce the resulting dissonance will be taken (Tajfel, 1981; Turner, 1982). The motivational theories may have focused upon the uncomfortable pressures, which supposedly lead people to create consistent views, but the cognitive theories show how people go about their lives comfortably acquiring consistent information. Both theoretical perspectives, in consequence, see the end result of psychological processes as the production of consistent mentalities.

Inconsistencies of Thought and Ideology

The social psychological processes of dissonance reduction and the self-confirmation of schemata lead one to expect individuals and groups to possess neatly arranged, and well-barricaded, systems of thought. Social psychologists have demonstrated how disconfirming evidence can be deflected, or discounted, by the totalitarian ego, which is intolerant of everything not fitting the ego's own self-serving ideology. However, this picture of psychological functioning is one sided (Billig, 1987). It deals only with those processes, which appear to work against any ideological or attitudinal complexity. Just as not all states are totalitarian, so not all the functions of the ego necessarily produce the uncritical confirmation of stereotypes and the creation of prejudice. Both on an individual and a group level, there are social psychological processes that suggest that the ego can be perplexed, contradictory, and critical, as well as being rigidly totalitarian.

Individual Level

Much of cognitive social psychology, with its emphasis upon the processing of information by schemata, has tended to ignore the fact that humans need not be held in thrall by their schemata. In addition to the unthinking use of schemata, we can examine critically our schemata and those of others. Bartlett, who introduced the concept of "schema" into psychological theorizing, emphasized this very point. Discussing his own unease with the term *schema*, he stressed that we can transcend and "turn around" our schemata (Bartlett, 1932; for a recent appreciation of the subtlety of Bartlett's ideas on cognition, see Edwards & Middleton, 1986). However, it is this critical aspect of cognition that tends to be ignored, with the result that prejudice is seen as the inevitable, and depressing, consequence of thinking.

Billig (1985, 1986a, 1987) has proposed a theoretical way out of the "depressing dilemma." He argues that the cognitive theorists have tied their models of thought too closely to perceptual models (see also Moscovici, 1982, for a critical analysis of the perceptual bias in cognitive theorizing). The result has been a neglect of the role of language, especially in the formation and transmission of prejudiced beliefs. When the cognitive theorists discuss language, they tend to assume that its prime function is to enable the world to be categorized meaningfully. In this way, the categories of language are seen to be functionally equivalent to perceptual rules for combining sights and sounds into meaningful wholes. However, this view overlooks one of the key aspects of language: the faculty of negation. Because language possesses negativity, it enables us to argue and to criticize, as well as to sort and arrange. The assumptions of schemata can be critically negated, and, in fact, it can be suggested that all attitudes possess a negative dimension: They are critical negations of opposing views, situated within a wider context of controversy. Billig (1986a, 1987) stresses the controversial, and argumentative, aspect of attitudes; this is not an aspect that is conventionally stressed by social psychologists (Jaspars & Fraser, 1984).

Billig (1985) has criticized the one-sidedness of a psychological account of thinking that sees categorization as the basic process of cognition. He suggests that the mental processes, which permit negation, come in opposing pairs. The process of categorization must be understood in relation to the opposing process of "particulariza-tion." Not only do humans have the faculty of categorizing a particular in a general category, but they also posses the ability to treat a particular as a particular, thereby refusing to surrender it to the category. Billig suggests that humans would not be able to categorize linguistically unless they were also able to particularize because these opposing processes are intimately connected. Because any particular can be either categorized or particularized, our acts of categorization are potentially controversial. In consequence, the cognitive skills, which allow us to categorize events in the world, also allow us to examine critically, and to unpick, uncritical assumptions. By shifting the image of the thinker from the information processor to the argumentative critic, a way out of the "depressing dilemma" is proposed. There is nothing about the forms of cognition to suggest that humans must inevitably hold self-serving prejudices and that their thinking processes must be controlled by such prejudices. Because prejudiced views are expressed linguistically, they are potentially controversial and can be opposed by tolerant views. Just as it is possible to interpret the actions of outgroup members in a prejudiced fashion, so it is also possible to argue against ethnic prejudices and to construct arguments in favor of tolerant interpreta-tions (for an alternative solution to the dilemma, see Brewer & Kramer 1985; Brewer & Miller, 1984).

Ideological Level

A simple reading of Pareto's account of the development of ideology would suggest that all groups should possess internally consistent, self-justificatory ideological systems. The premisses of dissonance theory might help explain how such ideological systems come into being, and the findings of cognitive social psychology would help explain how the systems are maintained. The problem is that for many groups, or societies, there is no single systematized ideology, which explains and justifies all significant social facts. Instead, there are conflicting beliefs, with the consequence that the members of the groups do not posses "belief systems" as such, but have contrary attitudinal themes. These contrary themes coexist in a way that contradicts a strict interpretation of dissonance theory or ideas about the "totalitarian" ego. In order to illustrate this, it is necessary to distinguish between two sorts of ideology: (1) the "forensic" ideology of a particular political or religious group, which seeks to interpret and often to change the world; (2) the general ideology, or patterns of beliefs that circulate within a society or social group (for a discussion of the different concepts of "ideology," see, for instance, Larrain, 1979, 1983; Billig, 1982; Eccelshall et al., 1984; the term forensic ideology is taken from Lane, 1960).

A forensic ideology offers a systematic explanation of important social events, or, as Aron (1977) wrote, such an ideology "presupposes an apparently systematic formalization of facts, interpretations, desires and predictions" (p. 309). For example, the forensic ideology of Marxism will explain major social events in terms of a limited number of premises about class oppression and the inevitable conflict between bourgeoisie and proletariat. The ideologists of Marxist groups will seek to develop an internally consistent and all-embracing view of the world; they will self-consciously attempt to do this by following certain basic principles, so that the ideological view resembles an axiomatic theory (see, e.g., Almond, 1954; Callaghan 1984; Newton, 1969). On the far right wing, groups frequently possess a conspiracy ideology, which fits the complex patterns of political events into the explanatory matrix of an overarching conspiracy (Billig, 1978; Cohn, 1967; Lipset & Raab, 1971). Anti-Semitic conspiracy theorists explain the major events of world history in terms of the machinations of a small number of Jewish conspirators, and, in this way, social complexity is reduced to a single explanatory mode.

Although the ideology of the conspiracy theory might appear so bizarre that it seems to require an explanation in terms of pathological paranoia, nevertheless, standard social psychological theories seem to offer adequate descriptions, at least *prima facie*. This can be illustrated by Henri Zukier's (1987) interesting social psychological analysis of medieval beliefs in a Jewish conspiracy. Zukier is able to show how the thinking of the conspiracy theorists is based upon "normal" cognitive processes, discussed by cognitive social psychologists. For example, attribution theorists have suggested that people wish to explain social events in terms of personal causation. Thus there is little "abnormal" in the conspiracy theorist wishing to explain politics *in toto*, according to the evil inclinations of the conspirators. Similarly, the desire to explain events, rather than leave them unexplained and indeterminate, is seen by social psychologists as a normal feature of social cognition. Zukier links the particular views of the medieval anti-Semites, and by implication the views of their modern descendents, to a general psychological aversion to indeterminacy.

Zukier's analysis offers a useful corrective to the assumption that all conspiracy theorists must possess abnormal personalities, but it does leave a problem for the cognitive theorists. To the extent that the "normal" processes of cognitive social psychology can explain abnormal, forensic ideology, then they seem less adequate for dealing with nonforensic ideology. To put the matter crudely: Hypotheses about the totalitarian ego might be adequate for explaining closed, totalitarian systems of thought, but more fluid and contradictory patterns of belief seem to require a different image of the ego.

The concept of "ideology" can easily be confusing because it is frequently used to denote a wider phenomenon than "forensic ideology." The concept is often employed, particularly by Marxist theoreticians, to refer to the patterns of beliefs and practices within a society, with the implication that such patterns possess functions for preserving the power, or class, relations within the society (e.g., Giddens, 1979; Mannheim, 1960). If a forensic ideology is characterized by systematization, there is no reason to expect the wider sort of ideology to be equally formalized. In fact, there are good reasons for thinking that the patterns of beliefs in the wider ideology are often looser and more contrary than those of the forensic ideology. For example, Abercombie and Turner (1978) have critically examined the thesis that there is a coherent ideology of capitalism. Instead of there existing a tightly formulated body of beliefs, to which all acquiescent members of a capitalist society adhere, there is a much more confusing pattern: "The so-called 'dominant ideology' of late capitalism is . . .at best an uneven and uneasy amalgam of assumptions about private property and about the importance of state intervention in economic life." (Abercombie & Turner, 1978, p. 163).

Billig (1982, 1985) has drawn attention to some of the social psychological implications of this rejection of the notion that capitalist society possesses a dominant forensic ideology. One aspect, in which the uneasy amalgam is revealed, is in the contrary ways people use for explaining social events. In place of the tightly ordered system of explanation to be found in a forensic ideology, there are contrary assumptions about individual and situational causes. Edelman (1977) has referred to the widespread existence of contrary myths in contrary society: There is the myth that poverty is caused by the actions and character of the poor themselves, and there is also the contrary myth that poverty is a result of societal factors beyond the control of the victims of poverty. Edelman suggests that both myths are simultaneously shared by most members of contemporary society. Edelman's myths about poverty are similar to what attribution theorists call "personal" and "situational" explanations (see Antaki, 1984, for a review of attribution theory). There is certainly evidence that political belief affects the willingness to explain poverty in terms of the personal characteristics of the poor or in terms of situational pressures, with conservatives preferring the former sort of explanation and left-wingers the latter (e.g, Feather, 1974; Feagin, 1972; Furnham, 1982, 1983, Pandey, Sinha, & Prakash, 1982). There is also evidence that blaming the poor for their fate is correlated with beliefs in a just world (Furnham & Gunter, 1984). However, these studies concentrate upon discovering differences between supporters of different political parties, and, in so doing, they overlook the more obvious fact that both the left and the right-wingers are willing to use both sorts of explanations, albeit with different emphases. Thus Nilson (1981) specifically examined both similarities and differences in explanations of poverty and concluded that the majority of people, as Edelman had predicted, see poverty both in situational and personal terms.

   Nilson (1981) uses her results to argue that there is a lack of serious ideological cleavage in American politics. In addition, the lack of clear-cut explanations for poverty, but widespread existence of contrary myths, provides further evidence that, if there is a general ideology of late capitalism, it is not of a forensic nature. Therefore, if one is examining the major patterns of belief in contemporary society, one should not be looking for consistent, or systematized, themes, but for inconsistent ones. As Billig (1984) suggested, the contradictions of the society might not be manifested by the existence of opposed groups, each possessing internally consistent but mutually contradictory ideologies; instead, "the contradictions of the society will be reproduced directly in the minds of most of those who live in the society" (p. 246).

Analysis of Ideology and Discourse

Following from the distinction between the consistent, forensic ideology and the inconsistent, general ideology, there are a number of social psychological implications for the study of intergroup ideology. Whereas the forensic ideology may be maintained at a level of strict internal consistency, as predicted by theories of dissonance reduction and the cognitive accounts of the totalitarian ego, one should expect the social psychological shape of general ideologies to be much looser. In consequence, one should be alert to the contradictory and ambivalent aspects of general ideology, rather than assuming *a priori* that there is consistency.

The detailed examination of the ambivalences of ideology may require a qualitative and ethnographic methodology, as opposed to the more quantitative methods traditionally employed by social psychologists. There is, at present, a detectable trend toward qualitative methods in social psychology, especially among younger social psychologists interested in ideological issues. The techniques of discourse analysis have been used with great effect by social psychologists, such as Edwards and Middleton (1986); Potter, Stringer, and Wetherell (1984); Potter and Litton (1985) Wetherell, 1986; Wetherell, Stiven, and Potter (1987); see also Potter and Wetherell, 1987, for a general discussion of the contribution of discourse analysis to the discipline of social psychology). Whereas the discourse analysts have tended to study what respondents say in situations created by interviewers, ethnographic social psychologists have recommended the study of naturally observing conversations and actions (Griffin, 1985a,b, 1986). This trend toward qualitative analysis has also seen a revival of interest in the study of rhetoric (e.g., Murray, 1984; Nelson & Megill, 1986; Shotter, 1986, 1990a, b). Billig (1985, 1986, 1987), arguing for a rhetorical approach to social psychology, suggests that the analysis of the contrary aspects of ideology should involve the detailed study of rhetorical strategies of argument; this is particularly useful, in order to see how inconsistencies are justified and maintained, rather than resolved in a simple sense.

The rhetorical approach involves examining the flexible aspects of the way people talk about themselves and the social world. Whereas social psychologists have traditionally assumed that individuals possess defined attitudes and belief systems, social psychologists examining rhetoric and discourse make no such assumptions. In fact, their attention is drawn to the contradictory elements, rather than the systematic aspects, of general ideological notions. Thus Wetherell et *al.*, (1987), examining the complex ways people talk about gender and equality, dispute the usefulness of assuming that people have an attitude on an issue. Billig (1987) stresses the need to situate the expression of attitudes in a wider rhetorical context. He argues that people not only change the way they express their beliefs depending upon the rhetorical context, but also they can change the very direction of their attitudinal arguments, when the rhetorical context is altered. For example, he points to the rhetorical context of the social psychological phenomenon of "reactance," which is normally explained in motivational terms (Brehm, 1966). Billig (1987) suggests that reactance occurs when the rhetorical context alters, and people find themselves arguing in a surprisingly novel direction. It is because such alterations in attitudinal expression are always possible, that attitudes represent "unfinished business" in unresolved controversies, rather than constituting a set system, which rigidly determines all attitudinal expressions (Billig, 1987).

If general ideologies contain contradictory elements, then they should not be conceived merely as large-scale schemata, which provide neatly arranged pictures of the social world. They also provide the dilemmas, about which members of society think and argue. In this sense, ideologies do not make the social world unproblematic so much as dilemmatic (see Billig *et al.*, 1988). Thus, as Edelman (1977) argues, poverty appears as a puzzle, in that it is seen to be caused both by the actions of individuals, as well as by social forces that leave the individual helpless. It is because poverty is seen as puzzling that the contemporary myths have a bias towards conservatism, rather than change. Thus poverty, according to Edelman, is simultaneously deplored and tolerated. In this way, pressure for radical change is deflected, not because the world is considered a just place, but because justice is helplessly deplored (Billig, 1982).

The Loughborough Discourse and Rhetoric Group has been exploring qualitatively these dilemmatic aspects of ideology. Not only does this entail a determination to look for the contrary aspects of attitudes but also a commitment to look beyond the social psychology of individual or interpersonal processes, in order to relate attitudes and actions to wider social, and ideological, patterns. For example, Edwards and Mercer (1987) have been investigating the practices and beliefs of teachers. They note the contradictions between teachers' views on the importance of developing individual creativity and assumptions about innate intelligence. In particular, Edwards and Mercer have explored a contradiction between the teachers' ideology of allowing the pupils to express themselves freely and the teachers' authoritarian behavior in the classroom. In this case the beliefs in

self-expression are being expressed by a practice, which contradicts
the very nature of the beliefs. Alan Radley (Radley, 1984; Radley &
Green, 1985) has been examining the thoughts and fears of those who
have suffered from heart attacks. In common with other investigators,
he has linked the proneness to heart attack with the possession of an
achievement-oriented, independent philosophy. However, what gives
Radley's work its particular rhetorical and ideological interest is that
he shows that this philosophy contains its own subtle contradictory
elements. On the surface, the heart-attack patients adopt an unambiguously masculine style, whereas at the same time they reveal, in a more
ambiguous way, a feminine style, which seeks nonobvious approval
and expresses a need for dependancy. Such is the subtlety of these
reactions, which are both embodied and embedded in social life, that
they are best studied by qualitative methods. In addition, the problems
of the heart-attack patients, caught between the dilemmas of masculine
and feminine modes, are not merely those of a few unlucky individuals, but they reflect wider dilemmas within contemporary society.

The Loughborough Group has also been examining the dilemmatic
aspects of ideologies more directly related to intergroup relations.
Susan Condor has been studying gender identity and women's conceptions of themselves and of men (e.g., Condor, 1986a,b). Instead of
assuming that women have a clearly defined identity, either for or
against men, she has been exploring some of the less obvious ways in
which women talk about gender relations. In particular, she has looked
at traditional women (a group, according to Condor, neglected, or
misunderstood, by many feminist investigators). The traditional
women were by no means unambiguously traditional, as their stereotype might suggest, but they supported a mixture of reform and
reaction. In this way, their thoughts were characterized by liberal and
conservative themes, simultaneously pulling in opposing directions.

Interestingly, Condor (1986a) draws a parallel between beliefs
about gender and those about race, referring to the beliefs of the
traditional women as a form of "new sexism." A number of investigators have commented upon the mixture to prejudiced and nonpreju-
diced themes that combine to form the 'new racism' (e.g., Kinder &
Sears, 1981; McConahay, 1981, 1982; McConahay & Hough, 1976;
McConahay, Hardee, & Batts, 1981). These authors suggest that
modern racists do not express their prejudices unambiguously but
present their opposition to black actions as an expression of traditional
values, such as the value for equality (see Weigel & Howes, 1985, for
evidence that this form of racism may not, in fact, be all that new). In
this way, racial values are not overtly expressed, and prejudiced
themes coexist with denials of prejudice. The result is a central

ambiguity in the modern discourse of race (van Dijk 1984). The same ambiguities are to be seen in a pronounced form in the discourse of the new right, which simultaneously contains authoritarian and liberatarian themes, as well as the expression and the denial of prejudice, all coexisting (Gordon & Klung, 1986; Seidel, 1985).

Billig (1987) discusses the rhetorical strategies,which are used to discuss the contrary themes of prejudice in everyday discourse. Often the disclaimer "I'm not prejudiced" acts as a defensive cover, which permits, although appearing to criticize, the expression of prejudiced views (see, Hewitt & Stokes, 1975, for a discussion of "disclaimers"). Cochrane and Billig (1984) report the conversations and arguments of adolescents, concerning race. The adolescents, whom they studied, did not, by and large, divide into groups of tolerant and prejudiced individuals, but the same person would be liable to come out with tolerant and prejudiced remarks, perhaps at different moments in the course of a discussion, and perhaps even in the course of the same statement. By setting up discussion groups, Cochrane and Billig were able to note how the adolescents aired contrary themes, admitted their own puzzlement of the issue, yet continued to deplore and simultaneously contribute to the prevalence of prejudice. Billig (1986b) reports an ethnographic study of a group of Young Conservatives. By and large the members, in talking of race, displayed the themes of modern racism, denying their own racism but introducing racist themes under the protective guise of uncontroversial values. In such a political group, the wider implications of this sort of discourse can be more apparent, than in conversations enacted in contexts with little overt connection to political life. Billig reports an incident in which an official in the senior party talked to the group of Young Conservatives about Southern Africa. The official had visited Southern Africa as part of a delegation from the World Bank. His discourse on apartheid, and his use of stereotypes of Africans, parallelled, and reinforced, the discourse of the young members about West Indians in Britain. In the case of the official, the contrary patterns of belief had a clear connection to a high level of international economic decision making.

All these investigations involve more than a methodological switch from the quantitative emphases in traditional social psychology to qualitative and ethnographic approaches. Over and above the commitment to a qualitative examination of discourse, there is a theoretical shift. This involves two factors. First, there is the emphasis upon dilemmatic and contrary aspects of thinking, which will be discussed more fully in the next section with particular reference to social justice research. Second, there is the commitment to situate psychological processes in a wider, ideological context, which relates the structure of individual dilemmas to the structural contradictions of society.

Concluding Remarks: Implications for Social Justice Research

There is a need to tie together some of the themes already discussed and to point to their implications for conducting research into the topic of social justice. In particular, the outlines of a rhetorical approach to the subject need to be sketched, in order to see how an emphasis upon rhetoric can lead to a different perspective on the study of social justice than is often entertained.

The first characteristic of such a rhetorical study would be that it would focus upon the ways that people conceive and talk of justice. It would be less interested in procedural outcomes, or in the ways that experimental subjects might allot rewards or penalties. Instead of seeking behavioral measures of justice, it would pay direct attention to the discourse of justice, studying the meanings of the term *justice* in everyday talk. For example, Wetherell, Stiven, and Potter (1987) were, in effect, doing this in their study of the discourse associated with gender equality. They were investigating what young people thought to be just and unjust—justly egalitarian and justly nonegalitarian—as they discussed the relations between the sexes. The authors were not concerned to produce a measure of "justice behavior" on the assumption that talk is less real than action, for they were interested in discourse itself. The complexities, contradictions, and evasions in this sort of discourse cannot be reduced to some sort of mathematically defined matrix, in which some payoffs are consensually agreed to be just and others unjust. To use the terminology of Serge Moscovici and his coworkers, such investigations aim to build up a picture of the "social representation" of justice in contemporary discourse (Farr, 1983, 1984; Jodelet, 1984; Moscovici,1982, 1983, 1984). Although some discourse analysts have criticized the concept of "social representations" (i.e, Potter & Litton, 1985), there is a basic compatibility between the two approaches, in that both advocate a qualitative sort of study, which pays special attention to language and communication (Moscovici, 1985).

A rhetorical approach, however, goes further than this, in that it directs attention to specific aspects of discourse. In particular, it pays attention to the argumentative features of discourse, thereby emphasizing the importance of negativity in thought (Billig, 1986a, 1987; Shotter, 1987). In order to develop such an approach, Billig (1987) has drawn upon the intellectual traditions of classical rhetoric. These traditions do not reduce rhetoric to the production of elegant phrases or empty adornment. Instead, classical rhetoric is centrally concerned with argumentation, and thereby, it recognizes the central place of argumentation in social life. Drawing upon this tradition and upon the "new rhetoric" of Perelman and Olbrechts-Tyteca (1971), Billig (1987) suggests that our attitudes, and indeed much everyday thinking, should be understood in an argumentative context. This would be particularly true of everyday meanings about justice. From a rhetorical point of view, the central point about a topic such as justice is not that there is consensus within particular societies about the meaning of "justice," but that there is disagreement. Justice is a matter about which people argue, have dilemmas, and express perplexity. In short, justice is a matter of controversy, and thereby of thought.

To illustrate this point, one can refer back to the example of the *Dissoi Logoi*. Early in the chapter, this ancient text was cited to suggest that different societies have different ideologies about justice: What one society believes to be just another will hold to be unjust. From a social scientific perspective, these different societal images can then be connected to economic and political interests, in order to show how different ideologies of justice serve different social functions. However, there is another aspect to the *Dissoi Logoi*. This anonymous text was originally intended to provide training exercises for aspiring orators. In fact, the text may comprise the notes taken down by a student attending a course in rhetoric. Although the precise origins of *Dissoi Logoi* are unknown, its author seems to have been a follower of the great sophist and early rhetorical theorist, Protagoras. What the author *Dissoi Logoi* aimed to do, in accordance with the philosophy of Protagoras, was to present opposing arguments on matters of controversy. Thus the argument in favor of a relativist approach to morality, quoted before, was opposed by an absolutist position, whose justificatory arguments were also provided by the author.

The point about these pairs of opposing arguments was not that they belonged to different social groups: They were all aimed at the same sort of Greek audience. Moreover, as rhetorical theorists in their textbooks stressed, such arguments were constructed from generally agreed "commonplaces," or to use the modern terminology, from social values (on the connection between "commonplaces" and "values," see Perelman & Olbrechts-Tyteca, 1971, and Billig, 1987). What this implies is that the commonplaces, or values, which are consensual within a particular society, or within a particular ideology, can be used to generate controversy by producing opposing arguments. Thus, each person sharing the values of commonplaces of the social group possesses the possibility for entertaining opposing arguments, which can be justified by these commonplaces or values. The possession of such values, which can be brought into conflict with one another, provides people with the material by which they can think, or argue with themselves, about social dilemmas.

This position contains an implication for the study of justice, in that justice is to be seen as an inherently controversial value. In an obvious sense, justice is noncontroversial, in that no one can sensibly deny in the abstract the value of this value. It makes little sense to champion outwardly, and without irony, the virtues of injustice. However, justice is inherently controversial in that its practice leads to conflicts with other self-evidently desirable values, or commonplaces. In fact, the example of "justice" is frequently found in classical rhetorical textbooks, such as Cicero's *De Inventione*, Quintilian's *Institutes of Oratory*, or the anonymous *Rhetorica ad Herennium*. All cite the way in which the commonplaces of "justice" are regularly brought into conflict with those of "mercy," especially in the law courts. Prosecutors are well advised to dwell upon the commonplaces of justice, stressing why the law should be applied in all its majesty, whereas defendants should counter these appeals by drawing upon the commonplaces of mercy. The point to notice is that the resulting argument between justice and mercy is not essentially between two separate populations, like the Spartans and Ionians disagreeing about the morality of female gymnasts revealing bare arms. It is an argument within a population. The members of the audience are presumed to possess both the commonplaces of justice and mercy. The dilemma arises because the commonplaces seem to conflict with each other, and the argument is necessary in order to establish which should have priority in the given case. The argument and the dilemma are only possible because the members of the audience possess conflicting values in their consciousness.

This emphasis upon the dilemmatic aspects of social thinking is different from those social psychological perspectives, that assume the necessary operation of some from of dissonance principle. As was mentioned earlier, social justice theories in social psychology often assume the operation of a dissonance-reducing motivation. Sometimes the link between social justice theory and dissonance reduction is made explicit. For example, Smith (1985) links Lerner's just world theory to dissonance theory, predicting that those who believe in a just world will also possess a number of other social attitudes if they are to avoid dissonance. Such a conception seems to assume that individuals, by force of psychological motivation, have to choose between justice and mercy. Having chosen, they will then possess a wide-ranging and internally consistent schema for categorizing the social world. This schema (whether liberally merciful or strictly adhering to the notions of a just world) will then permit the believer to avoid dilemmas, for everything will have been worked out in advance. That being so, such believers can only react to the world by categorizing dilemmas in a way that instantly resolves them. This social psychological perspective seems to overlook the dilemmatic aspects of thinking, for people are presumed to lack the conflicting values, or commonplaces, which are necessary for deliberation (Billig, 1987).

Some of the studies described earlier recognize, either implicitly or explicitly, the dilemmatic qualities of everyday thinking, and especially those dilemmas that arise from the age-old conflict between justice and mercy. Edelman's (1977) work is a case in point. The opposing myths about poverty, blaming and sympathizing with the poor, can be seen as modern versions of the opposing commonplaces of justice and mercy. To be sure, there may be individual and demographic differences to the extent to which some people and groups are likely to draw upon one or other myth. However, concentration upon finding statistically significant differences between populations with respect to their tendency to blame or sympathize may lead to a distortion. It may lead to an overestimation of the differences between "liberals" and "conservatives" and may ignore the simple but theoretically important fact that both possess the cultural values for sympathy and blame. In this respect, basic social dilemmas may not be so cognitively resolved that conservatives, stressing strict justice, will not feel the tug of liberal mercy and vice versa. Verba and Orren's (1986) study of American leaders' views on equality shows the complexity of attitudes. Even conservative business leaders, whose views could be described as exemplifying the just world ideology, nevertheless were prepared to recognize the injustice of some inequalities and possessed merciful commonplaces with which to articulate sympathy for the victims of social injustice.

The conflicts between just and merciful commonplaces can be seen in other examples that have looked at dilemmatic thinking. The teachers, studied by Edwards and Mercer (1987), find themselves in a position in which they oscillate between authoritarianism and liberalism. The new racists temper the harshness of racism with merciful phrases, without which the racism would appear socially unacceptable. Condor (1986a,b) reports an analogous intermixing of blame and sympathy with respect to gender attitudes. Of course, the intermixing need not be equally based, for the new racists and sexists has biased the balance in an unbalanced manner. The point is that the discourse expresses dissonant themes. The paradox is that this overt nonresolution of social dilemmas is used to express a position, which may be covertly and psychologically more resolved than it outwardly may appear (Billig, 1987).

What this suggests is that ideologies are not just characterized by consensually shared values. In addition, ideologies contain internal tensions, enabling there to be dilemmas, which are to be experienced, talked about, and argued over by the members of the ideological group. It is this aspect of ideology, which social theorists have tended to ignore, just as social psychologists have tended to look at the consistent, rather than ambivalent, aspects of attitudes. The rhetorical approach should not be interpreted as suggesting that there is no such thing as a motivation to be consistent nor that differences between liberals and conservatives' conceptions of justice do not exist. What it does recommend is that such conceptions should be examined within their argumentative context. This means more than situating attitudes within the context of arguments between groups or between ideologies. It also means recognizing those arguments that arise within ideologies and within the thinking of individuals. All this suggests that there are further issues for social justice research, beyond investigating how outcomes are allotted or looking at the differences between populations. There is also a need to study the dilemmatic aspects of thinking, as people talk and think about the continuing dilemmas of justice and mercy.

References

Abercrombie, N., & Turner, B. S. (1978). The dominant ideology thesis. *British Journal of Sociology, 29*, 149–170.

Adams, J. C. & Freeman, S. (1976). Equity theory revisited: Comments and annotated bibliography. In L. Berkowitz & E. Walters (Eds.), *Advances in experimental social psychology* (Volume 9, New York: Academic Press.

Adorno, T. W., Frenkel-Brunswik, E., Levinson, D. J., & Sanford, R. N. (1950). *The authoritarian personality* . New York: Harper & Row

Allport, G. W. (1958). *The nature of prejudice.* Garden City NY: Anchor Books.

Almond, G. A. (1954). *The appeals of communism.* Princeton, NJ: Princeton University Press.

Amir, Y. (1969). Contact hypothesis in intergroup relations. *Psychological Bulletin, 71*, 319–342.

Anderson, J. R. (1980). *Cognitive psychology and its implications.* San Francisco: W. H. Freeman.

Antaki, C. (1984). Core concepts in attribution theory. In J. Nicholson & H. Beloff. (Eds.), *Psychology survey* (Vol. 5,). Leicester: British Psychological Society.

Aron, R. (1977). *The opium of the intellectuals.* Westport: Greenwood Press.

Ashmore, R. D. & Del Boca. F. K. (1981). Conceptual approaches to stereotyping. In D. L. Hamilton (Ed.), *Cognitive processes in stereotyping and intergroup relations* (pp. 1136). Hillsdale NJ: Erlbaum.

Austin, W., Walster, E. & Ure, M. K. (1976). Equity and the law: The effect of a harmdoer's 'suffering in the act' on liking and assigned punishment. In L Berkowitz & E. Walters (Eds.), *Advances in experimental social psychology* (Vol. 9). New York: Academic Press.

Bartlett, F. (1932). *Remembering.* Cambridge: Cambridge University Press.

Bem, D. (1970). *Beliefs, attitudes and human affairs.* Monterey CA: Brooks/Cole.

Billig, M. (1978). *Fascists: A social psychological view of the National Front.* London: Academic Press.

Billig, (1982). *Ideology and social psychology.* Oxford: Blackwell.

Billig, M. (1984). Political ideology. In J. Nicholson & H. Beloff *(Eds.) Psychology survey* (Vol. 5, pp. 234–264). Leicester:British Psychological Society.

Billig, M. (1985). Prejudice, categorization and particularization:From a perceptual to a rhetorical approach. *European Journal of Social Psychology, 15,* 79–103.

Billig, M. (1986a). *Thinking and arguing: An inaugural lecture.* Loughborough: Loughborough University.

Billig, M. (1986b). Very ordinary life and the Young Conservatives. In H. Belorff (Ed.), *Getting into life* (pp. 67–94). London: Methuen.

Billig, M. (1987). *Arguing and thinking: A rhetorical approach to social psychology.* Cambridge: Cambridge University Press.

Billig, M. (1987). Anti-Semitic themes and the British far-left: Some social psychological observations on indirect aspects of the conspiracy tradition. In C. F. Graumann & S. Moscovici (Eds.), *Changing conceptions of conspiracy* (pp. 115–136). New York: Springer Verlag.

Brehm, J. W. (1966). *A theory of psychological reactance.* New York: Academic Press.

Brewer, M. B., & Kramer, R. M. (1985). The psychology of intergroup attitudes and behavior. *Annual Review of Psychology, 36,* 219–243.

Brewer, M. B. & Miller, N. (1984). Beyond the contact hypothesis: Theoretical perspectives on desegregation. In N. Miller & M. B. Brewer (Eds.), *Groups in contact* (pp. 281–302). New York: Academic Press.

Bruner, J. (1957). On perceptual readiness. *Psychological Review, 64,* 123–151.

Callaghan, J. (1984). *British Trotskyism: Theory and practice.* Oxford: Basil Blackwell.

Cantor, N., & Mischel, W., & Schwartz, J. (1982). Social knowledge: Structure, content, use and abuse. In A. H. Hastorf & A. M. Isen (Eds.), *Cognitive social psychology.* New York: Elsevier.

Cochrane, R., & Billig, M. (1984). I'm not National Front, but . . . *New Society, 68,* 255–258.

Cohn, N. (1967). *Warrant for genocide.* London: Chatto/Heinemann.

Condor, S. (1986a). Sex role beliefs and 'traditional' women: Feminist and intergroup perspectives. In S. Wilkinson *(Ed.), Feminist social psychology* (pp. 97–118). Milton Keynes: Open University Press.

Condor, S. (1986b). *Gender and social context: From sex categories to gender boundaries.* Paper presented at Annual Conference of the British Psychological Society, Sheffield.

Cook, S. W. (1984). Co-operative interaction in multiethnic contexts. In N. Miller & M. B. Brewer (Eds.), *Groups in contact.* New York: Academic Press.

Doise, W. (1982). *L'Explication en psychologie sociale.* Paris: Presses Universitaires de France.

Duncan, B. L. (1976). Differential social perception and attribution of intergroup violence: Testing the lower limits of stereotyping blacks. *Journal of Personality and Social Psychology, 34,* 590–598.

Eccelshall, R. *et al.* (1984). *Political ideologies.* London: Hutchinson.

Edelman, M. (1977). *Political language: Words that succeed and policies that fail.* New

York: Academic Press.

Edwards, D, & Mercer, N. (1987). *Common knowledge*. London: Methuen.

Edwards, D., & Middleton, D. (1986). Joint remembering: Constructing an account of shared experience through conversation discourse. *Discourse Processes, 5*, 125–138.

Edwards, D., & Middleton, D., (1987). Conversation and remembering: Bartlett revisited. *Applied Cognitive Psychology, 1*, 77–92.

Farr, R. M. (1983). Social representatons in the design and conduct of laboratory experiments. In R. M. Farr & S. Moscovici (Eds.), *Social representations* (pp. 125–148). Cambridge: Cambridge University Press.

Farr, R. M. (1984). Les repfesentations sociales. In S. Moscovici (Ed.), *Psychologie Sociale* (pp. 379–389). Paris: Presses Universitaires de France.

Feagin, J. R. (1972). Poverty: We still believe that God helps those who help themselves. *Psychology Today, 6*, 101–109.

Feather, N. T. (1974). Explanations of poverty in Australian and American samples: The person, society or fate? *Australian Journal of Psychology, 26*, 199–216.

Festinger, L. (1957). *A theory of cognitive dissonance*. New York: Row Peterson.

Freud, S. (1962). Five lectures on psycho-analysis. In *Two short accounts of psycho-analysis* (pp. 31–87). Harmondsworth: Penguin.

Furnham, A. (1982). Why are the poor always with us? Explanations for poverty in Britain. *British Journal of Social Psychology, 21*, 311–322.

Furnham, A. (1983). Attributions for affluence. *Personality and Individual Differences, 4*, 31–40.

Furnham, A. & Gunter, B. (1984). Just world beliefs and attitudes towards the poor. *British Journal of Social Psychology, 23*, 265–269.

Giddens, A. (1979). *Central problems in social theory*. London: Macmillan.

Gordon, P., & Klug, F. (1986). *New right, New racism*. London: Searchlight.

Greenwald, A. G. (1980). The totalitarian ego: Fabrication and revision of personal history. *American Psycholgist, 35*, 603–618.

Griffin, C. (1985a). *Typical girls?* London: Routledge & Kegan Paul.

Griffin, C. (1985b). Qualitative methods and cultural analysis: Young women and the transition from school to un/employment. In R. Burgess (Ed.), *Field methods in the study of Education*, London:

Hamilton, D. L. (1979). A cognitive-attributional analysis of stereotyping. In L. Berkowitz (Ed.), *Advances in experimental social psychology*. New York: Academic Press.

Hewitt, J. P., and Stokes, R. (1975). Disclaimers. *American Sociological Review, 40*, 1–11.

Hewstone, M., and Brown, R. (1986). *Contact and conflict in intergroup relations*. Oxford: Basil Blackwell.

Hewstone, M., and Jaspars, J. M. F. (1984). Social dimensions of attribution. In H. Tajfel (Ed.), *The social dimension*. Cambridge: Cambridge University Press.

Homans, G. C. (1983). Steps to a theory of social behavior; An autobiographical account. *Theory and Society, 12*, 1–45.

Jaspars, J. & Fraser, C. (1984). Attitudes and social representation. In R. M. Farr & S. Moscovici (Eds.), *Social representations* (pp. 100–124). Cambridge: Cambridge University Press.

Jodelet, D. (1984). Repfesentation sociale: phénomeñes, concept et théorie. In S. Moscovici (Ed.), *Psychologie Sociale* (pp. 355–377). Paris: Presses Universitaires de France.

Kinder, D. R. & Sears, D. O. (1981). Prejudice and politics: Symbolic racism versus racial threats to the good life. *Journal of Personality and Social Psychology, 40*, 414–431.

Larrain, J. (1979). *The concept of ideology.* London: Hutchinson.
Larrain, J. (1983). *Marxism and ideology.* London: Macmillan.
Lerner, M. J. (1977). The justice motive: Some hypotheses as to its origins and forms. *Journal of Personality, 45,* 1–52.
Lerner, M. J., Miller, D. T., & Holmes, J. G. (1976). Deserving and the emergence of forms of justice. In L. Berkowitz & E. Walster (Eds.), *Advances in experimental social psychology* (Vol. 9). New York: Academic Press.
Lipset, S. M. & Raab, E. (1971). *The politics of unreason.* London: Heinemann.
Mannheim, K. (1960). *Ideology and utopia.* London: Routledge & Kegan Paul.
McConahay, J. B. (1981). Reducing racial prejudice in desegregated schools. In W. D. Hawley (Ed.), *Effective school desegregation,* Beverly Hills: Sage.
McConahay, J. B. (1982). Self-interest versus racial attitudes as correlates of anti-busing attitudes in Louisville: Is it the buses or the blacks? *Journal of Politics, 44,* 692–720.
McConahay, J. B., Hardee, B. B., & Batts, V. (1981). Has racism declined in America? *Journal of Conflict Resolution, 25,* 563–579.
McConahay, J. B., & Hough, J. C. (1976). Symbolic racism. *Journal of Social Issues, 32,* 23–45.
McDougall, W. (1935). Pareto as a psychologist. *Journal of Social Philosophy, 1,* 36–52.
McGuire, W. J. (1966). The current status of cognitive consistency theories. In S. Feldman. (Ed.), *Cognitive consistency,* New York: Academic Press.
Mervis, C. B., & Rosch, E. (1981). Cateorization of natural objects. *Annual Review of Psychology, 32,* 89–115.
Murchison, C. (1935). Pareto and experimental social psychology. *Journal of Social Philosophy, 1,* 53–63.
Moscovici, S. (1982). The coming era of representations. In J. P. Codol & J. P. Leyens (Eds.), *Cognitive analysis of social behavior,* (pp. 115-150). The Hague: Martinus Nijhoff.
Moscovici, S. (1983). The phenomenon of social representations. In R. M. Farr & S Moscovici (Eds.), *Social representations* (pp.3–69). Cambridge: Cambridge University Press.
Moscovici, S. (1984). The myth of the lonely paradigm: A rejoinder. *Social Forces, 51,* 939–967.
Moscovici, S. (1985). Comment on Potter and Litton. *British Journal of Social Psychology, 24,* 91–92.
Murray, E. L. (1984). The significance of rhetoric in human science research. *Journal of Phenomenological Research, 15,* 169–175.
Nelson, J. S., & Megill, A. (1986). Rhetoric of inquiry: Projects and prospects. *Quarterly Journal of Speech, 72,* 20–37.
Newton, K. (1969). *The sociology of British communism.* London: Allen Lane.
Nilson L. B. (1981). Reconsidering ideological lines: Beliefs about poverty in America. *Sociological Quarterly, 22,* 531–548.
Nisbett, R. E., & Ross, L. (1980). *Human inference.* Englewood Cliffs, NJ: Prentice-Hall.
Pandey, J., Sinha, Y., Prakash, A., & Tripatti, R. C. (1982). Right-left political ideologies and attribution of the causes of poverty. *European Journal of Social Psychology, 12,* 327–333.
Pareto, V. (1935). *The mind and society.* London: Jonathan Cape.
Perelman, C., & Olbrechts-Tyteca, L. (1971). *The new rhetoric.* Notre Dame: University of Notre Dame Press.
Peterson S. A. (1985). Neurophysiology, cognition and political thinking. *Political Psychology, 6,* 495–518.
Potter, J., & Litton, I. (1985). Some problems underlying the theory of social representations. *British Journal of Social Psychology, 24,* 81–90.

Potter, J., Stringer, P., & Wetherell, M. (1984). Social texts and context. London: Routledge & Kegan Paul.

Potter, J., & Wetherell, M. (1987). Discourse and social psychology. London: Sage.

Radley, A. R. (1984). The embodiment of social relations in coronary heart disease. Social Science and Medicine, 19, 1227–1234.

Radley, A. R., & Green, R. (1985). Styles of adjustment to coronary graft surgery. Social Science and Medicine, 20, 461–472.

Rosch, E. (1978). Principles of categorization. In E. Rosch & B. Lloyd (Eds.), Cognition and categorization (pp. 28–48). Hillsdale NJ: Erlbaum.

Rothbart, M. (1981). Memory processes and social beliefs. In D. L. Hamilton (Ed.), Cognitive processes in stereotyping and intergroup relations, (pp. 145–182). Hillsdale NJ: Erlbaum.

Seidel, G. (1986). Culture, nation and 'race' in the British and French New Right. In R. Levitas (Ed.), The ideology of the new right. Oxford: Polity Press.

Shotter, J. (1986). Psychological theories as rhetorical constructions. Paper presented to The Rhetoric of the Human Sciences Seventh Annual Conference, Temple University, Philadelphia.

Shotter, J. (1986). A sense of place: Vico and the social production of social identities. British Journal of Social Psychology, 25, 199–211.

Shotter, J. (1987). Rhetoric as a model for psychology. Proceedings of the futures of psychology conference. Leicester: British Psychological Society.

Shotter, J. (1990). The rhetoric of theory in psychology. In J. F. H. van Rappard et al. (Eds.), Proceedings of the Founding Conference of the International Society for Theoretical Psychology. Amsterdam: North-Holland.

Singer, J. E. (1966). Motivation for consistency. In S. Feldman (Ed.), Cognitive consistency, (pp. 58-73). New York: Academic Press.

Smith, K. B. (1985). Seeing justice in poverty:The belief in a just world and ideas about inequalities. Sociological Spectrum, 5, 17– 29.

Snyder, M. (1981). Seek and ye shall find: Testing hypotheses about other people. In E. T. Higgins et al. Social cognition (Vol. 1). Hillsdale, NJ: Lawrence Erlbaum.

Sprague, R. K. (Ed.). (1972). The older sophists. Columbia: University of South Carolina Press.

Sumner, W. G. (1906). Folkways. Boston: Ginn.

Tajfel, H. (1981). Human groups and social categories. Cambridge: Cambridge Univerity Press.

Tajfel, H. (1984). Intergroup relations, social myths, and social justice in social psychology. In H. Tajfel (Ed.), The social dimension. Cambridge: Cambridge University Press.

Taylor, D. M, & Jaggi, V. (1974). Ethnocentrism and causal attribution in a south Indian context. Journal of Cross-Cultural Psychology, 5, 162– 171.

Taylor, D. M., & Moghaddan, A. (1987). Theories of intergroup relations. New York: Praeger.

Taylor, S. E. (1981). A categorization approach to stereotyping. In D. L. Hamilton (Ed.), Cognitive processes in stereotyping and intergroup relations, Hillsdale, NJ: Erlbaum.

Turner, J. C. (1982). Towards a cognitive redefinition of the social group. In H. Tajfel (Ed.), Social identity and intergroup relations (pp. 15–40). London: Academic Press.

Van Dijk, T. A. (1984). Prejudice and discourse: An analysis of ethnic prejudice in cognition and conversation. Amsterdam: Benjamins.

Verba, S., & Orren, G. R. (1986). Equality in America:The view from the top. Cambridge, MA: Harvard University Press.

Walster, E., Berscheid, E., & Walster, G. W. (1976). New directions in equity research. In L. Berkowitz & E. Walters (Eds.), *Advances in experimental social psychology* (Vol. 9). New York: Academic Press.

Weigel, R. H. & Howes, P. W. (1985). Conceptions of racial prejudice: Symbolic racism reconsidered. *Journal of Social Issues, 41,* 117–138.

Wetherell, M. (1986). Linguistic repertoires and literary criticism: New directions for a social psychology of gender. In S. Wilkinson (Ed.), *Feminist social psychology,* (pp. 77–96). Milton Keynes: Open University Press.

Wetherell, M., Stiven, H., & Potter, J. (1987). Unequal egalitarianism. *British Journal of Social Psychology, 26,* 59–72.

Wicklund, R. A. & Brehm, J. W. (1976). *Perspectives on cognitive dissonance.* London: Wiley.

Wicklund, R. A., & Frey, D. (1981). Cognitive consistency: Motivational versus non-motivational perspectives. In J. P. Forgas (Ed.), *Social cognition,* (pp. 141–163). London: Academic Press.

Zukier, H. (1990). Conspiracy as a crime in solidarity: The case of medieval Western European Jewry. In C. F. Graumann & S. Moscovici (Eds.), *Changing conceptions of conspiracy* (pp. 87–109). New York: Springer-Verlag.

8

Egalitarianism in the Laboratory and at Work

Morton Deutsch

This chapter focuses on the question: Is there, inevitably, the trade-off between economic efficiency and equality that is so commonly assumed (e.g., Okun, 1975)? It is divided into two major sections. First, I shall review the experimental research done in my laboratory that bears upon this question and, second, I shall summarize the diverse scholarly literature relating to work that is relevant to this issue: the literature dealing with different forms of work compensation, ownership, participation, and control. Elsewhere (Deutsch, 1985), I consider some of the problems associated with egalitarianism and discuss the conditions conducive to the effective functioning of an egalitarian system.[1]

Experimental Research on Egalitarianism

Studies of Cooperation–Competition

Although I was unaware of it as I conducted my early experiment on the effects of cooperation and competition upon group process (Deutsch, 1949b), this study has direct relevance to basic issues relating to the consequences of an egalitarian as compared to a meritocratic system of

---

[1]This chapter is based upon material presented more fully in my book, *Distributive Justice: A Social-Psychological Perspective.* New Haven: Yale University Press, 1985.

Morton Deutsch • Teachers College, Columbia University, New York, New York 10027

distributing rewards. As originally formulated, the experiment was meant to test my theory of cooperation and competition that focused on the social psychological effects of different types of goal interdependence in combination with different types of instrumental actions (Deutsch, 1949a). It was only much later, as my attention centered on distributive justice, did I realize that this early experiment was a study of the effects of two different distributive principles: a competitive–meritocratic and a cooperative–egalitarian principal.

The results of the experiment showed striking differences between the cooperative–egalitarian and competitive–meritocratic groups. The students in the groups that operated under the egalitarian principle (i.e., the "cooperative" groups) were not only more productive, but they also developed friendlier interpersonal relations and felt more esteemed and more self-confident as compared to those in the groups that functioned under the competitive "meritocratic" principle.[2]

Since my 1949 study of cooperation and competition, many hundreds of related studies have been conducted. They have investigated "individualistic" as well as cooperative and competitive groups; they have studied cooperative and competitive relations between groups as well as within groups; they have conducted research in classrooms and in work settings as well as in the laboratory; they have studied groups whose compositions were homogeneous and groups that were composed of individuals of diverse ability, or of diverse racial and ethnic background, or of people who were physically disabled and not disabled (see Johnson & Johnson, 1983.) The results of this large body of research are very consistent with my theory of cooperation–competition and with my early study of the effects of cooperation and competition upon group process. The findings are unequivocal in demonstrating substantial differences in the social psychological effects of the two distributive principles upon interpersonal relations, self-attitudes, attitude toward work, and group performance.

Experimental Studies of the Effects of Different Systems of Distributive Justice

My students and I (Deutsch, 1985) have conducted a series of studies that was stimulated by the assumption implicit in equity theory that

---

[2]It should be noted that the "meritocratic" principle is not always "competitive"; it is so only when a fixed amount (a constant sum) is being allocated: Hence, the more one person gets, the less is available for another. An "individualistic" form of this principle occurs whenever the amount of the allocated is variable and dependent upon the level of the total contributions: here, the allocations the individuals receive are independent of one another. Thus the results of this early experiment had no direct relevance to the individualistic form of "meritocracy."

people will be more productive if they are rewarded in proportion to their contribution. The research described in the preceding section on cooperation–competition had clearly demonstrated that this assumption is not correct when the individuals are working on tasks where it is helpful for them to cooperate, to share information and resources, or to coordinate their activities. Perhaps the assumption has validity only when the individuals are involved in noninterdependent tasks, in work that is not facilitated by effective cooperation.[3]

It is evident that the conditions described in footnote 3 are rarely found in the "real world" of work. However, they can be created in the laboratory. Our first two studies were fashioned to create the conditions likely to maximize the chance of finding support for the assumption that performance will be enhanced by the expectation of being rewarded in proportion to one's contributions. In them, the subjects worked in separate cubicles, on identical tasks that were neither interesting nor difficult. Both experiments systematically varied the type of distributive system, using the same task; the second also varied the magnitude of the rewards available to the subjects and used female as well as male subjects. In a third experiment, the subjects worked face-to-face on several different types of very brief tasks under different distributive systems. In contrast to the first three, the subjects in the fourth study worked alone under one or another reward system similar in character to the different distributive justice systems. In a fifth, the subjects worked face-to-face on a highly interdependent, extended task. In a sixth, the "good" being distributed within the group was "grades" rather than "money"; the grades were distributed either according to the "equality" or "proportionality" principle and were based upon either the "amount of effort" or the "level of performance."

Four different principles of allocating the group's earnings to its members were used in a number of the studies. These were described as follows:

---

[3]In fact, careful thought about the circumstances under which rewarding members in proportion to their contribution to a group (or rewarding individuals in proportion to their performance) would most likely induce relatively high productivity suggests that there are a number of basic requisites. These include the following: (1) the task to be accomplished must be clearly defined and specified; (2) the individuals involved must believe that their performance can be measured reliably, validly, and with sufficient precision; (3) achievement must be readily susceptible to continued improvement by increased effort, and this is believed to be so by the individuals involved; (4) the type of reward offered for performance must be desired by the individual, and its value to the individual must increase with the amount of reward he or she receives; (5) the dependence of an individual's reward upon his or her accomplishment must be known to the individual and subjectively salient during his or her work; and (6) neither individual nor group task performance should depend upon effective social cooperation.

- *Winner-takes-all:* Under this system, whoever performs the task best in the group wins all the money the group is paid.
- *Proportionality:*Under this system, each person is rewarded in proportion to his or her contribution to the group score. In other words, the person who contributes 50% of the group's total output will get 50% of the money to be distributed within the group; a person who contributes 10% of the group's total output would get 10% of the money to be distributed within the group, and so on.
- *Equality:* Under this system, each person in the group will get an equal share of the money to be distributed within the group. In other words, each person will get 1/3 of the group's total earnings.
- *Need:* Under the need distribution system, each group member will be rewarded according to the need expressed on the biographical data sheet. In other words, the person who needs the money most would proportionately get more money; the person who needs the money least would get the least amount of money,

The overall results of the six experiments will be presented in terms of a number of key questions asked of all the data.

1. *Did the different distributive system have differential effects on performance?* There is clear and consistent evidence in all of the relevant experiments that there are no reliable effects of the distribution system on individual or group productivity when neither individual nor group task performance depends upon effective social cooperation. This result is obtained when the individual is working in a group context and also when he or she is working alone. That is, there is no evidence to indicate that people work more productively when they are expecting to be rewarded in proportion to their performance than when they are expecting to be rewarded "equally" or on the basis of "need."

2. *Were there initial differences in attitudes toward the different distributive systems?* The subjects initially strongly preferred the "proportionality" over the other distributive system. The second most favored was "equality"; "need" was disfavored; and they had the most negative reaction to the "winner-takes-all" system.

3. *Were attitudes toward other group members affected by the different distributive principles?* Even when the groups were nominal rather than interacting groups (as in the first two experiments), there were some significant effects of the distributive system on attitudes toward other group members. The subjects in the "equality" and

"need" conditions reported having cooperative feelings toward one another; those in the "winner-takes-all" and "proportionality" conditions reported having "competitive' feelings toward one another.

4. *How were attitudes toward the tasks and work affected by the different distributive systems?* Under the "equality" system, the subjects found the tasks more interesting and more pleasant than in the other systems. They also reported the highest intrinsic motivation to perform well, the highest motivation to perform because of "task enjoyment," a high desire to increase the group's performance, and the lowest desire to outperform the other group members. Subjects, in all conditions, indicated very high intrinsic motivation to perform well, and this was rated as the strongest component of their motivation to perform well.

5. *Did the "high," "medium," "low" performers in the various conditions differ from one another in their preferences and attitudes?* Even before task performance had occurred, those who were to have different performance ranks in their groups had different preferences regarding the distribution principles: The better one's future performance, the more one preferred the "winner-takes-all" principle and the less one preferred the "need" and "equality" principles; the "medium" performers (those whose performance was neither best nor worst) preferred the "proportionality" principle more than either the "low" or "high" performers. In the nominal group, the relationship between task performance and preferences for distributive principle remained essentially the same from the pretask to posttask measurement Parallel results were obtained for the ratings of the "fairness" of the distributive principle.

However, in the face-to-face interacting groups, the relationship between task performance and preferences for the different distributive systems changed during the course of the experiment. After performing the various tasks, the "proportionality," "equality," and "need" systems were in each case just as likely to be chosen by "high" and "low" performers. Only the choice of the "winner-takes-all" system appeared to reflect self-interest: being chosen by "winners" only.

6. *What were the preexperimental correlates of initial attitudes toward the different distributive systems?* Preferences for "winner-takes-all" and, to a lesser extent for "proportionality" were associated with a sense of power, toughness, self-confidence, and a more conservative political orientation, a feeling of competitiveness, and a tendency to downplay one's groupmates. In contrast, preferences for the "equality" and "need" principles were correlated with more favorable attitudes toward one's fellow group members and less favorable views

of one's own chances and capabilities. The greater the tendency to be "Machiavellian," the higher the subject's preference for "winner-takes-all" and lower his or her preference for "equality."

Our results provide little support for the common assumption that productivity would be higher when earnings are closely tied to performance. Despite the fact that the tasks were neither particularly interesting nor demanding and despite participating in the experiment primarily to earn money, the subjects seemed more motivated to perform well by their own needs to do as well as they could rather than by the greater amount of pay they might earn from higher performance in the "proportionality" and winner-takes-all" conditions. Their motivation to perform was determined more by self-standards than by external reward.

These results are not surprising if one takes into account that the subjects were college students who were not alienated from themselves, their colleagues, or the experimenters. They had no reason not to do as well as they could whether or not they would earn money by so doing. If they had felt alienated from themselves and their capabilities and had little pride in their own effectiveness, then their performances might have been more influenced by the external reward. It is possible that the assumption that people will be more productive if they are rewarded in proportion to their contribution is valid only when people are alienated from their work.

Egalitarianism in the Workplace

The research that I have summarized in the preceding section clearly indicates that an egalitarian distribution of rewards or earnings within a group does not result in less effective individual or group performance than a meritocratic one; to the contrary, when the task required coordination, sharing, communication, or interdependent activity among group members, the performance of egalitarian groups was superior. However, these were laboratory and classrooom groups; the people involved were students; the rewards that were distributed did not affect the individual's standard of living; the groups had short lives; and so on. Perhaps the commonly assumed trade-off between efficiency and equality would appear in research on "real-life" egalitarian work groups, even if it does not necessarily occur in the laboratory or classroom.

Here, I shall briefly review the diverse scholarly literature dealing with different forms of worker compensation, ownership, participation, and control to see whether egalitarianism and efficiency are incompatible. However, before proceding with this review, I consider the meaning of "economic egalitariansm."

The Meaning of Economic Egalitarianism

In the literature on economic democracy, worker cooperatives, and the like, there is a clearly emerging social ideal of economic egalitarianism that has several key components. Central to the ideal of economic egalitarianism is the view that the workplace should be a cooperative rather than an authoritarian or adversarial system (Whyte & Blasi, 1982). A cooperative framework is required to do away with the oppositional, alienating tendencies inherent in the power differences between the bosses and the bossed as well as those implicit in the different economic interests of employers and employees. Worker cooperatives are democratically controlled by those who work in them. In small cooperative enterprises, decisions are usually made by the entire work group in frequent meetings. Larger ones have management positions, that are filled by election on the basis of one person, one vote. Such positions are usually subject to rotation and are open to all qualified members. Managers can be recalled by the members; ultimate authority rests in the work force. Full worker participation in decision making exists at all levels of the organization. The opportunity for informed and effective participation is aided by training and full access to relevant information.

How the income and surplus produced by the cooperative should be distributed is decided by the work force. The tendency is toward equality; differences, when they exist, between the highest and lowest paid workers are much smaller than in privately owned firms. Profit or surplus may be used for reinvestment within the firm to create new jobs, to improve working conditions, or to improve productivity; it may be invested in education, health clinics, daycare centers, or other social and community purposes; or it may be distributed in the form of bonuses or increased benefits.

Land, buildings, machinery, and other assets and liabilities of the cooperative are owned by the work force. Unlike the situation in employee-owned corporations, where the shares they own in the corporation can be sold to other individuals (including outsiders), members of a worker cooperative cannot sell their share of ownership except to the cooperative. The value of a cooperative member's share is determined by the value of his or her "internal account." The initial balance in this account is determined by the membership fee or the member's initial financial contribution at the start of the cooperative.

At the end of each fiscal year, the member's portion of the cooperative's surplus (or loss) is added to (or subtracted from) his or her
account balance. When a person terminates membership, the balance
in the member's account is paid out to the ex-member over a specified
number of years.

Patterns of Compensation

The available research on performance-based pay plans in industry
(summarized in Katzell & Yankelovich, 1975, and Lawler, 1971, 1981)
does not speak clearly nor reliably to the question of whether there is
a trade-off between egalitarian wage structures and work efficiency.
Thus there is some research evidence to suggest that individuals work
more efficiently when their pay is clearly linked to their performance.
But there are many qualifications that have to be added to this
statement. First, the research does not demonstrate that it is the
connection between pay and performance rather than the connection
with "accountability" (i.e., with performance appraisal and feedback)
or with other confounded factors that is instrumental. Second, as
Lawler has pointed out, merit pay systems can be dysfunctional and
lead to inefficiencies when the organizational conditions necessary to
their effective functioning does not exist. There is little reason to
believe that the necessary conditions for their effective functioning
exist in most work organizations.

There is also some research evidence suggesting that performance-
based pay plans where the performing unit is the group (department,
plant, or firm) can lead to more efficiency than pay plans based on
individual performance when cooperative work is required. Such
plans tend to be more egalitarian than plans based on individual
performance. Group plans, in addition, are less plagued by some of the
measurement and other administrative problems of individual merit
pay systems.

I could find no research evidence that directly addresses the
question of whether individual as compared to group merit pay
systems lead to more efficient retention of high-performing employees
and more efficient elimination of lower performing ones. On reason for
assuming that egalitarian pay systems are relatively inefficient is
because high performers presumably could earn more in a nonegalitarian system and, hence, would be likely to leave the egalitarian system;
this would not be the case in an individually based, merit system.
There are other reasons to suppose that the closer, personal attach-
ments and the more congenial interpersonal atmosphere associated

with the egalitarian as compared to the individualistic–competitive system might lead to a stronger desire to remain in the egalitarian system.

Patterns of Participation and Control

In the doctrine of economic egalitarianism, the ideal of equality of power—the ability to participate equally in making the decisions that control, directly and indirectly, one's work and the organization in which one works—is at least as central as the ideal of an equal standard of living. Worker participation in decision making within a firm can take place at three levels: the shop floor, the department and plant, and the corporate level. At the department and corporate levels, participation is usually indirect through delegates or representatives. Shop floor participation involves direct personal involvement as an individual or as a member of a small group in such day-to-day operating decisions as scheduling of work, work methods, workplace layout, quantity of output, quality control, training. Terms such as *job enrichment, job redesign, job enlargement, job rotation, work restructuring, autonomous work group,* and so on are often used to characterize worker participation and control at the shop level.

At the departmental and plant levels, worker participation is in the administrative decisions, through representatives to "work councils" or "joint labor–management consultative committees," that usually have consequences for weeks to months (at departmental level) or for a year or two (at the plant level.) At the departmental level, these include cost and quality control, resource allocations, achievement of targets and quotas, and planning and coordination of activities. At the plant level, the decisions center about product lines; production layouts; plantwide work arrangements; hiring, firing, and promotion of employees; and acquisition, organization, and control of resources needed for production. At the corporate level, worker participation is through representatives on corporate boards that are concerned with such long-range strategic policy decisions as setting goals and objectives; choice of products and geographic locations; pricing and marketing policies; major capital expenditures; diversification; mergers, acquisitions, raising of capital; and disposition of profits.

The meager available research evidence about the effects of a more equal sharing of power in the workplace suggests that it increases rather than decreases economic efficiency (see Katzell & Yankelovich, 1975, and Jain, 1980.) Although there is a significant push toward more participatory control in the workplace, propelled in part by the increasing education and sophistication of the high-tech work force, neither employers nor unions yet seem to be eager to extend coopera- tion to include the corporate board as well as the shop floor.

Employee Ownership

Two forms of employee ownership of firms are emerging in the United States (Woodworth, 1981.) Here, we briefly discuss one form, some- times labeled *worker capitalism*, in which employees, as individuals, typically acquire shares in the enterprise through an "employee stock ownership plan" or through direct purchase of a plant that is about to close, be relocated, or be subjected to a takeover by a conglomerate. The employees function as individual shareholders who have a per- sonal economic interest in the profitability of their firm; as sharehold- ers, even when they together own a majority interest (this is often not the case), the employees do not use their shares collectively to determine management decisions. "Worker capitalism" may or may not involve participation and control over their workplace. Rarely does it involve a fundamental change from a capitalist philosophy of ownership and management.

The results of the limited available research (see Conte & Tannen- baum, 1978) indicate that economic egalitarianism as expressed in the form of employee ownership of the firm appears to result in greater productivity and profitability as well as better attitudes. Again, there is little support for the widely held notion that increased egalitarianism has a trade-off in economic efficiency. Nevertheless, it is well to recognize that the atmosphere of euphoria that often characterizes a firm after its transformation to employee ownership, after several months, is often followed by growing dissatisfaction, sometimes ac- companied by severe conflict. As Whyte and Blasi (1982, p. 143) point out:

> The disillusionment of workers and the resulting conflicts arise out of a failure of management to recognize that an employee-owned firm cannot be managed effectively by following the authoritarian model.

Worker Cooperatives

A second form of worker ownership exists in worker cooperatives. These are usually owned by the work force of the firm or by the cooperative community in which the enterprise is located (as in the

Kibbutzim); many such cooperatives do not permit sale or transfer of individual ownership rights. Control of the firm is in the hands of the work force and is commonly distributed on the egalitarian principle of "one person, one vote." However, when the cooperative is part of a cooperative community (as in the Kibbutzim) or part of a complex of interrelated cooperatives (as in the Mondragon system), the larger community or cooperative system usually has an important voice in determining policy decisions that would affect the community or system of which it is a component.

There are many examples of successful, well-established, worker-controlled enterprises and of long-lived communes (see Lindenfeld & Rothschild-Whitt, 1982; Oakeshott, 1978; Simmons & Mares, 1983, for illustrations of worker-cooperatives and Kanter, 1987, for communes.) Later I discuss several examples of such enterprises that are structured on the egalitarian principle of "one member, one vote," including the U.S. Plywood Cooperatives, The Mondragon Cooperative System in Spain, and the Kibbutz Cooperative Sector in Israel.

The U.S. Plywood Cooperatives. Various studies have shown that the plywood cooperatives have consistently outperformed private plywood firms substantially (25 to 60%) in productivity and also in the wages received by the workers (about 25% higher.) A large portion of this productivity difference may result from the smaller number of management and supervisory personnel required in the cooperatives. In traditional firms, supervisory personnel are used to police the work force, checking on goofing off and careless or inefficient work. In the co-ops, workers police themselves and one another, saving an enormous amount of money that is traditionally spend for supervisors.

The Mondragon Cooperative System. The Mondragon Cooperatives in the Basque region in Spain have grown form a single industrial cooperative started by five young men in 1956, to a network of more than 87 cooperatives with 18,000 workers and $1.7 billion in annual sales. Thomas and Logan (1982, pp. 126–127), after a careful economic analysis conclude:

> Various indicators have been used to explore the economic efficiency of the Mondragon group of cooperatives. During more than two decades, a considerable number of cooperative factories have functioned at a level equal or superior in efficiency to that of capitalist enterprises. . . . Efficiency in terms of the use made of scarce resources has been higher in the cooperatives; their growth record of sales, exports, and employment, under both favourable and adverse economic conditions, has been superior to that of capitalist enterprises.

The Kibbutz Cooperative Sector in Israel Menachem Rosner
(Rosner et al., 1978), one of the foremost students of the Kibbutzim, has
written "The equality of mankind—not merely in its formal connota-
tion but in the true human and social sense as well--is the most
fundamental principle upon which Kibbutz society is based." Embodied in its basic values are two major conceptions: allowance for the
specific and diverse needs of various individuals (an individualized or
particularistic equality) and the separation of one's social contribution
from the material rewards one receives.

In 1979, there were 254 Kibbutz Communities with almost 120,000
members, comprising about 3.3% of the population of Israel (Rosner,
1982.) The contribution of the Kibbutzim to the Israeli national product
greatly outweighs their portion of the population (40% of the agricul-
tural and 6% of the industrial output), and its members have been and
are disproportionately represented in the parliament and among the
political and military leaders of Israel. At the same, time, the various
indicators of social pathology—crime, drug addiction, suicide, juve-
nile delinquency, mental disorder—appear to be disproportionately
low in the Kibbutzim.

A typical Kibbutz is an egalitarian, rural community of several
hundred families democratically governed by a general assembly based
on the principle of one member, one vote; the assembly meets on the
average of three times a month. A kibbutz is "owned" by its members,
but it cannot be sold, and its assets cannot be divided by its members.
If individual members leave, they have severance pay provisions based
on a number of clearly defined factors. Kibbutzim are organized into a
"holding company" that is affiliated with the general labor organization of Israel. Should the majority of a Kibbutz decide to dissolve it, the
Kibbutz's assets would be turned over to the holding company. (For
additional descriptions of Kibbutz life, see Blasi, 1980; Lieblich, 1982;
Rayman, 1982; Snarey, 1982.)

People who work together in a Kibbutz factory, no matter what their
positions in the factory, live together in the same community and have
equal standards of living as well as equal control over community
affairs. The decision-making process on issues related to the industrial
plant within a Kibbutz is partly determined by the nature of the
substantive issues. The Kibbutz general assembly usually makes the
decision on the election of a plant manger, the investment plan, the
professional training plan, and the hiring of outside workers; the
worker's assembly, within the plant, commonly makes the decisions
with regard to production plans, work arrangements, choice of candi-
dates for training, and election of other plant officials than the
manager; and the plant management decides with regard to technical

and professional problems. Even when the general assembly retains final decision power, it will receive suggestions and proposals from the worker's assembly and the plant manager with regard to the issue being considered.

For the Kibbutz as a whole as well as for its industrial plants and other branches, all managerial and coordinating positions are rotated in order to prevent the emergence of a managerial elite. Rotation implies not only a turnover of personnel but also that a factory manager will usually be assigned to other lower levels within the plant after completing his tour of duty as manager.

In addition to job rotation of managers, Leviatan (1980a, b) identifies two other mechanisms that are used in the Kibbutzim to counterbalance the ill effects of hierarchy in organization: direct democracy that provides rank-and-file workers influence over the selection (via the worker's assembly and the general assembly) of plant officers and influence over many aspects of the plant's functioning; and independence of status dimensions such that the individual's standard of living as well as his or her position in the Kibbutz community organization is uncorrelated with his or her position in the factory. That is, a manager has the same standard of living as a worker and is not any more likely to have a high position in the community.

Despite the "handicaps" under which they operate, Leviatan (1978, p. 11,) points out that studies and economic analyses of the functioning of Kibbutz work organizations have proved that the Kibbutzim not only compete with their rival organizations in Israel but that in many instances they function even better than similar organizations outside the Kibbutz. He indicates (1978, pp. 23–24) that the following general lessons can be drawn form the Kibbutz experience:

- The Kibbutz experience in the spheres of work and economy had proven the feasibility for the successful existence of a non-market economics, since the Kibbutz had broken down the traditional link between the contribution made by a person and the rewards conferred upon him.
- It serves also as a successful example of functioning of work organizations in a situation where material rewards or their equivalents cannot serve as such because of their nondifferentality. So, it highlights the effectiveness of psychological motivations of higher order needs.
- In the other words, the Kibbutz experience is inconsistent with the assumption of an inevitable trade-off between equality and efficiency.

Concluding Comment

I have reviewed an extensive literature (see Deutsch, 1985, for a more extensive review) that indirectly or directly bears upon the issue of whether egalitarian work systems are inherently less efficient than nonegalitarian systems. The existing research is meager and not of high quality, but its findings are concordant with the results of the more carefully controlled laboratory studies described in the first section. There is no reliable or consistent research-based evidence that justifies the conclusion that egalitarian systems are intrinsically less productive than the more traditional, nonegalitarian systems. To the contrary, the available research suggests that, when efficient work requires efficient cooperation, almost any movement toward a democratic, egalitarian, cooperative system and away from, the more traditional authoritarian, hierarchical, adversarial system of work improves productivity and lessens worker alienation. This is so whether the movement is from individual- to group performance-based pay, or from nonparticipation to worker participation in decision making and profit sharing, or from outside ownership to worker ownership, or from authoritarian control to democratic control. This is not to deny the importance of individual performance and accountability but rather to suggest that when everyone has a stake in your performance, your immediate coworkers as well as yourself, this enhances rather than reduces your accountability and your motivation to work and cooperate effectively. Nor is it to deny that one may work harder if one is paid more: When one is alienated from work (because of dissatisfying work), or from one's coworkers (because of competitive relations), or from those for whom one works (because of an adversarial system.)

As I have discussed elsewhere (Deutsch, 1985), egalitarian–cooperative systems have a tendency to break down and fail or to regress toward a more traditional, hierarchical, nonegalitarian system. It takes thoughtful, organized, and continual effort to sustain such systems. If egalitarianism were taken seriously and the serious effort necessary to establish and maintain such democratic cooperative systems were made, the odds are that we would be more productive and less alienated from ourselves and from one another.

References

Blast, J. (1980). *The communal future: The kibbutz and the utopian dilemma*; Philadelphia: Norwood Edition.
Conte, M., & Tannenbaum, A. (1978) *Employee ownership. A report presented to the Economic Development Administration, U.S. Department of Commerce.* Ann Arbor: University of Michigan Survey Research Center.

Deutsch, M. (1949a). A theory of cooperation and competition. *Human Relations*, 2, 129–51.
Deutsch, M. (1949b). An experimental study of the effects of cooperation and competition upon group processes. *Human Relations*, 2, 199–232.
Deutsch, M. (1985). *Distributive justice: A social-psychological perspective*. New Haven: Yale University Press.
Jain, H. C. (Ed.),(1980). *Worker participation: Success and problems*. New York: Praeger.
Johnson, D. W., R. T. Johnson, and Macugama (1983). Interdependence and interpersonal attraction among heterogeneous and homogenous individuals: A formulation and a meta-analysis of the research. *Review of Educational Research*, 53, 5–54.
Kanter, R.M. (1972). *Commitment and community: Communes and utopias in a sociological perspective*. Cambridge: Harvard University Press.
Katzell, R. A., & Yankelovich D. (1975). *Work, productivity and job satisfaction: An evaluation of policy-related research* New York: Psychological Corporation.
Lawler, E. E. (1971). *Pay and organizational effectiveness: A psychological view* New York: McGraw-Hill.
Lawler, E. E. (1981).*Pay and organizational development*. Reading MA.: Addison-Wesley.
Leviatan, U. (1978). *Some problematic aspects of the work sphere in the kibbutz society*. Haifa, Israel: Institute for Research of the Kibbutz and the Cooperative Idea, University of Haifa.
Leviatan, U. (1980a). *Counterbalancing the ill effects of hierarchy: The case of the kibbutz industrial organization*. Haifa, Israel: institute for Research of the Kibbutz and the Cooperative Idea University of Haifa.
Leviatan, U. (1980b). *Individual effects of managerial rotation: The case of the "demoted"office holder*. Haifa, Israel: Institute for Research of the Kibbutz and the Cooperative Idea, University of Haifa.
Lieblich, A. (1982). *KibbutzMakon* New York: Pantheon Books.
Lindenfeld, F., & Rothschild-Whitt J. (1982) *Workplace democracy and social change* Boston: Porter-Sargent.
Oakeshott, R. (1978). *The case for workers co-ops* London: Methuen.
Okun, A. M. (1975). *Equality and efficiency: The big tradeoff*. Washington, DC Brookings Institution.
Rayman, P. (1982). *The kibbutz community and nation-building* Princeton: Princeton University Press.
Rosner, M. (1982). *Democracy, equality and change: The kibbutz and social theory*. Darby, PA: Norwood.
Rosner, M., Ben-Devid, Y., Ovnat, A., Cohen, N., & Leviatan, U. (1978). *The second generation: Between continuity and change*. Tel-Aviv: Sifriat Poalim. In Hebrew.
Simmons, J., & Mares, W. (1983). *Working Together*. New York: Alfred A. Knopf.
Snerey, J. (1982) *The social and moral development of kibbutz sabras and founders* Cambridge, MA: Harvard University Project for Kibbutz Studies.
Thomas, H., & Logen, L. (1982). *Mondragon: An economic analysis*. London: George Allen & Unwin.
Whyte, F. W., & Blasi, J. R. (1982). Worker ownership, participation and control: Toward a theoretical model. *Policy sciences*, 4, 137–63.
Woodworth, W. (1981). Forms of employee ownership and workers' control. *Sociology of Work and Occupation*, B(2), 195–200.

9

The Model of Homo Economicus
Should It Be Revisited?

Janusz L. Grzelak

A widely accepted psychological assumption is that people respond to the world as they perceive it, not to the world as it is. In other words, it is assumed that people's behavior depends upon their cognitive representation of the external world, that is it depends upon their schemata and scripts that they acquire throughout their lives. So does our behavior, as social scientists. The way we theorize and do empirical studies is also determined by already available schemata and scripts. We call them "theories," "experimental paradigms," or the like. Moreover, in exploring the world of human behavior, we are not only channeled by theory itself but also attracted and channeled by particular interpretations of a theory and by methodological approaches that appear to be most commonly used and accepted within our scientific community. This bias effect seems to be as undesirable as inevitable.[1]

Psychological studies on allocation and exchange behavior have relied heavily on the image of man as a selfish being intent upon maximizing his benefits. This notion pervades much of our thinking, and it forms the core of many exchange theories, theories of decision

[1]The ideas presented in this chapter were partly developed within a research project sponsored by the Institute for Social Profilaxy and Resocialization (University of Warsaw). The chapter was written during my visit at the Catholic University of Brabant (Tilburg, The Netherlands). I wish to thank John Rijsman for arranging my visit and to thank Matthijs Poppe and Sandra Shruijer for their helpful comments on the first draft of the chapter.

Janusz L. Grzelak • Psychological Institute, University of Warsaw, 00-183 Warsaw, Poland.

making, collective action, and others. In the field of research on social dilemmas, it commonly manifests itself in narrowing down our approach to the theoretical framework of decision making and to experimental games as the main methodological paradigm.

Social dilemmas, often considered a subcategory of social traps, are characterized by two properties:

> (1) each person has an individually rational choice that, when made by all members of the group, (2) provides a poorer outcome than that which the members would have received if no members made the rational choice. (Messick & Brewer, 1983, p. 15)

Thus social dilemmas are conceptualized as a conflict of *interests* in which each person has a *choice* either to cooperate or to defect, to save (and possibly contribute to) common goods or to free-ride. How are the three concepts of "interest", "choice" (decision) and "n-person" related to the basic theoretical notions of social reality, people's interpretation of that reality, and research practice?

A comprehensive answer to these fundamental and complex questions is beyond my competence. However, in this chapter I intend to show at least some limitations of the present theoretical and methodological approach. They are chiefly illustrated by investigations of social orientations and social dilemmas, although, to a great extent, they apply to research on social justice as well.

The first section of the chapter is focused on choice consequences: the extent to which their meaning and their use is limited in experimental studies. The second section deals with the problem of cognitive representations and processes in interdependence situations and how they are related to social orientations. Next, a limitation of a two-person assessment of social orientation is shown, and an extension to a n-person assessment is proposed. The chapter ends with a discussion of some, especially cognitive, aspects of a multilevel interdependence structure of dilemmas in democratic and autocratic settings.

Many ideas presented in the first two sections originated from and were developed in collaboration with M. Poppe, Z. Czwartosz, and A. Nowak.[2]

Choice Consequences

Monetary Trap

Money and other material goods are a component of many but not all outcome structures of real social dilemmas. Yet, in experimental games

---

[2]A collaboration within the exchange program between the Catholic University of Brabant and the University of Warsaw.

and gamelike situations, outcomes, with almost no exception, are narrowed down to monetary payoffs. It is not surprising because financial incentives are the easiest to manipulate in laboratory settings and the utility function for money is fairly well studied. Money is also used in assessing individuals' social orientations and in investigating social (distributive) justice. It seems to be believed that in the exchange, allocation, or conflict situations, it is only the relationship between outcomes (and/or inputs) that counts, not the quality of them. Therefore, large portions of our knowledge about people's behavior come from research in which payoff structure, motivational variables, and social norms are manipulated, controlled, or measured by the use of monetary means.

The one-sidedness of this research raises the question of the extent to which this knowledge is valid when outcomes other than money are involved (Grzelak, 1986; Kemp & van Kreveld, 1986; Klandermans, 1986). The importance of the qualitative differences between various kinds of inputs and outcomes has been pointed out at the theoretical level (Foa & Foa, 1976). So far, only a very few empirical studies have investigated this problem.

In one of these studies (Grzelak, 1986) the differential effects of types of outcomes upon social orientations were explored.

Social orientations are defined by what people tend to achieve in interaction with others: to maximize own gain (individualism), partners' profit (altruism), joint profit (cooperation), a difference between own and partner's gain to the advantage of self (competition), to minimize a difference between own and partner's gain (equality orientation), or still other goals (Griesinger & Livingstone, 1973; Messick & McClintock, 1968; McClintock, 1976). A majority of techniques measuring individuals' value orientations is based either on choices made in matrix games (e.g., Messick & Thorngate, 1967) and in decomposed games (Kuhlman & Marshello, 1975; Kuhlman, Camac & Cunha, 1986; McClintock, Messick, Kuhlman, & Campos, 1973; Poppe, 1980; Pruitt, 1970) or on rank ordering outcome allocations to self and to partner (Grzelak, 1982; Radzicki, 1976; Wieczorkowska, 1982; also see the review by McClintock & van Avermaet, 1982). In one way or another, all these measurements consist in subjects making comparisons and expressing their preferences for various allocations of money. Can we, however, expect that someone predominantly concerned with his/her own monetary gains will also be motivated to maximize own gains when dealing with other kinds of outcomes, or might his/her orientation vary from one type of payoff to another?

In the aforementioned study by Grzelak (1986), three domains of outcomes/inputs were used to assess subjects' social orientations: (1) money that a subject and his/her partner could earn, (2) the amount of work that each of them contributed to a common task, and (3) the amount of control that each of them could have in selecting tasks they were supposed to work on. Subjects were to rank-order a number (9) of allocations from most to least attractive for each of the free domains separately. The rank orderings were then used to assess social orientations.[3] The results showed significant differences in subjects' social orientations depending upon the domain of inputs/outcomes. For instance, subjects displayed stronger individualistic and competitive orientations with respect to money than with regard to control. The rank-ordering method enabled us to examine the extent to which social orientations are correlated with one another. A significant, negative correlation between individualistic and equality orientation was observed only in the case of money, and it disappeared when work or control was at stake. In other words, in allocating money the more individualistic oriented a subject is, the lower is his/her concern for minimizing the difference between own and partner's gain, whereas in allocating work and control, high individualism can be accompanied by either high or low equality orientation. Equality orientation in one type of domain highly correlated with equality in each of the other two domains. On the other hand, individualistic and altruistic orientation in one type of domain did not correlate strongly with the respective orientations in any other domain. This suggests that people who are, for example, individualistic with regard to monetary rewards may not be individualistic when they face a problem of work division or the amount of control they can exercise. Therefore, it was shown that social orientations of the same person can vary from one choice situation to another because they are specifically related to the type of inputs and outcomes.

Kemp and van Kreveld (1986) examined the effect of allocation of either goods (money) or benefits (books) on subjects' preference for justice principles. The two types of resources did not differ in the kind of justice principle adopted by subjects. However, a significant difference was found in arguments that subjects used to justify their preferences. There were significantly more arguments referring to

---

[3] In the method adopted to this and to our other studies reported in the chapter, subject's actual rank ordering was compared with each of the five rank-order patterns typical of the pure (ideal) individualist, altruist, cooperator, competitor, and equality-oriented person. Therefore, each subject's social orientations were characterized by values (correlation coefficients in this study or the coefficients transformed into Z-scores in the next studies) of all the five parameters. This method seems to be very convenient whenever social orientations are dependent variables, although it has some disadvantages when it is used for classifying subjects into independent social orientations categories.

inputs (amount of work put into a task preceding allocation decisions) observed in goods than in the benefits allocations condition.

These findings should make us alert to the level of generality of conclusions drawn from experimental results. This, as a matter of fact, refers to all studies on social justice and conflict in which one type of resources is used, regardless whether it is money or any other type of input/outcome. In research on social dilemmas, money is almost exclusively used in the experimental game paradigm, but it is not so often applied within other than game theoretical approaches, for example, within social loafing theory (Latane, Wiliams & Harkins, 1979) or within theory of motivational losses (Kerr, 1983, 1986). Still, whatever domain of inputs or outcomes is used, the experimental results should not be generalized to other domains as long as we do not know how different types of domains are related to each other and what specific cognitive, emotional, and behavioral effects they produce.

Outcomes and Evaluations

The second problem is related to the meaning of choice consequences in theory and research.

As Grzelak, Poppe, Czwartosz, and Nowak (1986) point out, the theory of decision making assumes that an individual tends to maximize subjective value (subjective expected utility) of outcomes, not outcomes themselves. Contrary to this, in research practice we are used to pay attention to outcomes, not to their evaluations. When experiments are based on monetary payoffs, this seems to be justified by a commonsense assumption (the more money the better) as well as by psychological studies showing that subjective value of money is a monotonic function of its amount. It sounds reasonable as long as we expect an individual to be concerned only with his/her own gains. However, it becomes disputable when we adopt a broader view of social motivations, that is, that people care for others' gains and/or (dis) satisfaction, too.

For instance, a pure altruist is seen as a person who tries to benefit others, to enable others to make as much profit as possible. Does "to benefit" mean to care for their satisfaction or not? Again, it is implicitly assumed that maximizing others' outcomes is meant as maximizing others' satisfaction. Is this always a case? Certainly not. If the other is an altruist too or an equality-oriented person, giving him/her more money may cause his/her dissatisfaction rather than satisfaction. Paradoxically, the real altruist should be willing to take more himself or herself if he/she considers it as making another person feel better. It is then quite possible that judging others' motivation on a kind of surface basis, that is, their behavior, we often misinterpret their true intentions. In a number of relationships, especially in small groups, people seem to care for their own as much as for their opponents' and partners' (dis) satisfaction. It is likely that the importance of others' evaluations to us decreases as group size increases, that is, as the others become more strange and anonymous to us. Still, people have their schemata of others that include knowledge of what pleases others and what harms them. Therefore, both outcomes and subjective value of outcomes may account for people's decisions, actions, and justice judgments. There is hardly any research effort made to investigate this problem.

The study of Grzelak et al. (1986) was in part aimed at examining if there is any outcome/evaluation differential effect upon social orientation assessment. The five experimental conditions differed in what kind of consequences were allocated between a subject and his/her partner and how they were represented, that is, (1) numbers representing money (the traditional measurement technique), (2) iconic facial expressions of (dis) satisfaction with money, and rectangles of different sizes representing (3) money, (4) satisfaction with money, and (5) overall satisfaction with the exchange situation. Subjects were asked to rank-order a set of allocations according to their attractiveness to them. The correlational method (Wieczorkowska, 1982) was applied to assess subjects' social orientations. In addition, the assessment based on the five different consequence representations (the first dependent measure) was in each condition followed by an assessment done with the aid of an ordinary numerical representation of money (the second dependent measure). Only the latter three conditions—with rectangular representations of different consequences—are of interest at the moment. No major differences between these conditions were found with respect to the level of social orientations. However, there was some indirect evidence showing that the conditions differed in correlational patterns between orientations, that is, in a way orientations correlate with one another within each experimental condition. For instance, a correlation between individualism and equality orientation turned out to be more highly (negatively) correlated in the numerical representation of money than in any other type of representation. A correlation between individualism and competition appeared to be higher in the geometrical representation of outcomes than in the geometrical representations of satisfaction and in the numerical representation of money. All these differences between correlation coefficients were significant. Therefore, it can be said that social orientations did not mean exactly the same in all conditions.

They were "flavored" differently, depending upon what is represented as choice consequences.

Although this preliminary study failed to demonstrate in a direct way that the types of consequences influence the level of social orientations, it at least showed that there are some differences in how social orientations are related to one another. Therefore, the results create a promising basis for further explorations, explorations that shall also examine the outcome/evaluation differential effect upon justice judgments and choice behavior in social dilemmas.

It seems probable that subject's evaluations of own outcomes are spontaneous and automatic, whereas a special situational instigation might be needed to induce subject's attention being paid to the meaning of these outcomes to others. The instigation can be created by various situational cues, especially those coming from direct contacts with others. A plausible explanation of, for example, a repeatedly reported, striking communication impact on cooperation in conflict situations (Pruitt & Kimmel, 1977) could be that, at least in part, communication causes changes in a player's evaluation perspective, that is in his or her social orientations. The same refers to the discussion effect upon increase of group regardingness (van de Kragt, Dawes, Orbell, Braver, & Wilson, 1986). It seems likely that any direct contact with others before or during the conflict (especially a talk or a discussion about conflict related problems) may facilitate a process of adopting others' perspective. It may enhance one's sensibility to others' intentions and outcome evaluations. The same interpretation can be applied to the increase of contributing behavior as a result of the increase of group identity salience (Kramer & Brewer, 1986). Placing others in the same group category makes similarities between group members salient. The latter may include feelings of values similarities as well and increase in sensibility to others' well-being.

Deliberate Decision Making? Outcome Representation and Choice Processes

Numerical Trap

In studies on social dilemmas, a conflict is most often defined by numbers representing consequences (usually money, as it was said earlier) of choices made by the parties involved. Matrix entries in classic two- and n-person games, pool size, replenishment rate, harvest options in resource conservation simulations, inputs, and especially outcomes in experiments on equity—all are represented by numbers.

The first issue is how well numerical representation of outcomes reflects the most important features of social reality. Of course, it partly depends upon the domain of social life. The numerical representation is used in solving abstract, mathematical problems. The language of numbers is also natural and useful in economic type of situations. Prices, costs, profits, taxes, quantities of goods, and many of their properties are expressed by numbers. Certainly this is not the case in other interpersonal situations, like in everyday interactions with friends, colleagues, spouses. It seems more likely for numerical stimuli to activate schemata and scripts associated with the former types of situations than with the latter ones. In other words, the type of stimulation (this includes outcome representation as well) present in given situation strongly affects which schemata and scripts are activated, that is, it determines the interpretation of the situation. This, in turn, should influence people's motivation and behavior.

The importance of subjective, cognitive representation of a situation has been demonstrated by a number of studies (Abric, 1982; Markus & Zajonc, 1985). For instance, Abric and Vacherot (1976) showed that as many as a quarter of subjects playing a PDG (Prisoner's Dilemma Game) had spontaneously developed an interpretation of the PDG as an intellectual problem rather than as a game. This resulted in a marked decline in the number of those defecting choices that were made in response to the partner's defecting strategy. Eiser and Bhavnani (1974) had their subjects play the same PDG game, yet presented in four different contexts: as an experimental game, simulation of economic bargaining, simulation of international negotiations, and interpersonal interactions. The game and economic context evoked significantly fewer cooperative choices than both international and interpersonal contexts did. Whereas in the first two cases, notably in the second of the two, essentially competitive scripts must have been activated, the latter two cases tended to be associated with actions aimed at developing positive relations and at ensuring mutual satisfaction.

The second problem is how the numerical language representing the external world corresponds to the internal language in which subjective representations are formed (Grzelak, Poppe, Czwartosz, & Nowak, 1986). A number of recent theories on human information processing and a growing body of experimental evidence suggest that information is processed in at least two functionally autonomous systems: the propositional system and the imagery system (Ahsen, 1986; Kosslyn & Pomerantz, 1977; Paivio, 1972; Posner, 1978).

The propositional (discrete) system consists of propositions and relations among them. All the linguistic information is processed in this system. This includes logical and mathematical operations.

The imagery code is the system of images as internal analogs of the external world, where the basic functional property of mental representation is its isomorphism with the object (Shepard, 1978). The main operations done in the imagery system are holistic in their nature, and they correspond to changes of the external objects, like imagery movements, rotation, folding, changes in size, and the face. (Shepard & Cooper, 1982).

Some information is more likely to be processed in one of the two systems, some information in the other. It is claimed that very often both systems are involved in processing, one triggering and alternating the other, in a kind of a continuous interplay. However, it was shown that numerical and verbal situational cues appeal to and chiefly activate the propositional code, whereas visual material (pictures, figures, drawings, etc.) basically activates the imagery code. The code in which information is processed also depends upon individual predispositions, preferences (McLeod, Hunt, & Mathews, 1979). McLeod (1977) showed that when a sentence and a picture were compared with one another, some subjects tended to describe the picture in words, only to compare it with the sentence afterwards, whereas others first transformed the sentence into an image, which they compared with the picture.

The two systems result in important qualitative differences in both cognitive and emotional functioning. For instance, material that is imagined is remembered better than material that is processed verbally (Paivio, 1971). Images are strongly linked with body responses, and they produce somatic and emotional reactions similar to those elicited by actually perceived objects (Ahsen, 1986).

As Grzelak, Poppe, Czwartosz, and Nowak suggest (1986), investigations concerned with processing information on physical objects make it plausible that the imagery code is also utilized in social thinking. Images of persons, scripts of behavior, and a host of social scenes are expressed in this code rather than through words and numbers. The same may apply to some consequences of behavior. The sight of my partner who, previously hunched and dejected, now looks up and radiates in response to my cooperation, may reinforce my behavior much more effectively than any other, numerical, or verbal message expressing his satisfaction and appreciation. It seems likely that many values that people strive for in everyday life have imagery representations and that in the course of decision making, these representations may be even more salient than the propositional ones.

The differential effect of the way of outcome representation upon social orientations was examined in the forementioned study by Grzelak *et al.* (1986). As it was described earlier, choice consequences in this study were represented by numbers, rectangulars, and iconic faces. Analysis of variance showed that iconic representations of satisfaction resulted in a higher level of cooperation and altruism and in a lower level of equality orientation than geometric representation of satisfaction. Moreover, analysis of variance of differential scores (the first minus the second numerical measure) revealed that, in comparison with the second measure as the baseline, subjects were more altruistic and cooperative and less competitive when dealing with iconic than with numerical representations.

The results were explained by the properties of the imagery code. The imagery type of representation, especially facial ones being a very direct means for expressing emotions, could evoke stronger emotional responses, cause more attention being paid to another person and, possibly, induce stronger empathy with one's feelings than any other type of representation could do. In addition, numbers being strongly associated with economic types of scenarios could activate scripts typical of buyer–seller relationships, including scripts of competitive behaviors, whereas faces were more likely to activate scripts typical of a more ''personal'' types of interactions, including scripts of prosocial behaviors. There is still another possibility. In light of the earlier described results, we can also suspect that the type of representation changes the meaning of *what* is represented. Numbers, through an association with economic situations, may be more powerful in activating economic types of evaluations (i.e., value of money), whereas faces more interpersonal types of evaluations (i.e., making others' satisfaction a salient evaluation criterion).

The results of this preliminary study show that it does matter how we represent allocation of resources in our experiments. It cannot be assumed that findings based on numerical representations are valid in situations in which outcomes or their evaluations are expressed in another way.

A further, partial support of this thesis was also brought by the experiment by Grzelak, Ossewska, Bobrowski, and Wyszogrodzki (unpublished manuscript, 1986).[4] The study was aimed at testing changes in social orientations when more than two people are taking part in allocation of outcomes or satisfaction with outcomes. The assessment of social orientations was based on three different ways of

---

[4]The study was done within my MA seminar at the University of Warsaw and partially sponsored by the Institute of Social Profilaxy and Resocialization.

outcome and satisfaction representation: numerical representation of money, of satisfaction with money (5-point scale), and iconic representation of satisfaction with money (faces). Although there was no main effect of type of representation found, the appearance of changes in orientations turned out to depend largely upon the way in which outcomes or satisfaction was presented, that is, they were observed systematically in some conditions and not in others. The study will be discussed at some length later in this chapter.

Deliberate Decision Making?

A vast majority of empirical studies on dilemmas has been done by means of laboratory simulation of a conflict between individual and common interest (see the reviews by Dawes, 1980; Pruitt & Kimmel, 1977; Messick & Brewer, 1983; Stroebe & Frey, 1982). In the laboratory, be it by various manipulations, subjects are usually exposed to a very clear-cut conflict. They are presented with all choices that they and their partners can make and with what payoffs the possible combination of choices can result in. The decision problem then is well defined, and it enables an experimenter to observe what choices his subjects make: to save (and possibly contribute to) common goods or to free-ride. The transparency of conflict in the laboratory setting does not leave much room for subjects to interpret the situation in a way different from that intended by the experimenter. Moreover, one can say that the experimental scenarios and procedures are strongly coercive in a sense that they force subjects to make deliberate decisions.

The interdependence structure of a great number of dilemmas in social reality is unclear and hazy. It can be easily misperceived or not recognized at all. This refers to all aspects of interdependence, including as basic ones as the degree to which outcomes are contingent upon behavior of the involved parties (Poppe, 1986). Still, at a behavioral level (from an observer's perspective) people may act either against or in favor of common interest, although it does not necessarily mean that they do it intentionally. There is an impressive support of this supposition.

The classic experiments on the "minimal social situation" (Kelley, Thibaut, Radloff, & Mundy, 1962; Sidowski, Wyckoff, & Tabory, 1956) showed that subjects were able to "cooperate" even when they were completely unaware of the existing interdependence. In their original experiment, Sidowski and his associates (1956) had two subjects placed in a way that prevented them from either seeing each other or even suspecting each other's existence. Each subject was asked to press one of two keys either to gain maximal score or to avoid electric shock. Subjects did not know that their outcomes were interdependent and determined by a simple payoff matrix. However, after a series of trials and errors they had learned to coordinate their moves in a mutually rewarding way. So, in a sense, they cooperated (maximized joint profit) in a situation that did not appear to them as an interdependence situation. Kelley et al. (1962) explained this by the subjects' adopting a simple "win–stay, loose–change" strategy.

How much of everyday cooperation or free riding can result from such learning processes rather than from deliberate decision making? It seems to be a lot. Littering streets can become habitual if it is less costly to an individual than looking for a garbage can. Doing so he or she may not realize at all what will happen if everybody else were to do the same. This, of course, can apply to behavior testifying to one's tidiness as well. It can originate from rewarding experiences in the past, not from a person's conscious concern for the public good, such as cleanness.

Therefore, what we, as observers (channeled by our theoretical background) tend to consider as people's response to a dilemma situation is often likely to be an automatic, thoughtless reaction with no recognition of the existing conflict of interests. However, by focusing our research almost unexceptionally on well-defined, distinctly structured interdependence situations, we leave very little room to explore processes other than decision making.

Diversity of Conflict Perceptions

Even if a situation is recognized as a conflict of interest, it does not appear the same to all the parties involved. It varies, depending upon both situational and personal factors.

Poppe (1986) showed that people have their subjective theories of social values, an implicit structure of social motives. In his study, subjects were asked to judge the extent to which different social values (taken from McClintock model: McClintock, 1976) and justice rules are typical of various social relationships. Multidimensional scaling revealed that the perception of social relationships fell into a two-dimensional space of values, one dimension being cooperation and competition the other. If so, we can suspect that people tend to attribute certain social values to others quite spontaneously, and they can define their cooperative or competitive attitude to them merely on the basis of signs of another person's social role or status. In other words, an individual's perception of others' social orientations can substantially change (along the cooperative and the competitive dimensions) as he/she moves from one social relationship to another.

A number of studies revealed startling interpersonal differences in conflict perception (e.g., Maki & McClintock, 1983). Individual's own social orientations were proved to be one of the main factors accounting for these differences. For instance, in testing subjects in an initially ill-defined conflict situation and allowing them to ask any questions they wanted, Grzelak (1981) found individualists to inquire more eagerly for their own payoffs, altruists for their partner's payoffs, and equality-oriented subjects for both own and partner's payoffs, than subjects scoring low on each of these dimensions, respectively. In the same study, subjects were asked to recall the payoffs of the PDG matrix they had seen 10 minutes before. As many as 37% of them reproduced the matrix in such a distorted way that the game ceased to be a PDG. The most drastic changes were observed in equality-oriented subjects: They tended to reduce the difference between their own and their partner's payoffs. Eiser and Tajfel (1972) showed that in a game-resembling situation, cooperatively oriented subjects were more concerned with obtaining information on a partner's motivation than were competitively oriented subjects.

The motivationally based channeling and selectivity of perception result in individual differences in the generalized image of the social world, also in the perception of others' behavior and motivation. However, the experimental evidence on others' perception and expectations about their intentions collected so far is both rich and inconsistent.

Kelley and Stahelski (1970) discovered that people identified as competitively oriented were particularly prone to attribute the same motivation to others, whereas cooperators expected others to have a cooperative as well as a competitive motivation. The cooperators were also more flexible and responsive to a partner's moves than others. A similar effect was observed in the study of Kuhlman and Marshello (1975). The results reported by Maki and McClintock (1983) suggest that both individualists and cooperators are more aware of the heterogeneity of human motivation and can more readily recognize such motivations than altruists and competitors can.

On the other hand, Codol's (1976) reanalysis of Kelley and Stahelski's results as well as some other studies (e.g., Messe & Sivacek, 1979, for PDG; Kuhlman & Wimberley, 1976, for decomposed games but not for PDG; Liebrand, 1986, for limited resources games) showed that social motives are largely perceived in tune with one's own motivation. Dawes et al. (Dawes, McTavish, & Shaklee, 1977) reported that subjects four times as often attributed to others their own motivation than a different motivation. Kuhlman, Camac, and Cunha (1986) found that individualists revealed the highest generalized trust in others, competitors the lowest, cooperators occupying a position between the two.

Thus there seems to be evidence in support of both so-called egocentric attribution (or false consensus phenomenon) and the original Kelley and Stahelski hypothesis.

Liebrand, Jansen, Ruken, and Cuhre (1986) reported that cooperators tend to interpret others' behavior varying on a cooperation–competition dimension in evaluative terms ("good" or "bad"), whereas individualists in terms of power ("weak" or "strong").

Concluding, all these results suggest that a person's perception of choice situation is structured in a highly individualized manner. If so, it is likely that many social dilemmas are not perceived as such; secondly, even when conflict is recognized, perception of this conflict varies from one individual to another. It seems evident that the same well-defined experimental situations can be perceived in very diverse ways; thereby subjects in these experiments do not play the same game as the experimenters assume them to play, or they even do not play any game at all. Possibly, the logic underlying people's behavior in various interdependence situations is different as well.

N-person Social Orientations

Because the last 15 years brought a lot of experimental findings on a relationship between an individual's social orientations and his/her perception of the payoff structure, expectations about others, his/her actual behavior, and its flexibility, it seems worthwhile to note one of possible weak points of these studies whenever they were related to a n-person type of situation. So far, social orientations have been almost exclusively inferred from subject's preferences for two-person allocations of outcomes. The assessment techniques based on two-person allocations have also been used in studying behavior and perception in n-person situations (Liebrand, 1984, 1985, 1986, Liebrand, & van Run, 1985; Liebrand, Wilke, Vogel, & Wolters, 1986; Kuhlman, Camac, & Cunha, 1986). Knowing that people's behavior often varies quite markedly from dyadic situations to larger social settings (Messick & Brewer, 1983; Stroebe & Frey, 1982), can we expect a difference between two- and n-person orientations as well?

In the earlier mentioned study by Grzelak, Ossewska, Bobrowski, & Wyszogrodzki (1986, unpublished manuscript) there were two measurements used to assess subjects' social orientations: a two-person and a three-person version. In the three-person technique, subjects were presented with allocations of three outcomes: to a subject and to his/her two anonymous partners, labeled as A and B. A set of allocations (to be rank-ordered according to their attractiveness) was composed of 12 allocations selected in such a way that exactly the same pairs of values appeared in each of the three possible two-person combinations: subject–partner A, subject–partner B, and partner A–partner B. There were three experimental conditions differing in what was represented as allocation consequences and how: money allocations represented by numbers, satisfaction with money allocations expressed by numbers (points on a 5-point scale), and satisfaction with money displayed by iconic faces.

It was found that subjects revealed significantly stronger individualistic orientation in the three-person situation than in the two-person situation. The effect was observed in all the representation conditions (money, points, and faces).

In the three-person version, subjects' altruistic, equality, competitive, and cooperative orientations were calculated for the two persons: A and B, separately, and then they were compared with the respective orientations toward the only person in the two-person version.[5] There was no difference found between the two versions in subjects' orientation toward person A. However, a significant difference between the versions was revealed with respect to orientations toward person B. Subjects in the three-person situation displayed a higher competitive orientation toward person B than subjects in the two-person situation toward the only other person. The difference was significant in the iconic and the numerical representation of satisfaction with money, and it disappeared in the numerical representation of money.

Moreover, analysis of variance in the three-person situation also revealed sharp differences between subjects' orientation toward person A and toward person B (A vs. B being a within factor). Subjects were more competitive, less altruistic, and less cooperative toward person B as compared with person A. These effects were observed in the "money" and "faces" conditions but not in the "points" condition.

It has to be added that the two persons A and B differed only in the place in which their outcomes were displayed on a card: Subject's outcomes were on the left side, person A's in the middle, and person B's on the right side of each card. In other words, a spatial distance between subject and B was larger than that between subject and A. Thus social orientations toward other people seem to depend also upon

---

[5]Individualistic orientations are, of course, invariant of the allocation participants (A,B) because individualists, by definition, are concerned only with their own outcomes.

how others are related to the subject in physical space. This simple spatial effect—the shorter distance to another person is, the more prosocial orientation is activated—should, or course, occur in both two-and n-person situations. However, it becomes more visible in those situations in which there is more than one partner of interaction and in which partners' distances to the subject are differentiated. Certainly, the more partners present in a situation, the more of them are likely to be located beyond the bounds of one's space of close interpersonal relationship.

Therefore, an often observed decline of cooperation in large groups may not always require a very sophisticated explanation in terms of social interdependence and deliberate decision making. It can be hypothesized that the decline of cooperation following increase of group size may be also caused by changes in the basic social orientations toward others, the latter being in part a result of spacial distances between subject and others. As it was said before, the imagery code is the most natural code for processing spacial information. Thus it is suggested once again that the imagery processes may play an important role in the phenomena traditionally seen as being exclusively the effect of decision making, that is, the effect of information processed in the propositional code. This hypothesis is not considered as an exclusive explanation of the decline of cooperation. Spatial relationships are, of course, only one of many factors affecting prosocial motivation and behavior. In some situations they may not count at all, in some others, like in our experimental situation, they seem to constitute the most plausible interpretation of the observed decrease of prosocial orientations.

At the moment, any explanation of the results of this preliminary study seems to be more a matter of speculation than anything else. More important is that the study demonstrated that people's social motivation is not the same in two-and in n-person groups. The studies done so far have already revealed a strong relationship between social motivation and behavior in n-person situations. Yet it can be expected that we will gain a better, more accurate recognition of this relationship by applying a n-person rather than a two-person assessment of social orientations in our studies.

The findings reported here raise one more question, namely that about the nature of social orientations: To what extent can we still tend to consider social orientations as stable, traitlike characteristics of personality (as it is seems to be, suggested by Kuhlman, Camac, & Cunha, 1986). The results reported here demonstrate rather the interactional nature of preferences for outcome (or satisfaction) allocations. The lack of stability across various kinds of situations varying along such dimensions as what the choice consequences are, how they are represented, what is a kind of a social relationship in which an individual is placed, and what is a number of others who he/her is dealing with, or a relationship between his and another person inputs (Czwartosz, 1987)—all make the assumption about the existence of stable individual predispositions quite questionable. What may be stable and characteristic for a person is, at most, her or his individual pattern of preference variability across various situations (Czwartosz, 1985; Grzelak, 1982). Thus should a person's social orientations be defined as a result of interaction between his/her personal preferences and a number of situational factors (that is, in terms of a kind of stability of preference-situation configurations) rather than as his/her individual stable, personalitylike predispositions?

Me, We . . . They? N-Person Situtations and Social Helplessness

In the Hardin's (1968) classic example, size and quality of a common pasture depended upon each herdsman decision whether to increase or to keep his herd size constant. In energy conservation problems, all consumers are usually considered to be equally free in using their energy-consuming devices. This kind of dilemma can be viewed as a type of "me–we" conflict: What is best for me harms all of us (including myself) if we all do the same. "Me" and the rest of "us" are not differentiated in a sense that each party has the same or about the same control over outcomes. It is not always the case. In many real dilemmas, one more agent is present as well. It is "them": organizations, the state or local authorities, power groups. In other words, there is a two- or multilevel interdependence, where "they" are often more powerful than we are. "They" can narrow a range of options available to us, change payoffs or impose constraints on them, implement new rules regulating the use of common resources, and the likes. The fact that experimental studies are restricted to a one-level interdependence structure can be considered as an important limitation if our experiments are thought to be analogs of real situations, and it is believed that cognitive and motivational processes underlying choice behavior are the same in both our laboratories and social life.

The problem of structural changes in a one-level dilemma has been approached by several authors (e.g., Komorita & Lapworth, 1982; Messick, Wilke, Brewer, Kramer, Zemke, & Lui, 1983; Kramer & Brewer, 1986; Poppe, 1986; Poppe & Utens, 1986; Samuelson, Messick, Wilke, & Rutte, 1986; Wilke, Rutte, Wit, Messick, & Samuelson, 1986; Messick, Chapter 3 in Volume II). Almost all these studies are focused on which preferences for structural changes people reveal when they are unable to maintain the shared resources at a satisfactory level and on the extent to which some structural changes, like group partitioning [into a number of subgroups], (sub) group identification salience, changes in a pool size or in a common good contingency upon behavior, can provide a promising way for dilemma resolution.

The comments made in this section are limited to the two-level dilemmas in which the second level consists in the *already existing* leaders—authorities. In line with the main thread of the chapter, they will be focused on cognitive and motivational processes.

Water shortage can be caused by a drought or by a community council that decided to build poorly designed, inefficient water-supply networks. People in some countries suffer from food scarcity not only because of the limited natural resources but because the government is not able (and/or not willing to) run the national economy effectively. Needless to say that it does make a psychological difference what is perceived as the cause of a dilemma: natural, biological forces, or human, social factors. The distinction is clearly made in the literature when, for example, dilemmas of limited natural resources on one side and dilemmas of participation in social movements or other collective actions on the other side are considered. Actually, a superordinate, external social agent can be present in both types of situations, and it can markedly influence the way in which dilemmas are either solved or augmented. This influence consists in not only what the authority does itself but also in what its actions mean to people and how this meaning affects their behavior. The necessary precondition for the latter is that people perceive a causal relationship between their fate and the external social agent.

I fully agree with Messick (1991) that attributional processes are of extreme significance and that they probably appear in every dilemma as a spontaneous reaction to an unexpected failure situation.

Three types of attributions seem to be of special importance in all dilemma situations: (1) what is a cause of the dilemma, (2) what other dilemma participants intend to do, (3) the extent to which the situation can be controlled. These attributions may differ in their content, depending upon the structure of dilemma.

First, a full understanding of the nature of the dilemma always implies attributing a cause of an undesired state of affairs to others' as well as to one's own behavior. Because the latter is threatening, it seems quite likely that in a one-level dilemma an individual tends to attribute responsibility for a failure to external factors like fate, bad luck, and/or to others rather than to the self. Some experiments discussed earlier showed that this is especially true for competitors who tend to blame others for the undesired status quo most. This might create a vicious circle: Own competitive orientation leads to biased causal attributions—perception of others as overusing common goods that, in turn, may intensify motivation to compete (free-ride) as the best defense against others' competition. Causal attributions rely then either on the external factors or on a kind of intragroup differentiation: me versus they, where "them" means the other dilemma participants.

It can be expected that causal attributions are different in the case of more complex, two-level interdependence structures. The mere presence of another more powerful party provides a good and not-threatening explanation of the existing crisis: The more the other party is seen as responsible for the status quo, the less room is left for perceiving one's own behavior as a dilemma co-determinant and the weaker psychological reasons for blaming dilemma co-participants of the same level. In perception of two-level dilemmas, we should then observe more often an intergroup differentiation: we (me being a member of "we") versus they, where "they" means the other, external party.

Second, the two types of dilemmas should differ in attributions of intentions. Because knowledge of others' intentions is a basis for foreseeing others' behavior and predicting the future state of affairs, attributions of intentions in one-level dilemmas have to be restricted to intentions of other dilemma participants, whereas in two-level dilemmas, they should refer to intentions of both the same-level dilemma participants and the external party. Moreover, the more the other party is seen as responsible for dilemma occurrence, the more important knowledge about its intentions should become.

Third, we can suppose that behavior in dilemma situations depends largely upon the extent to which people judge their and others' behavior as controllable. For instance, Van de Kragt et al. (1986) demonstrated a strong positive impact of a group discussion on subjects' contributions to common goods. Messick et al. (1983), Samuelson et al. (1986), Wilke et al. (1986), and Messick (1991) showed that subjects revealed preferences for structural change (electing a leader) especially when they both failed to harvest successfully and perceived maintaining the pool as a difficult task. The results of these studies can be interpreted in terms of making the "uncontrollable" controllable. Electing a leader is a direct way of passing control over outcomes to a person seen as trustworthy and capable to handle the problem of using common goods more intelligently than any other group member. A group discussion leads to better understanding of others, to higher concern with others' interests, and to reduction of a fear of being cheated or exploited by others. It also gives an opportunity to *influence* each other's behavior, that is, to gain higher control over one's own outcomes by making each other do what is good (or at least better than it was) to all. Frequency and intensity of attempts to influence others should depend on the extent to which an individual views others as being flexible, susceptible to influence, and evaluates himself/herself as being able to use the effective "influence strategies." In one-level dilemmas, these beliefs and strategies are related to individuals; in two-level dilemmas—to groups and organizations.

Let us briefly consider two cases of two-level dilemmas that differ most with respect to the discussed attributional dimensions. They can be placed on the two poles of a continuum that, for sake of simplicity, I will label as a "democratic–autocratic (totalitarian)" continuum. This is only to mark a possible complexity of cognitive and motivational processes occurring in such situations, not to analyze them in an elaborated and systematic way.

1. If the elected authority in the *ideal* democratic setting is perceived as for a dilemma crisis then it is also expected to act according to people's will, that is to solve a dilemma in a way satisfactory to them. The authority's intentions are believed to correspond with inhabitants' interests and, due to the existence of democratic procedures, the inhabitants have a good basis to hope to be effective in making the authority do what they expect it to do. The city council is motivated to respond to the city inhabitants' complaints about the water supply. If the council members want to be reelected for the next term, they have either to reconstruct water networks or to do something else to lessen the crisis. It is likely that the community members, blaming the council for its unfortunate decision beforehand (i.e., perceiving it as the main cause of the water shortage), can suffer at the moment, but they do not feel helpless in improving their situation in the future. They face the problem of using the limited resource at present, and they have to cope with it somehow. However, they have an institutional and psychological basis to expect that the council will solve the problem in one way or another. If it will not, they can use a threat of withdrawing their support in the next elections or actually do it.

Social orientations toward power groups in the ideal democratic setting should be much more cooperative than in any other type of setting. If we operationalize n-party social orientations in the way we did in the previous section of this chapter and if one of the two others represents a power group, the second being another row participants of dilemma, then at least we should not expect orientations revealed toward the power group member to be much less cooperative (or more competitive) than those toward the other person. This should be basically caused by the electing experience, that is by passing control to others voluntarily. Those who originally were "one of us" and at present, by election, constitute the power group shall still be treated as in-group members. In other words, there is no basis to expect that in the ideal democratic setting an intergroup differentiation resulting in more competitive orientation toward the out-group members will occur.

2. The most dramatic situation is when dilemma participants perceive the authority as responsible for their fate, as having interests contradicting or at least not corresponding to their interests and, moreover, when they do not see any effective way of changing this state of affairs. The extreme case is that experienced in a totalitarian type of organization or state. Dictators are mainly concerned with maximizing their power, not with improving social welfare and society members' well-being. They can use various strategies to satisfy their interests. These strategies do not necessarily consist of reducing conflicts between the members of society. On the contrary, introducing and escalating everyday dilemmas can quite well serve dictators' interests, because it keeps people preoccupied with solving their everyday problems. They prefer people to compete with one another rather than to have them all moving against the existing establishment. So, regardless whether it is done on purpose or not, shortages of goods may be quite helpful in maintaining the totalitarian system. Following Tajfel and Turner's theory of social categorization (Tajfel, 1978, 1982; Turner & Oakes, 1986) it can be hypothesized that conflicting interests in dilemma situations facilitate personalization processes, that is, they make salient intermember dissimilarities and, in consequence, intensify conflict and lead to social disintegration. This should also manifest itself in a kind of induced social orientation: in an increase of nonsocial motivation (competitive and individualistic) toward both the dilemma participants and the authority and, possibly, an appearance of a strong aggressive component in the latter case.

Moreover, severe, continuous shortages and repeatedly experienced inability to control the perceived cause of them, result in, as it is frequently observed, syndromes similar to those described by the learned helplessness theory (Abramson, Seligman, & Teasdale, 1979; Seligman, 1975), that is in depression, feelings of helplessness, decline in motivation and activity, at least activity in the domains predominantly controlled by the totalitarian power.

However, unlike the case of an isolated individual deprived of control and chiefly attributing his/her ineffectiveness to his/her inabilities, in the case of social dilemmas, observations that others share the same fate should lead to external, stable attributions rather than to internal ones. Specifically, the autocratic setting makes it especially plausible to attribute a cause to the power group. And, unlike individual helplessness, helplessness in a social context can produce a variety of alternative behavioral ways of coping with control deprivation. One of them is a withdrawal from those domains of social life that are fully controlled by the external agent and moving to those domains in which personal control can be exercised. For instance, in some totalitarian countries, people deprived of a free access to mass media (which can be also considered as a kind of common good) either, taking some risk, develop underground networks of information exchange, or they narrow their social environment to small circles of friends and family members in which they can talk freely.

An elaborate discussion of this issue is beyond the scope of this chapter. However, it is surprising that in theories and research on social dilemmas so little reference has been made to the theory of learned helplessness, and almost no attempt to extend the latter to the social helplessness theory (Grzelak, 1987).

There are many nested dilemmas that can be placed between the two poles of the "democratic–totalitarian" continuum. To give an example, when a power group is not perceived as very strong and uncontrollable but is still seen as responsible for dilemmas, dissatisfactory experiences with resource shortages can give rise to social integration and mobilization—an instigation to move against the power group. Personalization can then be replaced by depersonalization (accentuating intermember similarities, perceiving them as falling into a category of sharing the same, undesired fate), feelings of helplessness by a hope for a positive change, and nonsocial motivations by a strongly cooperative orientation toward all belonging to the "we" category. The "we–they" conflict can underscore the hitherto "me–we–they" or "me–we" conflict.

It seems worth noting that the problem of attributional processes in situations in question is twofold. One of the major differences between the one-level and the two-level dilemmas is that in the latter some attributions can be easily used as a justification of one's competition and freeriding. It is in accordance with our everyday observation that whenever there is an additional, external party present at the social scene, some people tend to blame it for the status quo; saying, "It is they who caused my [our] misery," "It is they who are to solve the problem" then serve as rationalizations, as excuses for being concerned only with one's own interest. These misattributions are likely to occur even if the true causal contribution of the blamed party and its ability to solve the problems is low. It is needless to add that these misattributions augment the dilemma crisis. Through suppressing one's own responsibility for the status quo, they make people more free in displaying their individualistic and competitive orientations and in overusing the commons.

In sum, many dilemmas consist in more than one interdependence structure, and they are hierarchical in a way that the parameters of the lower-level parties largely depend on actions taken by the upper-level-parties. It is hypothesized that attributional processes can strongly differentiate social orientations toward members of the involved parties and have an even stronger impact on behavior in multilevel than in one-level dilemmas.

Summary

In this chapter, I attempted to show some limitations of the current approach to choice behavior in interdependence situations, especially the approach adopted in investigations of social orientations and social dilemmas. In most of the cases I also showed some still preliminary studies attempting to overcome these shortcomings.

The limitations of present studies are that they are restricted to a very narrow domain of outcomes; they often do not take into account the diversity and complexity of human information processing; they narrow down social orientations to two-person interaction; and they mostly deal with dilemmas of the simplest, one-level interdependence structure, whereas many real dilemmas are situated in a broad, multilevel interdependence structure.

More specifically, it was claimed that:

1. The structure of a conflict, as it is defined by its participants, is based on subjective evaluations of outcomes rather than on outcomes themselves.
2. Choices made by people result not only from deliberate thinking, "homo-economicus"-like calculating and balancing all the pluses and minuses but also from imagery type of information processing.
3. People's interpretation of choice situation varies from situation to situation and from one person to another depending upon situational stimulation and personal preferences: social orientations.
4. Individuals' social orientations toward others' interest can substantially change when there is not one but many others.
5. Cognitive (mainly attributional) and motivational (social orientations) bases of behavior are of special importance in multilevel dilemmas, where, besides the "row" participants, another party exists and (co)determines the conflict origins and its course.

Discussion of these problems revealed relevance of some theoretical perspectives (e.g., that of imagery information processing or social
helplessness) different from those commonly used in the field, that is,
different from social exchange, decision-making, and other economic
theories of social behavior. Theoretical ideas and experimental evidence presented in this chapter have questioned the model of homo
economicus, the model of man making rational decisions to maximize
his own interest in a kind of deliberate "mathematical" way. Should
be this model revised? The proposed answer is yes. It is my strong
feeling that in studying social orientations, social justice, and traps, we
are in a kind of trap ourselves, a trap of our experimental paradigms
and theoretical (pre)conceptions. We still lack a good psychological
theory of conflict between individual and social interest, and, I am
afraid, we are still quite far from having one. It seems worthwhile then
to look for possible inspirations coming from other fields of psychological studies and to try out new research methods. All these attempts
may somehow pay off in the future, even if some of the present ideas
look artificial or naive, even if some of them will turn out to be our
failures.

References

Abramson, L. Y., Seligman, M.E. P., & Teasdale, J. D. (1979). Learned helplessness in
    humans: Critique and reformulation. *Journal of Abnormal Psychology, 87*, 49–74.
Abric, J. C. (1982). Cognitive processes underlying cooperation: The theory of social
    representations. In V. Derlega & J. Grzelak (Eds.), *Cooperation and helping
    behavior. Theories and research*. New York: Academic Press.
Abric, J. C., & Vacherot, C. (1976). The effects of representations and behavior in
    experimental games. *European Journal of Social Psychology, 2*, 129–144.
Ahsen, A. (1986). The new structuralism: Images in dramatic interlock. *Journal of
    Mental Imagery, 10* (Whole No. 3).
Brewer, M. B., & Kramer, R. M. (1986). Choice behavior in social dilemmas: Effects of
    social identity, group size, and decision framing. *Journal of Personality and Social
    Psychology, 50*, 543–549.
Codol, J. P. (1976). Contre l'hypothese du triangle. *Cahiers de Psychologie, 19*, 381–394.
Czwartosz, Z. (1987). Sprawiedliwosc a preferencje podzialu wynikow [Social justice
    and preferences over outcome distribution]. In J. Grzelak (Ed.), *Problemy wspol-
    zaleznosci spolecznej [Social interdependence problems]*. Warsaw: Warsaw Uni-
    versity Press.
Dawes, R. M. (1980). Social dilemmas. *Annual Review of Psychology, 31*, 169–193.
Dawes, R. M., McTavish, J., & Shaklee, H. (1977). Behavior, communication and
    assumptions about other people's behavior in a common dilemma situation.
    Journal of Personality and Social Psychology, 35, 1–11.
Eiser, J. R., & Bhavnani, K. K. (1974). The effects of situational meaning on the behavior
    of subjects in the prisoner's dilemma game. *European Journal of Social Psychology,
    4*, 93–97.

Eiser, J. R., & Tajfel, H. (1972). Acquisition of information in dyadic interaction. *Journal of Personality and Social Psychology, 23*, 340–345.

Foa, U. G., & Foa, E. B. (1975). *Societal structures of the mind.* Springfield: Charles C. Thomas.

Griesinger, D. W., & Livingstone, J. W. (1973). Toward a model of interpersonal motivation in experimental games. *Behavioral Science, 18*, 73–78.

Grzelak, J. L. (1981). Social interdependence: Do we know what we want to know? *Polish Psychologycal Bulletin, 12*, 125–135.

Grzelak, J. L. (1982). Preferences and cognitive processes in social interdependence situations. In V. Derlega & J. Grzelak (Eds.), *Cooperation and helping behavior. Theory and research.* New York: Academic Press.

Grzelak, J. L. (1986). Money isn't everything: Differential effects of type of values upon social orientations. *Polish Psychological Bulletin, 17*, 147–154.

Grzelak, J. L. (1987). O bezradnosci spolecznej [Social helplessness]. In M. Marody & A. Sulek (Eds.), *Spoleczne sposoby radzenia sobie z rzeczywistoscia [Social ways of coping with reality]* (pp. 126–149). Warsaw: Warsaw University Press.

Grzelak, J. L., Poppe, M., Czwartosz, Z., & Nowak, A. (1986). *"Numerical trap." A new look at outcome representations in studies on choice behavior.* Paper presented at the East-West Meeting of the European Association of Experimental Social Psychology, Graz, Austria.

Hardin, G. (1968). The tragedy of the commons. *Science, 162*, 1243–1248.

Kelley, H. H., Thibaut, J. W., Radloff, R. & Mundy, D. (1962). The development of cooperation in the "minimal social situation." *Psychological Monographs, 76* (Whole No. 19).

Kemp, W. J., & Van Kreveld, D. (1986). Het verdelen van goederen and voordelen. In A. van Knippenberg, M. Poppe, J. Extra, G. Kok, & E. Seydel (Eds.), *Fundamentele Sociale Psychologie, 1,* Tilburg: Tilburg University Press. There is a version in English (unpublished manuscript, 1983): The allocation of goods and benefits: A multidimensional scaling analysis.

Kerr, N. L. (1983). Motivation losses in groups: A social dilemma analysis. *Journal of Personality and Social Psychology, 45*, 819–828.

Kerr, N. L. (1986). Motivational choices in task groups: A paradigm for social dilemma research. In H. Wilke, D. Messick, & C. Rutte (Eds.), *Experimental social dilemmas.* Frankfurt: Peter Lang.

Klandermans, B. (1986). Individual behaviour in real life social dilemmas: A theory and some research results. In H. Wilke, D. Messick, & C. Rutte (Eds.), *Experimental social dilemmas.* Frankfurt: Peter Lang.

Komorita, S. S., & Lapworth, C. W. (1982). Cooperative choice among individuals versus groups in an n-person dilemma situation. *Journal of Personality and Social Psychology, 42*, 487–496.

Kosslyn, S. M., & Pomerantz, J. P. (1977). Imagery, propositions, and the form of internal representations. *Cognitive Psychology, 9*, 52–76.

Kramer, R. M., & Brewer, M. B. (1986). Social group identity and the emergence of cooperation in resource conservation dilemmas. In H. Wilke, D. Messick, & C. Rutte (Eds.), *Experimental social dilemmas.* Frankfurt: Peter Lang.

Kuhlman, D. M. & Marshello, A. M. J. (1975). Individual differences in game motivation as moderators of preprogrammed strategy effects in prisoner's dilemma game. *Journal of Personality and Social Psychology, 32*, 912–931.

Kuhlman, D. M., & Wimberley, D. D. (1976). Expectations of choice behavior held by cooperators, competitors, and individualists across four classes of experimental games. *Journal of Personality and Social Psychology, 34*, 69–81.

Kuhlman, D. M., Camac, C. M. & Cunha, D. A. (1986). Individual differences in social orientations. In H. Wilke, D. Messick, & C. Rutte (Eds.), *Experimental social dilemmas* (pp.). Frankfurt: Peter Lang.

Latane, B., Williams, K., & Harkins, S. (1979). Many hands make light the work: The causes and consequences of social loafing. *Journal of Personality and Social Psychology, 37*, 822–832.

Liebrand, W. B. G. (1984). The effect of social motives, communication and group size in an n-person multi-stage mixed-motive game. *European Journal of Social Psychology, 14*, 239–264.

Liebrand, W. B. G. (1986). The ubiquity of social values in social dilemmas. In H. Wilke, D. Messick, & C. Rutte (Eds.), *Experimental social dilemmas*. Frankfurt: Peter Lang.

Liebrand, W. B. G., & van Run, C. J. (1985). The effects of social motives on behavior in social dilemmas in two cultures. *Journal of Experimental Social Psychology, 21*, 86–102.

Liebrand, W. B. G., Jansen, W. T. L., Ruken, V. M. & Cuhre, C. J. M. (1986). Might over morality: Social values and the perception of other players in experimental games. *Journal of Experimental Social Psychology, 22*, 203–215.

Liebrand, W. B. G., Wilke, H. A. M., Vogel, R., & Wolters, F. J. M. (1986). Value orientation and conformity: A study using three types of social dilemma games. *Journal of Conflict Resolution, 30*, 77–97.

McLeod, P. D. (1977). A dual task response modality effect: Support for bilingual episodic memory; acquisition and forgetting. *Journal of Verbal Learning and Verbal Behavior, 15*, 347–345.

Maki, J., & McClintock, C. G. (1983). The accuracy of social value prediction: Actor and observers influences. *Journal of Personality and Social Psychology, 45*, 829–838.

Markus, H., & Zajonc, R. B. (1985). The cognitive perspective in social psychology. In G. Lindzey & E. Aronson (Eds.), *The handbook of social psychology*. New York: Random House.

McClintock, C. G. (1972). Social motivation—a set of propositions. *Behavioral Science, 17*, 458–454.

McClintock, C. G. (1976). Social motivation in settings of outcome interdependency. In D. Druckman (Ed.), *Negotiations*. Beverly Hills: Sage.

McClintock, C. G., & van Avermaet, E. F. (1982). Social values and rules of fairness. In V. J. Derlega & J. L. Grzelak (Eds.), *Cooperation and helping behavior*. New York: Academic Press.

McClintock, C. G., Messick, D. M., Kuhlman, D. M., & Campos, F. T. (1973). Motivational basis of choice in three choice decomposed games. *Journal of Experimental Social Psychology, 9*, 572–590.

Messe, L. A., & Sivacek, J. M. (1979). Predictions of others' responses in a mixed-motive game. Self-justification or false consensus? *Journal of Personality and Social Psychology, 37*, 602–607.

Messick, D. M. (1991). Social dilemmas, shared resources and social justice. In R. Vermunt and H. Steensma (Eds.), *Social Justice in Human Relations, Vol. 2: Societal and Psychological Consequences of Justice and Injustice* (pp. 49–69). New York: Plenum Press.

Messick, D. M., & Brewer, R. M. (1983). Solving social dilemmas. A Review. In L. Whealer & P. Shaver (Eds.), *Review of personality and social psychology* (Vol. 4). Beverly Hills CA: Sage Publications.

Messick, D. M., & McClintock, C. G. (1968). Motivational basis of choice in experimental games. *Journal of Experimental Social Psychology, 4*, 1–25.

Messick, D. M., & Thorngate, W. B. (1967). Relative gain maximization in experimental games. *Journal of Experimental Social Psychology, 3*, 85–101.

Messick, D. M., Wilke, H., Brewer, M. B., Kramer, R. M., Zemke, P. E., & Lui, L. (1983). Individual adaptations and structural change as solutions to social dilemmas. *Journal of Personality and Social Psychology, 44,* 294–309.

Paivio, A. (1971). *Imagery and verbal processes.* New York: Holt, Rinehart & Winston.

Poppe, M (1980). *Social comparison in two-person experimental games.* Tilburg: Van Spaendonck.

Poppe, M. (1984). *An implicit structure of social motives.* Paper presented at the General Meeting of the European Association of Experimental Social Psychology, Tilburg, The Netherlands, May 8–12.

Poppe, M. (1986). Effects of change in a common good and choice behaviour in a social dilemma. In H. Wilke, D. Messick, & C. Rutte (Eds.), *Experimental social dilemmas.* Frankfurt: Peter Lang.

Poppe, M., & Utens, L. (1986). Effects of greed and fear of being gypped in a social dilemma situation with changing pool size. *Journal of Economic Psychology, 7,* 61–73.

Poppe, M., Croon, M., & Sluytman, A. (1986). *The implicit structure of social values and justice rules in a context of social relations.* Paper presented at the East-West Meeting of the European Association of Experimental Social Psychology, Graz, May 27–31.

Pruitt, D. G. (1967). Reward structure and cooperation: The decomposed prisoner's dilemma game. *Journal of Personality and Social Psychology, 7,* 21–27.

Pruitt, D. G. (1970). Motivational processes in the decomposed prisoner's dilemma game. *Journal of Personality and Social Psychology, 14,* 227–238.

Pruitt, D. G., & Kimmel, M. J. (1977). Twenty years of experimental gaming: Critique, synthesis, and suggestions for the future. *Annual Review of Psychology, 28,* 363–392.

Radzicki, J. (1976). Technique of conjoint measurement of subjective value of own and other's gains. *Polish Psychological Bulletin, 7,* 179–186.

Samuelson, C. D., & Messick, D. M. (1986). Inequities in access to and use of shared resources in social dilemmas. *Journal of Personality and Social Psychology, 51,* 960–967.

Samuelson, C. D., Messick, D. M., Wilke, H. A. M., & Rutte, C. G. (1986). Individual restraint and structural change as solutions to social dilemmas. In H. Wilke, D. Messick, & C. Rutte (Eds.), *Experimental social dilemmas.* Frankfurt: Peter Lang.

Shepard, R. N. (1978). The mental image. *American Psychologist, 33,* 125–137.

Shepard, R. N., & Cooper, L. A. (1982). *Mental images and their transformations.* Cambridge: The MIT Press.

Sidowski, J. B., Wyckoff, L. B., & Tabory, L. (1956). The influence of reinforcement and punishment in a minimal social situation. *Journal of Abnormal and Social Psychology, 52,* 115–119.

Stroebe, W., & Frey, B. S. (1982). Self-interest and collective action: The economics and psychology of public goods. *British Journal of Social Psychology, 21,* 121–137.

Tajfel, H. (1978). *Differentiation between social groups.* London: Academic Press.

Tajfel, H. (1982). *Social identity and intergroup relations.* Cambridge: Cambridge University Press. Paris: Editions de la Maison des Sciences de l'Homme.

Turner, J. C. I., & Oakes, P. J. (1986). The significance of the social identity concept for social psychology with reference to individualism: Interactionism and social influence. *British Journal of Social Psychology, 25,* Special Issue on the Individual–Society Interface.

Van de Kragt, A. J. C., Dawes, R. M., Orbell, J. M., Braver, S. R., & Wilson, L. A. (1986). Doing well and doing good as ways of resolving social dilemmas. In H. Wilke, D. Messick, & C. Rutte (Eds.), *Experimental social dilemmas.* Frankfurt: Peter Lang.

Wieczorkowska, G. (1982). A formal analysis of preferences. *Polish Psychological Bulletin, 13, 73–77.*

Wilke, H. A. M., Rutte, C. G., Wit, A. P., Messick, D. M., & Samuelson, C. D. (1986). Leadership in social dilemmas: Efficiency and equity. In H. Wilke, D. Messick, & C. Rutte (Eds.), *Experimental social dilemmas.* Frankfurt: Peter Lang.

10

Membership, Intergroup Relations, and Justice

Ronald L. Cohen

Introduction

I begin with a quotation from a recent book on justice and a biblical tale to identify the issues I hope to discuss. After a slight diversion required to map out the territory of justice in which I see these issues residing, I will suggest some ways that social scientists, and most particularly social psychologists, might address these issues.

First, the quotation. In his book on justice, the political philosopher Michael Walzer (1983) departs from the recent predominant trend in Anglo-American philosophy by opting for a radically particularist approach to justice. Rather than search for universal principles on which to base a theory of justice, as do Rawls (1971) and Kohlberg (1981), Walzer examines the historical and anthropological literature and outlines a theory of justice based on the notion of "complex equality."[1]

The very first arena Walzer discusses at length is the political community, and in that context he provides me with one of my starting points:

---

[1]This notion requires "a diversity of distributive criteria that mirrors the diversity of social goods" and an open-ended distributive principle: "*no social good x should be distributed to men and women who possess some social good y merely because they possess y and without regard to the meaning of x.*" (Walzer, 1983, p.20) The effect of this principle is that "different goods [go] to different companies of men and women for different reasons and in accordance with different procedures." (p. 26)

Ronald L. Cohen • Bennington College, Social Science Division, Bennington, Vermont 05201

> The idea of distributive justice presupposes a bounded world within which
> distributions take place: a group of people committed to dividing, exchang-
> ing, and sharing social goods, first of all among themselves. . . . The
> primary good that we distribute to one another is membership in some
> human community. And what we do with regard to membership structures
> all our other distributive choices: it determines with whom we make those
> choices, from whom we require obedience and collect taxes, to whom we
> allocate goods and services. (Walzer, 1983, p. 31)

Thus the very idea of distributive justice presupposes boundaries,
boundaries that define membership, and importantly, nonmembership
in a human community.

And now the biblical story. In First Kings (3:16–28), Solomon is
confronted with two women, each of whom claims to be the mother of
a child. Solomon commands that the child be cut in half and shared
between the two women. The first woman agrees, but the second
refuses and offers to let the first have the child. Solomon knows then
that the second woman is the mother and gives the child to her. One
commentary on this suggests that it may actually be an adaptation of a
common folktale and that it is a "typical example of that Oriental
wisdom which is concerned with the actual business of living rather
than with abstractions." (The Interpreters Bible, 1954, pp. 44–45). One
among the many themes this tale suggests is the complex relationship
between justice, on the one hand, and mercy and caring on the other.

Conceptual Properties of Justice

What links might there be between these two sets of issues: membership as the primary good at issue in matters of distributive justice and
the relationship of justice and mercy. I want to suggest that work
following the lead of Gilligan's (1982) critique of Kohlberg (1981) lays
out many of these links and suggests fruitful lines of inquiry on
intergroup relations.

I begin here with a clear statement by the contemporary ethical
philosopher William Frankena:

> Justice, whether social or not, seems to involve at its center the notion of an
> allotment of something to persons—duties, goods, offices, opportunities,
> penalties, punishments, privileges, roles, status, and so on. Moreover, at
> least in the case of distributive justice, it seem centrally to involve the
> notion of comparative allotment. (1962, p. 9)

Justice is done when those who should have, do have; when each gets
his or her due; when what people do have is appropriate to what they
should have.

If at the central core of justice lies the idea of an allotment of something to persons and at the core of distributive justice the idea of comparative allotment, what are the key conceptual dimensions of distributive justice? There appear to be four: (1) the things allotted, which I call *receipts;* (2) the persons to whom these receipts are or may be allotted, which I call *recipient units,* and characteristics of those units; (3) a functional *rule* that describes the statistical distribution of receipts among recipient units; and (4) a *standard* against which a specific statistical distribution, or set of distributions, of receipts among recipient units is evaluated. I will begin with, and say very little about, the dimensions of functional rule and standard because they are less relevant to my present purpose. Then I will go on to the first two— receipts and units.

Functional Rule

The third major conceptual dimension I have identified is the rule (the function) that describes the relationship between receipts, on the one hand, and recipient units and their characteristics, on the other hand. In some cases, this rule will refer only to the distribution of receipts and the composition of the recipient class as a whole. For example, a rule of equal allotment among recipient units may be stated in such a way as to preclude identifying any recipients save that they are bona fide members of the recipient class. "Equal income for persons" is one such rule, and it provides a description of the complete distribution of receipts. There are similar rules that refer only to the distribution of receipts but that do not provide a complete distribution, such as those specifying a certain distributional shape, variance, minimum, maximum, and so forth.

Whether they provide complete or only partial descriptions, rules that refer only to the distribution of receipts and not to characteristics of recipient units, might be called *nondifferentiating* or *nonindividuating* rules because they do not differentiate or individuate recipient units.

Most of the rules that are familiar to us may be called *differentiating rules.* They specify a characteristic or set of characteristics in terms of which recipient units are to be differentiated. Thus, each according to his or her or their need, merit, worth, contribution, sex, class, and the like, all these are differentiating rules. Such rules may also include a specification of the function that relates these characteristics to receipts. The rule most familiar to social psychologists is the ratio rule that, in Homans's (1974) terms, links profits and investments, or in equity theory terms, links inputs and outcomes. Differentiating rules may range from a rather weak rank-order consistency to a strong ratio proportionality.

I have tried (1) to identify several descriptive rules linking receipts to units, (2) to distinguish them in terms of whether they did or did not differentiate among recipient units according to their characteristics, and if they did, (3) to distinguish among the types of functional rule describing that relationship, ordinal, or ratio. Two other rules should be mentioned because of the important roles they have had in controversies about distributive justice. The first, equality of opportunity, describes a situation in which each recipient unit has equal likelihood of obtaining receipts. The common understanding of this rule, captured in the image of a fair race removing "handicaps," is that recipient characteristics or contextual features thought to be irrelevant to the distribution of the particular receipt are held constant. The resulting actual distribution of the receipt is thought, then, to be systematically related to (or reflective of) other recipient characteristics that *are* thought to be relevant to the distribution of the particular receipt.

One final, and closely related descriptive rule, is the random rule. This specifies that each recipient unit has equal opportunity to obtain a receipt, but that the actual, eventual distribution of the receipt not be systematically related to any other recipient characteristic. If, upon inspection of the actual distribution, there is a systematic rule that can describe the relationship between receipts and recipient characteristics, one begins to suspect that the allotment was not conducted randomly.

Torstein Eckhoff (1974) has suggested that the random rule is often employed when the receipt to be allocated is either extremely important or extremely trivial, that is, when the stakes are either very high or very low. When stakes are very low, it may be felt that the application of a specific rule is too costly. When the stakes are very high, for example, in allocating the opportunity to go into combat, literally a matter of life and death, a random rule may be preferred.

Standard

The fourth conceptual dimension of distributive justice concerns the nature of the standard against which a certain relationship between receipts and recipient units is to be judged. This dimension differs from the third in the following respect. The question most relevant to third dimension is: "How are the receipts under consideration *actually* allocated (or how might they be allocated) among a class of recipients?'' The question most relevant to the fourth dimension is, instead: "How *should* the receipts be allocated among recipients?'' Nicholas Rescher, like Frankena a contemporary moral philosopher, calls attention to the same dimension in discussing a *philosophical* theory of justice:

> The task of a theory of distributive justice is to provide the machinery in terms of which one can assess the relative merits or demerits of a distribution, "the assessment" in question being made from the moral or ethical point of view. (1967, p. 7)

I think it is important to distinguish this standard, both from a broader standard of moral rightness [2] and from standards that are not normative or ethical ones. For example, one might evaluate a distribution of receipts according to the effects it has on the instrumental productivity of individual recipient units or the recipient class as a whole. Such a standard is not necessarily less important than a standard of distributive justice, but it is certainly a different standard of evaluation. Distributions of receipts may be efficient and unjust, and they may also be inefficient and just.

There are other standards, not necessarily moral ones, in terms of which one might evaluate a distribution. One that has appeared often in the research literatures on reward allocation and on work productivity is the positivity of relationships among recipients. Another, less often identified explicitly, is the willingness of recipients to accede to the distribution and to accept an allocator's legitimacy in producing it. Interpersonal solidarity, productive efficiency, order and stability, and justice are several standards against which a particular distribution might be evaluated.

Receipts

Receipts may be material or social goods, conditions, roles, opportunities, obligations, and the like. And I will shortly examine the implications of Walzer's suggestion that membership be considered what I call here a receipt. They may have positive or negative value, and various degrees of either. The classification of receipts best known among empirical social scientists is probably Foa and Foa's (1974) classification of "resources." The Foas identify two dimensions, con-

---

[2]The relationship of justice to other moral standards is one of the issues on which Kohlberg (1981) and Gilligan (1982) disagree most strongly.I will examine this issue in some detail.

creteness and particularism, and then locate six "classes" of resources (services, love, goods, status, information, and money) at various levels of the intersection of these two dimensions. These types of resources were originally distinguished for purposes of understanding human social exchange, a process related to, but not identical with, the comparative allotment of receipts central to distributive justice. It is interesting to note that, of these six classes, the two that have occupied the most central roles in discussions of distributive justice are money and goods, resources categorized as concrete and universalistic. Whether this suggests that the issue of distributive justice is most likely to emerge in considering comparative allotments of concrete receipts that have widely shared social meanings is not clear.

Apart from this, whatever the type of receipt, those relevant to distributive justice appear to have two other features that are crucial to identify. First, receipts relevant to distributive justice must be thought of as distinct and separable from recipient units. By this, I mean that it must be possible to conceive of the receipt either as attached to, or owned or controlled by, a recipient. Receipts currently attached to recipients must be seen to be detachable, alienable, in both practical and moral terms. And receipts currently unattached to recipients must be seen as potentially attachable, controllable, or ownable.

A second characteristic of the receipts most often discussed when considering distributive justice is related to the first; such receipts must be, and must be believed to be, part of an aggregate "storehouse" of receipts. There must be some aggregate storehouse of receipts from which shares might be allotted in the future, or from which currently allotted shares can be understood to have come in the past. The contemporary political philosopher Robert Nozick (1974) points to what he sees as a lack of clarity on this issue in discussions of distributive justice. Nozick claims that arguments about distributive justice often fail to distinguish a distribution that is merely a statistical description of the current receipts of an aggregate of recipients grouped together from a distribution that results from an identifiable act or acts of allocation from a collective storehouse. I agree with Nozick that this is an important distinction but disagree with him on what follows from it. In fact, that disagreement itself can be seen to flow from different understandings of the source of the receipts in question and from importantly different understandings of the concepts of ownership and property.

Receipts relevant to distributive justice are thus aggregative storehoused social values conceptually independent, in the first instance, of the recipient units to which they may already be, or may become, attached.

Recipient Units and Their Characteristics

Recipient units are those entities, most often individual persons, to whom receipts are allocated; it is the justice of the resulting distribution to which the general concept of distributive justice refers. With the last dimension, I come to a series of observations related to the quotation from Walzer and the biblical story I mentioned at the beginning of this chapter. There I suggested that the very *idea* of distributive justice presupposed a bounded world within which distributions take place, that the primary good people distribute to one another is membership in some human community, and that we needed to pay closer attention to the relationship between justice and mercy or caring. In the remainder of this chapter, I want to explore several issues related to these observations: (1) the nature of the boundaries drawn to define membership; (2) relative size of the membership group; (3) members (individual or collective) and the relations among them; and (4) the nature of the distinctions drawn among members.

Issues of Membership

Drawing Boundaries to Define Membership

Questions of distributive justice circumscribe boundaries that *include* some and *exclude* others. A class of recipients must be circumscribed before any judgment of justice or any allocation is made. We may learn as much about justice, or a conception of justice, by noting how boundaries are drawn and membership thus defined as by noting how receipts are allocated within the recipient class.

Votes are distributed among citizens of a certain age but not (usually) among convicted felons and noncitizens. Instructional salaries are distributed among faculty members but not among students or food service workers. Obligations for national (military) service are distributed among (most often male) citizens of a certain age, and not among women, the young, the old, the infirm, and the alien. All of these situations involve circumscribing an aggregate, if not a group, of recipients among whom goods are distributed and a grouping that is left out of any receipts. The differentiation and the boundary in the examples so far cited are lateral and spatial. As in many of the examples mentioned, the boundaries of inclusion and exclusion involve the nation-state. In other cases, much smaller spatial boundaries count, as for example, neighborhoods, work groups, clubs, and the like.

But there are temporal boundaries as well. Recently many controversial issues have arisen over the justice or injustice there may be when we consider the imposition of boundaries over time. What rationales have been offered for excluding the not-yet-born from equal protection of the law? What arguments have been made for excluding the interests of members of future generations from the health requirements of clean air and water or a radiation-free (or minimally radiated) atmosphere? And how do people justify the absence of a population policy that will make *any* calculations about the benefits or costs to future generations impossible because the size of what I have called the recipient class is incalculable?[3]

A review of some work undertaken to examine the nature of these boundaries suggests that from any perspective that employs "equal consideration" as an aspect of the formal principle of justice (of Buchnan & Matheiu, 1986), focusing only on "those inside the relevant [spatial or temporal] borders seems a kind of unjustified ethnocentrism" (Fishkin, 1983, p. 359). In this, and perhaps other, ways, merely circumscribing the group(ing) to which the concept of justice will be applied, may be controversial. And perhaps unjust. Questions concerning the distribution of income *within* a circumscribed population are certainly among those considered crucial in understanding justice, but should those persons who maintain households be included among those to receive incomes? And if so, is not including or excluding them a matter of justice?

This kind of issue is perhaps easiest to see in controversies surrounding admission to groups that border the uneasy distinction between "public" and "private." Must anyone who wants to be able to join private clubs, such as fraternal organizations, and recreational and educational organizations (such as the Scouts and "private" colleges), and more public groupings that gather in privately owned settings such as luncheon clubs and bars? Is denial of entrance, access, and membership considered a matter of justice? And, if so, does this

---

[3]Questions concerning spatial boundaries, and the possibility of extending them, and those concerning temporal boundaries, and the possibility of extending them, may be relatively controversial (at least theoretically). Issues concerning species boundaries may be highly controversial. Excluding from consideration under this rubric the question of whether or in what measure human fetuses before birth are fully human, there is a healthy degree of controversy, some of it touching those engaged in psychological research, about whether nonhuman animals, and if so, which ones, should be included within the boundaries of those to whom justice of some sort is due.

suggest that justice is seen not only or primarily as a public virtue but a private one as well? (cf. Pitkin, 1982)

There are, of course, some groups to which denial of membership would seem unjust to very few of us. Whereas all would probably agree that denying any citizen entrance to a public park, access to a public education, or membership in the body politic constituted an injustice, we would all also probably agree that denying any citizen membership in a particular family would *not* constitute an injustice. Only if that particular citizen happened, on further examination, to be previously a member of that family might an issue of justice seem to arise. And this would move us to a slightly different issue anyway, not denial of entry to membership, but expulsion, excommunication, or exile from previous membership, all of which might also be seen to involve matters of justice.

I have spoken of "membership" and "group," and much of the social psychological research on justice is meant to be addressed to an understanding of just distributions of receipts among members of various types of groups. However, most of that research also ignores the *temporality* of both concepts. Individuals confronting a single allocation task or judgment, or strangers brought together for one relatively brief time to make an allocation or judgment, are unlikely to consider themselves, or others, members of any group. This is another way in which the "one-shot," ahistorical nature of most of our research misleads us.[4] If we wish to understand justice and the role it plays in social life, then understanding how we draw the boundaries of the "moral community" within which all matters of justice are confronted is crucial.

(Relative) Size of the Membership Group

Setting the boundary establishes the size of the membership group and, by implication, the size of the group not eligible for resources. With a fixed resource pool, the larger the size of the membership group, the lower the average level of resources within the group, This may suggest a concern about keeping the membership group relatively

---

[4] Though they are not referring explicitly to research on justice, Fraser and Foster (1984) justifiably refer to the sets of individuals employed in most of the research on small groups as "nonsense groups."

small, or about ensuring that the inclusion of additional members is accompanied by an increased store of resources.

Most of the social psychological research on distributive justice not only has predetermined the boundaries of the recipient group but has employed the smallest size recipient class, two. Among the most interesting models for describing distributive justice judgments are those that suggest that individuals take account of several pieces of information about each of the recipients, and integrate this information in an overall judgment. It is difficult to imagine how the complex cognitive models hypothesized to describe such judgments (e.g., Anderson, 1974, 1976; Leventhal, 1976, 1980) would be relevant to judgments of distributive justice involving groups of several, much less several hundred, recipients.

There is both reasonable speculation, and there are some data, to indicate that individuals differ in the complexity of the information they take into account in making such judgments and in justly allocating resources. As the number of dimensions on which information about recipients is increased, so too will be the difficulty of integrating all of the information in a final judgment. A similar consequence might be expected for a large increase in the size of the recipient group. Such an increase might lead individuals (1) to adopt justice principles that ignore characteristics of individual recipients, or (2) to group recipients into aggregate units. On the other hand, rather than reflecting the difficulty of integrating judgments for a large group of recipients, endorsement of justice principles more readily applied to large groups and the tendency to think in terms of larger recipient groups, might, instead, reflect a preference for inclusion. I will return to this and other possibilities later in the discussion of gender.

Drawing boundaries of inclusion and exclusion establishes membership and nonmembership groups simultaneously. The drawing of any boundary line would seem both to reflect some implicit theory or set of assumptions about relations between the two groups and to create the context for future intergroup relations. If membership is the (or even a) major receipt allocated, then conceptions of relations between kin and nonkin, the familiar and the alien (the stranger), become critical to understand.

"Members" (Individual or Collective) and Relations among Them

The recipient group may be large or small. So, too, may be the size of the recipient units that are distinguished from each other within the group. For example, it may be considered just that all workers in a factory share in an enterprise's profits, but such a position does not make clear whether shares are justly allocated to small work groups or to individual workers. Most current empirical research on distributive justice in social psychology employs individual persons as recipient units, but recipient units can be, and sometimes are, comprised of small or large numbers of individual persons. Not only individual persons but families, statistical aggregates (such as regional populations or age-defined aggregates), and self-conscious collectivities (such as classes, gender-based groups, etc.) may be the relevant-sized units among which the just distribution of receipts is at issue.

As these distinctions should make clear, the nature, or internal structure, of the recipient unit may vary. The relevant units may be statistical aggregates or self-conscious collectivities. Internal relations may vary in the extent to which individual members of the unit are, and consider themselves to be, part of a solitary group with (at least partially) common interests rather than simply occupants of a similar social place. The dimension I am discussing here is captured well by the concept of "catnet" developed in the resource mobilization literature on social movements. A *catnet* is a set of people both "rhetorically distinguished by a common label and interconnected by social ties" (Rytina, 1986, p. 144). As these are relatively objective characteristics of the set, it might be well to add as an additional dimension for consideration, degree of "collective self-consciousness" as an important characteristic of the set.

Nature of Distinctions among Members

Finally, in addition to circumscribing a recipient class of a certain size and composition and distinguishing it from the class of nonrecipients, discussions of distributive justice also often include an identification of certain dimensions along which recipients do, or may, vary. "Standing" on these dimensions, of course, serves in the first instance to determine who is "inside," and who is "outside," the entire recipient class. These, or other, dimensions, may also then serve as a potential basis for determining the amount and type of receipt appropriate to each recipient. [5] Status at birth, sex, ethnicity, age, religion,

---

[5]The functional rule dimension of distributive justice links (amounts of) particular receipts to members of the recipient class. Differentiating rules focus on a particular dimension and correlate standing on that dimension to particular amounts of a specific receipt.

and the like have all been employed as dimensions on the basis of which potential recipients are included or excluded; and these and other dimensions, such as work output or need, have been employed as dimensions for allocating receipts other than membership among units of the recipient group.

Summary

Understanding justice requires exploring the nature of the boundaries that delimit the group within which valuable resources may be distributed and the group from which any such resources are withheld. In most of the social psychological literature addressed directly to matters of justice, matters of the size, internal structure, and nature of the group of persons among whom receipts are to be allocated are not at issue. They are predetermined by the researcher and serve only as background to issues of explicit concern.

Membership in the relevant group is confined to participants in the research who confront two or three distinct individuals brought together as members of a (bogus) fleeting group that exists (to the extent it does) for the sole purpose of a single allocation. The participant may be led to think of the two or three persons among whom resources are to be allocated as a group, often by participating in a task, by being told of the other's(s') participation, (at times) by having a common label (workers or employees) applied to the them, and (at times) by having all experience a common fate, as when the resources to be allocated among them (are said to) depend on their joint performance. For purposes of convenient definition, we might consider them (and they might consider themselves) a group in two senses relevant here: (1) Each has status as an equal constituent part of a collectivity with a common task and a common prospect of reward, and (2) this collectivity is marked off from imaginable others who are neither members nor eligible for any of the specifed reward. In situations where membership and group boundaries are prefigured in this way, issues concerning the justice of allocation among individual group members may be described reasonably well by the current literature. But in other situations this is not likely to be the case. If membership is the primary good distributed in matters of justice, then the social construction of that membership needs to be better understood and to be addressed directly.[6]

---

[6]One relevant study (Major, McFarlin, & Gagnon, 1984) was designed to investigate the hypothesis that, if told to pay themselves a just amount, women would pay themselves

Issues of Personhood

I hope to have shown some of the most important ways in which issues
of justice and membership are linked. But each of the issues of membership discussed was based on an implicit understanding of (at least)
one central concept, the concept of the (individual) person, which I now
mean to examine more critically. Doing so will be illuminated by considering research that has uncovered difeerences in the way men and
women approach matters of just allocation and distribution.

Gender Differences and Their Implications

Though the social psychological literature on justice is not entirely
consistent on this point, much of it seems to suggest that, all other
things being equal, women tend to distributive resources more equally
than do men, who tend to distribute resources more unequally in
proportion to differences in task performance (Furby, 1986; Major &
Deaux, 1982). Several different explanations have been offered for this
difference: that males and females have different interaction goals—
females being oriented to harmonious and males to more competitive
goals; that people generally allocate equally when they see recipients
as people and equitably when recipients are seen as occupants of
positions—women being less likely to view people as occupants of
positions; and that, independent of whatever preference they might
have for harmonious social relations, women are more concerned than
men for the well-being of others.

   All of these explanations seem to suggest a difference in the way
women as opposed to men conceive of themselves, relations between
themselves and others, and justice. Carol Gilligan's (1982) work
presents evidence which suggests that women are more likely to approach justice in terms of caring, men to approach justice in terms of
rights. She suggests that the major theme informing women's development is an "ethic of care," whereas that informing men's development is an "ethic of justice." And this difference is related directly to

less than men would pay themselves. Not only did the data confirm the hypothesis, but
female research participants left the laboratory with the lower pay they had assigned
themselves. In this case, the way the researcher constructed groups, and understood
their meaning, directly affected the resource distributions that were produced. Two
levels of "group" were constructed: the "group" of research subjects and "groups" of
male and female subjects. The intent of the study was to demonstrate the unjust results
of different understandings of deserving and justice by men and women. The study
demonstrated not only that but inadvertently also demonstrated the unjust consequences
of certain social constructions of groups and membership, this time by the researcher.

the development of individual identity in men and women and to the way in which individual identity is linked to, or divorced from, others.

One way to understand some of Gilligan's work is to refer to the literature suggesting sex differences in empathy. This difference appears not to reflect any difference in the ability to assess another's state but rather a difference in a prosocial affective orientation, including a greater concern over hurting others. And, once again, empathy has direct implications for the construction and defense of boundaries, inclusion and exclusion, and membership[7]

How large or reliable the difference is between (at least) these two conceptions of morality and identity *as a gender difference* is not my concern here; nor, if the gender difference turns out to be large and reliable, is it my concern here which factors explain such a difference. Rather, I am interested to explore what appear to be (at least) two fundamentally different ways of understanding and conceptualizing morality and identity for hints they give about intergroup relations, membership, and justice.

What implications do these differences in conceptions of morality and justice, identity, and empathy have for issues of inclusion/ exclusion and membership? At the very least, they seem to suggest fundamental links among a conception of the individual person

---

[7]One excellent example of the kinds of differences Gilligan is discussing can be found in comparing the responses of two 11-year-old children, one girl and one boy, to Kohlberg's famous Heinz dilemma. In this dilemma, a man named Heinz considers whether or not to steal a drug which he cannot afford to buy in order to save the life of his wife. Whereas Jake conceives of the dilemma as a conflict between life and property, Amy sees it as "a fracture of human relationship that must be mended with its own thread" (Gilligan, 1982, p. 31). In response to the question from the interviewer ("Should Heinz steal the drug?"), it is clear from Amy's response that she does not conceive the situation as does the interviewer, and thus is responding to a different question than the one the interviewer thought had been posed.

> Amy is considering not "*whether* Heinz should act in this situation ("should Heinz steal the drug?") but rather "*how* Heinz should act in response to his awareness of his wife's need ("should Heinz *steal* the drug?"). The interviewer takes the mode of action for granted, presuming it to be a matter of fact; Amy assumes the necessity for action and considers what form it should take. (p. 31)

In another instance, in discussing the recent movement for women's rights, Gilligan suggests a reversal of the way many of us think about the relationship between justice and mercy. Gilligan suggests that this movement and actual changes in women's rights have changed women's moral judgments, "seasoning mercy with justice by enabling women to consider it moral to care not only for others but for themselves" (p. 149). Rather than the familiar admonition to "temper justice with mercy," uttered to a (presumably and prototypically) male judge out of a humane concern even for the convicted criminal, the injunction to women would emerge out of the recognition that justice requires caring for the self as well as others.

(personhood), a conception of the (type of) group in which such a person might have membership, and an understanding of justice consistent with those conceptions of personhood and group.

More specifically, a conception of personhood that stresses (supposedly) separate, self-contained individuals who enter into social relations out of a fundamentally selfish individual interest in order to further their (supposedly) individual goals seems linked to a conception of a group whose internal relations are only as strong and meaningful as calculation of individual advantage will allow. Membership in such groups is based on a calculation of individual advantage and is as strong and meaningful as such calculation will allow. In addition, relations between such groups are most easily conceived in terms of predatory standoffs between self-interested collections of narrowly bounded individuals. These understandings, in turn, are consistent with an understanding of morality that makes a particular conception of justice its foundation. That conception of justice both relies on boundaries for its definition and stimulates the narrowing or constricting of those boundaries rather than their expansion.

Justice

I argued earlier that the concept of distributive justice demanded boundaries, that it made no sense without them. Certain people were to be included in, and others excluded from, that set among which resources are to be justly distributed. Even though that may be the case, there may be important differences in the way these boundaries are drawn, and membership defined.

On one set of understandings I have just discussed, individuals conceived as separate entities, even when they join together as members of groups, do so for their individual, calculated advantage. From this perspective, justice may be seen as necessary to protect such individuals from each other and may be seen to consist primarily of provisions for the defense of rights and claims against others. It may be, as Sampson (1986) has argued, that our

> self-contained personhood ideal (e.g., Sampson, 1977) excludes the larger
> web of interconnections among persons and between persons and the rest of
> nature on which any genuine justice must be based. When the boundaries
> of the person dwell firmly at skin-level and go no further, the chances for
> including the larger whole of humanity and nature into our concerns is not
> likely. . . . Our exclusionary concept of personhood achieves an egocentri-
> cally based sense of justice. (pp. 89, 92)

Is another understanding of individuals, and groups, and thus, justice, possible? Apparently, yes.

Gilligan's work (1982) suggests that persons conceived as em-

bedded in social webs or networks and persons (for example, many of
the women in her research) who so conceive themselves, think about,
and may form, groups in very different ways. In addition, such persons
(may) think about justice and morality in different ways as well.

Gilligan (1982) characterizes the major theme in women's contemporary psychological development as caring and responsibility. The
implications are twofold. First, the major moral theme in women's
lives is an ethic of care; second, the major theme of identity in women's
lives involves connection and relation to others. The boundaries that
appear to be necessary concomitants of the concept of distributive
justice will be more difficult to impose, accept, and sanction for
persons whose self-understanding involves connections to others.

If this is the case, then such persons will, at the very least , tend to
be more inclusive in circumscribing a group of people among whom
resources should be justly allocated. Put another way, such persons
should be less likely to exclude any recognizable or imaginable others.
That being the case, such persons would most likely prefer distributive
principles more easily applicable to large groups. And within the
groups so circumscribed, such persons should prefer principles of
distributive justice that are less likely to differentiate members.

It may be reasonable to summarize the differences here this way.
Whereas some people conceive of themselves and others as self-
contained individuals, importantly distinguishable from each other,
other people conceive of themselves and others as part of a network or
web of interconnected nodules. Whereas the first type of person
assumes separation and considers the possibility of inclusion, the
second type assumes inclusion and allows for the possibility of
separation. For the first, exclusiveness in membership is assumed, and
the boundary question of justice becomes whether it is just to admit
potential new members. For the second, common membership is more
usually assumed, and the boundary question of justice becomes
whether it is just to exclude those currently seen as members. And
when boundaries have been drawn, the first sees the group thus
created as one constituted by members who as individuals are
basically separated from each other. Selection of distributive justice
principles for application among members of such a group will reflect,
and then reproduce, such separateness. Distributive justice principles
selected for application among group members who as individuals are
mutually constitutive will reflect, and then reproduce, such mutual
interdependence.[8]

---

[8]When told to prevent conflict, individuals make more equal allocations of receipts.
Particularly when made in the context of differences in performance, equal allocations

And Intergroup Relations

Much of the social psychological literature on distributive justice, though focused on the conduct and judgments of individuals, is meant to apply to an intergroup context. Much of this work involves situations where individuals are asked to imagine themselves as one of two or more employees of some business or industrial firm. Here explicitly, and more implicitly in research based on simulations of legal or political institutions (see, for example, Tyler, 1986), not only do individual persons act in conjunction with other individuals, but groups (of employees, defendants and attorneys, or citizens) act in conjunction with other groups (of employers or managers, judges and the criminal justice system, or governmental agencies) in an institutional context with social and political dimensions. Both competitive and cooperative relations among groups provide the context within which resources are actually distributed among them.

Concrete issues of boundaries and membership are played out among groups differing in power. One crucial aspect of differences in power among groups is the possession of resources (material and symbolic) that permit some, and discourage other, boundaries. Admission to citizenship, or membership more broadly, is often the result of struggles among groups varying in power. Even assuming admission has been granted or achieved, subsequent allocations of other receipts will be biased in favor of, and often directly controlled by, groups with greater power.

One way this is accomplished is through the deployment of resources which simultaneously aggregates others for the purpose of denying them full membership and undermines their ability to act as a collectivity. This process is very similar to the process of domination described by Apfelbaum (1979). She distinguishes two sequential stages in the creation of domination: the first, "grouping," involves marking and excluding member of the "other" category; while the second involves what sounds at initially to be a contradictory process of "de-grouping the to-be-subordinated group." (pp. 197ff) The grouping stage fits well the social categorization process (Tajfel, 1981; Wilder, 1986), particularly the social construction of boundaries, exaggeration of differences between in-group and out-group, perceived homogeneity of the out-group, and the ubiquitous in-group bias.

The de-grouping stage makes clear that the categorization process

---

tend to accentuate similarities and solidarity. Differential allocations seem to maintain or enhance status differences, to create strain, and to encourage competitive tendencies. (Cohen, 1986; Deutsch, 1985) serves crucial social functions and occurs within a particular social context. That context includes the ability to translate the psychological processes and consequences of categorization into "biased" allocations. This ability, in part, defines the position of a dominant group. At the same time it distinguishes itself from the subordinate group, the dominant group maintains control over subsequent allocations *and* prevents the emergence of solidarity among subordinates, in part by employing certain rules of allocation (Cohen, 1986).

Conclusion

Distributive justice involves an ethical or moral judgment concerning the comparative allotment of scarce and valuable resources. In order for such a concept, and the corresponding judgment, to have meaning, one must imagine a bounded space within which are included all those who are members of what might be called a "moral community."

Justice, membership, and personhood are closely related concepts, and they reflect closely interwined social processes. These processes unfold in intergroup contexts addressed only indirectly by most of the social psychological research on justice. Those intergroup contexts involve groups with varying amounts of power that are more or less able to assert their collective self-understandings, impose their understandings of others, and define and set the boundaries between selves and others. Until these processes are more closely investigated, our understanding of the just allocations of resources other than membership will be incomplete.

References

Anderson, N. H. (1974). Cognitive algebra: Integration theory as applied to social attribution. In L. Berkowitz (Ed.), *Advances in experimental social psychology* (Vol. 7, pp. 1–101). New York: Academic Press.

Anderson, N. H. (1976). Equity judgments as information integration.*Journal of Personality and Social Psychology, 33,* 291–299.

Apfelbaum, E. (1979). Relations of domination and movements for liberation:An analysis of power between groups. In W. G. Austin & S. Worchel (Eds.), *The social psychology of intergroup relations* (pp. 188–204).Belmont, CA: Wadsworth.

Buchanan, A. E., & Mathieu, D. (1986). Philosophy and justice. In R. L.Cohen (Ed.), *Justice: Views from the social sciences* (pp.11–45). New York: Plenum Press.

Cohen, R. L. (1986). Power and justice in intergroup relations. In H. W.Bierhoff, R. L. Cohen, & J. Greenberg (Eds.), *Justice in social relations* (pp.65–84). New York: Plenum Press.

Deutsch, M. (1985). *Distributive justice: A social-psychological perspective.* New Haven, CT: Yale University Press.

Eckhoff, T. (1974). *Justice: Its determinants in social interaction.* Rotterdam: Rotterdam University Press.

Fishkin, J. (1983). The boundaries of justice. *Journal of Conflict Resolution, 27*(2), 355–375.

Foa, U. G., & Foa, E. B. (1974). *Societal structures of the mind.* Springfield, IL: Charles C Thomas.

Frankena, W. K. (1962). The concept of social justice. In R. B. Brandt (Ed.), *Social justice* (pp. 1–29). Englewood Cliffs, NJ: Prentice-Hall.

Fraser, C., & Foster, D. (1984). Social groups, nonsense groups, and group polarization. In H. Tajfel (Ed.), *The social dimension: European developments in social psychology* (Vol. 2, pp. 473–497).

Furby, L. (1986). Psychology and justice. In R. L. Cohen (Ed.). *Justice: Views from the social sciences* (pp. 153–203). New York: Plenum Press.

Gilligan, C. (1982). *In a different voice. Psychological theory and women's development.* Cambridge, MA: Harvard University Press.

Homans, G. C. (1974). *Social behavior: Its elementary forms* (Rev. Ed.). New York: Harcourt Brace Jovanovich.

The interpreter's Bible: The holy scriptures and revised standard versions (Vol. III). (1954). New York: Abingdon.

Kohlberg, L. (1981). *Essays on moral development. Vol 1: The philosophy of moral development.* New York: Harper & Row.

Leventhal, G. S. (1976). Fairness in social relationship. In J. Thibaut, J. Spence, & R. Carson (Eds.), *Contemporary topics in social psychology* (pp. 211–239). Morristown, NJ: General Learning Press.

Leventhal, G. S. (1980). What should be done with equity theory? In K. Gergen, M. Greenberg, & R. H. Willis (Eds.), *Social exchange theory* (pp.27–55). New York: Plenum Press.

Major, B., & Deaux, K. (1982). Individual differences in justice behavior. In J. Greenberg & R. L. Cohen (Eds.), *Equity and justice in social behavior* (pp. 43–76). New York: Academic Press.

Major, B., McFarlin, D. B., & Gagnon, D. (1984). Overworked and underpaid: On the nature of gender differences in personal entitlement. *Journal of Personality and Social Psychology, 47*, 1399–1412.

Nozick, R. (1974). *Anarchy, state, and utopia.* New York: Basic Books.

Pitkin, H. F. (1982). Justice: On relating public and private. *Political Theory,9*(3), 327–352.

Rawls, J. (1971). *A theory of justice.* Cambridge, MA: Harvard UniversityPress.

Rescher, N. (1967). *Distributive justice.* Indianapolis, IN: Bobbs-Merrill.

Rytina, S. (1986). Sociology and justice. In R. L. Cohen (Ed.), *Justice: Views from the social sciences* (pp. 117–151). New York: Plenum Press.

Sampson, E. E. (1977). Psychology and the American ideal. *Journal of Personality and Social Psychology, 35*, 767–782.

Sampson, E. E. (1986). Justice ideology and social legitimation: A revised agenda for psychological inquiry. In H. W. Bierhoff, R. L. Cohen, & J. Greenberg (Eds.), *Justice in social relations* (pp.87–102). New York: Plenum Press.

Tajfel, H. (1981). *Human groups and social categories: Studies in social psychology.* Cambridge: Cambridge University Press.

Tyler, T. (1986). The psychology of leadership endorsement. In H. W. Bierhoff, R. L.

Cohen, & J. Greenberg (Eds.), *Justice in social relations* (pp. 299–316). New York: Plenum Press.

Walzer, M. (1983). *Spheres of justice: A defense of pluralism and equality.* New York: Basic Books.

Wilder, D. A. (1986). Social categorization: Implications for creation and reduction of intergroup bias. In L. Berkowitz (Ed.), *Advances in experimental social psychology* (Vol. 19, pp. 291–355). New York: Academic Press.

11

Interpersonal and Intergroup Injustice
Some Theoretical Considerations

J. E. M. M. Syroit

Introduction

In social psychology a distinction is made between interpersonal or interindividual injustice and social injustice. The former refers to the analysis of injustice problems as they occur between individuals; the latter refers to "relations between large-scale socially defined and evaluated categories of people" (Tajfel, 1982, p. 695). Although it is recognized that perceptions and cognitions giving rise to intergroup behavior reside in individuals, the position repeatedly advocated by Tajfel that it is not possible to extrapolate the social psychology of intergroup relations from the social psychology of interpersonal relations is widely accepted (Tajfel, 1978; Turner, 1975). Until now, most of the research on (in)justice had an interpersonal focus (see Adams & Freedman, 1976). It seems unwise to use only this body of research for developing an intergroup injustice theory. Austin (1979) is somewhat more optimistic by assuming that the structure of the interpersonal and intergroup theories can be the same and that only processes differ between the two levels of analysis. It is possible that Austin is right with his assertion about the analogy between interpersonal and intergroup analyses of individual behavior. We are inclined, however, to

J. E. M. M. Syroit • Department of Social and Organizational Psychology, University of Utrecht, 3584 CS Utrecht, The Netherlands.

follow Doise's reasoning about the relation between "psychological" and "sociological" explanations of behavior. Doise (1978) defends the thesis that "psychological," that is, individual explanations of behavior will be enriched by taking into account sociological or group variables. Individuals in social psychology experiments do not solely act as experimental subjects, but they bring with them their social positions that they occupy outside of the laboratory. Therefore, it seems wise not to reduce the individual level of analysis to the group level of analysis (or vice versa), but to take explicitly into account the sociological, that is, the group variables, in the psychological explanations of persons' behavior. In line with this reasoning, we will not try to reduce the interpersonal model of injustice to an intergroup injustice model (or vice versa) but to present both models of injustice separately in the conviction that this way of presenting our theories gives the best guarantee that injustice in everyday life might best be explained and understood.

In this chapter we will present some theoretical considerations about interpersonal and intergroup injustice. The former will be based on a theoretical analysis of interpersonal injustice (Syroit, 1984), whereas social identity theory (Tajfel & Turner, 1979) will be the point of departure for the intergroup injustice analysis. We will adduce some theoretical arguments in support of the thesis that these two theoretical frameworks constitute a solid basis for a future theoretical framework for injustice that, according to Tajfel:

> must be capable of taking into account both the interindividual relations within a socially homogeneous milieu and the relations—interindividual and collective—which obtain across a variety of barriers dividing social categories of people who perceive themselves as belonging to different communities. (1982, p. 158)

Interpersonal Injustice

For the sake of conceptual clarity, interpersonal injustice is analyzed in an indirect exchange relation (Von Grumbkow & Wilke, 1974) or allocation situation (Eckhoff, 1974), in which (at least) two persons P and O contribute to an exchange with a common exchange partner J, who provides the outcomes for P and O (see Figure 1A). This kind of situation allows for making a clear distinction between, on the one hand, the exchange relation between P and O and the exchange partner J, and on the other hand, the social comparison relation between P and O. In a direct exchange relation or reciprocation situation the roles of contributor and resource allocator show a great deal of overlap (see

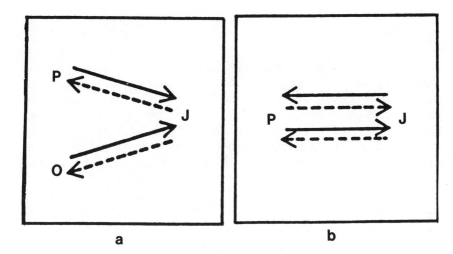

Figure 1 Schematic representation of the indirect (Part A) and direct (Part B) exchange situations.

Figure 1B). The situation is analyzed from the point of view of person P, who evaluates his exchange relationship with person J.

Inputs and Outcome Newly Defined

In inequity theory (Adams, 1965; Walster, Berscheid, & Walster, 1973, 1976), the concept of *inputs* refers to many different things, such as observable characteristics of an individual (e.g., race, height), psychological attributes explaining individual behavior (e.g., intelligence, skill, effort), and to actual behavior or behavioral effects (e.g., performance, quality of performance). In line with a distinction made by Rijsman (1983) between the cues an individual uses to form an impression about self (and others) and the self-(other-)referent meaning attached to these cues, a distinction is made here between the perceptual aspect of inputs, that is, *the input-cues*, and their cognitive–evaluative aspect, that is, the *input-meaning*. Input cues can be categorized into four classes: (1) bodily characteristics, (b) actions, (c) possessions, and (4) group memberships. Input meaning is the overall judgment about self, relative to others, which is based on the perception of the input cues belonging to self and to relevant others. The process through which a person makes this relative judgment is a process of comparative appraisal (Jones & Gerard, 1967). This relative judgment is expressed in the input ratio:

$$\frac{I_p}{I_o}$$

A similar distinction must be made on the *outcome* side. *Outcome cues*, the perceptual aspect of outcomes, consist of different kinds of rewards and punishments, received by P and O from the exchange partner J. These outcome cues are converted into *outcome meaning*, that is the relative judgment of the self. The most important difference between inputs and outcomes on the perceptual level, and thereby on the cognitive–evaluative level as well, is that outcome cues necessarily consist of behavior of the exchange partner directed at self and other. Outcome meaning is the appraisal of self and other as reflected in the rewarding or punishing behavior of the exchange partner. This reflected relative appraisal is expressed in the outcome ratio:

$$\frac{O_p}{O_o}$$

Both the input ratio and the outcome ratio express a person's *relative value in exchange*. These redefinitions imply first that the separate inputs and outcomes of self and other are no longer considered to be the basic elements of the unjust situation, and second, that because outcome cues are necessarily provided by the exchange partner, other rewarding aspects of the situation, such as intrinsically rewarding job characteristics, cannot be conceived as true outcomes in the context of injustice.

The Perception and Experience of Interpersonal Injustice

An exchange relationship between two individuals (P and J) is perceived as unjust by P when he perceives that his comparative relative value in exchange does not correspond with his reflected relative value in exchange. In other words, a relationship is perceived as unjust when the exchange partner (J) does not behave towards the individual (P) according to the latter's judgment of his value in exchange. Injustice represents an instance of not being validated by exchange partner (Rijsman, 1983). Injustice, thus defined, cannot be reduced to a particular case of cognitive inconsistency. It is necessarily an *interpersonal* event or, otherwise stated, a characteristic of the relation between the exchange partners. Cognitive dissonance, a mere *intrapersonal* state, is conceived of as an emotional state accompanying the interpersonal *conflict*.

Social comparison plays an important role in the construction of the comparative and reflected relative value in exchange. An important question is to what extent and in which way social comparison dynamics (tendency toward uniformity, tendency toward superiority, and the tendency to compare oneself with others [Festinger, 1954; Rijsman, 1974; Syroit, 1980] interfere with or influence the perception of injustice? For answering this question, it is useful to consider again the different relationships within the indirect exchange situation (See Figure 1A). Between P and O exists a social comparison relation, whereas between P and J exists an exchange relation. Social comparison dynamics directly affect the relation between P and O. Injustice on the other hand is a matter between P and J. The total indirect exchange situation can be conceived of as a Gestalt in which the relation P–J is the figure and the relation P–O forms the ground. The comparison other functions only as a standard for evaluation. This standard becomes more relevant the more the person P tends to compare himself with the other O. The tendency to compare oneself with others, which increases with a decrease in difference between the comparison partners, is an indication of the relevance of the other as a standard for evaluating one's own exchange relationship. It is hypothesized that the perception of injustice is not only a function of the perceived discrepancy between the comparative and reflected value in exchange but also a function of the tendency to compare oneself with the comparison other. This hypothesis has been supported in a series of studies ranging from evaluating hypothetical work situations (Syroit & von Grumbkow, 1977) to evaluations of actual pay of employees in a field study (Syroit, 1984).

The question about the relation between injustice perception and injustice experience has recently been raised by Greenberg (1984). Greenberg adopts the position that not every instance of perceived injustice is accompanied by feeling distressed. Factors that influence the transfer of perception to experience are, among others, the expectation of injustice, and individual or situational constraints preventing or inhibiting expressions of distress.

Reactions to Unjust Situations

The (psychological) conflict interpretation of injustice perception and experience implies that the actual restoration of an unjust event must be situated in the interpersonal context of the exchange situation. The appropriateness of the mechanisms described by Adams (1965) for resolving injustice problems is questioned. First, these mechanisms mainly focus on restoring cognitive balance within the person experiencing injustice. And second, insofar as these mechanisms have an interpersonal orientation, they are directed at the relation between the person experiencing injustice and his comparison other and not at the exchange partner. The mere reduction of cognitive dissonance, without changing the conflict relation with the exchange partner who is at the basis of the unjust treatment, seems like removing the symptoms without curing the disease. Reduction of injustice implies resolving or influencing the interpersonal conflict. Reduction of injustice takes the form of a direct or indirect negotiation process between the exchange partners, aimed at convincing the exchange partner of his unjust treatment and at changing his evaluation of the unjustly treated individual. Factors that codetermine the choice of the negotiation process are for example, personal characteristics such as assertiveness, locus of control; relational characteristics such as perceived status differences and power differences, the type of relationship between the exchange partners; and of course the more global, cultural characteristics of the larger system (group, organization, society) in which this particular unjust exchange is embedded (e.g., politeness rules, norms, and values governing interpersonal relations, traditions and history with respect to modes of conflict resolution, etc.).

Empirical evidence supporting the interpersonal conflict interpretation of injustice is scarce, because most studies on injustice were guided by the cognitive consistency approach. Studies done by Ross, Thibaut, and Evenbeck (1977) and Ross and McMillen (1973) show that injustice leads to social protest against those responsible for it. Schwarzwald and Goldenberg (1979) report that subordinates show less compliance to an inequitable than to an equitable supervisor. Lawler (1975) and Lawler and Thompson (1978) demonstrated that subordinates form revolutionary coalitions against inequitable managers. More complaints, less buying, and leaving a shop without buying were clearly related to inequitable price and service conditions in shops, as reported in a study by Huppertz, Aronson, and Evans (1978). There is some anecdotal evidence showing that inequitably paid subjects in inequity experiments protested against the experimenters, who were held responsible for the injustice and that they tried to sabotage the experiment (Hinton, 1972; Wilke & Steur, 1974; von Grumbkow & Wilke, 1978). In one of the author's studies, indirect evidence was found for the fact that in cases where face-to-face contact between the subject–employee and his experimenter–employer was less likely, people made use of indirect modes of injustice reduction (working less attentively, leaving the workplace earlier than agreed upon, producing bad quality work). These indirect modes of getting even with the experimenter–employer were less apparent in condition where future face-to-face contact with the experimenter was hypothesized to be high (Syroit & Sleypen, 1981; Syroit, 1984). In a field study, it was found that the use of mechanisms affecting the comparison other's contributions and outcomes did not correlate with reported feelings of underpayment, whereas mechanisms affecting the person's own situation did significantly correlate with feelings of underpayment (Syroit, 1984).

Intergroup Injustice

So far, we have described the interpersonal injustice model. Now we will briefly present the main elements of social identity theory (Tajfel & Turner, 1979) and comment on some parallels between these two theoretical models. The existence of such parallels makes us feel confident that these two models can fully contribute to the development of a theory of distributive injustice that applies in interpersonal as well as in intergroup settings. In the remainder of this chapter we will present some preliminary features of an intergroup injustice model.

From Interpersonal to Intergroup Injustice

The first question that needs to be answered is: When does interpersonal behavior becomes intergroup behavior? Or, when will an individual perceive an unjust event as an instance of intergroup injustice rather than one of interpersonal injustice? This question has been dealt with *in extenso* by Tajfel and his colleagues (Tajfel, 1978, 1981; Tajfel & Turner, 1979; Turner & Giles, 1981). The answer is closely related to the definition of a group. Definitions of groups, such as the one given by Sherif (1967), have been elaborated within the context of intragroup research, and they offer *no* explanation for the nature of intergroup behavior. The Bristol group defines a group as

> a collection of individuals who perceive themselves to be members of the same social category, share some emotional involvement in this common definition of themselves, and achieve some degree of social consensus about the evaluation of their group and of their membership of it. (Tajfel and Turner, 1979, p. 40).

According to these authors behavior can be placed somewhere on the continuum going from purely interpersonal to purely intergroup. Tajfel defines these anchors as follows:

> What is meant by "purely" interpersonal is any encounter between two or more people in which all the interaction that takes place is determined by the personal relationships between the individuals and by their respective individual characteristics. The "intergroup" extreme is that in which all of the behavior of two or more individuals toward each other is determined by their membership in different social groups of categories. (1978, p. 41)

Behavior that lies more to the intergroup end of the continuum is characterized by

> (a) the presence of at least a dichotomous social categorization so that individuals are identifiable as members of distinct social categories;
> (b) "low intersubject variability within each group. . . . This is, group members tend to behave in a homogeneous or uniform fashion;
> and (c) "low intrasubject variability in the treatment and perception of different outgroup members, . . . That is, the same person tends to act uniformity towards a wide range of different others. (Brown & Turner, 1981, pp. 37–38).

Turner (1982) has formulated the self-stereotyping hypothesis to explain behavioral variations along the interpersonal–intergroup continuum. The shift from interpersonal to intergroup behavior corresponds with the transition in self-concept functioning from personal to social identity. Personal identity refers to self-descriptions in terms of personal or individual attributes. Social identity refers to self-descriptions in terms of group memberships or social categories. Turner argues further that once a specific social identification has become salient, a person attributes to self and others the characteristics that are typical for his or her group or category. This self-stereotype has been derived from characteristics of persons belonging to his group. Members of out-groups, that is, groups or categories to which the person does not belong, are stereotyped in an analogous way. Individuals see members of the outgroup as undifferentiated and homogeneous, and they perceive their ingroup members likewise. Turner has called this process a process of "depersonalization." An encounter is interpersonal when the identification of self and other is based on individual, idiosynchratic characteristics of the individuals; an encounter is intergroup when the social identification of self and other is based on group memberships, enhanced and filled out through a process of self and other stereotyping and depersonalization. Brown and Turner (1981) enumerate a number of factors that make social identity become salient: conflict, confrontation or encounter with an outgroup, distinctiveness of the group in a given environment, number of group members present, similarity, common fate, proximity, being a representative of a group, and homogenity of the outgroup (pp. 42–43).

Parallel with the interpersonal–intergroup continuum, Tajfel

(1978) describes another continuum going from "social mobility" to "social change." Social mobility is defined as: "an individual's perception (most often shared with many others) that he can improve in important ways his position to another, as an individual" (1982, p. 52). Social change "as the term is used here, refers to the other extreme of the subjective modes of structuring the social system in which an individual lives. It refers basically to his belief that he is enclosed within the walls of the social group of which he is a member; that he cannot move out of his own into another group in order to improve or change his position or conditions of live" (p. 53). Four variants of conditions that help to determine the development of a social change structure of beliefs are distinguished: (1) the existence of a rigid stratification system, which becomes more and more unstable or illegitimate; (2) the creation of a social change system of belief; (3) the needs of certain individuals to establish clear-cut and impenetrable social dichotomies; and (4) intense conflict of interest that makes it unlikely for individuals to move to the adversary party (Tajfel, 1978, p. 58). The more a person adheres to a social change belief system, the more he will move toward the intergroup end of the behavioral continuum.

The analysis of the transition form interpersonal to intergroup behavior sets some prerequisites for a theoretical model of intergroup injustice. First, the person evaluating the exchange with another person must psychologically define himself as being a member of a group or social category and perceive the other person as belonging to another group or social category. One of the difficulties to be solved has to do with the division of social reality in two or more social categories, and the location of the person, the comparison other and the reward allocator in this social system. Second, in order to be able to speak about intergroup injustice and intergroup reactions to injustice, it must be assumed that the functioning of the person's social identity has been triggered in the exchange situation, instead of, or more than, his personal identity functioning. That is, the individual must act in terms of self–other identifications largely or exclusively based on their respective group memberships, further enhanced and filled out by the postulated self and other stereotyping process. Third, in order to behave more in the intergroup than in the interpersonal mode, a person evaluating the exchange must adhere more to a social change structure of the belief than to a social mobility belief structure.

It is now possible to make a preliminary statement about the transition from interpersonal to intergroup injustice. With respect to the perception of an unjust exchange situation, it is expected that the more a person relates the injustice to differences between himself and others in terms of their respective group memberships and the more this person structures the social system according to a social change belief system, the more likely it is that he will perceive the injustice as an instance of intergroup injustice and that his consequent behavioral reactions to or in the unjust situation will be positioned to the intergroup end of the interpersonal–intergroup continuum.

Aspects of Social Identity Theory Relevant for Intergroup Injustice

Social identity theory (Tajfel & Turner, 1979) starts with the basic assumption that individuals have a need for a positive self-concept and are thus motivated to maintain and/or establish this positive self-concept. Three main processes are described: social categorization, social identity, and social comparison.

Social categorizations "provide a system of orientation for 'self-reference': they create and define the individual's place in society" (Tajfel & Turner, 1979, p. 40). The social groups to which people belong provide their members with an identification of themselves in social terms, that is, a social identity that is a subsystem of the self-concept (Turner, 1982). This social identity is relational and comparative. It has positive or negative value connotations associated with the respective group memberships. Social comparison, in this case intergroup comparison, defines the evaluation of one's own group. This comparison takes place along value-laden attributes and characteristics.

The striving to maintain or enhance one's self-esteem takes the form of striving toward a positive social identity and leads to the tendency to differentiate one's own group from another group in a positive way. Some conditions must be fulfilled: (1) the individual must have internalized his group membership as an aspect of his self-concept; (2) situations must allow for intergroup comparison along relevant attributes, and (3) the outgroup must be perceived as a relevant comparison group (Tajfel & Turner, 1979, p. 41). The outcome of the social comparison, that is, the relative position of the group on an evaluative comparison dimension, is referred to as the group's status. Groups or individuals within groups have different modes of reacting to a negative or threatened positive status. Individuals can move out of inferior groups and join superior ones (individual mobility). Another set of reactions grouped under the label social creativity aim at redefining or altering elements of the comparison situation: (1) creating new comparison dimensions, which have to be legitimized in both groups; (2) changing the values assigned to the attributes of the group, and (3) changing the outgroup. A third possible reaction, labeled *social competition* is aimed at reversing the relative positions of the ingroup and the outgroup on a salient comparison dimension. Whether this social competition will lead or will not lead to real intergroup conflict depends on the security of the comparison. A comparison is called insecure when members of a group perceive cognitive alternatives to the actual outcome of a comparison with the outgroup. Two variables affect the security of the social comparison: (1) the legitimacy of the status difference, that is, whether the status difference is or is not in conflict with a superordinate value of justice, and (2) the stability of the status difference, that is, the feasibility of changing the groups' respective status positions. The security of status differences is questioned in cases of so-called nonconsensual status systems, in which groups do not agree on the values attached to the outcomes of comparison, or when the subjective status of a group does not correspond with its accorded status (Tajfel & Turner, 1979; Turner, 1982).

It is time now to point out some analogous and some different features of the two theoretical models presented here. Two important differences should be pointed out. First, the interpersonal injustice model is a heuristic framework that explicitly deals with injustice perception and individual reactions to or in unjust exchange situations. Social identity theory treats the problem of a person's striving to establish, maintain, and/or enhance a positive social identity. The second main difference is that the interpersonal injustice model gives an interpersonal analysis, predicting perceptions and behavioral reactions of individuals qua individuals, whereas social identity theory is an "intergroup" model, predicting perceptions and behavioral reactions of individuals qua members of groups or social categories. These differences are crucial and must be kept in mind when reading that some features of both theoretical models parallel each other.

The first parallel is the accentuation of the role of a person's identity in both theories: the personal identity in the interpersonal injustice model and the social identity in social identity theory. In the presentation of the interpersonal injustice model, the concept of personal identity has not been explicitly mentioned, but it is not difficult nor farfetched to translate the concept of value in exchange into the personal identity concept. Value in exchange refers to a person's relative and comparative evaluation of himself in a particular interpersonal situation, and it is based on the perception of differences between self and other with respect to individual characteristics. The core concept of social identity in Tajfel and Turner's theory refers to a comparative evaluation of self, relative to others predominantly defined in terms of characteristics of the groups to which they belong.

The distinction made between comparative and reflected value in exchange finds its parallel in the distinction made between subjective group status and accorded group status. Comparative value in exchange is the outcome of the social comparison of input cues. This process is initiated by the person who evaluates the exchange. Reflected value in exchange is the outcome of a reflected appraisal process, initiated by the reward allocator. An analogous distinction is made by Ng (1990) with respect to the status of a group "Unlike subjective status, which is the outcome of self-instigated comparison, accorded status is the outcome of other-instigated social comparison" (p. 22).

The third main parallel lies in the accentuation of social comparison processes and their role in establishing a person's identity: the personal identity or value in exchange in the interpersonal model and the social identity in social identity theory. In the two models, the tendency to compare oneself with others, on the interpersonal or the intergroup level, is an important variable influencing consequent behavioral reactions in the social situation. It is fully recognized that the nature of social comparison in an interpersonal context differs from the nature of these processes in an intergroup context. According to Festinger (1954), status differences and status hierarchies develop as the consequence of the incomparability of individuals, thereby implying that social comparison only can take place *within* a group or social category. Social comparison in social identity theory is by definition an intergroup comparison, and other factors than similarity may affect the salience of the other group for comparison (e.g., perceived illegitimacy).

The fourth parallel between the interpersonal injustice model and social identity theory is to be found in the conflict interpretation of the interpersonal relation and at least under some circumstances of the intergroup relation.

Finally, it is worthwhile to point out the occurence of the concept of injustice in the two theoretical models. It is explicitly present, of course, in the analysis of interpersonal injustice, and it is implicitly present in social identity theory through the concept of perceived illegitimacy of status differences between groups.

Although we were able to find some important corresponding themes in the two theoretical models, it does not seem wise as has been indicated in the introductory statement to incorporate the set of propositions of one model into the other. The two major differences, pointed out at first, do not allow for such a straightforward theoretical integration. But, as has been said before, social identity theory provides some valuable concepts and processes for building up an intergroup injustice model. It might be unfair to call it *first moves* because these have already been made by others (Austin, 1979; Caddick, 1981, 1982; Ng, 1984c; Tajfel, 1984). Their comments on this topic will be evaluated and used in our efforts.

Toward an Intergroup Model of Injustice

In this paragraph, comments will be given on four topics. Some considerations will be given about the structure of the intergroup situations in which injustice concerns might become relevant. Next, some ideas will be presented with respect to the antecedents of intergroup injustice, the perception and experience of injustice and its meaning, and finally about intergroup reaction to or in unjust intergroup situations.

The Structure of Intergroup Situations

The distinction made between direct (reciprocation) and indirect (allocation) situations is also relevant with respect to the intergroup analysis of injustice. Caddick (1981) points out this difference in his comments on his own study and that of Commins and Lockwood (1979b). In the Commins and Lockwood study, the inequitable treatment was induced by the experimenter who is in fact a third party, whereas in Caddick's study the outgroup was made responsible for the unfair task assignment. Most or all of the intergroup allocation studies belong to the direct relation category: group members are asked to allocate money or points to members of their group and of the other group. Austin (1979) also cites a difference between these two intergroup situations. In his analysis of injustice in an intergroup setting, he explicitly starts from an indirect intergroup situation in which the outcomes of the two groups are affected by allocation decisions made by a third party (e.g., the government). The examples he starts from are the school busing problem and the affirmative action policy in the United States in which black and white Americans are differently affected by governmental decisions.

In the context of intergroup relations, the picture is however more complex than in the interpersonal exchange situations. In the direct relation, the allocator can be an ingroup member or an outgroup member. In the indirect exchange relation, one can reasonably put the question whether this third party is really perceived as a neutral allocator of resources or as a member of the ingroup or of the outgroup, and thus profiting from the allocation? It is quite possible that perceptions about the location of the allocator are strongly influenced by the actual allocation. The question of the position of the reward allocator in the intergroup relation structure has relevance for the prediction of the kind of reactions of groups to perceived injustice.

Antecedents of Intergroup Injustice: What Are the Inputs and the Outcomes?

According to Austin (1979), the dominant justice principle in interpersonal as well as in intergroup relations is equity or proportionality. Equity is treated as the main justice principle in a number of studies on the relation between justice and intergroup behavior (Caddick, 1981; Ng, 1984a, 1990). And in the notion of fairness operationalized as equality in the numerous intergroup studies and in the studies by Branthwaite, Doyle, and Lightbown (1979) and by Branthwaite and Jones (1975), proportionality is implied. Equality is seen as fair mainly because of the absence of a real performance input factor.

The main question is: "What are inputs and outcomes on the intergroup level?" The way inputs and outcomes have been manipulated or measured in intergroup studies throw some light on the implicit conceptions about inputs and outcomes of researchers in the field of intergroup behavior. In the Branthwaite and Jones study, inputs are represented in the form of an initial status difference related to nationality (English vs. Welsh). In the Branthwaite et al. study, initial status difference (university vs. college students) and the performance on a word generation task are treated as inputs. In the studies by Commins and Lockwood (1979a, b), performance on a dot estimation task is used a means to induce initial status differences. In the studies done by Ng (1981, 1984a, b; 1990) performance feedback about production in a word generation task, a color guessing task, and a spot-the-ball task are used as input cues that supplement social categorization. In Caddick's 1981 study, performance on a spot-the-ball task is the input. Finally, in a study by Ancok and Chertkoff (1990), performances on a numerical and verbal test are used as input cues.

Outcomes are mainly monetary rewards. Commins and Lockwood (1979a) have used points, too. In Caddick's study, subjects are asked to divide rewards and evaluate the performance of others. In most of these studies, inputs refer to pure individual characteristics superimposed on a social categorization manipulation. The attenuating–accentuating effect of this interpersonal element on intergroup allocation is studied. It is hard to believe that subjects in these studies incorporated these purely individual characteristics into self-stereotypes, especially in conditions where individual input differences were manipulated *within* one social category. As in the case of interpersonal injustice, a distinction must be made here, too, between input cues that is , inputs on the perceptual level, and input meaning, that is, inputs on the cognitive–evaluative level. On the perceptual characteristics, but on the cognitive–evaluative level they must be integrated in the image. This is the situation-specific elaboration of social identity. It is almost needless to say that the evaluation of persons' inputs is a relative and comparative matter.

Outcomes are the material and immaterial resources given to members of groups by a reward allocator in return for their contributions. Outcome differences reflect the allocator's relative appraisal of the contributions of members of a group compared with those of members of another group. It is necessary that outcome differences are predominantly based on differences of group characteristics and not or much less on individual, idiosyncratic characteristics. As such, an outcome is an "outward and visible sign of the worth of a recipient's work in others' eyes" (Ng, 1990, p. 3). In an intergroup context, it should be added that a recipient is conceived as a member of a group or social category.

Input differences in an intergroup setting represent a group's subjective status, that is, the result of a self-instigated social comparison along dimensions that are relevant or salient in that particular intergroup exchange situation. Outcome differences represent a group's accorded status, that is, the result of other-instigated social comparison. These are necessarily provided by other persons.

The Perception of Intergroup Injustice

"An accorded status provides a social validation or invalidation of the (subjective) status which members of a group claim for their group" (Ng, 1990, pp. 21–22). Injustice can be conceived of as an instance of the invalidation of one's subjective status, thus as the perception of a mismatch between subjective and accorded status. Traditionally, injustice is seen in relation to the illegitimacy of the status difference between groups (Caddick, 1981, 1982). Illegitimacy is defined as a status difference that is in conflict with a superordinate value of justice, fairness, or equity. Illegitimacy can therefore, in our view, not be applied to the subjective status because a subjective status is the status group members claim for their own group. Thus, only the accorded status, which is provided by others, can be perceived as being illegitimate. This illegitimacy can be "caused" by procedural errors in the allocation process, or it can be implied in every situation where the accorded status does not match the legitimately claimed subjective status. In order to perceive injustice, the allocator (or allocating group) must be held responsible for the illegitimately, incongruent status allocation.

As in the case of interpersonal injustice, we also hypothesize with respect to intergroup injustice that a given mismatch between subjective and accorded group status will be perceived as more unjust, the more the outgroup becomes relevant for social comparison. With respect to illegitimacy, we hypothesize that a given mismatch between subjective and accorded group status will be perceived as more unjust, the more the accorded status is perceived as illegitimate.

Intergroup Reactions to Unjust Intergroup Situations

It is assumed that the perception of injustice motivates people to restore justice. Perceiving injustice is conceived as a conflict between the group and the allocating party who is responsible for the unjust allocation. The distinction made by Turner (1982) between real conflict and social conflict is relevant in this context. Real conflict refers to a conflict between groups about the allocation of (scarce) resources; social conflict is a conflict about the relative social identity. In most unjust allocation situations, both aspects of a conflict are assumed to be present.

The way people react in intergroup settings is dependent on the kind of belief structure they adhere to: social mobility versus social change. This distinction is highly relevant for predicting the kind of behavior to be expected from individual members of the unjustly treated ingroup in relation to the outgroup. Its relevance for predicting group members' behavior toward a third party allocator is not analyzed, yet. It is rather unlikely that people react in a purely individual way to instances of intergroup injustice, such as leaving the unjustly treated group in order to move into the justly or overrewarded group because it is very unlikely that a social mobility belief structure will develop under conditions of real or psychological intergroup conflict. The reactions of ingroup members towards outgroup members that belong to the social change category of reactions can be seen as in direct modes of influencing the allocator's opinion about the ingroup, in order to have restored him the unjust allocation. In a direct exchange situation, in which the outgroup is responsible for the unjust allocation of resources, these social change strategies are direct ways of bringing the accorded status in line with the ingroup's subjective status.

References

Adams, J. S. (1965). Inequity in social exchange. In L. Berkowitz (Ed.), *Advances in experimental social psychology* (Vol. 2, pp. 267–299). New York: Academic Press.

Adams, J. S., & Freedman, S. (1976). Equity theory revisited: Comments and annotated bibliography. In L. Berkowitz & E. Walster (Eds.), *Advances in experimental social psychology* (Vol. 9, pp. 43–90) New York: Academic Press.

Ancok, D., & Chertkoff, J. M. (1990). Effects of group membership, relative performance, and self-interest on the division of outcomes. *Journal of personality and social psychology 45*, 1236-1262.

Austin, W. (1979). Justice, freedom, and self-interest in intergroup conflict. In W. G. Austin & S. Worchel (Eds.) *The social psychology of intergroup relations (pp. 127–143).* Monterey, CA: Brooks/Cole.

Austin, W., & Walster, E. (1974) Reactions to confirmations and disconfirmations of expectancies of equity and inequity. *Journal of personality and social psychology, 2*, 208–216.

Branthwaite, A., Doyle, S., & Lightbown, N. (1979). The balance between fairness and discrimination. *European Journal of Social Psychology, 9*, 149–163.

Branthwaite, A., & Jones, J. E. (1975). Fairness and discrimination: English vs. Welsh. *European Journal of Social Psychology, 5*,323–338.

Brown, R. J., & Turner, J. C. (1981). Interpersonal and intergroup behavior. In J. C. Turner & H. Giles (Eds.), *Intergroup behavior* (pp. 33–65). Oxford: Basil Blackwell.

Caddick, B. (1981). Equity theory, social identity, and intergroup relations. In L. Wheeler (Ed.), *Review of personality and social psychology* (Vol. 1, pp. 219–245). London: Sage.

Caddick, B. (1982). Perceived illegitimacy and intergroup relations. In H. Tajfel (Ed.), *Social identity and intergroup relations* (pp. 737–754). Cambridge: Cambridge University Press.

Commins, B., & Lockwood, J. (1979a). Social comparison and social inequality: An experimental investigation of intergroup behavior. *British Journal of Social and Clinical Psychology, 78*, 285–289.

Commins, B., & Lockwood, J. (1979). The effects of status differences, favoured treatment and equity on intergroup comparisons. *European Journal of Social Psychology, 9*, 281–289.

Doise, W. (1978). *Groups and individuals: Explanations in social psychology.* Cambridge: Cambridge University Press.

Eckhoff, T. (1974). *Justice: Its determinants in social interaction.* Rotterdam: Rotterdam University Press.

Festinger, L. (1954). A theory of social comparison processes. *Human Relations, 7*, 117–140.

Greenberg, J. (1984). On the apocryphal nature of inequity distress. In R. Folger (Ed.), *The sense of injustice: Social psychological perspectives* (pp. 167–188) New York: Plenum Press.

Grumbkow, J., & Wilke H. (1974). Sociale uitwisseling en billijkheid. Toetsing en evaluatie van de billijkheidstheorie [Social exchange and equity. A test and evaluation of equity theory]. Nederlands tijdschrift voor de psychologie, 29, 281–316.

Grumbkow, J., & Wilke, H. (1978). Extreme underpayment in a simple and complex comparison situation. European Journal of Social Psychology, 8, 129–133.

Hinton, B. L. (1972). The experimental extension of equity theory to interpersonal and group interaction situations. Organizational Behavior and Human Performance, 8, 434–449.

Huppertz, J. W., Arenson, S. J., & Evans, R. H. (1978). Application of equity theory to buyer-seller exchange situations. Journal of Marketing Research, 15, 250–260.

Jones, E. E., & Gerard, H. B. (1967). Foundations of social psychology. New York: Wiley.

Kayser, E., & Schwinger, T. (1982). A theoretical analysis of the relationship among individual justice concepts, layman psychology and distributions decisions. Journal for the Theory of Social Behavior, 12,; 47–51.

Lawler, E. J. (1975). An experimental study of factors affecting the mobilization of revolutionary coalitions. Sociometry, 38, 163–179.

Lawler, E. J., & Thompson, M. E. (1978). Impact of leader responsibility for inequity on subsequent revolts. Social Psychology, 41, 264–268.

Ng, S. H. (1981). Equity theory and the allocation of rewards between groups. European Journal of Social Psychology, 11, 439–443.

Ng, S. H. (1982). Power and intergroup discrimination. In H. Tajfel (Ed.), Social identity and intergroup relations. Cambridge: Cambridge University Press.

Ng, S. H. (1984a). Equity and social categorization effects on intergroup allocations of rewards. British Journal of Social Psychology, 23, 165–172.

Ng, S. H. (1984b). Intergroup allocation bias before and after group discussion. Journal of Social Psychology, 124, 95–103.

Ng, S. H. (1984c). Social psychology and political economy. In H. Tajfel (Ed.), The social dimension (Vol. 2, pp. 624-645). Cambridge: Cambridge University Press.

Ng, S. H. (in press). Equity and bias in reward allocation: effects of performance, group membership, and status insecurity. Mimeographed copy.

Rijsman, J. (1974). Factors in social comparison of performance influencing actual performance. European Journal of Social Psychology, 4, 279–311.

Rijsman, J. (1983). The dynamics of social competition in personal and categorical comparison situations. In W. Doise & S. Moscovici (Eds.), Current issues in European social psychology (Vol. 1, pp. 279–312). Cambridge: Cambridge University Press.

Ross, M., & McMillen, M. J. (1973). External referents and past outcomes as determinants of social discontent. Journal of Experimental Social Psychology, 9, 437–449.

Ross, M., Thibaut, J., & Evenbeck, S. (1971). Some determinants of the intensity of social protest. Journal of Experimental Social Psychology, 7, 401–418.

Schwarzwald, J., & Goldenberg, J. (1979). Compliance and assistance to an authority figure in perceived equitable and nonequitable situations. Human Relations, 32, 877–888.

Sherif, M. (1967). Group conflict and co-operation. London: Routledge & Kegan Paul.

Syroit, J. (1984). Interpersonal injustice: A theoretical analysis illustrated with empirical research. Tilburg University, Doctoral dissertation.

Syroit, J., & von Grumbkow, J. (1977). Hoe billijk is billijk? Toetsing van een social vergelijkingsmodel van billijkheid [How equitable is equity? Test of a social comparison model of equity]. Nederlands tijdschrift voor de psychologie, 32, 471–482.

Syroit, J., & Rijsman, J. (1980). Effecten van sociale vergelijking: Effecten van belonings-vergelijking [Effects of social comparison: effects of reward comparison]. In J. B. Rijsman & H. A. M. Wilke (Eds.), *Sociale vergelijkingsprocessen Theorie en onderzoek* (pp. 176–186). Deventer: van Loghum Slaterus.

Syroit, J., & Sleypen, J. (1981) Inter- en intrapersoonlijke vergelijking van bijdragen en opbrengsten als maatstaven voor (on)billijkheid [Inter- and intrapersonal comparison of input and outcomes as standards for (in)equity]. *Gedrag, 9,* 326–340.

Tajfel, H. (Ed.) (1978). *Differentiation between social groups.* London: Academic Press.

Tajfel, H. (1981). *Human groups and social categories.* Cambridge: Cambridge University Press.

Tajfel, H. (1982). Psychological conceptions of equity: The present and the future. In P. Fraisse (Ed.) *Psychologie de demain.* Paris: Presses Universitaires de France.

Tajfel, H. (1984). Intergroup relations, social myths and social justice in social psychology. In H. Tajfel (Ed.), *The social dimension* (Vol. 2). Cambridge: Cambridge University press.

Rajfel, H., & Turner, J. (1979). An integrative theory of intergroup conflict. In W. G. Austin & S. Worchel (Eds.), *The social psychology of intergroup relations* (pp. 695–715). Monterey, CA: Brooks/Cole.

Turner, J. (1975). Social comparison and social identity: Some prospects for intergroup behaviour. *European Journal of Social Psychology, 5,* 5–34.

Turner, J. C. (1982). Towards a cognitive redefinition of the social group. In H. Tajfel (Ed.), *Social identity and intergroup relations* (pp. 15-42). Cambridge: Cambridge University Press.

Turner, J. C., & Giles, H. (Eds.), (1981). *Intergroup behaviour.* Oxford: Basil Blackwell.

Walster, E., Berscheid, E., & Walster, G. W. (1973). New directions in equity research. *Journal of Personality and Social Psychology, 25,* 151–176.

Walster, E., Berscheid, E., & Walster, G. W. (1976). New directions in equity research. in L. Berkowitz & E. Walster (Eds.), *Advances in experimental social psychology* (Vol. 9, pp. 1-42). New York: Academic Press.

Wilke, H., & Steur, T. (1972). Overpayment: Perceived qualifications and financial compensation. *European Journal of Social Psychology, 2,* 273–284.

12

Aggressive Reactions to Social Injustice by Individuals and Groups
Toward a Behavioral Interaction Model

J. M. Rabbie and H. F. M. Lodewijkx

Introduction[1]

In a discussion about the applicability of equity theory to aggressor–victim relationships, Donnerstein and Hatfield (1982) propose that groups will reward members who behave equitably and punish those who will not. When enmeshed in inequitable relationships, they argue, people experience distress that can be reduced by trying to restore the equity in their relationship. The greater the inequity, the more distress will be experienced and the more they will try to restore equity. According to equity theory, it is to be expected that the provoked victim will feel most comfortable when he or she retaliates appropriately. Consistent with this notion, it has been found that people retaliate both in kind and amount to the level of aggression they receive from others (O'Leary & Dengerink, 1973).

Retaliation may be inhibited by fear of reprisal. In a number of

[1]This chapter is based on earlier versions (Rabbie & Lodewijkx, 1983, 1986b). The research was supported by the Netherlands Organization for the Advancement of Research (NWO, 55-97). The authors wish to thank Ernest De Vroome and Bert Alberda for their assistance in the development, execution, and the data analysis of this experiment. The authors are indebted to Sjef Syroit for his constructive comments on this chapter.

J. M. **Rabbie** and H. F. M. **Lodewijkx** • Institute of Social Psychology, University of Utrecht, 3584 CS, Utrecht, The Netherlands.

studies it has been shown that people are less likely to behave aggressively when they know that their potential victims have the power to retaliate then when they know they cannot (e.g., Bandura, 1983; Donnerstein & Donnerstein, 1973; Jaffe & Yinon, 1983).

Donnerstein and Hatfield (1982) recognize that equity theory cannot explain all instances of aggression. There are some conditions in which equity considerations seem surprisingly ineffective in explaining how people behave. In their view, "people seem to behave most in accord with Aristotle's ideal—and most equitably—when they are calm, cool, and collected. When people are intensely angry, or intensely aroused, considerations of equity seem to go by the wayside" (p. 329).

The notion that emotional arousal may interfere with cognitive appraisal processes, for example, in group decisions, is one of the main issues in the present experiment. In this chapter we are interested in the question to what extent groups or dyads react with more angry aggression than single individuals to the norm violation of another more powerful party on which their outcomes seem to depend. Aggression is defined here as an intentional act to harm another interdependent party: a person or group.

According to the enhancement hypothesis, derived from our Behavioral Interaction Model (BIM), it is assumed that intragroup interaction strengthens the cognitive, emotional, motivational, and normative orientations that are already present in individual members prior to the group decision, as they try to cope with an uncertain external environment (Rabbie & Lodewijkx, 1985; 1986a,b; 1987). In this view, groups are not inherently more competitive or aggressive than single individuals, as is sometimes asserted (Jaffe & Yinon, 1983; Turner, 1981), but it will depend on the dominant psychological orientations in the group whether group members will act more or less aggressively than individuals to perceived injustice. When it seems legitimate or justified to punish another interdependent party for one's norm violation, group members will stimulate each other to express more aggression to the other offending party than socially isolated individuals are capable of doing. More specifically, the enhancement hypothesis predicts that the anger and indignation about the norm violation of another interdependent party will be enhanced through intragroup interaction. The emotional arousal and anger is assumed to interfere with the cognitive capability to suppress their angry aggression in a cool, calculated, and instrumental effort, not to antagonize a more powerful party and to avoid retaliatory action from him or them. We also expect that groups, as compared with single individuals, are less willing to restrain their angry reactive aggression because they have a greater need to assert themselves and are probably more inclined than individuals to use coercive aggression in an instrumental attempt to influence the behavior of the other party (Janis, 1982).

These hypotheses are based on a Behavioral Interaction Model in which an attempt is made to integrate a variety of theoretical approaches to the research on conflict and aggression of individuals and groups (Lodewijkx, 1989; Rabbie, 1987, 1989; Rabbie & Lodewijkx, 1987; Rabbie, Schot, & Visser, 1989). For a more complete understanding of the hypotheses, measurements, and the experimental variations employed in this study, the model will be reviewed in some detail.

The Behavioral Interaction Model

The Behavioral Interaction Model, depicted in Figure 1, builds on Lewin's (1936) famous formula that behavior B, including aggressive behavior, is a function of P, a person or a party and the environment E. The parties or actors involved may be persons, groups, organizations, and other social systems that have to cope with an uncertain, unpredictable environment.

In the external environment, three components can be distinguished: (1) the (physical) task environment, (2) the social internal and

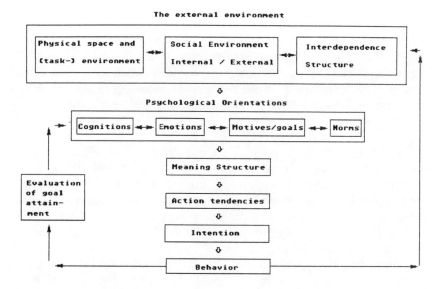

Figure 1. The Behavioral Interaction Model (BIM).

external environment: the behavior of other people within and outside the group or social system, and (3) the nature of the interdependence structure between the parties, with respect to goals and means and the power relationships between the parties or actors (Raven & Rubin, 1983). In an asymmetric interdependence relationship, the greater B's dependency on A the greater power A has over B (Emerson, 1972).

In the present experiment, three components of the environment were manipulated in the following way:

1. A physical task environment was constructed in which two parties, individuals or groups (dyads), had to play a mixed motive game: the Power Allocation Game (PAG) against a programmed party: another individual or a dyad that was prerecorded on videotape. For the subjects, the other party were fellow subjects just like themselves who were allegedly seated in a different room. The pseudo-other party could be seen on a TV screen in front of the subjects.

2. The external social environment: the behavior of the other party during the four trials of the game was identical for individuals and groups. The internal social environment of the two parties differed from each other: the individuals were socially isolated and had to rely on their own internal resources to deal with the situation, whereas the dyads had to make collective decisions about their choices in the game and about their aggressive responses to the norm violations of the other party. Thus they could use the internal resources of the group in making their decisions. In this way we could study the effects of the changes in the internal social environment of the dyads as they responded to the changes in their external social environment: the behavior of the other party during the four trials.

3. The interdependence structure between the parties was designed to be an asymmetric one: the subjects, after their own initial choice, were expected to make themselves more dependent upon the actions of the programmed party for attaining their outcomes than the other (more powerful) party was dependent upon them (Emerson, 1972).

According to the model, the three components of the external environment activate, in interaction with each other, specific kinds of cognitive, emotional, motivational, and normative orientations that enable people to cope with an uncertain and unpredictable environment. The psychological orientations may vary from relatively stable personality dispositions or traits at one pole of the dimension or can be considered as situational or "state" variables that are elicited in particular situations at the other pole of the continuum (Magnusson & Endler, 1977; Snyder & Ickes, 1985). The main function of these psychological orientations is to reduce the uncertainty in the external environment to such a manageable level that it enables the individual or group to achieve desirable and to avoid undesirable outcomes (Rabbie et al., 1989).

Cognitive orientations, and related concepts such as scripts (Abelson, 1976), social schemata (Taylor & Crocker, 1981), and hypotheses (Snyder, 1982), refer to the structure of expectations people have about themselves and their environment that reflect their organized beliefs about different physical and social situations (Deutsch, 1982, p. 24). They determine the encoding, interpretation, retention, and retrieval about people and events in the external environment. In an effort to measure these cognitive orientations, the subjects in the present experiment were asked to indicate what their expectations were about the game behavior of the other party and the extent to which they made internal or external attributions to explain the behavior of themselves and the other party.

Emotional orientations refer to subjective experiences and perceptions of relative sudden changes (emotions) or more slowly evolving fluctuations (moods) of physiological arousal in the autonomic nervous system (Frijda, 1986). Emotional orientations have cognitive as well as motivational functions. They alert people to threatening or pleasing events in the environment, which motivates them to avoid or approach them. These emotions and feelings were measured in this study by asking subjects how pleased, irritated, or disappointed they were about the behavior of themselves and the other.

Motivational orientations direct one to the possibilities of gratification or frustration of certain kinds of needs, motives, and goal attainments in a given relationship as they change over time in reaction to the behavior of oneself and others (Deutsch, 1982; Rabbie, 1987). Some of the motivational orientations of our subjects were measured by asking them from time to time how strongly they were motivated to maximize their own outcomes (max own); whether they wanted to earn as much as their opponent (equality or fairness); to compete with them (relative gain); to what extent they wanted to defend themselves against the other party (defensiveness); or whether they were strongly motivated to influence the other party.

Normative orientations orient one to the rules and regulations that govern the attitudes and behavior of people in a given relationship that may be enforced by positive or negative sanctions. Norms have a moral, prescriptive quality: they refer to obligations, rights, and entitlements and prescribe what people ought or not ought to do in certain circumstances (Deutsch, 1982; Turner & Killian, 1972). They have also a descriptive, informational quality in the sense that they provide people with consensually validated evidence about the social reality they are faced with (Deutsch & Gerard, 1955). Information about normative orientations of the subjects was obtained by asking them how they felt the money between the parties should be distributed between them: in an equal or equitable way, taking account of the power differentials between them. How they felt about the violations of the equality, equity, and reciprocity norms by the other party, and how justified and legitimate they felt their aggressive reactions had been to the norm violations of the other party and whether they had moral objections to administer painful white noise to the other party.

Meaning Structure

The cognitive, emotional, motivational and normative orientations, at any given time, produce an organized meaning structure of the external environment. Although many different meaning structures may exist, in our research we have focused on two broad orientations: an instrumental task orientation that emphasizes the power and control over others and a social–emotional orientation that stresses the relational orientation to others. For instrumentally oriented people, the relationship with the other is not an end in itself but a means or an instrument through which he or she may attain economic or other tangible outcomes (Rabbie, 1989a, b). Dependent on the nature of the interdependence structure between the parties, they will engage in instrumental cooperation or competition to maximize their outcomes.

Socioemotional oriented people are engaged in social or relational competition or cooperation if the external task environment allows these kinds of behaviors. Social or relational cooperation is aimed at achieving a mutually satisfying relationship with the other as an end in itself rather than as an external goal to the relationship. Relational orientations are often designed to effect changes in the internal social environment. Social or relational competition is aimed at differentiating oneself from another, in an effort to achieve prestige, status, recognition, or a positive social identity in comparison with another relevant party: another individual, group, or organization (Festinger, 1954; Lemaine, 1974; Snyder & Fromkin, 1982; Tajfel & Turner, 1979, 1985).

These analytic distinctions between instrumental and relational cooperation and competition bear a close relationship to the distinction that has been made between instrumental and reactive aggression (Buss, 1961; Feshbach, 1964). In instrumental aggression, the actor threatens to hurt or actually harms another party in order to achieve nonaggressive external goals that could have been attained by other means as well. Like instrumental cooperation or competition, instrumental aggression is primarily motivated by extrinsic incentives.

On the other hand, the goal of angry or reactive aggression is intrinsically motivated. Reactive or angry aggression is aimed at inflicting bodily and psychological harm to another interdependent party who can be held accountable for the frustration of one's goals or other aversive events (Berkowitz, 1983). The aim is to hurt another party as an end in itself, a goal that only can be achieved through aggression. Angry or reactive aggression is "annoyance motivated" because its primary function is to reduce or terminate an aversive or noxious state (Zillmann, 1979). In actual aggressive interactions, it is often very difficult to determine whether the aggression is intrinsically or extrinsically motivated. In the present experiment, we have tried to manipulate an instrumental orientation in the subjects by giving them the idea that by the suppression of angry aggression they could hope for valuable incentives provided by the other party. There is some evidence that adults are likely to restrain their aggression when this restraint holds promise of preventing, reducing, or eliminating aversive stimulation (Zillmann, 1979). Thus, if people have reason to believe that the expression of reactive aggression to the norm violations of a more powerful party will lessen their chances of obtaining valuable outcomes from that party, they are likely to restrain their aggression in an effort not to antagonize him or her and to invite retaliation.

In the context of this chapter, the angry or reactive aggression to the norm violation of another interdependent party can be considered as a reaction to different forms of social injustice. When the retaliatory aggression is undertaken to compensate for injury and harm suffered in an earlier attack (Zillmann, 1979, p. 40), we are dealing with the Aristotelian theory of retributive justice, that is, justice in compensation for harm and punishment of injury. The study is also concerned with distributive justice: justice in the distribution or allocation of goods and services (Homans, 1982). Finally, it also refers to various forms of procedural justice, as we will see (Leventhal, 1976).

Meaning structures generate various action tendencies. Consistent with the expectancy value models of Lewin (1936), Vroom (1964), and Ajzen and Fishbein (1980), it is assumed that among competing action tendencies that action will be chosen that is expected to result in attaining highly valuable goals and outcomes at minimal costs. According to the theory of reasoned action of Ajzen and Fishbein (1980), the intention or commitment to perform or not to perform an act is the best predictor of behavior.

The action or the behavior may lead to outcomes or a present state that has to be evaluated against the desired future state: the goal or standard the party wanted to achieve. When no discrepancy is observed between the present and desired state, the action is terminated. When a discrepancy still remains, the party has to revise or reconsider the psychological orientations, which led to the behavior that was not successful in reaching the standards or goals the parties set for themselves. The mismatch or discrepancy between the actual behavioral outcomes and the desired goals may induce a change in the psychological orientations symbolized by an arrow from the "evaluation of goal attainment" box to the psychological orientations in Figure 1, which may initiate a new cycle of action sequences that will be terminated until the goal is achieved or when different and more reachable goals are substituted for the original ones. The direct arrow at the right-hand side of Figure 1 from the behavior to the external environment at the top of the figure expresses the notion that acting on the external environment may have the effect of changing it, leading to different psychological orientations and meaning structures of the situation, which in turn may induce different action tendencies, intentions, and behavior until the original or modified goals are achieved. Just like other cybernetic action models, for example, the control model of Carver and Scheier (1981), the TOTE-concept of Miller, Galanter, and Pribram (1960), and the information-processing model of emotions of Frijda (1986), our model can be considered as a self regulating, negative feedback system, modulated by multiple feedback loops that results in a reorganization of meaning structures, action tendencies, and the kind of goals the actor wants to achieve in interaction with other parties until some steady state is attained between them.

In the present experiment, the subjects were frustrated in their legitimate expectations about the attainment of their goals by the illegitimate actions of the other programmed party. In his revised version of the frustration–aggression theory, Brown (1986) has proposed that frustration—the blocking of a goal response by another party—is only a stimulus to aggression when the frustrated party experiences an unfair or illegitimate disadvantage in comparison with another party. An unfair or illegitimate disadvantage is conceptualized in his theory as a state of inequity between the perceived ratio of outcomes and investments of one party in comparison with the ratio of the outcomes and investments of another relevant party (Brown & Herrnstein, 1975; Brown, 1986, p. 575).

In our view, retaliatory aggression is not only a response that is used to restore equity or distributive justice in an inequitable relationship, as equity theorists seem to suggests (Brown, 1986; Donnerstein & Hatfield, 1982), but aggression also occurs when procedural justice norms seem to be violated (Eckhoff, 1974; Leventhal, 1976). In a number of experiments, it has been shown that the intentional violation of a procedural norm, for example, a breach of a promise, and not so much the inequitable relationship between the parties per se, aroused angry aggression in individuals and groups (Lodewijkx, 1989; Rabbie & Horwitz, 1982; Rabbie & Lodewijkx, 1984 a,b, 1986a,b, 1987; Rabbie, Lodewijkx, & Broese, 1985). Generally, the greater the perceived intention that the other party was out to exploit them by illegitimate means, the more retaliatory aggression that did occur (Cf. Ferguson & Rule, 1983). In other words, actions of another party may not only be perceived as illegitimate because they produce inequitable outcomes, but they also are considered to be illegitimate because these actions violate norms of procedural justice: how the distribution of goods and services is arrived at and the manner in which it is implemented (Leventhal, 1976). In our experiment, in which the other programmed party abused his power to gain an unfair advantage over the subjects, at least both types of illegitimacy were involved.

One of the main objectives of the experiment was to find out whether groups would show more angry aggression than socially isolated individuals in reaction to the norm violations of the other party. According to our enhancement hypothesis described earlier, social interaction, or even the mere presence of others (Zajonc, 1965, 1980), enhances the psychological orientations in the group that are already present in individuals when they are confronted with the same external environment. There are a great variety of theories that deal with influence processes in groups for example, group polarization (Lamm & Meyers, 1978; Rabbie et al. 1989); social facilitation (Zajonc, 1965, 1980) deindividuation (Diener, 1980; Festinger, Pepitone, & Newcomb, 1955; Prentice-Dunn & Rogers, 1983, Rabbie, Lodewijkx & Broese, 1985; Zimbardo, 1970); the impact of emergent norms (Rabbie & Visser, 1984; Turner & Killian, 1972), diffusion of responsibility (Jaffe & Yinon, 1983), groupthink (Janis, 1982; Hart, 1990); modeling and observational learning (Bandura, 1983, 1986; Rabbie & Goldenbeld, 1988), and social and emotional comparisons (Festinger, 1954; Gerard & Rabbie, 1961; Rabbie, 1964) to name only a few. Although different psychological mechanisms may be involved, most of these theories have in common that they predict an enhancement of the orientations, attitudes, and behaviors that are already present in individuals prior to the intragroup discussion. Our enhancement hypothesis refers to the enhancement of existing orientations, but up to this time it does not specify the kind of specific mechanisms that may be involved in this enhancement process.

It is likely that in the present experiment, group members may share cognitive, emotional, motivational, and normative orientations about the structure of the conflict and the behavior of the other party. Group polarization studies have shown that through social comparison processes and the exchange of persuasive arguments, groups polarize in their aspirations, attributions, and other cognitive orientations, in the direction of the opinions and beliefs held by the individual group members prior to the group discussion (Lamm & Meyers, 1978; Rabbie & Visser, 1972).

At an individual level of analysis, social facilitation theory assumes that the mere presence of others creates a state of physiological arousal or drive, which strengthens the dominant, well-learned responses of the individual (Zajonc, 1965, 1980). The stimulating intragroup interaction and the irritation and anger evoked by the norm violations of the other party enhance the emotional arousal of the individual members in the group. If individuals have learned to act in an aggressive manner against the norm violation of the other party, the heightened emotional arousal in the group will strengthen the dominant aggressive responses of group members as compared with the emotional orientations and behavior of single individuals, particularly when the other members show approval and encouragement about the expression of aggressive behavior (Rabbie & Goldenbeld, 1988).

Individuals and groups differ in their level of motivation. In earlier research it has been found that groups as compared with individuals are more instrumental and less relational oriented (Rabbie, Visser, & Van Oostrum, 1982). They were more inclined than individuals to maximize their outcomes, attach greater weight to their interests (Horwitz & Rabbie, 1982), have higher aspirations than individuals about what can be accomplished in negotiations (Rabbie & Visser, 1972), and were less willing to develop a mutually satisfying relationship with the other group (Rabbie et al., 1982). If groups are more instrumental in their motivational orientations than individuals, the frustration caused by the illegitimate actions of the other party will be greater for groups than for individuals. In that case it is to be expected that they are less inclined to placate the other party, have a greater need to assert themselves, and are more likely than individuals to use coercive aggression as one of the behavioral options to influence and control the other party in an effort to obtain valuable outcomes or incentives from him or her (Tedeschi, 1983).

With respect to the normative orientations, it has been argued that groups are convinced of their moral righteousness vis-à-vis other groups (Janis, 1982; Simmel, 1964). Especially when they are unfairly disadvantaged by the other party, they feel more justified than individuals to punish the other for his or her norm violations.

The Behavioral Interaction Model assumes that the aggressive behavior in this experiment is a combined function of changes in the external environment, that is, the manipulated independent variables, and the cognitive, emotional, motivational, and normative orientations of the subjects. To explore the effects of these mediating variables on the aggressive behavior of individuals and groups, regression and path analyses will be calculated on the aggression data that were obtained at the third and fourth trial of the game.

To summarize our arguments, this experiment was designed to test and explore the following hypotheses:

1. The abuse of power and norm violation of another interdependent party leads to a greater increase in reactive aggression than adherence to the norm to distribute outcomes in a fair and equitable way.
2. Groups will show more aggression than unaffiliated individuals will do to the norm violations of another interdependent party.
3. The more people have reason to believe that the expression of aggression toward a more powerful party will lessen their chances of obtaining valuable outcomes from him or her the more they will suppress their aggression in an effort not to antagonize the other and to risk their chances of being rewarded by the other party.
4. The more people expect valuable outcomes from the other party, the more they will choose an alternative that makes themselves dependent upon the other more powerful party. Obversely, the less people expect valuable outcome from the other party, the more choices they will make that are intended to deprive the other party from his or her allocation power and to inflict a loss on him or her even at some costs to themselves.
5. The difference in aggression between individuals and groups will be greater in a condition in which the suppression of aggression can be considered as an instrumental response to avoid retaliatory actions from a more powerful party than in a condition in which the suppression of aggression does not serve such an instrumental purpose.
6. When they are put at an unfair disadvantage by the norm violation of another powerful party, groups are more inclined to set higher negotiation demands, will report greater assertiveness, and will use more aggression in a threatening and coercive way than individuals will do.

Method

The physical task environment and the asymmetric interdependence structure between the parties was manipulated by a Power Allocation Game (PAG), modeled after a game developed by Smyth (1989). The outcome matrix of the game is presented in Figure 2. As can be seen, each party can make an A- or B-choice. If the Blue party, (the subjects themselves) in a simultaneous play makes an A-choice and Green (the programmed party) does the same, Blue confers power to Green to divide the 6 guilders between them. (The way in which the 6 guilders could be divided is depicted at the left of Figure 2). If Green divides the money in an equal or equitable way, each party receives three guilders that is more than each party could have gained by making any other combination of choices. In principle, then, a mutual A-choice is clearly the most dominant strategy for the two parties to maximize their individual and collective outcomes. Thus an equal distribution between the two parties appears to be the most fair and equitable resolution of the conflict of interest between them.

In the present experiment, 20 dyads and 20 individuals, all male students at the University of Utrecht, volunteered to take part in the experiment. They received Dfl. 15.00 (about $ 8.00) per person plus the money they could earn in the bargaining task they would participate in.

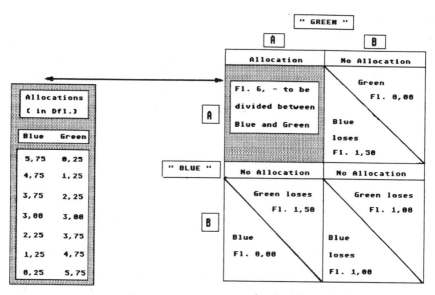

Figure 2. The outcome matrix of the Power Allocation Game (PAG), (to the left the possible allocations of the Green party in case both Blue and Green choose A).

Procedure

At each trial of the four-trial game the parties had various opportunities to communicate with each other:

1. Before they made their definite A- or B-choice, each party could make a tentative proposal how he felt that the money should be divided when both parties would make an A-choice. It was expected (and actually found) that subjects would propose an equal division of the money in the first three trials of the game.
2. After the interchange of these proposals, the parties had to make their definite simultaneous choices, which could depart from the tentative proposals they had made earlier.
3. When both parties made a definite A-choice, only Green received the power to allocate the money between the two parties in any way he (or they) wanted. Again, the definite distribution between the two parties could be quite different from the distribution proposed earlier.
4. At the end of each trial, only the Blue party could indicate his approval or disapproval of the actions of Green by means of a aggression apparatus that would send high frequency white noise blasts with intensities varying from 1 to 8 to the earphones of the other party. The Green party did not have such an apparatus so they could not retaliate in kind. The subjects knew what they were doing to the Green party because they had heard sample noises before, which were rated by them as either very soft (level 1: 10 dBA) or as very disturbing and almost unbearable (level 5: 80 dBA). There was only one aggression apparatus per group, so the members in the dyad had to make a collective decision how much white noise should be administered to the other party. The actions of the other party at the four trials represented the changes in the external social environment for the subjects.

The hypotheses were tested in a $2 \times 2 \times 4$ repeated measurement design with the four trials as repeated measures of choice behavior and levels of aggression. In the group condition, the two members in the dyad were told that as a Blue party they would work on an intergroup task with two fellow subjects, called the Green party, which were seated in a separate room but could be seen on a TV screen in front of them. In fact—unknown to the subjects—the two individuals of the Green party were prerecorded on videotape. In the *individual* condition, a single Blue individual was faced with a single Green person who also could be seen on the screen.

The subjects were told that they had to reach a limit of at least Dfl. 6.50 within the four trials of the game; otherwise they would lose all the money they had earned during the game.

In the *reactive* condition, half of the subjects in the group and individual condition were informed that only one of the two parties could reach the limit and could keep the money that was earned during the game. The party who had reached the limit for the first time had won; the other had definitely lost. At the third trial, the (programmed) Green subjects abused their power to allocate the money by giving much more money to themselves than to the Blue subjects, enabling them to reach the limit first. At that time, the Blues realized that they had lost the chance of reaching the limit and that it made no sense anymore to suppress their aggression in an effort not to antagonize Green and avoid retaliation from them.

In the *instrumental* condition, half of the subjects were told that *both* parties could reach the limit and that it did not matter who was the first one to reach it. In this condition, the subjects still had some hope that Green would give them the extra money on the fourth trial they needed to reach the limit. Therefore, it was expected that they would be more inclined than subjects in the reactive condition to make themselves dependent upon Green by making an A-choice at the fourth trial. Subjects in the instrumental condition would also be more motivated than subjects in the reactive condition to restrain their aggression in an effort not to antagonize the other party.

At the first two trials, the Green party adhered to the equality norm by proposing and actually dividing the money in an equitable, equal way. So after two trials, each party had earned Dfl. 6.—in total, just Dfl. 0.50 short of the limit they needed to reach. On the basis of their previous experience with the behavior of Green and his tentative proposals, the Blue party expected Green at the third trial to divide the money equally, but contrary to that expectation, he gave Dfl. 5.75 to himself and Dfl. 0.25 to the Blue party, enabling himself to reach the limit but leaving Blue only Dfl. 0.25 short of reaching the limit. Thus, at the first two trials, Green adhered to the equality norm and acted according to his proposals, but at the third and critical trial, he violated these norms to the disadvantage of Blue. At the fourth trial, Green again proposed an equal distribution but instead of choosing an A, he made a B-choice that in fact immunized him against the possible retaliatory action of Blue, who also could have made a B-choice.

It should be noted that at the end of the fourth and last trial, subjects in *both* the instrumental and reactive conditions realized that they had definitely lost the chance to reach the limit and that it made no sense anymore to restrain their aggression against Green. So, in the fourth trial no difference in aggression should be expected between the two conditions. However, because it made no sense to restrain one's aggression at the fourth trial for subjects in both conditions, an increase was expected in aggression from the third to the fourth trial for our instrumental subjects, but no difference or even a decrease in aggression for subjects in the reactive condition who had already expressed their anger and aggression at the third trial. Thus Hypothesis 3 is tested in two ways: by means of a "between-group" design at Trial 3 and a "within-group" or repeated measurement design, comparing the behavior at Trials 3 and 4 with each other.

After each trial, the subjects were asked to indicate their reasons for their choices and their verbal reactions to the behavior of themselves and Green. These questions were designed to measure changes in the psychological orientations of the subjects over time.

Results

Check on Experimental Manipulations

In the first two trials of the Power Allocation Game, the programmed opponent adhered to various norms for appropriate social behavior. He adhered to the equality norm by proposing an equal division of the money, if both parties would make an A-choice. He acted in accordance with his proposal, so he did what he said he would do, thereby conforming to the norm that actions should be consistent with one's words. In line with the reciprocity norm (Gouldner, 1960) that we should treat others as they treat us, he reciprocated the proposal of the subjects by making an A-choice and distributed the money in a fair and equal way. Thus he also adhered to a norm of fairness and equality (Leventhal, 1976).

In accordance with our expectations, all subjects, regardless of the experimental conditions, favored the equality norm: without exception they proposed an equal distribution of the money between the two parties. All subjects made also an A-choice on the first three trials, indicating that this choice was indeed the most dominant strategy to maximize their outcomes in this game. At the same time by making an A-choice, all subjects conferred allocation power to their opponent. In view of the adherence to the appropriate social norms by the other party during the first two trials, there is no need to apply negative sanctions to this behavior, and as a consequence very low levels of white noise were delivered to him. These very soft noises can be considered as a sign of acknowledgment and approval rather than a sign of disapproval. As can be seen in figure 3a and 3b, the overall mean levels of white noise in the first trial and second trial were very low: respectively .45 and .44. As expected, there were no significant differences between the experimental conditions on these measures. Thus in the first two trials, preconditions were created needed to test our hypotheses.

Our manipulation of the reactive or instrumental condition, designed to allow the expression or restraint of reactive aggression to the norm violations of the other party, did also have the desired effects. Subjects in the instrumental condition (M = 6.27) expressed a greater desire to "reach the limit at the fourth trial" than subjects in the reactive conditions did (M = 2.00; F = 64.04, df = 1,37; p < .00001) (see Table 1, 2.4).

Hypotheses

In the first two trials, the opponent adhered to various norms of appropriate social behavior. As will be remembered in the third and

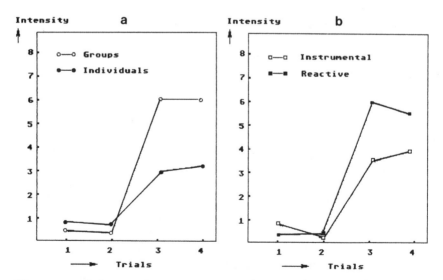

Figures 3a and 3b. Mean level of intensity of white noise blasts for individuals and groups (Figure 3a) and for subjects in the instrumental and reactive condition (Figure 3b) during the four different trials of the game.

critical trial, the other party deviated from these norms in various ways. First of all he did not conform to his earlier pattern of behavior. Blalock and Wilken (1979) have pointed out that

> regularization of patterning in an exchange relationship may become imbued with normative connotations. In other words, if individuals in an ongoing exchange relationship continually respond in the same way to a given action by the other party, the other party is likely to develop normative expectation regarding that response. (p. 195)

In our experiment, the programmed opponent violated these normative expectations by suddenly giving himself much more than to the other party. He made a different division of the money he said he would do in his earlier proposal, and he violated the equality norm. In our first hypothesis (H.1), it was expected that the infringement of these moral precepts would lead to an increase in aggression from the first two trials to the last two trials. The white noise data for the last two trials are presented in Figures 3a and 3b. There is strong support for H.1. The overall increase in aggression (white noise) from the first two trials to the last two trials is highly significant (Effect trials: $F(3,35) = 59.28$; $p < .0001$.). Consistent with Hypothesis 2 this trial effect is stronger for groups than for individuals (Gr/Ind $\times$ Trial $F(3,35) = 6.45$, $p < .01$) (see Figure 3a). In line with Hypothesis 3, this effect is stronger for subjects in the reactive conditions than in the instrumental conditions (I/R $\times$ Trial $F(3,35) = 4,10$, $p < .01$) (see Figure 3b).

Consistent with earlier findings that groups are more instrumental in their orientations than individuals (Rabbie et al., 1982), questionnaire responses show that group members were more "incentive motivated" than individuals. During the first two trials prior to the norm violation, group members indicated that they were more motivated to reach the limit than individuals ($p < .04$); they wanted more than individuals "to earn as much as possible" ($p < .04$), and they showed also somewhat more reluctance than individuals to be dependent upon Green to obtain valuable outcomes from him ($p < .06$) (see Table 1, 2.1). These results suggest, consistent with BIM, that the intragroup interaction enhances the motivational orientations of the group members.

In view of the greater outcome orientation of groups than individuals, it was expected in Hypothesis 2 that groups would feel more frustrated and aroused by the illegitimate actions of the other party and considered it more justified to punish the other group for their norm violations. In line with Hypothesis 2, the level of the white noise aggression at the third trial was higher for groups than for individuals ($p < .002$) as can be seen in Figure 4a. Generally the level of

Table 1. Mean Level of Aggressive Reactions, Mean Ratings on Dependent Measures and ANOVA Summary ($df = 1,37$)

	Group instrumental	Groups reactive	Individuals instrumental	Individuals reactive	Groups vs. individual F(A)	$p <$	Instrumental vs. reactive F(B)	$p <$	F(A × B)	$p <$
1. Aggressive reactions										
1.3 Mean intensity of white noise blasts third trial	5.26	6.83	1.70	5.00	11.45	.002	13.87	.001		
1.4 Mean intensity of white noise blasts fourth trials	6.67	5.42	2.00	4.92	12.62	.001			8.06	.01
2. Dependent measures[a]										
2.1 Reaching limit 1° trial	5.86	6.50	5.00	5.20	4.47	.04				
To earn as much as possible 1° trial	5.59	5.30	3.50	4.70	4.77	.04				
Reluctant to be dependent on Green 1° trial	2.95	3.05	2.20	1.70	3.78	.06				
2.3 Irritation 3° trial	5.73	6.00	3.40	5.30	8.07	.01	4.05	.05		
Disappointment 3° trial	5.64	5.85	3.80	4.90	5.83	.02				
To assert oneself 3° trial	5.86	6.45	3.40	5.70	10.09	.003	8.05	.01		
To influence Green 3° trial	6.55	6.10	3.50	6.20	11.01	.002	5.95	.02	12.37	.001
Perceiving aggression as a threat 3° trial	5.55	6.25	2.90	6.00	7.80	.01	13.38	.001	5.46	.03
To apeace Green 3° trial	3.91	3.15	4.80	4.30	3.03	.09				
Proposed allocation by Blue 4° trial	6.45	4.80	4.40	3.10	9.69	.004	5.79	.02		

2.4 Reaching the limit 4° trial	5.95	1.80	6.60	2.20		64.04	.00001
To earn as much as possible 4° trial	5.41	3.05	3.50	2.40	3.78	.06	6.44	.02
To earn as much as Green 4° trial	4.91	3.35	4.20	2.60			4.23	.05
Wanting a fair division 4° trial	5.23	4.45	5.40	3.10			4.37	.04
Depriving Green of allocation power 4° trial	2.36	4.00	1.20	3.50			7.40	.01
Thwarting Green party 4° trial	2.45	5.20	1.40	2.70	7.17	.01	10.18	.003
To inflict a loss on Green 4° trial	1.82	5.05	1.70	2.90			11.37	.002
Percentage of A-choices 4° trial	90%	70%	0%	40%			18.00	.0001

[a] For all variables the higher the score the more subject agree, feel that it is important, and so forth.

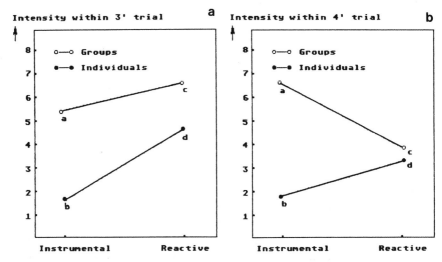

Figures 4a and 4b. Mean intensity of white noise blasts for groups and individuals in the instrumental and reactive conditions during the third trial (Figure 4a) and the fourth trial (Figure 4b).

aggression, especially by groups, was surprisingly high. We were struck by the fierceness by which groups reacted to the behavior of the other party. The level of aggression was higher than in any of the other aggression experiments we have conducted earlier (e.g., Rabbie, 1989a; Rabbie & Horwitz, 1982; Rabbie & Lodewijkx, 1983, 1984, 1987; Lodewijkx, 1989). As can be seen in Table 1, 1.4, and Figure 4b, the level of aggression of groups was also much higher than that of individuals at the fourth and last trial of the game ($p < .001$).

In Hypothesis 3, it was predicted that subjects in the instrumental condition would show greater restraint in expressing their aggression than subjects in the reactive condition. According to Table 1, 1.3, and Figure 4a this hypothesis received also strong support: Less aggression occurred in the instrumental than in the reactive condition during the third trial ($p < .001$).

As can be expected, subjects in the instrumental condition were more optimistic about the final outcomes than subjects in the reactive condition. The instrumental subjects had higher aspirations than reactive subjects in "what they could earn in the game" ($p < .02$); they wanted to earn as much as Green ($p < .05$), and they attached more importance than the reactive subjects did to a "fair" and "honest" division of the money between the two parties ($p < .04$) (see Table 1, 2.4).

In view of this optimism, it was predicted in Hypothesis 4 that instrumental subjects would make themselves more dependent on

Green by making an A-choice than reactive subjects would do. Consistent with this hypothesis, much more A-choices were made in the instrumental condition (95%) than in the reactive condition (55%), $F(1,37) = 18.00$, $p < .001$) during the fourth trial. The motivational significance of the greater number of B-choices than A-choices made in the reactive condition becomes quite clear if the reasons are examined the subjects gave for their choices. As can be seen in Table 1, 2.4, subjects in the reactive condition expressed a greater desire than subjects in the instrumental condition to deprive Green from his allocation power ($p < .01$), to thwart and frustrate the other party ($p < .003$), and to inflict a loss on him ($p < .002$).

Hypothesis 5 predicted that there would be a greater difference in aggression between individuals and groups within the instrumental than within the reactive condition. In line with our interaction model, it was expected that intragroup interaction would enhance the cognitive, motivational, emotional, and normative orientations in the group. The high level of anger and emotional arousal could interfere with the interchange of relatively cool and deliberate arguments in favor of suppressing the aggression in an effort to placate the other party. It was expected that single individuals would experience a lower level of emotional arousal than groups, making them cognitively more capable to restrain their aggression for instrumental reasons as compared with groups. There is some support for this hypothesis. As expected, the difference in intensity of the (aggressive) white noise between individuals and groups during the third trial is greater within the instrumental condition (see Figure 4a: contrast a-b $F (1,37) = = 12.01$; $p < .001$) than within the reactive condition (see Figure 4a, contrast c-d $F (1,37 = 4.35 \ p < .04)$). During the fourth trial these contrasts were respectively a-b: $F(1,37) = 32.09$; $p < 0001$; c-d: $F(1,37) = 1.41$, $p < .24$ (see Figure 4b).

In line with the BIM, the emotional arousal was higher in groups than in individuals because groups reported more irritation ($p < .01$) and disappointment ($p < .02$) at Trial 3 than individuals did. However, consistent with Hypothesis 6, the questionnaire results indicate that groups may not only be more *aroused* and frustrated but also less *willing* than individuals to restrain their aggression in an effort not to antagonize the other party. Results in Table 1, 2.3, show that groups expressed greater needs than individuals to assert themselves ($p < .003$), wanted more strongly to influence the other party ($p < .002$), hoped that their aggressive reactions would be seen as a threat ($p < .01$), and were somewhat less inclined than individuals to placate the other party ($p < .09$). Groups seem also more assertive on a behavioral level. In their negotiations how the money should be divided, they demanded a greater share of the six guilders (Dfl 4.75 to themselves and Dfl 1.25 for Green), whereas the individuals proposed an equal division of the money (Dfl 3.00 - Dfl 3.00) (F (1,37) = 9.69; p < .004).

There are other results that indicate that groups, despite their higher levels of emotional arousal, are at least as capable to restrain their aggression than individuals are. At the fourth trial, subjects in the instrumental condition realized after the B-choice of the opponent that they could not reach the limit anymore. They knew that they had lost the game, and in this respect they were in the same position as the reactive subjects had been at the third trial. Because it made no sense to restrain their aggression at this time, no differences in aggression between the two conditions were expected at the fourth trial. A significant interaction was obtained between the two experimental variables (F (1,37) = 8.06; p < .01). This interaction is mainly due to the higher level of aggression in groups as compared with individuals in the instrumental condition (see Figure 4b). The level of group aggression was also higher in the instrumental than in the reactive condition. This finding may imply that groups reacted with more aggression than individuals did to the B-choice of the opponent. Apparently, groups reacted with greater aggression than individuals when it appeared that their restraint shown at the third trial did not have the desired effects in influencing the other party. Because the expression of aggression at the fourth and last trial could not serve any other instrumental purpose than to punish the other party for his norm violation, it was expected that there would be an increase in aggression from the third to the fourth trials for the subjects in the instrumental condition, but no difference or even a decrease in aggression for subjects in the reactive condition. Subjects in the latter condition had already experienced their disappointment at their loss at the third trial of the game and had already expressed their unrestrained aggression to the other party. As can be seen in a comparison of the data presented in Figures 4a and 4b, this hypothesis receives some support, but more for groups than for individuals. Also, in this case, intragroup interaction seems to enhance the psychological orientations already present in single individuals (Lamm & Meyers, 1978; Rabbie & Visser, 1972, 1986; Rabbie & Lodewijkx, 1985; Rabbie et al., 1989).

The basic assumption of the Behavioral Interaction Model is that the aggressive behavior is a combined function of the changes in the external environment: the manipulation of the independent variables that is, the Individual-Group (IG) and the Instrumental-Reactive (IR) conditions and the interaction between them (IG × IR), and the intervening psychological orientations measured by the questionnaires on the other hand, which may mediate the effects of the independent variables on the main dependent variable: the aggressive (white noise) behavior. Path and regression analyses were performed on the aggression data obtained at the third and fourth trials of the game. The path diagram, describing the determinants of the aggressive behavior at the third trial, is presented in Figure 5a . In Figure 5b, a path diagram can be found relating the independent and intervening variables to the aggressive behavior occurring at the fourth and last trial of the game. Only those questionnaire items were included in the diagrams that showed a significant relationship with the aggressive behavior. The variables presented in Figure 5a can be characterized as follows: IG refers to the independent Individual-Group variable; IR refers to the instrumental and reactive variable, whereas IG X IR represents the interaction between them. *Internal attribution* is a cognitive orientation, which was measured by the answer to the question, "To what extent can your aggressive behavior be attributed to your own personality characteristics?" The *Irritation-coercion* scale is based on the following 7-point questionnaire items: 7 = strongly irritated; 7 = strongly motivated to influence the other; 7 = aggressive behavior is meant as a threat; 7 = wanted strongly to assert oneself; 7 = felt very disappointed; 7 = did *not* want to keep on good terms with the other. Although the factor analysis yielded a very homogeneous scale (alpha =.91), inspection of the questionnaire items on which the scale is based reflect a combination of two distinctive orientations: an emotional orientation, reflecting irritation, disappointment, and other indications of emotional arousal and a coercive motivational orientation directed at influencing the other party. The combination of both orientations in one single factor suggests that the aggressive behavior at the third trial can be more characterized as an instrumental than as an angry, reactive response to the provocations of the other party. It should be noted, however, that most of these (retrospective) questions were asked after, rather than before, the aggressive reaction of the subjects because it was felt that the administration of the questionnaires would interfere with the spontaneity and impulsiveness of the aggressive reaction. Therefore, retrospective questions were used to measure the psychological orientations involved in the aggressive behavior. It might well be that this procedure may have introduced a greater instrumental deliberateness on the part of the subjects than was actually the case prior and during the actual expression of the aggression. Because of this procedure, the causal ordering of the variables in the path diagram should be interpreted with some caution.

The correlations in Figure 5a between the level of white noise at Trial 3 (Aggression 3) and IG ($r = .48$), IR ($r = .42$), and IG × IR 3 ($r = -.16$), indicate the direct effects of the independent variables on the aggressive behavior. The standardized beta weights or regression coefficients indicate the strength of the direct relationships between

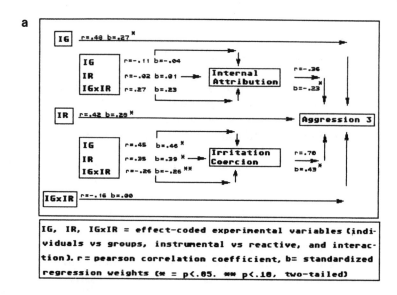

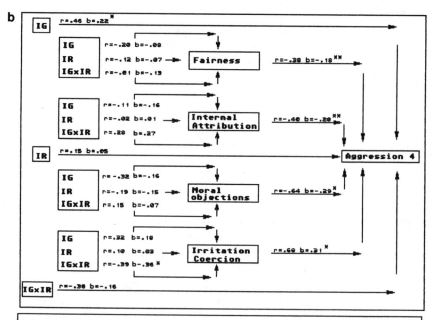

Figures 5a and 5b. A path analysis of variables contributing to the explanation of the variance of the aggression expressed at the third trial of the PAG (Figure 5a) and the fourth trial (Figure 5b).

the independent variables and Aggression 3, when one controls for the effects of Internal attribution: the extent to which one's aggressive behavior is attributed to oneself, and the effects of the Irritation-coercion variable. The betas between Aggression 3 and IG (.27) and IR (.28) are still statistically significant but explain less of the variance. The effects of the independent variables are mainly mediated by the Irritation-coercion variable. The beta weights between IG, IR and IG × IR and Irritation-coercion are respectively .46 (p < .001), .39 (p < .005), and −.26 (p < .10). The negative sign of the last insignificant beta weight indicates that the dyads are more irritated and coercive in the instrumental condition, whereas individuals feel more irritated and coercive in the reactive condition.

The tendency to attribute one's aggressive behavior to oneself seems to be dispositional rather than a state variable (Magnusson & Endler, 1977; Snyder & Ickes, 1985). This cognitive orientation is not induced by the experimental conditions: none of the beta weights relating the independent variables to the internal attribution factor are statistically significant. The less people attribute the aggressive behavior to their own personality characteristics, the stronger the aggressive reaction to the other (beta = −.23; p < .04). Apparently, the more the other party can be held accountable for one's own behavior, the less inhibitions people feel to hurt the other as a punishment for his illegitimate actions (Ferguson & Rule, 1983; Lodewijkx, 1989).

The changes in the external environment and the psychological orientations explain a considerable amount of the variance in the aggressive reaction. The independent variables explain 48% of the variance ($F(3,36)$ = 10.07, p < .001). After the inclusion of the emotional–motivational orientations Irritation and Coercion, the explained variance increases to 58% ($F(4,35$ = 11.91, p < .000), and when the cognitive Internal attribution variable is added, the explained variance is raised to 63% ($F(5,34)$ = 11.40, p < .000).

According to our model, every change in the external environment evokes different psychological orientations, meaning structures and consequent behaviors. At the fourth and last trial the subjects realized that everything was lost, that there was no chance to reach the limit, and that the B-choice of the other made it impossible for them to deprive the other from his allocation power. At the fourth trial, there was no effective difference any more between the instrumental and reactive condition. The subjects in these conditions had only different experiences with the game situation that could have affected their aggressive behavior at the fourth trial. As a consequence, it is likely that different psychological orientations are elicited by the changes in the external environment at the fourth trial. The path diagram presented in Figure 5b confirms these expectations.

As compared with the path diagram in Figure 5a, there are not two but four intervening variables: (1) *perceived fairness*: the degree to which the other had been fair or honest in his allocations; (2) *internal attributions*: the degree to which the aggressive behavior was ascribed to the personality characteristics of the subject; (3) the extent to which the subjects indicated *moral objections* to deliver painful white noise to the other; (4) the *Irritation-coercion* scale (alpha .87) that was at this time based on the items: very disappointed, irritated, not at ease, tense, willing to assert oneself, aggression is meant as a threat, do not want to be on good terms with the other, and strongly motivated to influence the other. The effects of the independent variables on the level of aggression at the fourth trial (Aggression 4) have already been discussed on the basis of the analyses of variance. The beta weights indicate that the effects of the IG variable and in particular the IG $\times$ IR interaction are mediated by Irritation-coercion variable (beta = $-.36$). The greater the irritation and the need to influence the other, the greater the aggression ($b = -.31$). The other intervening variables show a negative relationship: the greater the unfairness attributed to the other, the greater the aggression ($b = -.18$); the less the aggression was attributed to one's own personality characteristics the more aggression was expressed to the other, ($b = -.20$) and finally, the stronger the moral objections to deliver painful white noise to the other, the lower the level of aggression ($b = -.29$). The independent variables and the interaction between them explained 39% of the variance in the aggressive behavior ($F(3,35 = 7.61, p < .000)$; the addition of the Irritation-coercion variable explained 57% of the variance ($F(4,34) = 11.73, p < .000$), and the inclusion of the other cognitive and normative orientations in the regression analysis raises the amount of explained variance to 71% ($F(7,31) = 11.10, p < .0001$). This figure is even higher than the one obtained in the regression analysis presented in Figure 5a.

Both sets of data show strong support for the basic assumption of our model that the important mediating or intervening psychological variables should be taken into account to provide a fuller explanation of variations in aggressive behavior between individuals and groups.

Discussion

This experiment clearly indicates that parties, both individuals and groups, are willing to confer power to another party by making themselves dependent upon him, in the expectation that they will receive valuable rewards from that other party.

They also will restrain their aggressive reactions toward that party in an effort not to antagonize the other and forfeit valuable outcomes from him. Consistent with earlier findings, there is considerable support for our enhancement hypothesis derived from our model: that intragroup interaction stimulates greater aggression of groups than of single individuals (Lodewijkx, 1989; Rabbie & Horwitz, 1982; Rabbie & Lodewijkx, 1984, 1985, 1987; Rabbie, Lodewijkx, & Broese, 1986).

One of the main questions in this experiment was whether the greater emotional arousal in groups than in individuals would interfere with their cognitive capacity to restrain their aggression toward the other party in an effort to avoid retaliation from him. An answer to this question seems important in view of the opinion of Donnerstein and Hatfield (1982) who assume that intensely angry people who are strongly aroused are incapable to take account of equity considerations and presumably are unable to act on these considerations. It was expected that single individuals would experience a lower level of emotional arousal, making them more capable to suppress their angry aggression for instrumental reasons as compared with groups. Consistent with these expectations, the difference in aggression between individuals and groups was greater within the instrumental than within the reactive conditions. However, groups may not only be less capable but also less willing than individuals to restrain their aggression. According to their answers to the questionnaires, groups as compared with individuals, had stronger needs to assert themselves, were less willing to placate the other party, and were more inclined to use coercive aggression in an effort to influence the other party. The finding that irritation and other indices of emotional arousal are strongly related to coercive efforts to influence the other, and more so for groups than for individuals, suggests that group members seem as capable as individuals to restrain their aggression for instrumental purposes but are probably less willing to do so for social competitive reasons such as preserving one's self-esteem and group identity, attain prestige and recognition, and are more strongly motivated to avoid losing face than individuals (Lemaine, 1974; Pruitt & Rubin, 1986; Tajfel & Turner, 1979).

This experiment was not designed to test any particular theory in the area of group aggression and social justice but to obtain some evidence for the usefulness of a general Behavioral Interaction Model, which has guided our research efforts for the last few years. The regression analyses presented in the path diagrams in Figure 5a and 5b provided some support for our model. Consistent with the model, it appeared that cognitive orientations such as attributions to oneself contributed to the strength of the aggressive reaction. The emotional and motivational orientations, represented by the irritation and coercion scale, explained a great deal of the variance in the aggressive reaction. Finally, a normative orientation, such as a moral objection to delivering painful white noise to the other, inhibited the expression of aggression to a significant degree. These findings suggest that the meaning structures of social injustice situations should be taken into account to explain the instrumental and angry aggression of individuals and groups in situations of social conflict between them.

References

Ajzen, I., & Fishbein, M. (1980). *Understanding attitudes and predicting social behavior.* Englewood Cliffs, NJ: Prentice- Hall.

Abelson, R. P. (1976). Script processing in attitude formation and decision-making. In J. S. Carol & J. W. Payne (Eds.), *Cognition and social behavior.* Hillsdale, NJ: Lawrence Erlbaum Associates.

Bandura, A. (1983). Psychological mechanisms of aggression. In R. G. Geen & E. L. Donnerstein (Eds), *Aggression, theoretical and empirical reviews. Theoretical and methodological issues.* Vol. 1. New York: Academic Press.

Bandura, A. (1986). *Social foundations of thought and action: A social cognitive theory.* Englewood Cliffs, NJ: Prentice- Hall.

Berkowitz, L. (1983). The experience of anger as a parallel process in the display of impulsive "angry" aggression. In R. G. Geen & E. I. Donnerstein (Eds.), *Aggression, theoretical and empirical reviews (Vol. 1).Theoretical and methodological Issues.* New York: Academic Press.

Blalock, H. M., & Wilken, P. H. (1979). *Intergroup processes: A micro-macro perspective.* New York: Free Press.

Brown, R. & Herrnstein, R. J. (1975). *Psychology.* London: Methuen.

Brown, R. (1986). *Social psychology, the second edition.* New York: Free Press.

Buss A. H. (1961). *The psychology of aggression.* New York: Wiley.

Carver, C. S., & Scheier, M. F. (1981). *Attention and self-regulation: A control theory approach to human behavior.* New York: Springer.

Deutsch, M. (1982). Interdependence and psychological orientation. In V. J. Derlega & J. Grzelak (Eds.), *Cooperation and helping behavior.* New York Academic Press.

Deutsch, M., & Gerard, H. (1955). A study of normative and informational influence upon individual judgement. *Journal of Abnormal and Social Psychology, 51,* 629–636.

Diener, E. (1980). Deindividuation:The absence of self-awareness and self-regulation in group members. In P. Paulus (Ed.), *The psychology of group influence.* Hillsdale, NJ: Erlbaum.

Donnerstein, E., & Donnerstein, M. (1973). Variables in interracial aggression: Potential in group censure. *Journal of Personality and Social Psychology, 22,* 143–150.

Donnerstein, E., & Hatfield, E. (1982). Aggression and inequity. In J. Greenberg & R. C. Cohen (Eds.), *Equity and justice in social behavior* (pp. 309–336). New York: Academic Press.

Eckhoff, T. (1974). *Justice: Its determinants in social interaction.* Rotterdam: Rotterdam University Press.

Emerson, R. M. (1972). Exchange theory. Part II Exchange relations and network structures. In J. Berger, M. Zelditch, & B. Anderson (Eds.), Sociological studies in progress (Vol II, pp. 58–87). Boston: Houghton Mifflin.

Ferguson, J. T., & Rule, B. G. (1983). An attributional perspective on anger and aggression. In R. G. Geen & E. I. Donnerstein (Eds.), Aggression, theoretical and empirical reviews Vol. 1. Theoretical and methodological issues. New York: Academic Press.

Feshbach, S. (1964). The function of aggression and the regulation of aggressive drive. Psychological Review, 71, 257–272.

Festinger, L. (1954). A theory of social comparison processes. Human Relations, 7, 117–140.

Festinger, L., Peptone, A., & Newcomb, T. (1955). Some consequences of deindividuation in a group. Journal of Abnormal Social Psychology, 47, 382–389.

Frijda, N. H. (1986). The emotions. New York: Cambridge University Press.

Gerard, H. B., & Rabbie, J. M. (1961). Fear and social comparison. Journal of Abnormal and Social Psychology, 62, 586–592.

Gouldner, A. W. (1960). The norm of reciprocity: A preliminary statement. American Sociological Review, 25, 161–178.

Hart 't, P. (1990). Groupthink in government: A study of small groups and policy failure. Dissertation, University of Leyden.

Homans, G. C., (1982). Foreword in J. Greenberg & R. L. Cohen (Eds.), Equity and justice in social behavior (pp. xi–xviii). New York: Academic Press.

Horwitz, M. & Rabbie, J. M. (1982). Individuality and membership in the intergroup system. In H. Tajfel (Ed.), Social identity and intergroup relations (pp.) Cambridge University Press: Editions de la maison des Sciences de l'Homme.

Jaffe, Y., & Yinon, Y. (1983). Collective aggression: The group-individual paradigm in the study of collective social behavior. In H. H. Blumberg, A. P. Hare, V. Kent & M. Davis (Eds.), Small groups and social interaction (Vol. 1). New York: Wiley.

Janis, I. L. (1982). Victims of group think: A psychological study of foreign policy decisions and fiascos. Boston: Houghton Mifflin.

Lamm, H., & D. G. Meyers, D. G. (1978). Group-induced polarization of attitudes and behavior. In L. Berkowitz (Ed.), Advances in experimental social psychology (Vol. 11). New York: Academic Press.

Lemaine, G. (1974). Social differentiation and social originality. European Journal of Social Psychology, 4, 17–52.

Leventhal, G. S. (1976). Fairness in social relationships. In J. Thibaut, J. Spence, & R. Carson (Eds.). Contemporary topics in social psychology. Morriston, NY: General Learning Press.

Lodewijkx, H. (1989). Aggression between individuals and groups: Towards a Behavioral Interaction Model. Dissertation, University of Utrecht (in Dutch).

Lewin, K. (1936) Principles of topological psychology. New York: McGraw-Hill.

Magnussen, P., & Endler, N. S. (1977). (Eds.). Personality at the crossroads: Current issues in interactional psychology. Hillsdale, NJ: Erlbaum.

Miller, G. A., Galanter, E., & Pribram, K. H. (1960). Plans and the structure of behavior. New York: Holt, Rinehart & Winston.

O'Leary, M. R. & Dengerink, H. A. (1973). Aggression as a function of the intensity and pattern of attack. Journal of Research in Personality, 7, 61–70.

Prentice-Dunn, S., & Rogers, R. W. (1983). Deindividuation in aggression. In R. G. Geen & E. I. Donnerstein (Eds.), Aggression:Theoretical and empirical reviews. Vol. 2, Issues in Research. New York: Academic Press.

Pruitt, D. G., & Rubin, J. C. (1986). Social conflict: Escalation, stalemate and settlement. New York: Random House.

J. M. Rabbie (1964). Differential preference for companionship under threat. *Journal of Abnormal and Social Psychology, 67,* 643–648.

Rabbie, J. M. (1986). *Interpersonal and intergroup aggression.* Paper presented at the symposium, "Aggression: Interaction between individuals or social groups," at the 21st International Congress of Applied Psychology, July 13–18, 1986, Jerusalem, Israel.

Rabbie, J. M. (1987). Armed conflicts: Toward a behavioral interaction model. In J. von Wright, K. Helkama, A. M. Pirtilla-Backman (Eds.) *European Psychologists for Peace.* Proceedings of the Congress in Helsinki, 1986.

Rabbie, J. M., (1989a). Group processes as stimulants of aggression. In J. Groebel & R. H. Hinde (Eds.), *Aggression and war: Their biological and social bases.* Cambridge: Cambridge University Press.

Rabbie, J. M. (1989b). *A Behavioral Interaction Model: A theoretical frame work for studying terrorism.* Paper presented to the International Society on Aggression, 5th European Conference, June 25–30. 1989.

Rabbie, J. M., & Goldenbeld, C. (1988). *The effects of modeling and accountability on aggressive intergroup behavior.* Paper presented to the World Congress of ISRA, July 1988, Swansea, Great Britain.

Rabbie, J. M., & Horwitz J. M. (1982). Conflict and aggression between individuals and groups. In H. Hiebsch, H. Brandstätter, & H. H. Kelley (Eds.), *Social psychology,* revised and edited version of selected papers presented at the XXII International Congress of Psychology, Leipzig D. D. R., 1980, no. 8.

Rabbie, J. M., & Lodewijkx, H. (1983a). *Differences in reactive and instrumental aggression between individuals and groups.* Second European ISRA Conference on group processes and intergroup conflicts, Tel Aviv, Israel, October 14–17, 1983.

Rabbie, J. M., & Lodewijkx, H. (1983b). *Aggressive reactions to the abuse of power by individuals and groups.* The second European ISRA conference, Zeist, 1983.

Rabbie, J. M., & Lodewijkx, H. (1984). *Aggression between individuals and group members.* Sixth Bi-annual ISRA Meeting. The International Society for Research on Aggression, Turku, Finland, July 12–15, 1984.

Rabbie, J. M., & Lodewijkx, H. (1985). The enhancement of competition and aggression in individuals and groups. In F. L. Denmark (Ed.), *Social/ecological psychology and the psychology of women* (pp. 177–187). Elsevier Science Publishers B. V. Amsterdam, North-Holland.

Rabbie, J. M., & Lodewijkx, H. (1986). *Conflict and aggression between individuals and groups.* Paper presented to second International Kurt Lewin Conference, sponsored by the Society for the Advancement of Field Theory. September 11–14, 1986, Philadelphia, PA.

Rabbie, J. M., & Lodewijkx, H. (1986b). *The expression of anger and aggression to social injustice in interpersonal and intergroup conflict:A test of a Behavioral Interaction Model.* International Conference on Social Justice in Human Relations, University of Leiden, July 28–30, 1986.

Rabbie, J. M., & Lodewijkx, H. (1987). Individual and group aggression. *Current Research on Peace and Violence, 2-3,* 91–101.

Rabbie, J. M., Lodewijkx, H., & Broeze, M. (1985). *Individual and group aggression under the cover of darkness.* Paper presented to the symposium, "Psychology of Peace," at the third European Congress of the International Society for Research on Aggression (ISRA) devoted to Multidisciplinary Approaches to Conflict and Appeasement in Animals and Men, Parma, Italy, September 3–7, 1985.

Rabbie, J. M., J. C. Schot, & L. Visser (1989). Social identity theory: A conceptual and empirical critique from the perspective of a behavioral interaction model. *European Journal of Social Psychology, 19,* 171–202.

Rabbie, J. M., & Visser, L. (1972). Bargaining strength and group polarization in intergroup relations. *European Journal of Social Psychology, 4*, 401–416.
Rabbie, J. M., & Visser, L. (1984). Deindividuatie en de ontwikkeling van normen in groepen toeschouwers, een veldexperiment. In R. v. d. Vlist (Ed.), *Sociale Psychologie IV. Samenleving en Individue.* Deventer: Van Loghum Slaterus.
Rabbie, J. M., & Visser, L. (1986). *The attribution of motives to oneself and others in mixed motive-conflicts.* Paper presented at the 9th International Meeting of the International Society for Political Psychology (ISPP). Amsterdam, June 29– July 3, 1986.
Rabbie, J. M., Visser, L., van Oostrum, J. (1982). Conflict behavior of individuals, dyads and triads in mixed-motive games. In H. Brandstätter, J. H. Davis, & G. Stocker-Kreichgauer (Eds.), *Group decision-making* (pp. 315–343). London: Academic Press.
Raven, B. H., & Rubin, J. Z. (1983). *Social psychology.* New York: Wiley.
Simmel, G. (1955). (K. H. Wolff, transl). *Conflict.* New York: Free Press of Glencoe.
Smyth, L. (1989). *Power, threat and justice behavior: A social psychological study in the context of Northern Ireland.* Dissertation, University of Utrecht.
Snyder, C. R., & Fromkin, H. L. (1982). *Uniqueness: The human pursuit of difference.* New York: Plenum Press.
Snyder, M. (1981). On the self-perpetuating nature of social stereotypes. In D. Hamilton, *Cognitive processes in stereotyping and intergroup behavior* (pp. 183–202). Hillsdale, NJ: Erlbaum.
Snyder, M., & Ickes, W., (1985). Personality and social behavior. In Lindzey & A. Aronson (Eds.), *The handbook of social psychology* (Vol. II, pp. 883–947). New York: Random House.
Tajfel, H., & Turner, J. C. (1979). An integrative theory of intergroup conflict. In. W. G. Austin & S. Worchel (Eds.), *The social psychology of intergroup relations* (pp. 33–47). Monterey, CA: Brooks/Cole.
Tajfel, H., & Turner, J. C. (1986). The social identity theory of intergroup behavior. In. S. Worchel & W. G. Austin (Eds.), *Psychology of intergroup relations* (pp. 7–24). Chicago: Nelson-Hall.
Taylor, S. E., & Crocker, J. (1981). Schematic bases of social information processing. In. E. T. Higgins, C. A. Harman, & M. P. Zanna (Eds.), *Social cognition: the Ontario symposium on personality and social psychology.* Hillsdale, NJ: Erlbaum.
Tedeschi, J. T. (1983). Social influence theory and aggression. In. R. Geen & E. Donnerstein (Eds.), *Aggression: Theoretical and empirical reviews.* New York: Academic Press.
Turner, J. C. (1981). Intergroup behavior. In. J. C. Turner & H. Giles (Eds.), *The experimental social psychology of intergroup behavior.* Oxford: Basil Blackwell.
Turner, R. M. & Killian L. W. (1972). *Collective behavior* (2nd ed.). Englewood Cliffs, NJ: Prentice-Hall.
Vroom, V. H. (1964). *Work and motivation.* New York: Wiley.
Zajonc, R. B. (1965). Social facilitation. *Science, 149*, 269–274.
Zajonc, R. B. (1980). Compresence In. P. B. Paulus (Ed.), *Psychology of group influence* (pp.). Hillsdale, New Jersey: Erlbaum.
Zillmann, D. (1979). *Hostility and aggression.* Hillsdale, NJ: Erlbaum.
Zimbardo, P. G. (1970). The human choice: Individuation, reason and order versus deindividuation, impulse and chaos. In. W. J. Arnold & D. Levine (Eds.), *Nebraska symposium on motivation.* Lincoln: University of Nebraska Press.

Author Index

Subject Index